Lean Mastery

8 Books in 1

Master Lean Six Sigma & Build a Lean Enterprise, Accelerate Tasks with Scrum and Agile Project Management, Optimize with Kanban, and Adopt The Kaizen Mindset

Table Of Contents

Greg Caldwell

Book #1

Lean Six Sigma Simplified

How to Implement the Six Sigma Methodology to Improve Quality and Speed

Introduction

This book contains a detailed explanation of the Lean Six Sigma principle.

This book is for executives, leaders, and managers who are looking to keep their businesses profitable by maximizing employee productivity while conversing company resources. The Six Sigma Methodology provides businesses with techniques and strategies that will increase productivity and reduce overall waste.

Readers will be provided with solutions that can easily be understood and implemented. This book will also provide what companies stand to gain when they apply principles of Six Sigma. There will also be a section on the common mistakes made and how avoid them.

Thanks for purchasing this book, I hope you enjoy it!

Chapter 1 Introduction to Lean Six Sigma

What matters the most when in a business?

Any person who has ever been into a business venture or project has encountered that question from time to time. And, if you think about it, there are a lot of things that do matter in a business. This includes the organizational structure of the business, its policies, and its people.

Those are all noteworthy issues, there's no doubt about that. But there is one other aspect that any business person should never overlook: the process.

Why the process? The reason is simple. The process is the manifestation of a company's vision and goals. If the policies are the standard, then the process is the mean by which those standards are made manifest.

And every business who has ever produced something will always be judged by two things: input and output. To be more specific about it, a production is gauged whether it is good or not by how it maximizes the available resources while producing goods and services that are of noteworthy quality. In essence, a good producer knows how to maximize their efforts and optimizing the value that they offer.

And this is where your product methodology comes in. But that does leave us with a question: What kind of methodology are you using for your business, if any? What guides your production from step 1 to 139? What quality should the end product possess once the production cycle is complete? How much items should your company even create for that project?

Here's a scenario: imagine that your company creates and assembles engine components for various clients. Let's say that you got an order for 32 engine parts to be delivered within 5 months.

If your company built 65 engine parts, did you truly meet the project goals or were you wasting a lot of effort by producing more than what was asked? Did every item go through sufficient quality assurance checks before being shipped out? You have to remember that you were only asked for 32 components so did you actually meet the project goals without overextending your resources?

Or what if you produced the exact amount ordered but incurred several delays in the production process that spans weeks or months. No matter how good those components are, they would still not have met the project specifications and you, of course, lost some valuable clients.

This constant clash between producing good quality, delivering on time, and minimizing unnecessary byproducts is something that could stress out any business owner. And you have to remember that resources are finite no matter how many they are. Eventually, and if you are not careful, you'd bleed out precious materials through overproducing and over-processing.

Undoubtedly, you have been trying or looking for different methodologies to guide your operations. But, if you are the one that is looking to optimize every move your business makes in the production process and optimize the results, then perhaps the Lean Six Sigma methodology might be the best solution for you.

What is the Six Sigma methodology? Without giving away too much right now (since you're going to read about it later on anyway), the Lean Six Sigma methodology was designed to help business optimize how their production processes for a single project or multiple ones by streamlining the process.

This way, at least on paper, your company should be able to provide more value to the clients while eliminating unnecessary waste, regardless of what form that takes.

At the same time, the process also focuses on building up on where your team is the most effective at. Continuous improvement of the current business layout should allow for organic growth for the company as it takes on bigger, more elaborate projects in the future.

But how should you apply it for your project? Like all other methodologies, Lean Six Sigma is only applicable in certain conditions, but the good news is that the methodology has a rather wide range when it comes to compatibility with project types and production process.

All that is necessary, then, is for you to find out how you can implement the method to your current business layout. This includes identifying your goals, understanding your current processes, and finding out potential areas for improvement.

In addition to this, you should understand that Six Sigma is not exactly the most fool-proof system out there. If one is not careful, it is easy to encounter pitfalls and create mistakes during the production process. Fortunately, such problems can be easily addressed so as long as you are quick enough to identify and act on them.

Of course, you might be asking yourself: is the process complicated to apply? The answer is no. To make things easier to understand, I have set everything up so that you learn the process step by step. Some situations based on real-world scenarios would also be provided so that you can understand that the process is highly applicable in real life.

And if that is still too complicated for you, don't worry. The truth is that the Lean Six Sigma methodology is not as demanding a process compared to other methodologies. It works with what you have and helps you improve on your overall performance based on where you are the strongest.

And, of course, the methodology is highly open towards change. By acknowledging the more unpredictable elements of the process, you can optimize your system to address change and come up with something that meets the new standards without making too much waste.

The point is that the process is highly sustainable and allows for multiple opportunities for improvement down the line. The more you adhere to the Lean Six Sigma methodology, the better you are in addressing its core issues while also applying its principles.

And if you have no further questions, now is the time to prepare yourself as we step into the world of the Lean Six Sigma Methodology.

Chapter 2 Some Preliminary Considerations

As was established, Lean Six Sigma is a process that is designed to streamline your operations on a continuous basis. The premise is that the constant cycle of improvement in how you produce value to your clients should make your business more capable of delivering on what it promises to its clients on time.

However, what you might not have known is that Lean Six Sigma is actually a hybrid concept. To put things simply, Lean Six Sigma is the combination of two concepts named, well, Lean and Six Sigma. To prevent some confusion later on, it is best that we tackle the basics of the concepts first.

What is Lean?

The most basic definition of Lean is that it is a process that aims to reduce waste and wasteful activities in a production cycle. In essence, it focuses on eliminating the steps in a process that are wasteful, either replacing them with ones that do or just simplifying the entire process.

Lean as a process is highly effective when it comes to:

- Reducing the time for each process cycle.
- Improving the delivery time for products and services.
- Reducing the chances that defects would occur in the production process.
- Reducing inventory levels while maximizing space.
- Optimizing available resources through strategic improvements in the production process.

Lean is also cyclical in nature. This means that it primarily promotes a continuous method of improvement in the systems and facilities in order to remove waste.

What is Value under Lean?

Value is a rather vague term when you think really think about it. However, Lean keeps things simple and just defines value is anything that is related to how a customer perceives a product or service that you are offering to them. And this just does not limit itself to customer perception but would also factor in their willingness to pay for such.

To put it simply, Value is the thing that people are looking for in your products and services to the extent that they would go out of their way to pay top dollar for it. And, in the production process, value dictates what steps must be included in it. Of course, a process is simply any activity wherein base materials are turned into components and components turned into actual products or services.

As a matter of fact, Lean defines several categories that processes can fall under. They are as follows:

A. Non-Value Added Activity – These are simply the activities that do not add value to the product or service. In short, they are wasteful steps that must be removed from the overall production process.

On the customer's perspectives, NVAs are activities that they think are not paying for when they purchase what you offer. In fact, if they know that such wasteful steps are included in the process and at a considerable amount, their perception of the product decreases considerably.

B. Value-Added Activity – These activities add value to the process and are deemed essential. They are steps that either improve productivity and quality or simplify the process, so things get done at a far more efficient rate.

C. **Value-Enabling Activity** – These activities are not something that the customer expects to pay for when they are purchasing your products/services. However, they are integral to delivering value in the production process.

Believe it or not, every production process out there is comprised of 80-85% Non-Value Adding Activities. In short, there are quite a lot of unnecessary steps in a process aimed to turn raw materials into something tangible and functional.

The aim of Lean, then, is to identify these steps in the process, eliminate them, and simplify the entire cycle.

Waste and Removing it

The Lean traces its origins to the Toyota company through its Toyota Production System. The TPS model is something that was designed for production environments where a high volume of raw materials are to be processed to create an equally high volume of products as ordered.

However, Lean now can be applied to various environments because of its strong focus on waste, specifically process waste. Using the Japanese word "Muda" which translates to "garbage" or "useless" in English, the Lean method has identified several wastes that could be generated in any process. They are as follows:

- **Defects** – Inherent flaws in a product/service that occur in the middle of their creation.

- **Overproduction** – The facility simply creates more than what was necessary or demanded by the client.

- **Waiting** – This is the time spent by materials, resources, people, information, and equipment being idle as they are still not needed. This could also include the time necessary to set up important phases of the development process or the time spent processing valuable data.

- **Non-Utilized Talent** – Primarily a Human Resource based waste, this occurs when the company does not properly leverage the skills of their workforce. This includes placing people on positions where they are either underqualified or overqualified.

- **Transportation** – These are wastes that occurred when transferring equipment, materials, and personnel from Points A to B and onward. An important aspect here is that the movement itself does not add value to the final product or service.

- **Inventory** – The storing and stockage of unnecessary materials. This includes works in progress (WIPs) and other unfinished components.

- **Motion** – These are unnecessary movements of equipment and personal that take up time, energy, and other resources but do not necessarily add value to the product. Worse, they can result in work fatigue which decreases the productivity of the workforce.

- **Extra Processing** – This is where all the NVAs of a production process should be included once identified. Aside from that, any activity or task scheduled for a period such as performing work beyond what was specified by the customer should be included here as well.

The Principles of Lean

In order to be applicable for various projects and industries, Lean has adopted a rather simplistic process. In fact, these steps would form the pillars of the Lean movement and they are the following.

1. **Define Value** – You'd think that this process involves you identifying the value that your product has to its customers, but it doesn't. The thing about value is that nobody else (including you) can define it but the end user himself.

Identify your customers. Who are they? What problems do they face? What solutions to those problems can your product/service offer?

Upon identifying what your customers expect from the product, you can then start classifying them into the Non-value added, Value Added, and Value Enabling groups.

2. **Mapping the Value Stream** – So how does a raw material turn into a working product? What steps does it take? This will show that as you map out all the necessary steps that must be taken to materials and components into the end product.

This is also where you can identify all those NVAs and eliminate them. This should help your company reduce potential delays in the process while also improving the overall value of the product you offer.

3. **Create the Flow** – Once the stream of production is identified, you must then identify how that product is going to be delivered to your customers. The point here is that flow must be continuous so that the company can identify when and how to deliver on its promises on time.

The flow must also be designed to maximize the efficiency of the process. This means that unnecessary motions must be reduced, and wasteful activities avoided at all costs.

4. **Establishing Pull** – meet system beat time, which is simply the rate of which a product is created and optimized to meet the demands of the customer.

This is where the tool called Just in Time (JIT) comes in as it helps in establishing the pull through ensuring a workflow smooth enough that disruptions are completely done away with. This also helps in addressing inventory management and space-related issues.

5. **Seeking Continuous Improvement** – Lastly, your team must establish a sense of consistency in all of your processes. Constant

effort for efficiency in terms of delivery time and product quality should be ensured, while also preventing the team from going back to older, inefficient standards.

By continuously improving, your business can identify more areas that generate waste and reduce the amount of defects and quality-related problems with your end product.

Six Sigma Defined

Alternatively, Six Sigma is a methodology that focuses on solving problems and is heavily reliant on cold, hard production data. Where Lean focuses on eliminating waste, Six Sigma primarily focuses on reducing defects and imperfections in the end product.

The Goal

Six Sigma has a rather bold goal. To be more specific, every product that you create under the Six Sigma system should have a 99.99996% quality rate. This means that the process you use should have only 3.4 duds out of a million good products or, better yet, less.

Six Sigma is best done with the use of the DMAIC system. DMAIC is an acronym that stands for:

- **Define** – Problems and objectives in the production process must be identified and set.

As such, it is important to create the project charter in this phase. This is basically a blueprint that the six-sigma system would follow. It would also include:

- Business case
- Goal statement

- Problem statement
- Project scope
- Timelines
- Resources
- Estimated benefits

In essence, the charter is an outline of how the six-sigma system is going to be implemented in the project.

- **Measure** – What is the current state of the production layout? What can be done to make it better? What are the metrics for success in this particular production process?

The variables in the process are going to be measured, hence, the process data will be analyzed and collected.

Once done, the baseline should be established, and metrics set. When compared against the final performance metrics, the overall process capability for the project can be identified.

- **Analyze** – The existing process and production system must be scrutinized. The goal here is to identify the factors that influence success, failure, and the generation of defects in the production process.

In this process, it is necessary to perform a root cause analysis. This can be done by using complex analytics tools to identify what caused a defect in the product. References like Pareto charts, histograms, fishbone diagrams, and other graphical data will come in handy at this point of the process.

- **Improve** – Come up with strategies that can enhance the systems and processes and then implement the improvements. The steps must include identifying, testing, and implementing solutions to a problem, and this can be done through simulation studies, design experimenting, and prototyping, among other analytical technics.

- **Control** – Once changes are made, the challenge then is to make them sustainable. Come up with policies and processes that make sure that your team does not slack off and go back to the older standards. This is to ensure that improvements are continuously seen in their output.

In other words, a control system must be put in place to monitor the performance of everyone in the project post-improvement. Also, a response plan must be done to address failure if ever it occurs.

One other important task here is Process Standardization which will guide all of your employees that handle the production process from this point on forward. This can be done through the setting up of policies as well as a manual that would instruct people how to conduct each process in the development cycle.

Finally, benefits will be reviewed here and estimated if they were met. All in all, this part of the process is focused on making sure that whatever gains were made during the improvement phase are not lost over time.

Similarities and Differences

Obviously, you must not conflate Lean with Six Sigma since they are entirely different frameworks. However, that does not mean that they don't share similarities or, better yet, complement one another. After all, why would you think anyone would bother combining them into one tool if they are not compatible with each other?

Just keep in mind that the differences are there to ensure that there is no shortage of available analytical tools and strategies that could improve your processes even further. And as for the similarities, they are there to drive home the point that Lean and Six Sigma can be done simultaneously or, for the purposes of this book, under a unified framework.

A. Similarities

- Both are reliant on the definition of value which is based on customer experience and perception. In short, the customer is the King.

- Both use a flow mapping approach to easily understand how the process could be improved. Even if the analysis is focused on the product or service, the end goal is still to make improvements on the process wherein such product or service will be made and delivered.

- Both rely on data when determining current performance as well as the impact of future performance. This is why the data collected in Lean Six Sigma can still be used in to support either of its parent frameworks.

- Both are applied using improvement projects that will be implemented typically in a cross-functional team. The duration of a singular project and the composition of the team under both framework is determined by the scope and scale of the project.

- Both were primarily designed for manufacturing process but have adapted into other processes.

- Ultimately, either framework is highly effective in reducing waste and variation, whatever form either takes.

B. Differences

- Lean is focused on waste while Six Sigma focuses on Variation or any deviation from the target standards or performance.

- Lean uses visual techniques for analysis and problem solving and is supported by extensive data analysis. Six Sigma is more statistical in nature which is supported by data visualization. In essence, Lean is visual while Six Sigma is numerical.

- A lean solution is always supported by a value stream map. This would then lead to changes in work flows as well as work instructions through various steps in the production cycle.

Alternatively, the Six Sigma solution is supported with changes in the setup procedures and the control plan for monitoring the process to prevent deviations from the standard. This will also impact work instructions and would frequently lead to changes in the measurement approach and other similar systems.

These differences and similarities just emphasize that they have always been compatible to one another. As such, it is easy to merge them into one methodology that allows you to minimize your waste as well as deviations from the standards in your development process.

What is Lean Six Sigma?

And now we come to the most important part of this chapter.

Lean Six Sigma is a system that is driven be facts and data that is focused on preventing or minimizing defects in the end product while also eliminating whatever is considered as wasteful in the production process. It is something that is purely driven in minimizing variations in the cycle, eliminate waste, and improving the overall perception of the public towards the product or service.

And to do this, Lean Six Sigma combines the philosophies and principles found in its parent frameworks. To put it simply, it is designed to make the production process more efficient which, in turn, should translate to a better product. And not only do improvements occur on a one-time basis, they must be done continuously and whenever necessary.

Why Has it Become Important Today?

You might be asking "why is Lean Six Sigma becoming popular today"? The answer lies in the fact that the world has become much more dynamic today than it was in the past.

Shifts in fields like technology, economics, politics, and even culture means that consumer behavior can change at the drop of a hat. And not only do people like different things in a short period of time, the tools and technologies that you deem are superior today can become inferior in a moment's notice.

To better explain this, here's an example. Supposed that you are creating a videogame that runs on a graphics engine that allows for 1080 frames per second gameplay. What if, in the middle of your development, that graphics engine was rendered obsolete by an even more powerful engine that runs on 2040 frames per second?

Or what if an ambitious project was just dropped on your team and you must deliver on the vague promised features within 18 months or so? And, in the middle of the process, the people higher up decided to add new features or systems on top of what you are already working at.

Under normal circumstances, you and your team would be tempted to drop everything that you have worked so far and start from scratch. This means you'd be incurring delays, not meeting project specifications, and losing a valuable client in the process. And, as far as videogames are concerned, there are too many examples of such situations including Anthem, Mass Effect: Andromeda, and the infamous ET game from the 1980s.

The Lean and Six Sigma systems cannot meet such dynamic demands on their own, even if they are rather effective frameworks. As such, the most sensible option was to integrate the two frameworks into a singular but more comprehensive tool.

As was previously stated, the ultimate objective of Lean Six Sigma is to eliminate waste, reduce variation, and ensure a continuous improvement of systems and the end product. How the process can be effective is dependent on the project and your business's current layout. However, there is no doubt that the framework will ultimately help you in streamlining your processes.

As proof of that, Lean Six Sigma is used in various industries and sectors today, not just in car manufacturing where they originated from. Whether oriented towards products or in providing services, Lean Six Sigma has found a home in many businesses and corporations today.

The Takeaway

To summarize things, Lean Six Sigma is a methodology that works best if you are particular about eliminating waste and variation in the processes for your business. In essence, it is an integrated method that takes the best of what Lean and Six Sigma have and using them to great effect.

If done right, lean Six Sigma is particularly effective in improving process efficiency, optimizing resources, and satisfying customer expectations. And, of course, it is so adaptable that it has seen use in various industries today.

What that simply means is that Lean Six Sigma has worked well for others which means it can work for you. The only challenge, then, is to make sure that you implement it properly for your project.

Chapter 3 The Lean Six Sigma Principles

As of now, you might be asking yourself "What makes Lean Six Sigma effective?"

Just like its parent methodologies, Lean Six Sigma is guided by several principles that would determine whether or not is implementation is successful in your business. If you want your business to get optimized with its processes, it is best that you get acquainted with the following principles.

I.   Addressing a Real-World Problem

By design, Lean Six Sigma is a methodology that focuses on the process from top to down and from bottom to top. The top-down aspect is often associated with the identification of a tangible issue in the process and then addressing it with the best possible strategy.

Lean Six Sigma is always focused on not only problems but problems that have continuously impeded a company's production processes as well as the overall reception of the end product. More often than not, the team will have to address such major problems through repairing and overhauling the production process while also addressing customer complaints.

In essence, Lean Six Sigma is not there to make people busy for busyness sake or to apply the proverbial band aid on a deep wound. It's there to apply something that would address an issue once and for all.

Did you remember the Quality Circle programs which were all the rage in companies during the 1980s? Basically, the premise was that the team has the full autonomy in choosing what projects they focused on.

This is all well and good for empowering a team and giving them ownership over their work. However, more often than not, teams had the tendency to choose problems that are surface-level or are mere symptoms of something greater. In essence, they are not addressing the root cause of the issue.

For instance, you run a restaurant that has been floundering for years. On the analysis phase, you found out that the problem points to the product i.e. the services and food that you offer. Perhaps the food is sub-par, your wait staff are not responsive, or the overall state of your kitchen is an utter mess.

So, how do you go about solving the problem? Do you renovate the place and add new equipment? Do you retrain your team to provide better food and services? Do you hire new chefs or wait staff? Or do you just lower the prices and offer discounts?

Only you can answer that dilemma but let's just say that the solutions that directly address the core problem most certainly does not involve gimmicky promotions.

The point is that Lean Six Sigma is there to offer your business a chance at real improvement. An actual overhaul, if you may, instead of a mere makeover.

But here is the problem, though. It is often hard to get an organization to recognize just how important it is for the methodology to succeed in order for the entire business to succeed. It is here where your ability to diplomatically tell your staff why it is important to change without dictating them what to do next will come in.

II.   Team-Based Analysis

Cross-functional collaboration is a key aspect of the Lean Six Sigma methodology. The reason for this is quite simple: business processes, no matter what they are comprised of, are always cross-functional by nature. This means that every aspect of the process must correlate to one another and this is all the more important when it comes to analyzing problems in the process.

To put it simply, it is not enough to enhance a step. If you improve one aspect of the process at the expense of another, you are not exactly eliminating waste nor are you removing the probability of defects in the end product. You just made the problems move to another, and sometimes weaker, aspect of your production process.

And this is where the Lean Six Sigma methodology will encounter a lot of problems during implementation. Leaders, for instance, tend to find and address a problem on their own without informing the rest of the cross-functional team.

This might be permissible if the project is small in scope and the group composition is no more than 10 people. But in projects that are larger in scope or in cases where the leader has no previous experience with the process being analyzed, doing things on your own can be time-consuming or, worse, disastrous.

This is why Lean Six Sigma insists that you get the cross-functional team involved with the analysis. By having multiple people doing the analyzing with you (or for you), you can draw from a wider pool of knowledge and look things from different perspectives. In paper, this means that you can come up with a more comprehensive solution to a problem.

III.   Process Focus

As of now, you should realize that the Lean Six Sigma method is best used for analyzing process. In fact, even if a problem being investigated points towards the product being the main source, Lean Six Sigma will address the problem by changing the process that designs, builds, and delivers the product.

The reason for this is that Lean Six Sigma is meant to analyze and improve on actions which, in turn, is part of the overall process. Actions do not happen for no reason and rarely do they leave no impact to succeeding steps.

As such, you are best not ignoring every action that occurs and why they are made. And if you think that's complicated, don't worry. This is where the Value Stream Map is going to come in and you'd learn more of that later on.

With a Value Stream Map, everybody understands what's happening every phase of the process and how they correlate to one another. With this, you and your team gets an understanding as to the underlying problems that are otherwise hidden if you look everything from an isolated point of view.

For instance, if you recognize that there is a defect in the product, the Lean Six Sigma allows you to approach the problem through correlating the product with the steps that made it in the first place. Perhaps the fault was created on step 3 which was carried over in the succeeding phases. Once identified, you can now single out the problem and address it. It's like surgery; just with less blood and more charts.

IV.   Data

Lean Six Sigma is not a predictive framework. It does not rely on guesses (even calculated ones) but instead insists that you use data that can be verified and supported. Things like the current condition of your business's setup, the state of the production facilities and equipment you have, and the quality of the product and service that you offer are going to be scrutinized in the Measure phase.

In essence, Lean Six Sigma focuses on what is actually happening and not what you THINK is happening or might happen. It only through identifying the current state of things that you can hope to understand what must be fixed to make things better.

And, of course, data is not just for identifying problems. Once a solution has been mapped, data will then be gathered to determine if that solution is properly addressing the issue or not. And if it does solve the problem, data will be gathered again to find out how to make the solution sustainable or build on what has been achieved.

Why is data that integral to Lean Six Sigma, you ask? Here's the answer: no matter how you think you are transparent or open to change, the reality of your business's current state is often a tough pill to swallow. It may not be you per se or your team, but businesses often have a tough time accepting the fact that there is something wrong with their place.

Think of it this way: if you tell somebody that what they are doing is wrong, more often than not they'd resist the idea. But, if you come in heavy and present them with indisputable data through charts, graphs, and visual ideas, the more logical portion of their brain can put two and two together and come to the conclusion, for themselves, that what they are doing is wrong.

Simply put, you cannot hope to inspire change in your data by mere words alone. You have to back your claims with numerical and scientific data to appeal to the more reasonable part of your organization. If done right, this could lead to them making the necessary paradigm shift and implement sustainable changes.

V.   Solutions that Address the Root Cause

Some methodologies start with the assumption that every problem has a unique or special cause. And if that cause can be identified, eliminated, or controlled, the problem will go away.

There are other methodologies that start with the assumption that the problem is a naturally occurring element within the process i.e. the process itself is flawed. And if the process were to be changed, the problem will go away.

To be truthful, both approaches are effective, if not admirable. But Lean Six Sigma understands that the best way to fix a problem is to put in place a system where problems can be easily spotted first. This, in turn, can control the occurrence of that problem or give way for the overhaul of the entire process.

And in order to make sure that the solution does not make things worse, Lean Six Sigma uses tools that can help you identify whether a problem is unique to your current layout or is a generally occurring one across businesses and production processes similar to what you have.

By making this distinction, your team can go about finding and isolating the root cause of the problem. Once identified, the team can create a solution strategy that will properly address the issue.

For a common cause, your team has the option to redesign the entire process, eliminating unnecessary steps and activities. If the problem is more special in nature, then a more laser-focused solution is needed.

VI.   Making Solutions Sustainable

Lean Six Sigma is a methodology that is not content with identifying a problem and then solving it. The final phase of the process is something called Control, and this is where the challenge of keeping changes sustainable comes in.

You must expect resistance to come in all forms when implementing changes. Why is this so? Because, for many people and organizations, change is hard and uncomfortable. Security is best expressed in stability. The longer something remains as the status quo, the more comfortable people are in working along those systems and standards.

And this is can be a tough obstacle to deal with when implementing changes under the Lean Six Sigma method. New information has to be learned, old habits broken, and new methods have to be mastered. And while the rest of the organization is doing that, your team must also monitor how the implementations are carried out while setting up support systems, so everything does not revert back to the old standard.

In essence, you do not declare a victory under the Lean Six Sigma method just because you identified the root issue and came up with a winning solution for it. If the solution was successful once, the challenge then is to make it successful for a thousand times more. Consistency and sustainability are the two major indicators that whatever solution you came up with works and that the people behind the project are capable enough of applying it.

The Main Takeaway

Although these principles form the core of the methodology, you are not exactly required to follow them to the letter. They are only there to guide you to understand what needs to be improved on your business and how you go about bringing about those improvements.

As a matter of fact, you can have your own principles based on those mentioned above to guide how your staff goes about implementing the methodology. However, you must understand the intentions behind Lean

Six Sigma and these principles do explain why things must be done in this way or that.

By understanding the "spirit" behind these principles, you and your team can come to an agreement as to how Lean Six Sigma can be applied under your current layout. After all, you are not expected to succeed in doing anything without first understanding why you should focus on certain aspects or perform certain tasks.

Chapter 4 Benefits and Other Matters

Lean Six Sigma is promoted as a continuous improvement methodology. However, you might have a question that can boil down to this phrase "Improve on what?" Does the method improve product sales and increased customer engagement? Does it lower complaints due to defects or poor deliveries?

What about the human resource side of things? Will it improve employee morale? Can it make the workplace more conducive to individual development?

The answer to all of these is one big "YES". But, to make things simpler, let's look at the more general benefits that a well implemented Lean Six Sigma strategy can bring to your business.

I.   Organizational Benefits

The methodology was primarily meant for organizational application unlike other methodologies, especially Agile. As such, you can expect for the methodology to bring some tangible advantages for your organization which would include the following.

A. A Simplified Process

A direct result of eliminating waste and variation is that the overall process used by your business gets optimized. And by optimized, Lean Six Sigma means simplified. The cross-functional value stream maps will identify areas where waste is created the most, remove them, and create rework and workarounds for more persistent issues.

Once the waste is removed and the workarounds are no longer needed, what you would end up with is a process that is simpler and easier to manage. What happens, then, if the process no longer has unnecessary steps?

For starters, things get done faster now and end products can be delivered on time more consistently. This also leads to products of better quality which results in higher customer satisfaction ratings and, of course, increased sales.

Also, the faster process will lower overhead costs which will increase your profit margin.

B. Fewer Errors

The Lean Six Sigma process always starts with you defining what quality is acceptable for the entire project. This is of course based on what customers perceive to be valuable to them. This external focus on quality puts great emphasis on continuous improvements which makes the method effective in addressing actual root causes in a problem.

Also, the reliance on hard, irrefutable data over predictions and instinct will drive home the point that this method is all about solving actual problems, not just surface-level ones. The end result then is that the improvements implemented are more effective in addressing an issue while bringing the quality to a level more acceptable to customers. In essence, Lean Six Sigma is used not just to address problems. It is there to address the problems in your business that matter the most.

C. Better Performance Predictability and Control

It goes without saying that simpler processes are easier to control and manage than complex ones. The reason for this is that simplicity does away with variation which makes things even more predictable. To be more specific about it, the method helps you get better control on the process's cycle times, output quality, and overhead costs.

Think about it this way: If a process involves 3 steps, the chances of your staff mucking things up are fewer. Compare this to a process with 7 steps and 5 sub-processes where the margin of error is wider.

And when you make your processes more predictable and controllable, you give your business a tremendous advantage especially if you operate in an industry who has a nagging tendency to change standards from time to time. The Tech sector, for example, is quite notorious for consistently pushing the boundaries which means companies have little time to adjust to new tech standards before a new one is introduced.

Aside from changing technology, customers nowadays can be fickle which creates an even more unstable environment to do business on. With a predictable and controllable process, your business can adapt quickly without losing any momentum of sorts.

D. Active Control

Lean Six Sigma shortens cycle times and puts in control plans and support systems that are based on real-world data. And if you have short cycle times and data-based control systems, you and your staff are at a position to make better decisions that impact the way the entire process performs and at a faster time too. This should help in improving performance while also making boosting the morale of your team.

Aside from that, operators can now understand how their work can impact the overall process while also getting instant feedback. With this, operators won't feel like they are not in control with the process as they now can directly manage the process and also improve on it.

And with shorter cycles, the organization is better equipped to respond to changes in the marketplace. This means that you can make the necessary updates to your process to meet new standards without overspending or making things complicated again.

II.   Personal Benefits

Lean Six Sigma is something that must be applied on an organization level and has benefits that cover the same scope. But what about the individuals that make the implementations happen? What does the method offer to them on a personal level? Here are some of its personal benefits.

A. Personal Effectiveness

Lean Six Sigma has always been about solving problems which means that operating under it makes you even more competent in any position and industry. The methodology guides you through a clear-cut process that involves inquiry, identification, and solution creation.

In fact, you don't have to be a manager of some big-time company to even apply Lean Six Sigma. The tools that it offers to you can be applied on everyday situations, not just scenarios found in board room meetings and production facilities.

And even if you don't use all the tools given to you, the Lean Six Sigma process will make you more inclined to assert greater control in finding problems and fixing them. In essence, Lean Six Sigma might be a business method, but its application is practically unlimited.

B. Leadership Opportunities

The methodology was designed for project implementations and projects naturally require leaders. In Lean Six Sigma, not only is a manager required to exercise all their leadership skills, but they are given the chance to be exposed to other functions and departments within the organization. Of course, the exposure comes in the context of finding and addressing a real issue in the process.

Constant interaction with teams will improve your communication skills while directly addressing changes in the marketplace trains in you making strategic decisions at a moment's notice.

And, if you do succeed under Lean Six Sigma, you open yourself up for advancements in the organizational chart. After all, what would make the higher ups be more receptive of your presence than the fact that you led a project which helps them save on expenses, improved their product, and reduced unnecessary by products in the production process?

C. Higher Pay and Upper Movement

Here's one benefit that the Lean Six Sigma method can offer to all of its practitioners: Credentials. The method has a "ladderized" system of certification. The more "belts" you get, the more qualified you become (for any higher-paying positions).

The reason is quite simple on a management perspective. Lean Six Sigma is easy to understand but there is a certain challenge to its application. Those that do manage to implement it effectively for projects gives higher ups an impression that they are ready for bigger responsibilities.

Of course, that promotion comes with its perks which always includes a higher salary. The rate may vary from one industry or country to another but it's easy to say that LSS certified people tend to land more rewarding jobs. As such, if you are the one that wants to quickly move through the ranks of your organization, then mastering Lean Six Sigma might help you do just that.

But what if you are already on the top of the organization chart? Since there is technically no upper movement possible, Lean Six Sigma is highly effective in making sure that your tenure in the organization is secured. It does this not through some underhanded, political maneuvering but through an honest, concerted effort to overhaul things below you so that they bring about the best of everyone in the organization.

In essence, by bringing about necessary changes and overseeing their implementation, you put yourself in a position where people can attribute whatever benefits they are reaping from the method to you. It's one way of making sure that you stay where you are in the organization for as long as humanly possible.

Where is Lean Six Sigma being used?

Right now, you might be wondering as to what industries and functions have Lean Six Sigma been used. The short answer is "Everywhere". Here's the more comprehensive answer, if you are wondering:

As was stated, Lean originated from Japan's automotive industry and Six Sigma from a high-tech system manufacturer. What this means is that Lean Six Sigma found its home in manufacturing industries. However, it was found out that the method can also be applied for other projects that do not necessarily revolve around process engineering and quality control. Here's a list of departments where the methodology has also found a place in:

- Logistics
- Information Technology
- Legal Services
- Maintenance
- Marketing
- Research and Development
- Sales
- Customer Service
- Human Resources
- Finance
- Engineering
- Product Testing

And Lean Six Sigma has also extended its reach into several well-known industries across the world including:

- Agriculture
- Aviation
- Banking and Finance
- Electronics
- Government
- Educational Services

- Healthcare

- Medical Products and Services

- Mining

- Energy

- Pharmaceuticals

- Retail

- Transportation

- Telecommunications

What Does this All Mean?

So, what does these benefits and wide range of applicability in Lean Six Sigma mean to you? For starters, it should give you the idea that the methodology is highly applicable regardless of what project you are undertaking in whatever industry that you are working on. As a matter of fact, you don't need to be that business-savvy in order to have an appreciation of what Lean Six Sigma has to offer.

Second, the methodology is potentially effective in addressing issues in your organization while also making its output better. All that is needed, then, is for you to understand how the process should be implemented into whatever system you currently have for your organization.

Chapter 5 Ranks, Tools, and Techniques

So far, you have been told why Lean Six Sigma is good and what guides it. However, you might be asking yourself now "When will I get to know how it's going to be done?"

Fortunately for you, that time is now. And to fully understand how the methodology is applied, you'd have to know the different ranks, tools, and techniques that are made available to you and your team.

Lean Six Sigma Ranks

The methodology takes a lot of cues from its parent Six Sigma framework as far as rank naming conventions are concerned. To put it simply, Six Sigma took its ranking names from Japanese martial arts.

In short, think of your team as a Karate Dojo; just minus the bamboo flooring and the need to punch somebody in the face. And since this is based on Karate, each rank has its own set of required training and certification.

Each organization used to set their own standards when it comes to applying Lean Six Sigma in the past. However, most groups today refer to the standards set by organizations like the American Society for Quality and the International Association of Six Sigma Certification.

Also, you don't have to use these names for your group per se if you find them a bit corny. Just get familiarized with what responsibilities each rank has to take in order to pull off Lean Six Sigma right.

A. The White Belt

This is where everyone who wishes to master the Lean Six Sigma methodology starts with. And just like in martial arts, Lean Six Sigma white belts are novices. The concept has just been recently introduced to them which means that they have yet to master any skill, tool, technique, or even principle.

As far as your Lean Six Sigma project team is concerned, White Belts should not take any active role as their focus is to complete the basic program. However, there is no harm in letting them try out simpler tasks such as gathering data to assist the higher ranks.

B. The Yellow Belt

Forming the base line of the Lean Six Sigma hierarchy, the yellow belts serve as the primary implementation agents of the method for various projects. As they are the starting rank, anyone who wants to become a yellow belt must simply learn the basics of the methodology and its various tools and techniques.

- The yellow belters are expected to take part in team meetings and would serve the role of a subject matter expert for their assigned function. Of course, that function is to be exercised in tandem with their full-time job.

- Depending on the size and scope of a project, there can be more than 3 yellow belts that form part of the team. Some of these yellow belts would have to divide their time performing tasks for multiple project teams.

- Training for yellow belts would mostly focus on the structure of the methodology and the use of various cross-functional tools and techniques.

- For analysis, the yellow belt is mostly relegated to assisting the green and black belt through collecting pertinent information. However, they may be able to help in interpreting the results provided that they already have the skills for it.

- Yellow belts are primarily required to lead the implementation of a solution within their own function or discipline.

C. The Green Belt

Like the yellow belts, green belts can also be numerous within an organization and usually serve the role of a project leader. The green belt is expected to work on Lean Six Sigma projects that fall within their own areas of expertise.

And since this is one rank higher, a green belt is expected to have mastered the basic Lean Six Sigma methodology and structure. They are also capable of applying the analytical tools and strategies for their respective projects.

- The green belt would lead various small projects that focus on one function or area of the entire business process. This is also performed in conjunction with their full-time job.

- Most green belts would also lead projects that is associated with improving one aspect of the business process. But there are also cases where green belts can take part in large cross-functional projects often lead by a black belt.

- As the project leader, the green belt will do the analytical portion of the Lean Six Sigma process, often leading it or observing the work of yellow belts.

- As the leader, the green belt is also expected to make sure that Lean Six Sigma is implemented properly and the tools and techniques it uses are employed appropriately.

- At Phase Gate Reviews, the green belt will do the presentation of data and the subsequent discussions. Their advanced training under the Lean Six Sigma methodology also means that that they are the most capable of interpreting the information they are presenting for the rest of the team or organization.

- The green belt is not exactly the subject matter expert for all aspects of the Lean Six Sigma implementation process. However, they can be an expert for some part of the process, product, or service.

As such, they can bring their expertise in the discussion the same way that a Yellow belt does. But that does not mean that everyone must expect for them to know everything about the process. And if they do encounter a problem in implementing a solution, they can turn to the black belt for advice and instruction.

D. The Black Belt

Organizations can have multiple black belts, although not as numerous as green and yellow belts. The black belt serves as the subject matter expert for a specific function or location within the organization. They are tasked with leading large cross-functional projects while serving as mentors for green and yellow belts within a particular group or department.

As a black belt, a person is not only required to master the basics of the Lean Six Sigma methodology, but they must also know how to appropriately apply the same. A black belt's day would include the following tasks:

- Conducting a team meeting for one of the projects that they are leading.

- Meeting with green and yellow belts to review what progresses they have made and provide instruction for the next steps.

- Performing an analysis on the value stream map for one of the projects that they are leading.

- Provide training for prospective green and yellow belts regarding the Lean Six Sigma methodology and tools.

- Meet with the organization's stakeholders, leaders, and even clients to discuss the status of the projects that they are leading. They must also identify various issues and problems which must be avoided in future projects.

Clearly, the black belt is expected to lead various projects simultaneously while acting as a mentor for the ranks below them. The projects that they lead are also large in scope and cross-functional by design.

However, the most challenging part of their "duties" would have to be dealing with many different stakeholders. And once they do complete several projects, a black belt must be reassigned to a new function or department so as not to stagnate in their position.

E. The Master Black Belt

The last level of the Lean Six Sigma method, the Master Black Belt serves as the one managing the entire initiative of implementing the method in the organization. Unlike the previous ranks (and like Connor Macleod from Highlander), there can only be one Master Black Belt for every Lean Six Sigma organization.

Master Black Belts are full-time position and it comes with a number of responsibilities which include:

- On the perspective of training and certification, there is actually nothing that distinguishes a master black belt from your regular Lean Six Sigma black belt. However, their responsibilities are larger in scope and reach.

- The master black belt will not be managing a particular project. Rather, they are going to make sure that the Lean Six Sigma initiative is maintained for as long as possible.

- Master Black belts normally work closely with senior management to determine how many black, yellow, and green belts are needed and which functional departments and locations would get them first.

- They are required to maintain a status portfolio of projects. Here, they will detail what projects have been completed, which ones are currently being implemented, and what has been proposed in the most recent meetings.

In relation to this, they are able to assess the impact of the overall Lean Six Sigma program on the organization and they can determine which improvement efforts must be prioritized depending on what strategy the organization agrees to.

- The master black belt also work with the Human Resources department to maintain training records of all yellow, green, and black belts currently operating in the organization.

- If an organization is rather small or the Lean Six Sigma initiative is limitedly applied, the role of Master Black Belt can be assumed by any of the available black belts.

Important Note: Although the naming of the ranks are taken from martial arts, they do not come with the notion of Seniority in Lean Six Sigma. Nobody is nobody's "senpai" (senior) or "kouhai" (junior) in Lean Six Sigma. As such, you cannot use an LSS title to pull rank with your team (not that it is advisable to do so in recent years, mind you).

What the organizational structure simply implies is that the workload for implementing the Lean Six Sigma methodology is evenly distributed across the chart. No one is supposed to do less or more than what they were trained to do but each must make sure that they contribute to the initiative to the best of their abilities.

And, as was stated, you don't have to use this particular organizational structure for your group. Just make sure that everyone has a workload that reflects their skills and expertise while laying out a clear line of communication. This way, your team can know who reports to who and what tasks they must focus on for every phase of the project.

Tools and Techniques

Now that you know of the organizational structure of a Lean Six Sigma team, it's time to look at the tools and techniques that you are going to equip them with. A lot of these tools are older than even Lean or Six

Sigma, having only been incorporated to Lean Six Sigma as the years went on.

One of the best features of Lean Six Sigma is that you don't have to master all of these tools at once. They are divided into phases meaning they only come necessary at certain points of the business process. This means that any team can pick and choose which tools to use depending on the situation. In fact, every organization has their own set of favorite tools and techniques under the Lean Six Sigma method.

But, all the same, it's time to get acquainted with you and your team's Lean Six Sigma arsenal.

1) Process Analysis

These tools are mostly associated with the Lean portion of the method. As such, they are meant to describe the process for you while also identifying what could make it efficient.

- **The Process Map** – This is a graphical display that shows how each step and process correlate with one another. In turn, this gives your team an idea as to how one decision you'd make for one part of the process would affect the rest. Each process and step will be marked as a separate item on the map.

- **Value Stream Map** –. This process map shows the primary flow of processes if every step goes as planned. A major focus here is how value is created and delivered in every part of the process.

- **As-Is Process -** This is a special variant of the process map that shows all the steps of the process as they are carried out in the business's current environment. This is not something that is exactly similar as what is documented in procedural charts.

- **To-Be Process** – If the As-Is chart shows how things are done currently, then the To-Be process shows how things are supposed to be done. This is often reflected in the revisions of the business process and its documentation that is released as part of the implementation.

- **Data Boxes** — These are located in the process and value stream maps. They are used to record the metrics associated with a particular step such as cycle times, inventory, available resources, and value-added time.

- **TAKT Time** — This is a measure that is associated with the process being analyzed. It will reflect the amount of time allowed for each process that ensures that the process meets the demands of the customer.

- **Roll Throughput Yield** — This is an equation that determines the probability that an item will pass through every part of the process properly and creates something valuable. It is done by multiplying all the step yield values from the value stream map.

- **Work-cells** — This process structure is used to speed up the flow through the process. All process steps will be arranged together in a single work cell which reduces time spent in transitioning between steps.

- **Kanban** — A variant of the lean method, Kanban is a visual scheduling approach where the previous step provides a signal for the next step to commence. On paper, this allows your team to minimize on inventory as you only have to stock up on materials necessary for that step of the project.

- **Visual Control** — This is a signaling system which allows operators to anticipate potential bottlenecks in the process. Once identified, they can then set up activities meant to relieve pressure in those areas, preventing the bottleneck from happening. It is an ideal tool for real-time process management.

2) Visual Analysis

A staple in every problem-solving methodology, visual analysis tools and techniques can be used in multiple phases in the process. And because they are visual by design, these tools are easy to understand.

They also make communicating ideas and proposals to senior management and operations easy to understand, especially in helping them see how one change can affect the solution and the process.

- **Histogram** – A vertical bar chart, this Histogram shows the relative size of different categories of various instances and occurrences. It is used for the identification of the biggest contributing attributes to a problem.

- **Pareto Chart** – This is a variant of the Histogram which organizes the biggest categories first down to the smallest. You may use this to determine which categories need to be prioritized when solving a problem.

- **Fishbone Diagram** – Also known as the Cause and Effect Program, this graph shows all the possible consequences that could occur because of an unsolved problem. This can be used as a tool to identify what caused a problem in the first place.

- **Scatter Diagram** – This chart plots two attributes that are associated in a data point. One attribute is shown on the vertical axis and the other on the horizontal axis. The diagram will show if there is a correlation or a tendency towards correlation between the two attributes.

- **Box Plots** – This tool shows the spread of data for a parameter and the nature of any attribute that tends to occur. The center half are shown in a box with a line going to value in the midpoint. The outer half of the data will then be placed in the upper and lower portions of the box, showing the extremes of what is most or least likely to occur if the attributes in the center are present.

- **Run Chart** – This diagram shows a sequence of values for a certain parameter used in a process. The values are either seen in each successive product or collected at set times in the middle of a production process.

- **Pie Chart** – This circular chart shows the relative size of categories in relation to a specific parameter. Each category gets a slice of the "pie", the ones with the heaviest correlation to a parameter getting the biggest slices.

- **Check Sheet** — A rather simple visual took, the check sheet only shows what needs to be measured in the end product. If the product meets a certain quality, that item will be marked with a check mark.

- **Solution Selection Matrix** — This matrix compares various options of a solution across several criteria. It takes inspiration from the Pugh Concept Matrix and assigns scores to each option, giving you and your team an idea as to which ones are the most applicable for a certain problem. Of course, the one that scores the highest will be the most applicable.

- **Quality Selection Matrix** — This is a matrix is a diagram that shows how the expectations and needs of the customer is met across the business process. You should use this to set performance goals for the process, identify potential waste, and any missed opportunity your team did not notice in the previous cycles.

- **Bottlenecks** — When tasks or processes start to get backed up in a part of the production cycle, this is what is called as a bottleneck. And it is at bottlenecks where the most waste is being generated including slow moving inventory, long wait times, and extra management needed just to decongest everything.

- **Five S** — This is a special set of workplace disciplines that focus on organizing assets and resources. How your team can abide by the 5 S rules (if you apply them, of course) will determine how smooth your operations will be.

- **Poka Yoke** — If Five S is about maximizing space and wise inventory management, Poka Yoke is all about making the workplace error-proof. Used in the design process, Poka Yoke uses quality checks and gates to ensure that there are no mistakes made for every segment of the process. Or, at the very least, Poka Yoke makes mistakes even more obvious that they are now easier to address before the product gets shipped.

3) Statistical Analysis

If the analytical tools lean more to the Lean side of things, the Statistical Analysis tools would lean more to the Six Sigma side of the method. Statistical analysis helps you and your team make sense of the data that you gathered and determine what is the most significant in addressing a problem.

For these tools, you might have to purchase software such as the Excess Analysis Tool Pak or the Minitab application since processing and interpreting the data they collect manually is nothing short of difficult. Of course, the people assigned to interpret the data in these tools must be trained to do so. This means that the tools as mentioned below are something that only green belts and higher can appreciate.

- **Process Capability** – This statistical ratio compares normal process variability with the specifications set by the customer. It is expressed through metrics like Cp, Pp, Cpk, Ppk, and other variables. In short, this tool is ideal for predicting whether or not a process has the ability to deliver on the specifications without creating defects.

- **Descriptive Statistics** – These set of statistical techniques describe a normal behavior for a process in relation with a specific parameter or the end product. This includes the median, mean, mode, and standard deviation.

- **Inferential Statistics** – This statistical method is used to relate the statistical performance of a sample to the statistical performance of the larger population. This approach is reliant on the sampling approach used and the confidence interval and level employed.

- **Measurement System Analysis** – This comprehensive analysis tool is used to inspect and test systems in their ability to correctly identify a measured value within a process or the product itself. It will include assessing the accuracy, precision, stability, linearity, and discrimination.

- **Gage R&R** – This tool is focused on determining how accurate your measurement systems being used are. It uses experiments that focus on comparing products and processes with a predetermined set of values and testing how frequently those values are being met in every production cycle.

- **Hypothesis Test** – This test is used to determine whether an assumption you set for a specific data can be verified or not. Typically, it is used in the Lean Six Sigma procedure to determine if the samples gathered are statistically similar to one another or there are substantial differences in each.

In case of dissimilarity, this would tell you and your staff that a change that you are planning to maintain can have a significant impact to the process or the end product. There are different sub-techniques that you can use here depending on the data and the number of parameters that have to be scrutinized.

4) Project and Team Management Tools

The ability to connect a project with the strategies of upper management and customers is also something that Lean Six Sigma also focuses on. Fortunately for you, there are tools and techniques that can help you manage the project and team in relation with external people.

Some of these tools are useful in understanding how external people view the project. Others are highly effective in streamlining the internal and external channels of communications. Either way, these tools can make handling your project marginally easier.

- **Critical to Quality** – These parameters focus on the product, process, and service especially on their ability to deliver on the value promised to customers. The CTQ attributes, however, is not something that you and your team would come up with. It is something that only external people like the stakeholders and the client can create for the team.

- **Project Charter** – This document is used to authorize the project and provide its scope. In essence, they give the direction and boundaries that a team needs in order to meet the specifications of the project. There is no proper format for the charter which means organizations use their own unique framework for this.

- **In-Frame/Out-Frame** – This technique is used to clarify boundaries for a project that the team must follow. As such, the scope will be determined in this frame as well as the areas that the team must not focus on during each phase.

- **SIPOC** – This stands for Supplier, Input, Process, Output, and Customer. It is another limit-identifying technique to define the limits of the process while also helping stakeholders understand how the project can be completed.

- **The Cross-Functional Team** - This simply refers to the Six Sigma Team that you have built up regardless of its composition and set of shared responsibilities. Normally, every function of the team will have a representative who will join in on team meetings and explain key issues in their subject matter of expertise.

- **Team Decision Making** - This decentralized form of decision making puts more focus on the team coming to a consensus first before acting. Although your teams still rely on hard data, they still have the ability to prioritize what needs to be done and who will be in charge for each segment of the implementation process.

- **Culture Change Management** - Implementing Lean Six Sigma on your projects is not going to be sustainable if you don't set up the proper support for it. This is where Culture Change Management comes in as it helps the rest of the organization get used to the new standards and master the new protocols for the business process.

A core focus in this management strategy is in building enough support during the Improvement and Control Phases. If done right, any change you would want to implement is not only effective but also sustained for a long period of time.

- **Stakeholder Management -** This is what you should use in identifying the key stakeholders in your Lean Six Sigma projects. Who are the stakeholders for each LSS project you would take? What are their performance goals and communication lines?

- **Implementation Planning -** This is a set of practices that will help the team understand how to execute a change in the project or a project itself. Matters such as the division of labor as well as the time period for which changes should be observed will be discussed here.

To Summarize

As was previously stated, you don't have to use all of these tools for your Lean Six Sigma projects. In fact, you might have noticed that there are some tools and strategies whose goals and functions are already covered by others or that some strategies are best used for smaller or larger projects, depending on the case.

With that being said, however, there are also tools and strategies listed above that form the core concept of Lean Six Sigma. Things like setting up a Cross-Functional Team or several analytical/statistical practices are things that you and your team must set up properly in order to carry out the LSS changes in your organization.

It's up to the team, then, to determine which tools and strategies are best for their current project. It would also help the teams if they do not become dead-set on using one particular strategy over and over throughout multiple projects. It's a good thing to master a tool but this should never be done at the expense of other items in the arsenal, especially if one tool or strategy answers an issue more efficiently than the others.

Chapter 6 The Lean Six Sigma Process

The process for problem-solving under the Lean Six Sigma methodology actually borrows from its Six Sigma predecessor. In short, the process is divided into 5 phases known collectively as DMAIC or Define, Measure, Analyze, Improve, and Control.

Each of the phases has a premise or question that must be answered. And if that question is answered, the project can proceed to the next phase.

So, how long should each phase last? That depends truly on what your project is trying to solve. Normally, at the end of each phase, there is a review to discuss what has been achieved so far and what must be improved before the next phase begins.

Now, let's take a look at these phases in detail.

Define

This is the first phase of the process and must answer this question "has the problem been identified from multiple perspectives?". Normally, in this phase, a Green Belt or Black Belt will be tasked with describing the problem to the rest of the team.

Aside from explaining the problem, the specifications for the project can also be identified. Thus, the number of yellow belts can be proposed by the team to the higher ups here as well as the scope of the entire process.

During this phase, those who will become yellow belts will have to undergo basic Lean Six Sigma training if there are no available yellow belts within the organization yet. The phase will then end with the team coming up with a project charter which identifies the problem and how the project is going to solve it. Of course, what goals must be achieved and how success will be determined may also be discussed in this phase.

Measure

In this phase, the baseline condition of the process is set up. This can be done by identifying the current performance of the progress, the product, or the service in relation to the critical attributes of quality or success as identified in the Define phase.

And what should be asked in this phase? It is "How much do we understand of the current process and can we gauge performance in each step?"

And this is where things get tricky. If you were not the one to document or even properly control every step of the process, this phase is going to take a while to complete. The reason for such is because you have to establish the current standards first so you could find out how to make improvements. And you cannot do this without documenting each step and measure of the current workflow.

The processes must be defined so that you and your team can determine the flow of one step to another especially in delivering that value until it reaches the customer.

More often than not, businesses do not have the appropriate system to measure and collect data, so they need to be developed first. This is where the subject matter experts (the green and yellow belts) will come in as they gather and interpret data from the business's current layout.

By the end of this phase, every problem and issue identified must be quantified or supported with hard data. But, most importantly, the "As-Is" state of the business process must be established so the "To-Be" Process can start to take form.

Analyze

This phase of the process is particularly focused on answering the question "What is the root cause of this problem?". In this part, every data gathered in the succeeding phases will be processed, analyzed, and interpreted by the green and black belts. As such, it is at this phase where the leader has to decide what kind of analytical and statistical tools they have to employ to determine what makes a problem tick.

It is at this phase where the concept of Hypothesis Testing comes into play. What is this, you may ask? The term might sound technical and scientific (and it is), the premise is rather simple.

When confronted with a problem, anybody of sound mind would usually come up with a theory on what caused it. Let's say, for example, that your business just had to recall batches of the products it shipped. As someone who has an understanding of the business process, you might have some hunches as to what caused it.

With your hypotheses as your base, you and your team will then conduct a series of analytical and statistical interpretation sessions to see if the data supports any of the causes you suspect produced the problem. And if not, the process will get your team acquainted with a bigger, underlying problem that has never been addressed before.

And don't worry about the math. The computations are rigorous but the process itself of comparing and contrasting data is rather straightforward. This is quite true if you and your team decide to use some tools like Excel's Analysis Tools.

Another important aspect of this phase is the accuracy of the problem you have identified. In essence, the team must be extra careful not to prepare a detailed problem statement. There is a strong chance that you might base your entire analysis on a wrongly assumed problem. This causes you to lose time and effort especially on the next phase.

Improve

It's important to remember that this is the 4th phase. Why? A lot of Lean Six Sigma teams make the mistake of rushing to this part of the process without thoroughly completing the previous three. And if your team does that, you create a solution that addresses what is merely a symptom, not the actual problem.

And thus, the question to be asked here is "Is there a solution for this problem that is viable, effective, and easy to implement?" Depending on the nature of the problem, your team members might have to assume a larger or smaller role to create a solution.

And, of course, this is going to be the more labor-extensive and expensive phase of the Lean Six Sigma process. This is where to the "To-Be" state of the process will be realized, after all, and that would involve changing equipment, adding new software, overhauling the entire production process, and re-training operators.

While implementation is on-going, the green and yellow belts do not stop in gathering and interpreting data. At this point, however, their focus is not on validating the problem but monitoring if the solution is effective in addressing a problem even at a controlled environment.

Either way, every viable solution must be thoroughly tested while the implementation materials are being developed. At the end of this phase, you and your team should have a solution ready for deployment.

Control

This is the final phase of the process and should answer the question "Can the solution now become the new standard?" To be more specific about it, the Lean Six Sigma team at this point should determine whether or not the solution has properly addressed the problem.

And not only should the solution address the issue properly, it must do so consecutively. A mistake that teams often make at this point is celebrating "false" successes where some effect they think is good occurs and they assume that this solved the problem.

All members of the project are to be involved in this phase especially in monitoring the implementation process in their respective departments. This phase will continue to remain in effect until a sense of stability can be observed. As such, this phase will take weeks to a month to occur.

In order to properly execute this phase, the team must have set up a control plan to monitor changes in the product or process. This will include thresholds wherein performance can be measured as well as corrective strategies to be implemented in case performance takes a dip.

This is a rather crucial part of the phase as the last thing you would want to happen is if everybody reverts back to the old process. In most cases, a plan of this type will also use statistical process controls.

Once the operators of the process no longer need the control and support of the project team, then and only then can you say that this phase is finished, and the entire Lean Six Sigma process is completed.

Phase Gate Reviews

So far, the Lean Six Sigma process will involve everyone in the project team and that includes the yellow, green, black, and master black belts. But they are not the only people that needs to do something in order to implement Lean Six Sigma properly.

Upper management and stakeholders also need to be aware of whatever is happening through the five phases. These people along with the master black belt, or any of available black belts, will conduct what is called as a Phase Gate Review.

So, what's a Phase Gate? It is simply that period of the process where one phase is about to end, and another begins. To be simpler about it, a Phase Gate Is that period in between phases. As such, a Phase Gate Review is simply a periodical reporting session where the team and the upper management discuss what has been achieved so far in the Lean Six Sigma methodology.

The review of Phase Gates is meant to achieve three purposes:

- Review the work of most recent phase completed to make sure that everything was done according to the LSS method. If anything, inadequate was discovered, the upper management may compel the project team to do over certain steps and come back for another review. It is here that the Black Belt will inform the team what was their perceived weaknesses or mistakes and will coach them on how to do address such.

- Take a look at whether or not the pertinent question of the phase has been sufficiently answered. Also, the review will cover any documentation and supporting data gathered. If the data does not support the answer, the team can be compelled to continue on the phase until the question has been sufficiently answered.

- Set up the boundaries for the project. This focuses on the specifications for the next phase based on the results of the previous phase. Some examples of a boundary include setting up a time-window for data gathering and interpretation of the Measure Phase or setting up a budget limit for implementations in the Improve Phase.

One Important Note: Of course, it is assumed that the people doing the Phase Gate Review are aware of the basics of the Lean Six Sigma process. After all, nothing can derail and demoralize a project more than a committee that asks the wrong questions for any given phase.

For instance, if the upper management persists on making the team find a solution for a problem when everybody is still in the Define Phase is a bit premature. The proper forum for that question is for the Phase Gate review for the Analyze Phase.

As such, it is the duty of the assigned Black Belt to make sure that the reviewing team are aware of what questions the team is trying to answer for each phase of the process. This includes cutting them promptly (politely, of course. Remember that they are still your superiors) and informing that such question should be reserved later.

And, of course, you should be ready for the possibility for resistance of miscommunication in this part of the process. Thus, you should find a way to make sure that everybody in the team and the higher ups are in the same page.

If your team has a concern that they need to be addressed or a special request for the next phase, they must not feel intimidated by the higher ups to ask for assistance in such. And if the higher ups feel that the project is getting out of hand, you must find a way to communicate the same without demoralizing your team.

An open and transparent line of communication will actually help you bridge the gap between your teams and the higher-ups that all of you have to answer to in the end. And if both parties are satisfied, any favorable response you get from either is a tell-tale sign that everybody has understood the important of the Lean Six Sigma initiative.

Chapter 7 Lean Six Sigma in Action

So, how do you go about applying the Lean Six Sigma Process?

This is a rather loaded question because the methodology is not something that is actually that easy to comprehend, especially if you are new to it. And talking about this methodology using complex, technical words without some illustration is not going to help matters.

But, don't worry. It is a rather straightforward process which is why it is best to discuss each phase of the methodology by using a real-world scenario.

The Problem

For the rest of the chapter, you and I are going to solve a problem that maybe hypothetical but is based on what is currently happening in various homes across the world. In fact, you might have encountered this yourself.

Every morning when you go out for work, what is the one thing that you always do aside from taking a bath and taking in your morning coffee?

If you answered, "look for my keys", then you and perhaps millions of other readers are correct. And here lies the problem: What if you can't find them quickly?

You rummage through the pants you've used last night, and they weren't there. You checked the countertop and it they aren't there. You check the hook where you usually hang them, and they aren't there. Now, you're getting frustrated. Let us say, for brevity's sake, that you found them at the couch to your immediate relief.

The question now is this: how many minutes every day that did you lose over finding your keys? How many times in a week were you at risk of missing the bus or train to the city? And, what if you arrive at your business only to find out that you brought the WRONG set of keys which means you can't unlock important storage units and containers until someone who has the duplicates does it for you?

The point is that this mild annoyance has occurred multiple times in the past and has been affecting how you start your day. And, you being the responsible kind of person, decided that enough is enough and would want to put up something that makes sure that this does not ever happen again.

Now, it is time to apply the Lean Six Sigma Methodology to solve this problem of yours.

A. Define Phase

First, let's start by considering this problem from the perspective of the customer. So, who's the person going to benefit greatly from your changes? Yes, that's right. You.

How are you going to benefit from this? For starters, you now have a definite place to store your keys every night. This means you cut down on time looking for them which means you don't leave your home in a hurry.

Next, there is the fact that you always have the right set of keys with you. Whether you are opening the business or a more personal storage container, you always have the right key for every lock that you encounter for a single day.

Either way, the keys can be in one place that you can immediately head out and pick up every morning. Based upon the In-Frame and Out-of-Frame, you can decide to limit the process to what you do with the keys every night and at morning of the next day. You will not include everything else that does not involve your fingers touching those keys such as taking a bath or eating your breakfast.

Thus, the goal of your project in the charter is to implement a system where you can immediately acquire the right set of keys before you head out of the house.

B. Measure Phase

At this phase, you should start creating a process map that shows what could possible happen to your keys from the moment you arrive at home and ends with your arrival at the office the next day. This process can have different branches depending on whether the following day is a regular workday, a weekend, or a holiday.

You can even differentiate things further to accommodate variables like you going out the night before or the weather was bad that you required additional preparation time the next morning. You might even have to factor in every unplanned shift in your usual activities like having to work overtime or encountering an emergency on the road.

Either way, you will find out that mapping the process for weekends and holidays are so varied that it is next to impossible. But the process for your weekdays can be predictable which makes mapping easy.

Your As-Is process may look something like this:

1. Arrive at home

2. Unlock Door

3. Put things on desk

4. Empty pocket

5. Change clothes

6. (Evening passes and morning comes)

7. Get dressed

8. Grab things on desk

9. Find your keys

10. Lock the door

11. Arrive at work

12. Unlock desk, cabinets, and other storage units

You can even add time metric and success metric for each step. Just keep in mind, however, that there are only three of those steps that have a value-added time element to them. Those steps are emptying pockets, finding the keys, and unlocking the doors and cabinets. And, of course, all of those steps have a high success metric except for Finding the Keys.

One challenge you will face in mapping the process is defining a pass or fail condition for each step. This can be obvious as you have to determine the purpose of each step to identify what outcome you desire the most.

You then have to collect data for these steps in a span of four weeks or more. You check sheets every night before bedtime and take notes of how much time each step must be completed. At the same time, you record everything that you have done with your keys if ever there you have to use them on a weekend or a holiday during that data gathering period.

One other challenge that you would have to face during this time is something called the Hawthorne Effect. This is where the measurement of a parameter changes what people do. Simply put, since you are now monitoring what you are doing, you subconsciously change your behavior to become more cautious.

It's similar to how wait staff behave if they know one of the diners in the evening happens to be a Michelin reviewer. If the subjects know that they are being measured, their behavior changes to respond to the test.

As such, you run the risk of not collecting data that would reflect your usual daily performance under the process. In this scenario, your brain might subconsciously remember where you left your keys, impacting the results in step 9.

C. Analyze Phase

Now that you have data, you can start analyzing your process. Sure, there is no data for weekends and holidays but the lack of such provides little variation for the process most of the time. The point is that you know have a sequence of events that depict what happens to your keys the moment you arrive at home and when you arrive for work the next; and backed up by hard data.

So, you create a Fishbone Diagram to determine the root causes. Perhaps you came up with six possible causes given your regular proximity to the place where you should place the keys every night or how active you are outside of work.

So, your diagram could look something like this:

Drops Keys   No proper key placement   Keys get stuck in couch

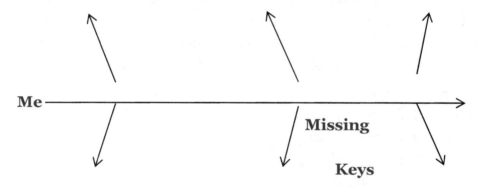

Got drunk last night   Increment weather   Housemates move them

Your Fishbone diagram can also be explained like this:

a) You don't have a designated place to store your keys at every night.

b) You just drop the keys wherever you place your baggage at.

c) You drop the keys right at your last known spike of activity I.e. the couch after binge-watching your favorite show.

d) In days when the weather is bad, where you have extra layers of clothing, you just place your keys at the pocket of your coat which hangs at the closet.

e) You have nightly drinking sessions with your friends which causes you to black out and not remember where you placed your keys in the morning after.

f) When someone you live with sees that your keys are placed in an unusual location, they might move it without asking your permission.

Now, which of these possible causes are most likely to occur? You can arrange the causes according to their order of possibility and frequency which might look like this:

1. No proper key placement

2. Drops Keys

3. Keys stuck in couch

4. Housemates move them

5. Increment weather

6. Got drunk

So, you can figure out that a lack of key placement is the most frequently-occurring possible root cause of your problem. But you think for yourself "Does it share elements with the rest?". You might be surprised that possible causes that share a common element might point you to the presence of a bigger, underlying issue. Let's take a look.

If you have a tendency to just drop your keys wherever you left your bags, that means that your brain does not recognize a system where you should place key items of your work at home. And if your keys do get left in the coach after your last nighttime activity, that also points to the fact that you don't have a set system for key placement.

If your housemates tend to relocate your keys, that means that there is no set system for proper key placement at home. And if you lose your keys because you blacked out last night, then your brain does not subconsciously recognize where to place the keys even at an inebriated state.

So, what do these possible causes share? Yes, that's right. You do not have a definite place where the keys can be stored every time you arrive at home.

If you want to be detailed about it, your analysis could look like this:

Problem: You take time finding your keys every morning.

Primary Cause: When arriving at home, you just place the keys wherever you feel like it. Sometimes, it just stays in your coat or back pocket hours after arrival.

Root Cause: No defined system for proper key placement established at home.

D. Improve Phase

This is now the time to come up with a solution. The question, however, is this: which solution is the best? There are many ways to address your key problem. Your first option was to put a lock on the door so that you can just place the keys there. But the strategy is not particularly good to look at and the hook is too small that you might end up forgetting it existed in the first place.

The next option is to connect your keys to your bag or belt. However, the connecting chains are too gaudy to look at and you run the risk of losing your keys if you lose your belt or bag. The third option was to place an RFID tag on your keys which can be monitored via an app. Your only concern here is that the RFID system is more expensive.

You could weigh the pros and cons of each but that is not exactly methodical as the Lean Six Sigma framework requires you to be. At this point, you can use a Solution Selection Matrix where each solution will be graded in several categories

Let us say that an option that gets a perfect score in one category should get 5 points and the lowest possible score is 1. So here's an example:

Solution	Low Cost	Aesthetics	Convenience	Total
Door Hook	4	2	5	11

RFID	1	5	5	11
Belt/Bag Chain	3	1	3	7
A bowl on the desk	5	5	5	15
Get a duplicate	2	3	5	10

At a glance, you noticed that the Bowl on Desk solution ranked the highest. Why? It is cheap to acquire, it blends well with your current table/counter layout, and it is big enough to be noticed whenever you enter the room.

And thus, you decided to use the Bowl on Desk strategy to address the issue. Now, how should it be incorporated to your process? It might look something like this:

1. Arrive home

2. Unlock Door

3. Put things on desk

4. Empty pocket

5. Place keys on bowl

6. Change clothes

7. Check keys if they are on the bowl before going to sleep

8. (Evening passes and morning comes)

9. Get dressed

10. Grab things on desk

11. Get keys from bowl

12. Lock the door

13. Arrive at work

14. Unlock desk, cabinets, and other storage units

And because the bowl is placed on the desk, it itself can serve as a Poka Yoke reminder of your key's status. Simply put, if the key is not there, it should be in the pocket of your coat or pants. Also, this solution addresses five out of six problems found in the measure phase.

There is now a process defined for every day of the week, including the weekends and holidays. You could even add another Poka Yoke to the solution like making sure that the keys are always placed in the same pocket regardless of whatever you are wearing. Or you could add an item like a tag to differentiate this set of keys from the others. This way, you don't mistakenly bring the wrong set of keys at work.

You might have noticed that we didn't take away any crucial step in the process but added more. Whether or not this would benefit the overall process would be seen in the next phase.

E. Control Phase

Since this problem did not require a cross-functional team, this phase should be easy to complete. To do this, monitor any change that has occurred in your process. Did you leave your home on time? Did you arrive at work with a calmer state of mind?

And as for the application of the process, were the new steps easy to achieve and maintain? Were you placing the keys at the bowl every night and then remembering to immediately go there before leaving work?

You need to monitor the process to make sure that it works, and this is where a control plan will come into play.

First, set up a response plan where you and your housemates would look for the keys if they are not on the bowl before bedtime. Second, you should also set up fail safes in case the process cannot be followed due to extraordinary circumstances.

For instance, you are about to go out for another drinking party with your friends. Knowing that you tend to black out and forget what you did last night, you might want to set up a system where your friend designated to be the most sober (or least drunk) of that night would place the key in the bowl. This way, you can be assured that your items are still in place even if you are trying to remember what happened to you last night.

Or you just don't get too drunk to the point of passing out. That works, too.

After three weeks if the solution is maintained, you can then be certain that the problem has been eliminated. And although the new process has 3 more steps which you think would defeat the purpose of the Lean system, it actually removed a huge portion of your time looking for the keys every morning.

With search times drastically reduced, overall efficiency in the process was increased and the margin of error was also dropped to non-existent levels. Customer satisfaction is guaranteed, and you could go about your day not worrying what will happen to your keys in the next morning.

The Takeaway

This is but one of the simpler applications of Lean Six Sigma. Of course, large business projects will require more steps and will most definitely go through a lot of processes, key issues, and collaborations across cross-functional teams. In fact, we did not do any Phase Gate review in this scenario since it was so simple and minor in scope.

The point is that the Lean Six Sigma methodology always follows the same straightforward sequence. It begins with you identifying a problem and ends with you making a solution sustainable.

Now, does that mean that every solution that you and your team discovered through Lean Six Sigma be really effective in the long term. The answer, sadly, is no. There are chances when your solution becomes too unmanageable and this could be caused by factors outside of your control.

A policy-based solution, for example, can be delayed by corporate politics and bureaucracy that its effects can get diminished the longer the solution is applied. A technology-based solution, on the other hand, can be rendered obsolete if a new system is introduced in the market mid-implementation.

What could this mean for you? It only tells you that you must do the Lean Six Sigma process again. Identify a key issue, find the latest solutions, and implement those before everything becomes too late.

Of course, you can also do things that take the concept of the Lean Six Sigma even further and come up with a system that is effective and sustainable for your organization. This will include addressing some key issues inherent with Lean Six Sigma itself.

Chapter 8 The Art of Decluttering

The core premise of Lean Six Sigma is the streamlining of your business processes. As such, it is important that you also deal with something that has plagued many businesses and private individuals in order to apply the Lean Six Sigma methodology. After all, the method is just as effective as the team and operator using it.

And thus, it is best that we have to confront one of business's dirtiest words: Clutter. Heck, even the way it rolls of the tongue sounds offensive.

It has been a fodder for reality TV shows like Hoarders and, on a business perspective, a bad business model regardless of your process methodology.

Of course, the remedy here is to un-clutter but that does pose a question: "How Do I Do It?"

To answer that question, let us start with the ABCs.

Why Get Rid of Clutter?

It is easy to talk about decluttering but why should you it? There are various legitimate reasons why you should make certain aspects of your business and personal operations less of a mess, particularly:

- **Space**

Basically, clutter takes up space that could have been used for more useful ventures. For instance, look at an LSS-optimized storage facility and one that is, well, not LSS-optimized.

The former may be filled with a lot of things, depending on the project, but you can be certain that every item stored there has a purpose relative to the phase of the project. The latter, on the other hand, is not only filled with a lot of things but 99% of these things cannot be used for any immediate reason.

Which of the two is maximizing the available space? Naturally, not the cluttered one.

And apart from taking up physical space, the clutter also tends to take over everybody's mind. The more clutter, the more things you and your team will have to maintain in a functional state in the hope that they'd be useful sometime in the future.

- **Prioritization**

Going back to hoarding, why do you think that hoarders can't get rid of what they own? They believe that these things are highly valuable, despite having greatly depreciated. Alternatively, they think that these objects might become important for some undetermined purpose for an undetermined future.

Simply put, everything is precious in a room which is why nothing should be thrown away – this is how clutter takes form.

The Lean Six Sigma method requires you to be as objective as possible, seeing the real importance of the things that you should keep over the things you think you should keep. Eventually, this can be applied in mental clutter, with which you and your team start prioritizing activities and steps that add value to the end product.

It is not practical to keep on doing things that don't contribute to work productivity.

- **Cost Effectiveness**

It goes without saying that you eventually spend less if you have need of less things in your business. But, even if you argue that the things that you acquired were cheap in the first place, maintaining them or sorting through them does cost you a pretty penny in the long run. You have to remember that the price of any item is not just limited to the one listed on the price tag.

Let's say that you bought a secondhand printer for your business which cost you $30.00. A printer nowadays will cost $60.00 at the very least. But the cheap printer malfunctions twice a month, it skips lines when printing, or the ink bleeds out of the canisters from time to time. So, adding the constant maintenance costs and the occasional expletive that your staff utters when using the printer, did you save on $30.00 or did you waste $30.00 or more instead?

This is the same thing that happens if you purchase unnecessary assets to your business. Do they need regular repairs and maintenance? Can you move them on your own or do you have to hire people to transport them? These kinds of operational cost make clutter expensive, eventually.

- **Profit**

This may be the most direct result of cleaning up your storage area in terms of the financial aspect. Take advantage of their value by simply transferring ownership to others. By selling items that you don't have a need of gives you profit – allowing you to declutter and earn a little. Your loss could be someone's gain. To make it easier for you, just think that you are simply giving others a chance to enjoy the things you used to be fond of.

"But is LSS about throwing away waste? Who's going to find my useless stuff valuable? You ask. The truth with the Lean Six Sigma method is that it deals with waste that personally hinders you from becoming efficient in your operations. If we were to make that simpler, it helps you deal with YOUR waste, the elements or byproducts of your actions that do not bring value but might be valuable to someone else.

And speaking of value, there is a huge possibility that you might discover the real value of the things that are taking up your physical space which may be higher than your perceived value over them. If you've caught an episode of the TV program, Pawn Stars, there are instances when the real value of an item considered by others to be trash, is made known – where an expert confirms a particular item is worth thousands of dollars.

That deck of trading cards collecting dust in your attic might be a collector's item. That piece of clothing that almost looks like a rag could be a relic from 100 years into the past. That thingamabob with some weird scribbles? A movie prop signed by a famous actor. And so on and so forth.

Sure, the pawnshop would do their best to give a low estimate but the sheer surprise as to knowing how valuable that thing is for somebody else is always entertaining to watch.

On a business setting, such instances are hard to find. That piece of equipment that is rusting in your storage areas might not even come up to a quarter of their original price. But let us just say that you are better off earning a few dollars by selling these things as opposed to them taking up useful space in your business.

- **It Helps you Comply with Lean Six Sigma**

Naturally, decluttering your physical space is compatible with your Lean Six Sigma Goals. Keep in mind that decluttering is more than just getting rid of everything useless that is taking up space in the room. It is also about arranging the layout of the room so that space is maximize and no movement is wasted being there.

For example, if you want the front desk moved so that your secretary has a better sight of people entering the door, that move is easier if there are fewer, unused tables or other fixtures standing in the way. Or what if a stack of magazines is starting to form in one side of the area and next to a naked power outlet? That's an obvious fire hazard right there for you and your staff.

By decluttering the place, you open up the area to be redesigned into whatever you want. Applying this with the Lean Six Sigma, you give your business the physical and mental reordering it needs to embrace the methodology better.

- **Decluttering the Right Way**

Getting rid of excessive items that you may have accumulated over the years can be quite challenging. Here are a few helpful tips to get you started:

A. For Physical Spaces

1. One at a Time

The biggest hurdle you'll have to face would be losing interest during the process of decluttering. For one, if you have acquired too many items, you are likely to go the easy way out – abandoning the task. The one big challenge in decluttering is

To make this less of a challenge for you, you and your staff should commit to identifying 1 item each that needs to go for that day. If your project team is made up of 10 people and there are hundreds of items to be disposed of, then you can create a system wherein your team will deal with them one at a time.

You don't need to get rid of them all at the same time, take it step-by-step. Remember it's a process, there is no shortcut to it. It may appear to be a slow process, but things can get done, rather successfully. That's more than important, and that's progress.

2. List them Down

A good way to making the cleaning initiative sustainable for your team is to provide some system for it. Firstly, divide the area into smaller sectors and list all the items which have been identified as "for disposal".

It will also help if you will also create a schedule for every area, to make decluttering more orderly and efficient. It even helps if the cleaning activity is a Lean Six Sigma project itself. That way, your decluttering drive has become part of the organizations LSS campaign.

Aside from helping you complete an inventory of the things that the business owns, listing everything down (and adding a schedule) makes it easier to identify the things that need to be kept and those that need to be discarded. You'll be surprised to find items you'll never even remember you had (or bought).

B. For People and Activities

1. Prioritize, Prioritize, Prioritize

A good strategy of taking control of the business's daily operations or your own activities is to create a to-do list, ranked according to importance (or urgency). Start by writing down all the goals that the group must achieve. After that, determine if the planned activities will help you achieve these goals.

But do remember to not bind yourself to this list. The order of priority can change according to external factors. The point here is that you must always check that every move that your business makes is serving the more immediate goals and achieving long-term plans.

2. Write Things Down

This might sound cliché but having a journal of important activities can help you in a number of ways. First, it helps you de-congest your mind and organize your thoughts.

The reason why the mind gets overworked is because you let your thoughts uncontrollably pile up. Writing them down helps you pause and reorganize.

Second, it helps you monitor your progress. This could help in the Improve and Control phases as the subtlest of changes in behavior and performance can be noted and recorded. And nothing can be rewarding than looking back at a journal and seeing how you and your team have gradually improved over a period of time.

3. Never Multitask

A cardinal sin that business owners and managers often make is encouraging people to do many things at once. This is even made more apparent if a deadline is nearing. Soon enough, you would be pulling people from their own projects and making them work overtime.

Do not get the wrong idea, though. Multitasking is effective but only in short (and I mean really, really short) bursts of activity. If there are a lot of things to accomplish, prioritize those that need to be done immediately. You can go back to the lesser items once you're done with the urgent tasks.

However, if it composes your entire business or personal strategy, then you are likely to generate more clutter than what you started with. If possible, complete items on your to-do list one at a time.

And this is where your Lean Six Sigma tools can also play a role in. The method can help you identify key areas where bottlenecks can occur. The better you are at predicting where everyone has to deal with a lot of work backlog, the faster your team can be in preventing bottlenecks from happening.

This way, everybody in your team can finish every important task without becoming too tired for the next phase of the Lean Six Sigma project.

The 5S Methodology

Efficiency is all about doing more while using less. The Lean Six Sigma also operates in ensuring that your business is as efficient as possible.

However, there are other methodologies out there that you can use in Tandem with Lean Six Sigma. One of these efficiency-focused methods is 5S.

What is it, exactly? 5S are a set of principles that help your business maximize its available space and resources while also eliminating waste. This means that it is highly compatible with Lean Six Sigma and your decluttering initiative especially since it aims to make your workspace organized, clean, and safe.

And like Lean Six Sigma, 5S is used by many industries today in tandem with other methodologies.

Why Implement It?

Lean Six Sigma already is focused on identifying waste. So why bother with another methodology with 5S? This is because the 5S method looks at waste differently. If waste in the LSS method impedes your ability to provide value to the end product, then waste in 5S directly impedes your operations by making it unsafe to be in your workplace in the first place.

For instance, leaks and spills on the floors increase the risk of people slipping there, costing your business more money in medical expenses and insurance coverage. Another example is the presence of byproducts like crumpled paper and disused periodicals like newspaper and magazines which easily ignite when exposed to a source of fire.

Therefore, the 5S is best if implemented along with Lean Six Sigma. Although, there is no stopping you from implementing the same as a standalone method.

Implementation

Like Lean Six Sigma, 5S is divided into, well, 5 phases. They are as follows:

1. "Seiri" or Sort

At this phase, your team should go through all items in the work area. This includes tools, supplies, raw materials, components, cleaning equipment, and others. The designated 5S leader should then evaluate and review every item contained within that group and identify which ones are essential for everyday operations and which ones are not.

Every essential and unessential item will then be cataloged and tagged with set markers. Also, there might be items that are essential but are not used frequently. The 5S leader must evaluate how often these items are used to limit their amount in the work area.

2. "Seiton" or Straighten

Once every item has been identified and marked in the work area, it is now time to divide the place into "zones". These zones are where your every item must be placed in order to eliminate waste of all types.

For example, in order to eliminate waste of movement, all essential items must be within the reach of an operator. Handheld tools must be found at desks within chest-level of the person and heavier tools at their feet. The less they have to go to one place of the room to get important items, the faster they can finish their work.

And what about waste in the form of unwanted byproducts or damaged equipment? The room must have a designed red zone where these items can be placed. Of course, the red zone must be cleared of items on a weekly or daily basis.

The labels for each item must also be detailed. It must show the designation of the item, where it should be stored, and where it must be placed if it becomes damaged. The recommended quantities for each item must also be provided.

3. "Seiso" or Shine

Once everything is in place, the third step is to remove every trash in the area. This includes regular disposals of garbage as well as cleaning of regularly used equipment.

Remember that unkempt process equipment increases variability as well as equipment failure. And the more that your equipment fails, the more waste in the form of delays occur in your business process.

Also, dirt in the area increases the presence of workplace hazards which leads to injuries, or worse. To prevent any of these, your team must set up a regular cleaning procedure. If possible, the workspace must be cleaned before and after every work shift.

The 5S leader must also check the place and make sure that it is free of potential work hazards. This includes exposed electrical cables, burnt out bulbs, and oily leaks. And if they do find such, they must notify the rest of the team in order to address the issue as quickly as possible.

4. "Seiketsu" or Standardize

Perhaps the most important step, this part involves setting up standards for everyone else to follow. What signifies a clean and safe workspace? What are the types of waste that people must dispose of? How should one dispose of waste?

In this step, the leader must set up instructions, checklists, and other documents for others to peruse. This can even come in the form of company memorandums where the rest of organization can be informed of how to do the 5S process.

The goal here is to simplify the 5S process in such a way that everybody understands how to clean their own workspaces. Operators must also be trained in detecting deviations from the standard and addressing them either on their own or with others.

Scheduling is also an important aspect of this phase. You must set up regular cleaning and maintenance processes for the equipment in each area.

5. "Shitsuke" or Sustain

One of the most challenging parts of any new standard is to make the changes sustainable. After all, the chances of people slipping back to old standards and regressing are always high in any organizational initiative.

During this phase, an audit system must be put in place. The goal here is to make sure that not only has 5S been properly implemented in the workplace but has been ingrained into the overall organizational culture.

In essence, people in your organization must be implementing 5S not because a memo says so but it's they identify with it as part of the company's core values. This phase can last for more than a month as habits can form within no less than 30 days.

Additional Step: Safety

Some groups added a "+1" step in their process, making the method 5S+1. The additional step focuses on Safety, specifically in identifying potential work hazards and removing them.

This step also includes the selection of standardized equipment, tools, and workstations that were designed with ergonomics in mind. In essence, this step answers the question "is Safety being put first in the organization?".

To Summarize

It goes without saying that cleaning the physical workspace is integral to the Lean Six Sigma methodology. However, the culture itself needs to embrace the notion of cleanliness and change in order for any methodology to be sustainable there.

After all, any system will not be followed, and people will regress to old standards if you don't place any system to make sure that people would actually work according to the new status quo. As such, in a lot of cases, the culture of the organization must be addressed if you want your decluttering and cleaning efforts to count in the long run.

This means that you have to deal with how your organization defines and sees the Waste that it produces, either unintentionally or deliberately.

Chapter 9 D.O.W.N.T.I.M.E.

The Lean Six Sigma methodology has always been rather obsessed with eliminating waste. And if you are running a business that offers any tangible product or service, you are bound to generate waste whether you are aware of it or not.

In the Japanese language, the closest term you can get to waste is "Muda" and the Lean system has identified 8 types of Mudas that anybody can create in their business operations. If you are serious about optimizing your work area, you should at the very least be able to identify what these wastes are, how they are formed, and how they could leave an impact to your business.

But to make this easier for you, let's called the 8 Deadly Wastes as DOWNTIME which is fitting since you are bound to make a lot of temporary halts to your process if these issues prevail in your business. DOWNTIME simply means: Defects, Overpopulation, Waiting, Not Utilizing Talent, Transportation, Inventory Excess, Motion Waste, Excess Processing.

Defects

The most basic definition of a defect is that it is a deviation from the set standard. If, say, your production process was meant to create 82 cans of fresh tomatoes, a defect in that system would be a can filled only halfway through or tomatoes stored in a dented can.

Or, in software development, defects could manifest through glitches in the code or program-crashing bugs that were not addressed before the program was mass produced and shipped to the market. Either way, any element in the product that does not reflect the quality that you are looking for in the production process or what a client expressly states that your business should create can be labeled as a defect.

Defects can be caused by a number of reasons which include:

☐   Poor Quality Assurance Checks or None at All.

☐   Poor equipment maintenance.

☐   Lack or improper documentation of the process (No standards set).

☐   Un-optimized processes or steps of the process.

☐   Not understanding customer specifications.

☐   No control of inventory levels.

☐   Poor overall production design.

☐   Design changes improperly documented.

You may ask yourself "can defects be eliminated entirely from the process?" The answer, sadly, is no. But you can actually minimize the chances of them occurring.

Under the Six Sigma method, good odds for the appearance of defects in your production process should be 1 to 3 over 1 million. If we are going to translate that to percentages, your production success rate should be 99.9999% at best.

Overproduction

You might think that producing more than what is required is good but, on the Lean Six Sigma perspective, it's actually detrimental to your business. When your staff blindly produce, you are reducing important business capital.

For instance, if you produced 40 car windows instead of 20, how much of those 40 windows are a sure sell? 50% only. As for the rest, they'd be collecting dust in a storage area where they are going to depreciate in value. So, your production team has just wasted their time, money, and effort on 20 windows that will not be paid for by customers.

This usually occurs in manufacturing business but there is a chance that this could happen to your work area as well especially if you have been facing bottlenecks in the past. Overproduction can happen when:

☐   You implement Just-in-Case production policies.

☐   The customer specifications are not properly defined or understood.

☐   Forecast-based production cycles.

☐   Long set up times.

☐   Changes in engineering.

☐   Unoptimized automation.

The most obvious solution here is to streamline the flow of work. It must be simple enough that the customer can understand it. And if they understand it, they can rein in their expectations and give you specifications that you can attain given your current layout.

If necessary, you must also change the sequence of steps by adding new ones, replacing old ones, or removing entire steps altogether. This is important in reducing bottlenecks which should prevent your business from either under-performing or over-delivering.

Waiting

When some part of the process gets backed up, the flow of materials and other resources stops. What happens then is that the subsequent steps have to stop functioning so that the backed-up step can be cleared.

Wait times usually happens because a machine breaks down. For example, your business designs and creates books for clients. What happens, then, if your primary printers are taken out of commission because they need repairs? Your team will have nothing to do but wait until the printers are repaired or replaced.

Aside from equipment malfunctions, waiting can happen since your team is waiting for raw materials to be approved or just because your inventory of important components ran out. Other causes include:

☐ Imbalance in the workloads (others have light ones and others have heavy loads).

☐ Emergency downtime due to equipment failure.

☐ Long set up times.

☐ Forecast-based production.

☐ Too many work absences.

☐ Poor process quality.

☐ Production miscommunications.

☐ Insufficient resources.

Whatever the cause was, the most important aspect you have to address here is the bottleneck. Adequate staffing and the proper balancing of workloads can do a lot to prevent this problem from occurring in the future. Or, at the very least, you can gradually minimize its magnitude until bottlenecking becomes insignificant to your business operations.

Not Utilizing Talent

Although this is not a form of waste recognized in the older Lean framework, the improper utilization of human resources has become a major problem for companies today. As far as this waste is concerned, any company can generate it in two ways.

First, you either assign people who are not properly trained for the task. This could mean that their skills are not compatible with the specifications of the task or that the administration simply did not give them enough tools to successfully complete their jobs.

Second, you may hire people who are overqualified for the job. If you hire a professional to do menial labor, are you really making full use of their talents? You are just paying them for their raw strength which anybody can do. In essence, you may be using your assets but the way they are being utilized is not optimized.

Regardless of the situation, your business is liable for not utilizing your worker's talent in the following:

☐   Assigning the wrong people for the wrong tasks.

☐   Wasteful administrative activity like micromanaging tasks.

☐   Poor communication, if any.

☐   Lack of team cohesion and collaboration.

☐   Poor human resource management.

☐   Insufficient training.

☐   Not providing workers with workspace conducive to their personal development.

All of these problems point to one source: a lack of effective human resource management. Fortunately, the solutions are equally simple which includes proper employee training, continuous employee development, and the ability to resist to micromanage everything in the business.

Transportation

This type of waste is something that is directly tied to company logistics. Transportation waste is often seen in manufacturers since they have to manage the logistics of products and raw materials in between facilities and the marketplace. But make no mistake. Even business offices can do this with the improper transportation of documents and other forms of correspondence.

The premise of this waste is simple: Transportation is costly. The more you make motions that do not involve delivering the end product to the customer, the more money you lose.

Also, transportation significantly exposes products and raw materials to elements beyond your control that would damage them or make them deteriorate. And there have been far too many instances when products and materials get damaged at the road or on the sea for factors that may have not foreseen.

Here are some ways that can create transportation waste:

☐ Poor business layout.

☐ Excessive process steps.

☐ Misaligned flow of the process.

☐ Unoptimized production and delivery systems.

The best method to minimize on transportation waste is to simplify the process. If one thing can be done in 3 steps instead of 5, the margin for error is considerably smaller. This could also be solved by optimizing the layout of the workplace or office, limiting the transition of products from facility to market, and shortening the distances between process phases.

Inventory Excesses

A direct effect of overproducing, excesses in your inventory happen when there are more products and components to store in your storage areas, waiting when they will be useful; if ever they become useful.

Think of it this way: a client ordered only 20 items from you and yet you made 40. Why would they go out of the way to pay for 40 when you were only asked for 20? The rest will be stored somewhere else in the hope that someone will order them in the future.

And while they are waiting, they are deteriorating. Soon enough, that thing which was in pristine condition would degrade until it is of no value when somebody does order for it.

This is a problem usually seen in manufacturing businesses, but food service providers often deal with this more given that their products have shorter lifespans. For instance, if one item in the menu is not in demand, a sensible chef would not order for its ingredients frequently. Or, they ask for a reservation a week before so they could add the food items to next week's market budget.

Because if that piece of meat or fish stays in the freezer too long and nobody is ordering for a dish that needs such, it is going to spoil. In essence, spending on $3,000.00 worth of food items without an assurance that they are going to sell on the next day is the same with wasting $3,000.00 on a poorly thought-out gamble.

- ☐ Overproduction and buffers.
- ☐ Poor QA and monitoring systems.
- ☐ Uncoordinated production schedules and paces.
- ☐ Untrustworthy suppliers.
- ☐ Long set up times.
- ☐ Miscommunication with customer specifications.

Motion Waste

This is where the Non-value Adding Activities will fall under. Simply put, any activity that your team makes that does not ultimately lead to delivering value through the production process is wasteful by nature. For instance, if a request for certain raw materials takes 10 steps to complete when it could have been done in 3, then the system is unoptimized.

Or what if your staff have to walk 100 meters to a separate building, go through a requesting desk, fill out the papers, wait for 30 minutes to get the request approved, and then return to their desks?

It might sound reasonable if the item in question is large like a laptop computer but what if the item being requested were a box of staple clips or even 10 reams of bond paper? They would have saved a lot more time if everything the needed were within arm's reach.

Other Motion wastes would include:

- ☐ Poorly designed processes.
- ☐ Poor workspace layout.
- ☐ Sharing of tools and machines.
- ☐ Congested workspaces.
- ☐ Isolated operations.
- ☐ Unnecessary bureaucracy and corporate red tape.
- ☐ Lack of standards.

The most effective solution here is to re-arrange the physical layout of the work area. By decreasing the distance between workstations and other fixtures, your staff can do their work at a faster pace.

Also, giving the organization policies and systems an overhaul would come in handy here. The system wherein items requests can be checked and approved must not take more than 10 minutes to complete.

Excess Processing

If products can be overproduced, they can also be over processed. Over processing can occur when an item goes through several steps which share many similarities with one another. Or it could happen when the production process is needlessly long, filled with phases that could have otherwise been removed.

For example, are three successive quality assurance checks that necessary when the quality of the product can be determined by just one or two? Or what if a bottling process features two automated capping machines, one that would twist the cap and the other to seal it? That is an over processed production layout right there.

Other cases of excessive processing would include:

- ☐ Too much reporting or documentation.

☐   Excessive paperwork.

☐   Reentering or duplicating recorded data.

☐   Overdesigned production equipment.

☐   Human errors.

As with other production wastes, over processing can be addressed by simplifying and optimizing the production layout. This includes removing unnecessary steps or spreading multiple checks and balance functions across the entire process and not successively.

Understanding Process Variation

How about the Six Sigma part of the process? How is waste manifested and understood with this statistical method? The answer lies in something called Variation.

What is Variation, then? To answer that, you must understand that there are actually eight dimensions of quality which are:

1. Conformance

2. Performance

3. Features

4. Reliability

5. Durability

6. Serviceability

7. Aesthetics

8. Perceived Quality

Each of these dimensions are self-exclusive from one another. What this means is that customers might think that a product or service is good in terms of Reliability but would be otherwise terrible in Performance or Aesthetics.

However, some dimensions work in conjunction with each other depending on the nature of the product. If a product is Durable, then it could also be Reliable.

But, as far as Six Sigma is concerned, it focuses on the dimension of Conformance. You have to remember that customer perception is important in the Lean Six Sigma method since it is they that will ultimately determine of what you offer was actually good.

To put it in other words, quality for a customer is determined by how well it conforms to their standards, whatever those standards may be.

What is Conformance?

This is simply the degree to which something that you offer to the market meets a predefined set of standards. It is important to remember as well that your services and products offered are a function or manifestation of your internal processes as well as the processes of other groups that do business with you.

So how does conformance come into play with your processes? Here are a few examples:

1. A loaning service promises to respond to their customers within 24 hours after an inquiry is made.

2. A local pizza joint assures customers that they would deliver pizzas to their doorstep in 30 minutes or its free.

3. A software developer required to write a program with 10 correlated features and no more than 3 bugs per a thousand lines of written code.

4. A kitchen crew told to cook 20 steaks, 15 of which are medium rare and 5 rare.

To understand conformance better, think of archery. Let us say that every Critical to Quality metric (CTQ) is the bullseye found on every target. To conform to customer standards, you must be able to hit that bullseye with every arrow you drew.

But, of course, we can't make perfect hits every time we shoot. You may hit a perfect bullseye once and the rest will just group around the first shot.

Believe it or not, this is okay. If any product or service you offer more or less hits most of the customer's set standards, then your product is to be deemed of good quality and you are deemed a consistent provider of such. Going back to the archery scenario, you are considered a good marksman if your shots group the bullseye.

But what happens if one of your shots was way off? Perhaps it did not even hit near the bullseye. Or perhaps it was so off-angle that it did not even hit the target.

This is a deviation from the standard. The outlier. That one freak occurrence where you did not meet the customer's expectations. This is what is called as Process Deviation.

Is Minimizing Variation Enough?

So, if you have little process variation, does this mean that you are hitting all of the needs of the customers? Not really. A more consistent process simply means that everyone managed to follow the process to the letter but the process itself does not assure that value is ultimately delivered to the customer.

When quality issues happen, you have to first determine whether or not it was caused by a variation in the process or some inherent flaw in the system. Things like a lack of training, old equipment, and mere negligence can cause problems. But, fortunately, they are easy to address since they are rather obvious manifestations.

However, if the system itself is flawed, the problem instantly doubles in size. Instead of having to merely do quick fixes, you now have to consider the idea of having to redesign your entire process.

To make a good judgement call on this situation, black belts and master black belts must clearly define the process and determine whether the problem was created by any of the wasteful activities mentioned earlier in this chapter or it was caused by a deviation from the process.

And the latter can be quite challenging to determine as you have to carefully track workflows, the allocation of responsibilities, and the formulated standards to get to the source of the problem.

Of course, the conclusions you can come up with are just as good as your interpretation of the data as provided. And if your information is not accurate, the best that you can do in addressing the situation is, well, get lucky.

Can Variation be Eliminated?

The answer, sadly, is one big NO. Unless your business process is found in a work environment where outside variables have little impact, there is always some process variation occurring. Let us say, for the sake of discussion, that you promised to deliver pizzas within 30 minutes after an order is placed.

What happens if there was heavy traffic going to that client's place? What if the delivery truck blew a tire or you were pulled to the site by patrolmen because of a faulty taillight? Surely, these would affect how you deliver on your promises.

Or what if you had contingencies like a spare vehicle or you knew some shortcuts in that place? They might help in you delivering your promises within the acceptable limit, but they won't always assure 100% success in that particular situation.

Reducing Process over Results

This can be rather counter-intuitive, but it is best that you focus on consistency over getting results. Why? You ask. Isn't the whole point of being in the business to produce great results?

Going back to the archery scenario, even the hits that group around your most accurate shot are still variations of the process. Unless you have the skills of Robin Hood, it is statistically impossible to get all shots hitting the bullseye with 100% accuracy.

But what if we had two archers? Let us say that Archer A varies his strategy every shoot. He might aim from the left in one shot, he might shoot from above in the other. He might even do handstands and draw his bow with his feet. But he keeps hitting the target.

And then we have Archer B. He stands on the same spot and aims his bow in exactly the same angle. He may score a perfect hit one or two times but the rest of his shots group around an area near the bullseye.

Which of the archers has the best chance of improving their accuracy and consistency? The answer is Archer B.

The reason for this is simple: He always sticks to the same process. This makes him easy to analyze and predict. Thus, you can set up a process map that allows you to detect where he makes the most and correct the same.

Archer A, though good, is all over the place. There is no way to identify what he is doing right when he lands a hit and where he went wrong should he ever miss a target.

Thus, by reducing variations in the process, you make the Lean Six Sigma implementation phase easier on everybody's part. As a result, what was seemingly counterproductive as a measure through reducing variations regardless of how good the results are can give your business more opportunities to expand later on.

One Important Note

What you have to understand is waste is a natural byproduct of your business's operations. If you do things wastefully, then you are bound to generate a lot of waste. It is as simple as that.

As such, you have to remember that Waste may be the focus of the Lean Six Sigma method, it is not the one that it addresses directly. After all, waste is just a manifestation of what is wrong with your business.

Thus, your chosen strategy in your Lean Six Sigma projects should be to address what was generating all that waste and variation. Because if you are going to just address the waste itself, you are merely applying the proverbial band-aid to what could be a festering wound.

For example, your production cycles generate defects by 20 to 30 items. The fault could be with your machines. It could be in your staff. It could even be in the organizational culture. You'd never know until you dig deeper.

And, eventually, you'd still end up dealing with increased business costs as well as lost time and resources. To identify waste, it is important that you analyze your organization and find out which part of the process generates the most waste.

After all, everything will be a matter of standardizing things and keeping the changes sustainable.

Chapter 10 Problems and Challenges

So, is Lean Six Sigma the best problem-solving methodology out there? Not really.

Don't get the wrong idea, though. A lot of companies have implemented Lean Six Sigma successfully and enjoyed its benefits including a better bottom line, increased productivity, and a reinvigorated workforce.

Unfortunately, others have not fared so well with Lean Six Sigma which causes the rest thinking about using the methodology themselves. So, will the methodology work on your business? That depends greatly on, well, you. But it is best that you learn everything that you have to about this methodology, even its ugly side.

Why Don't Businesses Use Lean Six Sigma at all?

There are many reasons why a lot of organizations don't use Lean Six Sigma. Many of these are unfounded but many are also rather valid. And, of course, some are based on misconceptions about the method.

Either way, here are some of the reasons blurted out by people why they won't even think about using Lean Six Sigma for their projects.

1. "It's a Fad!"

A lot of organizations don't use Lean Six Sigma because everybody else is using it. For them, LSS is similar to buzzword-heavy methodologies that rose (and fell) in recent years including Total Quality Management, Business Process Re-Engineering, and the Theory of Constraints.

And right from the premise you could get the idea that this reason is based on a rather faulty understanding of Lean Six Sigma. It's not a fad technically as the methodology has been in use by various industries for over several decades now.

What's more, Lean Six Sigma is not something that was cooked up by a boardroom meeting or a marketing session. It was first established in

Japanese industries which lead to the country's huge boom during the last half of the 20th century.

And, aside from that, it is spearheaded by several industry bigwigs like Henry Ford, Western Electric's Walter Shewhart, and Toyota's Shigeo Shingo. As such, the methodology would rather not have you think that is just this hot new business administration trend.

2. "I Don't Have the Time to Dedicate to the Program"

Think about it this way: if a person is too busy putting out trash fires, would they have the time to listen to you explain to them the finer points of how to throw a pail of water in a burning pit? Time is a commodity that not all companies have the luxury of. For you, there is a strong chance that you are racing against a deadline of sorts to meet an objective.

And Lean Six Sigma does demand time from you in order to learn it. You have to devote a portion of your workday learning the basics and then create strategies on how to implement. While you are doing those, you still have to make sure that the business functions normally on a regular basis.

This is why it was recommended that the Lean Six Sigma initiative starts small and in a self-sustained unit within the organization. A few would have to master the method first so that they, in turn, can teach the rest. If done right, the entire organization can embrace the methodology without wasting too much of their time learning it.

But what if your organization could not afford to apply the LSS drive in a small scale since, well, it is already operating in a small scale? This makes for a perfect segue into the next reason which is....

3. "We're too Small!"

One oft-repeated phrase in implementing Lean Six Sigma is "we've hit a wall". That "wall" can come in many forms.

For many small businesses, that wall comes in the form of possessing cash flow that is tied up in inventory (or receivables), even when the company is generating profits. For some, that wall takes the form of persistent employee turnover. And for some, the wall could be the frustration of having to deliver a different quality of product or service than the one you and your team were used to.

Either way, the wall signifies that processes being implemented are becoming insufficient in achieving the goals that you have set.

But the thing with Lean Six Sigma is that it is highly adaptable as a methodology. In fact, it can be an Agile methodology in the sense that it allows you to perfectly embrace change, whatever form that it comes in, and still provide value to your customers.

The truth is that Lean Six Sigma never asks you to completely overhaul your current business layout. It only requires for you to completely understand how your business is performing given its current tools and systems and how that might be improved through the LSS implementation process.

And if you do think that an overhaul is needed, the LSS method is compatible enough with other methodologies that its goals can fit with what you have already set to achieve with other projects. As such, the size of your business and team composition should never become a hindrance to your projects provided, of course, that you fully understand how the Lean Six Sigma methodology must be applied.

4. "I'm Not a Manufacturer!"

Here's another Lean Six Sigma myth that still prevails today. Since it was first formed and implemented to be use in a car manufacturing facility, then Lean Six Sigma is meant only for those companies that produce something tangible that is going to be used for mechanical and industrial purposes, right? Wrong.

You'd be surprised as to how many non-manufacturing companies were able to succeed in implementing Lean Six Sigma. These include:

☐   The Bank of America

☐   Coca-Cola

- [ ] Starbucks
- [ ] Wal-Mart
- [ ] AT&T

The reason for this is Lean Six Sigma is actually focused on waste and process variation, something that is shared by a lot of industries. In fact, food service sectors can benefit from Lean Six Sigma more due to the more perishable nature of their products and the fact that they can generate more business waste on a relative perspective than manufacturers.

The point is that the Lean Six Sigma method should be applicable to your business if it has a fairly repeatable process or cyclical activity, where data can be collected from such activities, and there is a need to produce the same item consistently regardless if the amount of repetitions is 10 or 1 million times.

5. "I'm Not an Engineer. I Don't Do Math"

Granted, the Six Sigma part of the methodology can be rather intimidating. Statistics, after all, is a subject that many who went to college are not exactly excited about, even those that ace on it. There's just something about number crunching that is a bit of a hassle for anyone who wants their analysis to be simple and straightforward.

But here's the thing, though: you don't need to have a strong grasp of mathematics in order to enjoy the benefits of the methodology. In fact, some of the most effective tools of the Lean Six Sigma arsenal like drawing a process map or a fishbone diagram requires your team to have a good pair of eyes (and a lot of common sense) in order to be properly utilized.

The diagrams are easy enough to put up and using them to identify bottlenecks and other problem areas are equally easy. Even asking the simple question of "why?" can yield you a lot of possible answers. The point is that you must never forget to understand what the consumer really needs in order to reduce waste and variance in the business process.

6. "We're Using Lean Already. Thank You"

Some businesses do not use Lean Six Sigma since they are using Lean already. Some even state that they are using Lean Six Sigma but would focus more on the Lean aspect.

However, Lean and Six Sigma are not exclusive concepts, nor do they need to be applied in a linear way. They, by design, can complement one another.

Lean speeds up the entire process while Six Sigma makes it more accurate. Lean reduces the waste produced by the inherent flaws in your system while Six Sigma reduces the probabilities of that one freak defect from happening in every successive good production run.

To put it on simpler terms, Lean is all about Efficiency while Six Sigma is all about Effectiveness. And those two things tend to produce dramatic results if you focus on them both. If you focus on Lean, you sacrifice quality for speed. Likewise, you sacrifice efficiency if you focus on Six Sigma.

7. "We Tried, and It Didn't Work out for Us"

Any business owner or project manager that uses this reason should ask themselves "Why did I fail?". Perhaps the fault lies in the people and the technology. Or perhaps it was the intentions behind the implementation of the initiative.

And what about the commitment levels of everyone involved in it? How did you define success and what were its metrics? Were the goals even realistic in the first place?

The point is that this is more of a problem of execution rather than an inherent flaw in the method. And if you do fail in applying the Lean Six Sigma methodology, there is always the option to get back to the drawing board. Just remember that any tool is just as effective as the people who use it.

The concept is rather simple and straightforward that you should get considerable results from it if only you and your team tried to understand the basics.

8. "I'm Afraid of Change and Failure"

This is perhaps the most legitimate and understandable. The only problem is that a lot of people would not admit of such and thus bluster their way out of even giving the method a chance.

Pride is indeed a factor, however, when you think about it dread and fear are more potent emotions. It may be paralyzing to the point that you can't implement any change that you want to see in the business out of fear that you are going to mess things up.

It prevents your team from learning new skills, taking on new roles, or implement more agile programs like the Lean Six Sigma methodology. If you want to succeed in Lean Six Sigma, or any other Agile methodology, that Fear must be eliminated.

Common Implementation Mistakes

Another aspect you should consider in the Lean Six Sigma method is its actual application in your project. What is barely mentioned by a lot of people is that there are a number of pitfalls that stand in your way of properly implementing the process.

And as we have mentioned a while ago in this chapter, no discussion of Lean Six Sigma is ever complete without addressing some of the mistakes that you could potentially make in implementing your strategies and how you could overcome such. And here are some of them:

1. Thinking Certifications are Enough

In order to make everyone in your Lean Six Sigma team as competent as possible, you might hire people who are trained and certified under the Lean Six Sigma methodology. And you think to yourself that these certified people are most definitely able contribute to the implementation phase.

But keep in mind that there is more to Lean Six Sigma than just certifications. If your team is more focused on becoming certified, you run the risk of doing things too by-the-book. This means that your team gets more tied up to doing things through set procedures rather than asking how the system could be improved for the better.

This could also come back to bite you in the rear later on when your initial trainees become mentors themselves. If they are too focused on the certification, they can't provide really valuable tactical advice to new yellow and green belts assigned to new Lean Six Sigma projects.

The Solution

If possible, train your Lean Six Sigma team to focus more on understanding customer specifications than doing things by the sequence. They should understand that the LSS method should adapt to the specifications of the project or the goals of the group, not the other way around.

And this is where your skills as the primary mentor would come into importance. You must know how and when to apply the tools provided and even provide constructive criticism if you feel that the team is becoming too focused on becoming certified, not adaptable.

2. Indifferent Higher Ups

You would think that resistance would come the most from people directly underneath you in the organizational chart but no. When it comes to convincing people that Lean Six Sigma works, employees are more than willing to give it the chance.

It is a senior manager who is so convinced that it won't be applicable to organization (and for the various reasons stated above, to boot) that would be your major source of frustration in the implementation process.

The reason for this is simple; the higher ups have a lot of influence in dictating how many people should become LSS certified and the overall scope of the initiative. In other words, their support can make or break the initiative irrespective of available resources.

The Solution

At this instance, your best strategy is to be diplomatic. After all, you still report to these people and you'd rather not derail the effort further by antagonizing them.

You have to be forthcoming with what the method requires and the benefits the company can enjoy from it. Its role should be emphasized and any misconception regarding the method should be sufficiently addressed.

If possible, have a meeting set up with the higher ups so you could explain the Lean Six Sigma methodology to them in a direct and open communication channel. There's no assurance that you can convince theme here, mind you. But at least you can explain the concept to terms easier to understand which sets up a future acceptance.

3. A Faulty Strategy

Regardless of the nature of your operations, it is still important that you synchronize your business goals to the goals of the Lean Six Sigma initiative. As such, a faulty strategy and misaligned goals will result in confusion among teams and the higher ups which prevents the organization from delivering the value they promised to customers.

If not addressed, this could reduce the overall effectiveness of all teams. Delays would start appearing, customers get frustrated, and everyone in the organization would start to question what was the point of Lean Six Sigma in the first place.

The Solution

As the project manager, you must make it a point to constantly align the goals of the Lean Six Sigma project with its core principles. This means that you must scrutinize the strategies to be implemented before the date of actual execution. Talk with your team constantly before the implementation phase starts. What are their concerns? Is there a problem that they have yet to air out? Maintain the line of communication between your teams as open as possible so that everybody understands the overall strategy to be implemented.

One key aspect to remember here is that the strategy should be tied to the changes in business results. This means that you have to monitor the implementation properly and the overall goals should be constantly remembered by all teams involved.

4. Selecting the Wrong Lean Six Sigma Project

A lack of project prioritization makes the team run the risk of wasting valuable resources. Aside from that, this results in processes becoming prioritized at a period earlier than expected as well as bottlenecks. Worse, your green and yellow belts might have to deal with tasks that they were not yet trained for resulting in haphazard results.

Whatever the case, not properly selecting which LSS project to complete first or simultaneously with the others can lead to lost time, money, and other valuable resources. This would even lead to a delivery of poor quality or delays in the completion of projects.

The Solution

During the training phase, it is important to take as much time as possible in helping the trainees understand how to prioritize tasks. You should hammer in the point that, yes, all projects are important, but they must be done in the right sequence, so you don't create unnecessary waste.

It would even be recommended that you take a leaf out of the Kanban process here and come up with a project scheduling scheme. Divide all projects into 3 groups: Proposed, Doing, and Done. This table will shift every time a new project is proposed or is completed.

With this Kanban visual signaling system, you and your team can have an understand of what needs to be done now and how that correlates to projects in the future.

5. Lack of Support and Collaboration

Where a lot of Lean Six Sigma teams fail is in making sure that everybody in the organization is in on the effort of implementing the method. This could be attributed to the team failing to properly communicate the benefits of Lean Six Sigma or it could be due to the failure of laying down the formal rules and guidelines in which the end goals are to be attained. Either way, everybody is just doing their own thing in the organization which leads to wasted efforts or, worse, huge losses.

The Solution

There is no other workaround for this problem but to make sure that the Lean Six Sigma initiative slowly works itself to becoming a part of the organizational culture. To be more blunt about it, you have to lay down the concept that what the organization truly wants and what Lean Six Sigma can offer are basically one and the same.

For instance, the organization wants to increase profit margins while optimizing the systems to becoming efficient. Lean Six Sigma is a method that can achieve those by removing waste and variance while also simplifying the process. If you can make the higher-ups and the stakeholders see that the conflict between organizational needs and Lean Six Sigma goals is just a matter of semantics, they are more inclined to support it.

Important Note: The rule of thumb when addressing implementation issues is always "The earlier, the better". You have to know when the organization is about to create a mistake in its Lean Six Sigma initiative and find ways to address it. If you take to long to address an issue, you run the risk of bloating the problem until it becomes too expensive to fix.

Mastering Lean Six Sigma

As was stated, the Lean Six Sigma method is just as good as the people implementing it. So, how is your group going to master it for your various projects?

Psychologist came up with 4 stages on how a person develops competency or learns a new skill. This is based on two dimensions which is a person's level of consciousness and their current competence.

Stage 1: Unconsciously Incompetent - At this point, a person does not understand how to do something or is unable to recognize that a problem exists. In short, you don't know what you don't know. In the Lean Six Sigma perspective, this means that you are not even aware of what Lean Six Sigma is and most definitely don't know how to apply it for your project.

Stage 2: Unconsciously Incompetent - This is the point you reach when you are aware that you do not know something or how to address a problem. This is the instance when the Lean Six Sigma method is introduced to you and you realize that there is a better way of addressing a situation. In essence, you have an idea of the solution but have yet to know how to implement it in your organization.

Stage 3: Consciously Incompetent - Here, whoever was teaching the group has demonstrate the skill and knowledge needed to implement to methodology, but it requires a lot of concentration and effort. This is a stage that usually happens when going through the Green and Yellow belt training.

In essence, the trainees now understand the methodology and how to use the tools, but it will take a lot of practice and discipline in order to become a master of the methodology. This is a rather critical stage of the learning process as you'd want to internalize the process. Without mastering the basics, you and your team run the risk of reverting to your previous standards and failed methodologies.

Stage 4: Unconsciously Competent - After putting in much time and effort in mastering the method, Lean Six Sigma has become second nature to the person. They can now implement it with minimal mistakes and can adjust their strategies to respond to sudden changes in customer specifications.

But, again, it takes a while to get to this stage. You need to master the method by applying it several times in different projects. Sure, you are going to make a lot of mistakes, but you can use those as opportunities to hone your craft. You can also undergo further training, read more Lean Six Sigma books, and attend meetings.

If you yourself feel confident enough to teach others how to master the skill or even do some presentations yourself, then you will know that you have finally reached this stage.

How Do I Continuously Improve?

You have to understand that Lean Six Sigma is not a one-off thing that you could forget about in time. It is the most effective not only if you have mastered it but also continuously seek ways to develop yourself.

Continuous Improvement is one of the major goals of any Lean Six Sigma initiative apart from eliminating waste and process variances. The question is, how should you do it? For starters, Continuous Improvement should not be seen as a strategy. Instead, it should be a way of life. A discipline, if you may.

And to maintain this way of life, there are a few tips that you should keep in mind.

1. Focus on Small Steps

This might sound counterproductive, but it is better if you can put more focus on the smaller, incremental changes that your business or group makes over the massive shifts done over a long period of time. The reason for this is simple: small changes are done quickly, regularly, and are rather inexpensive. By completing a set of daily tasks, you can see the changes take place as they occur.

More importantly, a focus on small changes removes the psychological barrier that prevents you from continuously improving. Think about it: When it comes to implementing changes, the first complaint that you or your team would utter would go along the lines "why is it taking so long for the benefits to come?" It can be frustrating at times to think that your efforts are seemingly not paying off which could kill the Lean Six Sigma initiative at its earliest phases.

But, with small changes, you and your team could see and reap the benefits and celebrate each victory earlier on. In time, you'll see the changes accumulate until you would notice your organization is in a far better state than what you started with.

2. Empower Employees

Yes, you and other leaders have a lot of influence in making Lean Six Sigma work but it's the employees that would make it successful. One key problem as to why Lean Six Sigma initiatives fail is that nobody down the line knows the principles by heart. As a result, they won't realize that the way they do things currently are not optimized or that there are more efficient ways to do their tasks.

Alternatively, a lot of people are resistant to change because change brings about uncertainty. Lastly, some are just reluctant to share ideas out of fear that they are going to be placed in the limelight.

It is your role, then, to educate your people on the tools and techniques as well as choosing the best ones for certain situations. But most importantly, you have to give them the assurance that there is nothing to fear out of trying something new.

The less reluctant your team is towards embracing the method, the quicker they can master it and move through the Lean Six Sigma ranks.

3. Feedback Always Matters

It goes without saying that everybody within the team should be encouraged to voice out their concerns as the Lean Six Sigma initiative is being implemented. You have to have a little bit of dissent within your teams not because you want people to undermine the rest of the group's efforts.

Instead, you need some people to remind everybody else that maybe, just maybe, all of you are going about this problem the wrong way. Seeing things from multiple perspectives allow you to detect problems before they get worse and course correct. But such feedback would not be available if people just keep to themselves.

Maintain an open and transparent line of communication between teams and management during the initiative and you should get the best possible results from the program.

To Summarize

Now, would these problems occur at your implementation phase? Or do the reasons above apply to your situation? Not exactly. There is no doubt that some Lean Six Sigma initiatives went smoothly and others, well, didn't.

That being said, it is still important to know that there will be flaws in your execution. After all, if you don't think that you are going to fail, you can't properly prepare a contingency in case that you do. And if you do fail, then at the very least you and your team could use that instance as an opportunity to learn and do better next time.

Conclusion

I'd like to thank you for transiting my lines from start to finish.

I hope this book was able to help you to understand the principles of Lean Six Sigma.

As of this point, there should be no doubt that the Lean Six Sigma methodology is effective. Sure, it might have some few flaws but that does not take away from its overall potential to optimize your organization's current process methodology.

But you might be wondering whether or not Lean Six Sigma is right for your organization. In other words, you might have no doubts that Lean Six Sigma works but would it work for your business or organization specifically?

If you still have any doubts whether or not Lean Six Sigma is the best option for your upcoming projects, it is best that you answer a few questions first.

What is the Goal of the Group/Business?

Regardless of what industry it operates in or the kind of products it offers, any organization has one goal to achieve: enjoy more from doing less. This does not mean that they cut corners or cheap out on their output, mind you.

The goal of every organization out there is to bring value to the customer without overextending themselves. And this is where Waste becomes an important factor as it the biggest manifestation that some areas of the process are not optimized.

Aside from showing the flaws of the system, waste does ultimately affect the quality of the end product. If only those wasteful activities and variations in the process were eliminated, you could have come up with a better offering to the market.

And this is something that Lean Six Sigma is quite good at. If helps you identify what goes wrong and where in the process and then come up with strategies that directly address such. In time and with support, that problem could either be minimized or eliminated.

What are Your Personal Goals?

On a personal level, you should also consider what you want to do in your chosen profession or career. For many, career growth could be either in movement or security. To put it in other words, there are those that want to stay in a rather lucrative position for as long as possible or move through a series of highly rewarding jobs and positions over various sectors in a considerably quick pace.

This is where a Lean Six Sigma certification would come in important as the methodology is widely recognized by various industries and sectors in the market. And, as far as upper management is concerned, they would like to invest on someone who knows how to optimize systems and deliver on the specifications of a project.

And if you are already in a position of considerable influence or power, the Lean Six Sigma certification could still help you make yourself relevant in the organization's strategic decision-making sessions. When it comes to eliminating waste or delivering value, your input would have a considerable weight in them which means that they are more likely to be implemented. And if that implementation was successful, the success could be attributed to you.

In other words, with the credentials offered by a Lean Six Sigma program, you can secure your tenure in any organization or allow yourself to move quickly through the ranks and reap more benefits.

But, of course, this is only possible if you continuously learn and improve. A Yellow belt in Lean Six Sigma is already good but the Green, Black, and Master Black belts will put you in more favorable positions.

Aside from that, credentials might be good, but they won't do you any favors if they don't allow you to be successful. What good is a Black Belt certification, for instance, if every project you have led has either generated mediocre results or was dropped because of delays and technical problems?

As such, the ultimate indicator of your mastery of the Lean Six Sigma method is not exactly your rank but your ability to apply what you have learned in actual scenarios. And that whatever you applied was actually effective and sustainable.

Are You Open to the Prospect of Change?

Change is a but a part of the natural order. However, a lot of managers tend to balk at it because of the uncertainty it brings. Why change something that has been proven to work?

But you have to remember that there is always a better way to do things and that there are issues that have to be fixed to enhance a system. This is what the Lean Six Sigma methodology is rather good it.

Through analysis, it brings problems that you were not aware of or, at least, deemed to be insignificant and then lay out the ways on how they could affect the process. By understanding how one thing leads to another, a Lean Six Sigma professional can map out a better flow of processes so that value is delivered to the customer at a more efficient rate.

As such, if you are not a believer of "If it isn't broke, don't fix it" and are always seeking for ways to develop yourself or your organization, then Lean Six Sigma might be a good fit for you.

And now we come to the end of this book. Now that you have understood the basics of the Lean Six Sigma methodology, all that is left to do is to get the proper training, get certified, and start applying all that you have learned.

If done right, you might just improve yourself and your organizational processes in such a way that you can deliver on the output that you have promised to clients; and on time to boot.

I wish you the best of luck!

Book #2

Lean Analytics

How to Use Data to Track, Optimize, Improve and Accelerate Your Startup Business

Introduction

I wrote this book basing from words of experts, online influencers, and personal opinions.

Many people already wrote books about this topic. Why still write one if that's the case? That's because of the explosion of information about this topic. It made it inevitable for people to generate different and new interpretations. Their words can confuse individuals who want to learn about it.

Unlike those books written before this, this book aims to serve as a short guide. Treat it as a supplementary source of information if you will. It will not pander on claiming that this is the one single book you need to master the subject.

Many people have already jumped on the bandwagon. They created websites with domain names using the words lean, startup, and analytics. Visit them and all they want is to get something from you instead of them giving anything worthwhile. It's easy for people to get misinformed when they research because of those sites. Not to mention that the web isn't exactly moderated and curated for its accuracy.

Aside from that, there are other factors that complicate things:

1. Experience and application of the theory resulted into a different realization
2. Different backgrounds of people influence a different opinion
3. Excessive recycling of facts and opinions passed from one person to the next

The goal of this book is to give its readers a primer about lean analytics. I'd be honest here: it's not actually complex. It will only become complex if you put it in action and you have already a lot of data to analyze.

Since that's out of the way, here's a short story I want to tell you.

As you might have already guessed, I'm an entrepreneur. My first business flopped. I wasted my savings and the money I loaned. And I learned little from my experience after the business fell.

Let me tell the optimistic people that the failure wasn't worth it. It's like learning that a wooden bridge will collapse if you walk on it by walking on it. You could have saved yourself by asking the guy living near the bridge if it's stable enough.

A failed first business is like that. You are going to enter an unfamiliar territory. The first thing you should do is to ask the people who are already in that place. It should've been common sense.

People should stop preaching that it's normal to fail on your first attempt. It's plain wrong. If you believe that, you're actually setting yourself into an expensive failure.

What I did after the blunder was to cool myself down for a while. I took some jobs to pay the loan. Some of those loans came from friends and relatives. Of course, I also needed to have money for the usual daily expenses and the dreadful monthly bills. It's a painful and shameful experience.

I cleared all the baggage that came with the failed startup. I decided that it was time to look back on what happened. I wanted to know if it's still possible for me to be the businessman I aspired to be.

As I found out, I was wrong with everything. That wounded my ego. But I suppressed it believing it's already too late for me to whine about something that's passed. There's no use crying over spilled milk, especially if it's already dried and spoiled.

Going back to my postmortem, there were two primary things that attributed to my failure.

1. I failed to perform intensive research. I thought the knowledge of relatives and friends was enough. I asked the ones who have established businesses. I was wrong.

    But it doesn't mean that what they taught me was wrong. They don't work anymore. I could have succeeded if I started my business two decades ago. But the entrepreneurship landscape has changed a lot in the past few years.

Let me use my previous analogy. They were miles away from the bridge I was going to cross. I asked them if I can cross the bridge that appears to be already collapsing. They said yes, having no idea about what I was talking about. That was dumb of me.

2. I relied on instinct. I was confident. I thought I can delve into the mind of my customers. I thought that I can predict their behavior. I was, again, dead wrong. And it was my fatal mistake.

It was stupid of me. Why do I need to do that in the first place? I should have asked the customers themselves. Why try to emulate them if they're already there waiting for me to ask them.

Of course, I wasn't able to think of those things right off the bat. I was able to get some help. And the help I got was in the form of a book, The Lean Startup, written by Eric Reis.

But before I delve into that, I want you to know that both Lean Startup and Analytics helped me with my new venture. It's not that my business became one of the Fortune 500, but running it feels different and much better.

During my first venture, I was always lacking sleep. I always pushed myself harder every day thinking about all the things going on with the business. And despite the effort and sacrifices, nothing worked out.

I was borderline depressed after the catastrophe, which was my first business. But now, I didn't have to do too much. Well, I still do more since I'm running lean. I don't have full time employees, instead I have a few freelancers.

But I don't have to think too much. Instead of scrambling my brain on how I can improve my business, I can ask my customers. They are more than willing to tell me what I need to do and what they want. I do what they say, and I can sustain them and make them loyal.

I don't have to dizzy up myself with numbers, trying to measure if I am doing the right things or not. Currently, my Only Metric That Matters is sales count. If I have more sales, I'm doing better. If there's few then that's the time I need to put in more effort.

There are no guessing games anymore or prioritization. My business expenses are also a lot lower now. I don't rent an office or warehouse anymore. Everything's done at home. When it comes to logistics and other services, I hire the right businesses and people that can do the task I need to do.

I guess that's enough stories for now.

What I can promise you is this. Doing lean startup and lean analytics can make your mind rest easy. It's not the surefire success method, I admit that. Because if it is, I won't even bother to write this book. I would instead enjoy my vacations and earned money.

I can't say that it's a surefire method to prevent your business from failing. But I can promise that it will reduce the risk of losing your business.

Sure, some say that the amount of success is relative to the risk you are willing to take. I take that as truth. I would rather be a semi-successful businessman if it means I can keep my sanity. I wouldn't want to live a life filled with anxiety thinking how I can repay my loans when my business fails.

For those who want to start a business. I recommend running lean. It doesn't matter if you're a layman who wants to turn his life around and be the boss or if you're a business graduate. Running lean is the best way to start a business today.

With that said, the book contains information on how you can exactly do that. I would like to repeat that this book is a result of research and experience. But I promise you that after you finish this book, you'll have a different perspective as an entrepreneur who wants to establish a startup business.

Chapter 1

Lean Startup and Analytics The Discussion You've Been Waiting For

"Lean Startup isn't about being cheap [but is about] being less wasteful and still doing things that are big."

— Eric Reis

This chapter's goal is to let you understand the basics of Lean Startup and Analytics. It will talk about their definitions and how they work, and why they have been developed. Also, it will teach you on how to have a data driven mindset. Having a data-driven mindset will make it easier for you to apply lean analytics in your business.

What Is Lean analytics?

Benjamin Yoskovitz is one of the authors behind the Lean analytics book. According to him, lean analytics is an approach to improve your business. It relies on you focusing on one single metric to measure your progress toward your goals. The book refers to that metric as the One Metric That Matters. It's pretty straightforward, don't you think?

To start with Lean analytics, you should have great knowledge of the industry you're in. You should also know the current state of your business. Is it on its way to success? Is it failing? Or everything is doing fine with no signs of sudden success or failure?

The next step is to set a goal. It can be better sales or it can be company expansion. Once the goal is set, you will need to determine your One Metric That Matters. If your goal is better sales, your One Metric That Matters is the number of sales your company will make.

Lean analytics isn't a static approach—it was before. Every business has its own unique needs and it changes, depending on the state it is in. This means that you need to change your One Metric That Matters from time to time.

You need to reevaluate your company's performance and goal to know the proper metric to use next time.

Startups and Lean analytics

Lean analytics restrains a business from losing its focus on its goal. Startups benefit from it. It helps them overcome the initial pitfalls of starting a business. That pitfall is the fervor to do all things at once and recover investments made.

Lean analytics pushes startups away from going through premature scaling or growth. Instead of expanding, it pushes a business to establish a solid foundation. Businesses using lean analytics become solutions specialists.

It gives the company a direction, and a very narrow one at that. As mentioned before, lean analytics uses a single metric to measure progress. This approach has been developed from a business methodology called Lean Startup.

Lean Startup

Lean startup is a business methodology that promotes running a business as lean as it can. Steve Blank and Eric Reis helped popularize it.

The methodology encourages an entrepreneur to start a business with minimal resources. This includes minimizing employees, products, and services.

Regular and large-scale businesses use a Swiss knife to operate. A lean startup only uses a sharp and flexible single knife.

As the business operates, it improves and adds elements to the business when needed. Progression means the business obtains essential tools to help the single knife.

Build, Measure, and Learn

When it comes to product and service development, a Lean Startup uses lean analytics. Lean analytics follows a simple build, measure, and learn development cycle.

For example, if the entrepreneur has an idea for a product, he'll start to build. He'll then measure and test the product. He'll then gather data from the measurements. And then he'll learn how he can improve the product based on data and lean analysis.

The improvements learned are ideas that he'll use to build again. The cycle repeats until he creates the perfect product.

During the measurement and learn cycles, companies undergo five stages:

1. Empathy: Connecting to customers and knowing what they want.
2. Familiarity: Making your brand, products, and services stick to customers' minds.
3. Virality: Making non-customers discover your brand, product, or service.
4. Revenue: Developing methods to further improve revenue from your products and services.
5. Scale: Enlarging your reach and customer base.

For example, you have built a new car model. You will first deal with the customers and test the product. Once they finish testing the car, you will gather data from them by asking for feedback. You then enter the learn and build phase again.

In the next measurement phase, you will then make your way to introduce the car to more people. You'll do that by making the car more appealing. Then another cycle goes by.

After that, you will focus on the revenue aspect of the new car. If you learn that the model is viable for your business, then you can start scaling your production.

To move through the stages, you need to follow the hook model. The hook model has four phases. They are:

1. Trigger: Event that needs to be done to start the lean analytical stage.
2. Action: Action that needs to be done to act upon the trigger.
3. Variable Reward: Motivator to make the action continue.
4. Investment: Motivator to make the stakeholders proceed to the next stage.

The Pitfall

Amateurs, like me before, always tend to get trapped in the wrong mindset. When they start a business, they tend to think that it's as simple as:

1. Think of a product
2. Develop the product
3. Sell the product
4. Profit!

Mind you, that's not a bad mindset to have. After all, you can simplify a business like that. The only problem is that they get stuck with that simplification. They fail to see or discover the intricacies behind every process.

For example, an entrepreneur wants to start a coffee shop. He finds a location for it. Build the shop. List the menu he wants to be present on the shop. And opens it. And like before, his business fails. Why did that happen?

The problem is that the coffee shop owner thought that he's done after the initial stage. He thought that the business will grow by itself.

Unfortunately, you can't plant a seed, water it for a few days, let it grow by itself, and harvest the fruit after. You can't treat a business that way. You don't stop and wait.

For one, you should never end the connection between you and the customer after he buys your product. Your job isn't done yet if someone gets your service and product. You should get feedback.

Customer feedback is the most important element in a successful business. The wants of the customer are your ticket to success.

For example, do you still remember Twilight? Do you remember the time when it was the most popular romance book title on the market? Because of its immense popularity, many amateur and veteran authors had an idea. They took it to themselves to write books about vampires.

What happened? Did another vampire story become popular? No. What happened was that Fifty Shades of Gray took the throne. Was that a vampire story? No. So why did it become popular?

The author of that book is a fan of Twilight's author. And she knows well what made Twilight good. She was a customer. It wasn't about the vampires. It was about the kind of romance that made the book sell well.

It's the same for other products. Just because bubble tea is popular doesn't mean that people will buy bubble tea from you. Customers have individual needs. And if you want your product to sell, your product must meet those needs. If a certain bubble tea is popular, get one and analyze it. Talk to the people who drink that product, and ask what they like.

Use the feedback and imitate the tea. Sell it. And you now have a higher chance of having a successful business.

Lean Startup: Your Business Doesn't Matter, Your Customer Does

The core concept in lean startup is communication to customers. It's the crucial element that shouldn't be ignored.

Entrepreneurs should create and develop businesses because of love of people. That sounds cheesy and cringe worthy. But businesses should be built to serve first; make their owners profit second.

Businesses are solutions providers and product suppliers. Products and services must fix a problem and please the desire of customers. A business' existence and its success depend on the needs and wants of people.

If you already have a lean startup running, it's never too late to shift your focus to your customers. You can start by doing these four steps:

1. Customer Discovery. Test ideas on what the customer needs, interest on the product, and business viability.

2. Customer Validation. Test the viability of the business through product sales. A product sales road map is generated. If the road map is doable and repeatable, the business is viable.

3. Customer Creation. Business plans are executed to expand and scale customer acquisition. Create customer demands to direct and improve sales.

4. Company Building. The last process. The transition from being a lean startup to a real business. It focuses on completing the business. Employees, products, and functionalities that it needed before are added.

Supply and Demand

A business is there to complete the equation of supply and demand. Most entrepreneurs nowadays either don't know that or are focused on other things. This is especially true about new entrepreneurs who're running their first startups.

It is somewhat understandable. You'll feel that you need to focus on how you can get your money back fast. The feeling intensifies if you have limited or loaned money. Believe me. I was in that situation, too.

Unfortunately, it's difficult to shift your attention to anything else. You are pressured. You must achieve results. There's no time to waste. You'll jilt the existence of your role to meet the demands of your customers. This then leads to your imminent failure.

In lean startups, you need to treat your businesses as an experiment. This experiment aims to answer two core questions.

1. Do people need this product?
2. Can I build a business around it?

You don't create a product and push it to people. It's true that if there's no need for a product, you should create one. It's a sound approach, but why would you try to do that if you can pick a product that there's already a need for? Again, supply and demand.

If your answer to the first question is yes, then you should deal with the second. Answering that question will lead to tons more. Here are a few of the follow up questions:

1. Is the product you have profitable?
2. Is there demand for your product?
3. If it isn't, can you make it so?
4. What are the steps you need to do to get that?
5. Can you even compete with the other businesses offering the same product?

In your quest to find answers to those questions, you need to use Lean analytics and have a data driven mindset to do so. And that's going to be discussed in the next chapter.

Takeaway

Lean startup is a methodology in running a business. It encourages entrepreneurs to have a bare-bones startup. It makes business owners focus on two things: customers and products.

Lean analytics is an approach developed with lean startup in mind. It encourages data analysis and logic to measure and act upon a business' progress. This leads to the introduction of the one metric that matters.

The one metric that matters is a chosen metric that's used as a measurement tool. Its purpose is to track the progress of the business towards the owner's goal.

Lean analytics also empowers lean startup's product development cycle. The cycle involves three stages: build, measure, and learn.

- The build phase takes an idea and turn it into an actual product.
- The measure phase tests the products to get useful data.
- The lean phase uses data gathered to improve the product or gain insight on what's the next business step.

You must be focused on customers and be data driven. You need to be like that to harness the effectiveness of both the methodology and approach. Both will be discussed in the next chapter.

Chapter 2

Your Journey to Become a Data Driven Person

"The price of light is less than the cost of darkness."

—Arthur C. Nielsen

For you to take full advantage of Lean analytics, you should become a data driven person. You should value the importance of every snippet of data you can gather. And give utmost care when processing them a logical manner.

Two things that you should remember when approaching matters in a data driven manner:

- Never ignore existing data, and never prioritize new data over old data.
- Squeeze out huge amounts of data as possible.
- Make data presentable and understandable
- Legally and ethically get data
- Data should back your every decision

A data driven mindset can also help you:

1. Learn industry knowledge. The industry has its own methods, techniques, skills, and tactics. They were developed to make things fruitful and easier for entrepreneurs. They didn't appear out of nowhere. They were developed, thanks to the continuous work to gather and process data. If you were able to do the same, you'll have one that you can call your own.
2. See all the opportunities. Have an eye out for every small thing happening in your business. It'll allow you to have greater insight and idea on what to do next if a problem arises. You'll also see every opportunity that you can take advantage of.
3. Understand your competitors. Things happen for a reason. If your competitors are having the upper hand or failing hard, you'll know

the reason why using analytics. It allows you to imitate best practices and avoid game losing actions.

4. Have full grasp of lean analytics. Lean analytics is useless if you don't value data and think logically. And it isn't restricted to analytics alone. A data driven mindset can help you create logical and proper business decisions. This is true regardless if you have a lean startup or not.

Remember that lean analytics seeks to remove any wasteful actions and decisions. It promotes valuable actions during the early stages of your company or startup. And with those benefits, it will effectively raise your chances of success.

Now, it's time to get more intimate with Lean analytics. At this point, the previous chapter has already given you many pointers. Those hints on how to apply lean analytics on your business or startup are there to get got your feet wet. This chapter will provide you with a chance to do some deep diving.

The One Metric That Matters

Later in this chapter, you will learn about data collection, relation, and types. If you can, it's a good time to decide the one metric that matters for you.

To make it easy for you to know that metric, follow the simple steps below.

The Customers

The first and crucial step is to get acquainted to your customers and extract data from them. There are many ways to do this, and the step you need to do depends on how you do business.

Up Close and Personal

The subtitle says it all. Just talk to them. You don't need to interrogate them or shower them with questions. You don't need to think of leading questions. Build rapport and connect to them.

Build a connection with them, and data gathering will be easier. Do that, and they'll comfortably give you feedback and other information you need. Plus, they will appreciate the effort and time you give to them.

Of course, this is highly effective on startups. And the ones that rely on foot traffic and walk-in customers will benefit from this strategy.

Customer Service

Customer service representatives get the most interaction with customers. Actually, whoever's on phone duty will have the most interaction.

You can get friendly and establish rapport on the phone like with the previous method. But unlike personal conversations, phone calls often end short.

Be sure to take the opportunity to ask for feedback at the end of each call. Be polite and don't push the customer too much for information.

Customer Feedback Form

A customer feedback form will be impersonal, regardless of how you word it. It'll never be considered warm and friendly for customers. It's a cold way to gather feedback and it's often considered a bother.

Also, customers who actually fill up feedback forms often have negative things to say. Consumers have the tendency to not bother themselves with surveys. This is especially true if they're okay with the product or service they received.

If they are pissed, you'll likely hear from them. As long as they're given the chance to talk, they definitely let you know what's on their minds. This makes customer feedback forms a good way to fish out negative impressions.

Observe Your Business Processes

Making your business lean is like taking all the fat out of a cut of meat. But unlike meat, not all fat in your business can be seen easily by the naked eye.

Because of that, you need to devote some of your time to observe the processes happening in your business.

The things you can find and remove from your business can vary. Some of those are:

1. Employees who slack off too much
2. Inefficient work processes
3. Unnecessary business expenses
4. Unproductive overtimes
5. Wasteful usage of electricity, Internet, water, etcetera

Removal of the Unneeded Elements

The next step after finding the inefficiencies in your business is to remove them all.

Check the Changes in Your Metric

After doing all the previous steps, check if there is some improvement in your metric. If there is, it means that you have done something right and the metric is spot on. If there isn't, the metric isn't a good indicator, and you should come up with another one.

Oiling the System

Removing people and inefficiencies have one inevitable result: change. People hate change. In case you still have employees, be sure to reward them for their good work. Assure them that they are essential.

Introduce Improvements

Once your business is working at its best state, it's time to introduce some improvements. This part of the process is entirely up to you.

You can try to imitate some of the processes your competitors do. You can check out some books about businesses to learn more on how you can improve your operations.

Of course, you can focus on the One Metric That Matters, and check the data you gathered to get an idea on what to do next.

The Data for Your Analytics

Analytics is a measure of progress towards one's goals. You need to learn your goals first before you can consider a metric. It's been iterated before, but here are some extra things that you should learn.

The first and most important step in creating a good metric is to gather good amounts of proper data. The data should pass certain qualities and requirements. And those qualities and requirements are:

Comparable

A single point of data only gives little information. For example, selling three products today provides little and useful information. It can't help you measure your progress alone.

It gives you a starting point. Yet it needs another point of data for it to be actually useful in measuring your progress.

Say that you sold three products today and sold nine products yesterday. You can generate much more measurable information from that situation.

You can synthesize the two data points and evaluate it. You can learn that your product performed poorly today compared to yesterday. Collect comparable data points to measure your progress.

Understandable

If you don't understand a data point, it becomes irrelevant. For example, if you live in the UK, you'll be much more familiar with kilometers rather than miles.

Ask an American how far a place is from where you're standing. Expect that he will give you a distance value using the Imperial miles.

The answer you'll get is correct and true. But, it becomes irrelevant because you might have no idea how far a mile is.

Because of that, you should know how to process data to make it understandable and relevant. Here's a quote often attributed to Einstein, "It should be possible to explain the laws of physics to a barmaid."

Actually, Ernest Rutherford said that. Anyway, if it's possible, then you can understand and explain the data you got.

Rate-able

A data point is convertible or translatable to numbers. It should be always in the form of a ratio or percentage. After all, you can always process raw data or numbers to ratio or percentage.

For example, you sold three phones yesterday and nine phones today. It's easier and informational if you interpret the data by using ratio or percentage. You can say, there is a 300% increase of phone sales in your retail store today.

But of course, play safe with this one. As William Bruce Cameron said it best in his book Informal Sociology: A Casual Introduction to Sociological Thinking, "Not everything that can be counted counts, and not everything that counts can be counted."

Relevant

As mentioned before, the metric or data must be relevant. A relevant metric can make you think of improvements and changes. An irrelevant metric is something good to know.

A customer bought three things from your company today. Sure, you can understand what it means. But does it tell you anything? Is it relevant? What did the customer buy? It's true that it is understandable. The data is simple: customers bought three things from you.

It becomes irrelevant because it doesn't provide any context. It doesn't have any accompanying information to make it relevant as a metric. When gathering understandable data, it's much better to have your data points to be specific and detailed.

For example, the customer bought three iPhone units from your retail store today. The context changes and you understand the relevance of the information. You can evaluate that your iPhone units are getting more popular than other phones in your store.

Remember that it's much better to have more data and discard the excess. Having less data only restricts you to what you can learn.

Eight Types of Data

This is where it gets interesting. You should know that there are at least eight types of data. You can use those to create a business metric to measure your business' progress. Most lean analytics use the first two types for the one metric that matters.

But it should help you out if you know the eight data types to prevent you from improperly using them. Other types aside from qualitative and quantitative can help you create unique metrics. Those metrics might not help you measure progress, but can help you in other things such as marketing, company management, and the likes.

Qualitative

This includes customer interviews or anything that doesn't involve numbers. It can be in the form of gut feeling or personal feedback. This gives you insights. This allows you to think on how you can gather or collect data for the next type of metric.

Qualitative data is often converted to quantitative. For example, feedback can be converted into numbers: 5 for positive, 0 for negative. A product's success can be measured this way.

However, data in its qualitative form is useful in lean analytics. The comments from customers can help in the development cycle of your products.

Quantitative

This is mostly numbers. It's the most used type of data that businesses use regardless if they're running lean or not. The data you get from this type of metric allows you to know the data you actually need to gather.

Unlike qualitative, you can't easily revert quantitative data to qualitative. What you can do is to interpret it. Data can be reformed or skewed through interpretation.

Vanity

It only makes you feel good. It does not help you create actionable plans that matter for your company. And it's often wrongly used as a metric to measure progress. It still serves as a good motivator and marketing material for businesses.

Actionable

Actionable often comes internally from your organization. But it can be gathered from customer feedback, too. Actionable data and metrics can provide you with insights. These insights can directly affect and influence your business decisions.

Exploratory

This is speculative data, one that's generated using currently available data on hand. This can involve predictions on how metrics will change over time. It can also show how the metrics can be influenced to achieve the result you want.

Reports

Data gathered from reports can be actionable, vanity, exploratory, or lagging. It can be generated internally or you can source it from third parties. It is often acquired by businesses periodically, depending on how you set it.

Lagging

People usually call lagging data as historical data. Not all data can be acquired instantly. Some of your business actions require some time to see results. This results can be interpreted as usable data.

Leading

The biggest difference between leading and exploratory data is the time range it predicts. Exploratory data are often predictions set to the far future. Leading is predicted for data in the near future.

Data Linking: Causality and Correlation

Data are often related or linked in one way or another. Two types of data relationship are causal and correlational.

1. Correlational: Two data points behave in a similar way because of another data point. For example, the number of umbrella sales goes up and the number of people getting flu goes up, too. You know that people buying umbrellas do not actually increase people getting sick. But you can say that it's the rainy season, which can cause umbrella sales go up and flu victims go up.
2. Causal: Two data points behave in a similar way because one of the two causes the other to change. The two data points can be considered independent or dependent. For example, it's rainy and it causes people to get sick. The independent data is the rainy weather. And the dependent data is people getting sick. People getting sick does not cause rainy weather, but rainy weather can cause people to get sick.

What does data relationships have to do with Lean Analytics?

1. Correlational data can help you predict events. For example, next month is the start of the rainy season. You can predict that the number of people buying umbrellas and getting sick will skyrocket.
2. Causal data can help you affect the future. If you sell umbrellas before the rainy season starts, you can help prevent people from getting sick.

Data Link Testing

Unfortunately, the relationship between data is not always obvious. You can just say that two data points are causal or correctional.

To know the relationship between your data, you must perform these processes.

1. Find correlation
2. Test causality
3. Optimize causal factor

You now have a full grasp of lean startup and analytics. You are also more data driven than ever. The next step is to learn more about the technical side of things. We're going to talk about Minimum Viable Product. And we will apply what you have learned so far using examples.

Takeaway

Lean startup and analytics won't work without a data-driven mindset. Lean analytics is a research focus method of running a business. Without data, it's useless.

Don't rely on passive experience and mistakes. Focus on actively learning all the things you can with lean startup and analysis.

Of course, an unguided research doesn't bring anything to the table. You need to be precise with the information you gather. Because of that, you need to handpick the data you get to make your analyses fruitful for your company.

The center of it all is the one metric that matters. It's the single data point that will guide and tell you about the progress of your company. The only challenge is that you need to know what that metric will be.

The first thing you should do when you start operating is to realize what your company's goal is. The metric you choose should be directly tied to your goal. It should be also capable of measuring your progress.

To make your business lean and efficient, you need to work on the following:

First, have a metric that's actually useful. You should know how to figure it out, and where and how to get the necessary data for it. The best source is your customers. That is why lean analytics pushed you to be customer and product centric.

There are three common ways on how you can get your data from them. They are: up and personal, customer service, and customer feedback form.

The next steps are to observe your business processes. After that, remove unneeded elements from it and check the changes in your metric. If the metric says you progressed, proceed on oiling your system. Lastly, introduce improvements and repeat everything.

The data you gather will flood you as your business operates. Ideally, getting all the data you can get will be excellent for your analytics.

Since you're running lean, you might be the only person working on the data. It's okay be a bit selective on the data you harvest.

There are four characteristics that your data must have. They must be comparable, understandable, rate-able, and relevant. Without those qualities, you're wasting your time collecting data.

Some of those useless data can be converted into something useful. But you wouldn't want to spend the little amount of time you have, considering that you have a lot of things to do.

And then there's also the eight types of data. You have qualitative, quantitative, vanity, actionable, exploratory, reports, lagging, and leading. Be sure to choose the right of data for your metric and analyses.

Lastly, you have data linking or defining the relationships of the data you have. Always be sure to know the difference between causal and correlational data. Causal is simply a pair of data with one data point affecting another. And correlational data is simply a pair of data with both being affected by an external data.

Chapter 3

Minimum Viable Product: The Root of All Profitable Products

"The MVP has just those features considered sufficient for it to be of value to customers and allow for it to be shipped or sold to early adopters. Customer feedback will inform future development of the product."

—Scott M. Graffius

To obtain that One Metric That Matters, you need to be already data driven. You should have collected the right data. Choose the type of data you wish to use. Figure out their relationships. And then evaluate them.

But to be honest, you don't need to be too intense on finding that metric. You can actually decide upon it for a few seconds. This is especially true if your business is simple.

Once you get to this point, everything will be up to you. Again, the metric depends on the type of business, your goals, and situation. A chosen metric for one business will not work for another.

Anyway, this chapter will talk about minimum viable product. But before that, here are some examples you need to study.

An Example: The Profitable Hotdogs

Saying it like that seems irresponsible and can get you confused and baffled, so here's an example.

Say that your startup is a humble food cart that sells hotdogs. By starting your business lean, it means that you'll man the store yourself. You will also handle everything else. Manage finances, buy the supplies, and market. Also, you will have your single core product: the hotdogs.

You already have a data driven mindset. You care now for statistics and analytics. Together with your cooking equipment, you have a tablet with an inventory and sales app. That app will make it easy for you to track and record data about your stores and customers.

Deciding that the number of hotdogs sold is the One Metric That Matters is a good choice. It's a no-brainer. Your business is too lean and simple for it to need complex analysis. Nonetheless, you still want to gather data for your business just in case.

All you need to do now is operate the business and set your goal. Say that your goal is to make your business handle your daily expenses. You can add the fact that it should also cover at least a percent of the amount you loaned for the business per week.

Thanks to your business setup, you can easily connect with your customers. You can take advantage of connecting with them personally. It's a good opportunity to talk to them while they wait for their food.

Through this, you can easily gather enough information from your customer. You can ask how they like your product. You can also fish for information if there's anything they would want from it that will make them buy more from you. At this rate, forming connections with them will be fast and easy. In return, they can give you tons of feedback.

You've heard what they have to say about your stall, product, and you. Now you know that they would prefer their hotdogs to be sandwiched. You got a new idea, and you have now a new product: hotdog sandwich.

As you go about your business, you then check the efficiency of your operations. You found out that there was no need for you to have an ice box. You used to keep your hotdogs cool inside it to prevent spoilage. Now you don't need it since all your stocks are consumed the same day you bought them.

You then removed that unneeded element and made your stall a bit more efficient. Removing the icebox removed the expense of buying dry ice for it. Also, completely removing it from the business process made it faster to cook the hotdogs. It's faster to cook because they're not ice cold, so you don't need to thaw them.

After the change, you noticed the number of customers increased. It was most probably because of the faster cooking time, which was the result of eliminating the ice box. Your One Metric That Matters is showing you now that your business is getting better.

The next step you did was to apply some improvements. It was an easy thing to think of. You just need to buy more hotdogs because you always come home without any hotdog. The move is beneficial since you can sell more of your products. It also reduced the number of times you need to visit your supplier.

Since your business is doing well now, it's time for you to check on the data you gathered. What you have primarily is your sales history. The data it contained was easily comparable, understandable, rate-able, and relevant. You have complete control of your business.

You were able to know that you sell very well during the weekends. That's thanks to your sales history. You decided to bring more hotdogs during those days to maximize your sales.

Counter Example: The Demand for Ice Cream

Of course, the previous example seems too good to be true since the customers are just gobbling up the hotdogs. But here's a similar example, but didn't have the same customers. The entrepreneur has used lean startup methodology and lean analytics, too.

The example again is a food cart that sells hotdogs. It's running lean; the only difference is the owner chose a bad location. Low foot traffic, and nobody's really interested in buying hotdogs on the street.

Hotdogs sales is still the One Metric That Matters. The owner of this hotdog stall started operating with the same goal as the previous example.

With a measly number of customers and foot traffic, the owner can't connect to customers well. Nonetheless, he pursued gathering data by interviewing the locals. He was able to know that people in the area don't particularly like hotdogs.

He then asked them what they preferred. They preferred ice cream instead. In this case, the product he built failed in the measurement cycle. In the learn cycle, he learned that he'll get nowhere with hotdogs, but ice cream has a higher chance of getting sold.

Thankfully, he didn't hire anyone. He only bought a simple stall with a propane tank, gas burner, fryer, ice box, and acrylic food display. So, if he wants to convert into an ice cream stall, all he need is to get rid of the tank, burner, and fryer. He needs to replace them with an ice cream canister and an ice cream scooper. He can place the cones and containers on the acrylic display.

He has done that, and he settled for a single flavor: vanilla. After a few days, he sold a decent amount, but the metric is telling him that he's still not doing well. After a week, he realized something. The low foot traffic in his location is really hurting his business.

He now has to decide on two things since even if his product has potential, he can't build a business around it. He could either call it quits; or he could move to a place with more people.

Either way, he can freely decide without stressing himself. The amount of money he has spent on the business was minimal; the losses he incurred was not great.

Application Overview

The examples showed how simple and convenient lean startup and lean analytics is. And there's a high chance you were already doing it before you stumbled upon this book.

Doing things lean made the operation of the startup easier simple and easier. It also removed the fear and stress of failure. It's not that you expect yourself to fail. But with lean, you know that you'll not hit rock-bottom if your first attempt doesn't work out.

And even if doesn't work out, you still have the option to continue or just stop. You have full control. You don't actually fail, but you'll just experience a setback.

On the other hand, you might have noticed that both examples only have one product to sell. That's because both examples are using a minimum viable product or MVP. The term has been thrown in the previous sections a few times. But what is it exactly?

Minimum Viable Product

Most people don't just view lean analytics as a product development cycle. They view it as the best approach with producing a minimum viable product or MVP.

Most lean startups mainly rely on MVPs. They are products that can solve a problem. They can satisfy a need. They don't have the bells and whistles or any secondary features or functions.

An MVP is a product in its simplest form. It can give you profit with minimal effort and resources. Putting it like that, it's fundamentally similar to lean startup. Instead of a lean business, MVPs are lean products.

For example, if you have a food cart or stall, you can treat a simple scrambled egg as your minimum viable product. The ingredients of this scrambled egg are egg, a bit of salt, and cooking oil for frying. Access to the ingredients is a non-issue since they are commercially available anywhere.

Processing the ingredients to make a scrambled egg requires minimal effort and skill. And on its core, it can simply alleviate the hunger of your customer.

You can develop your MVP using the BML (build, measure, and learn) development cycle. This process can make your scrambled egg a more profitable product.

To get started with BML, you need to start with an idea, which is parallel with your goal. Say that your goal is to develop a tasty product or scrambled egg. One of the most viable ideas you can build into your product is to improve your ingredients.

You can start with replacing your cooking oil with butter. Build the idea, and test it out to your customers to start the measuring process. Select the one metric that matters in this phase. You can just use the number of sales you gain or loss as the metric. Record the data you gathered and analyze the data.

If the number of sold scrambled eggs improves, start the cycle again and build the new idea. That idea is the usage of butter. If you experience losses, then you can let go of the butter, and rethink of a new idea. Using sea salt instead of regular fine salt might be a good idea to implement.

The Perfect Product

As you progress and go through countless BML cycles, your MVP becomes a perfect product. A perfected product can help you answer the second core question in your business. Can you build a business around your product?

This perfect product can help you sustain your business. But if the metric goes down, you can just retreat your product for another round of development cycle.

Why MVPs?

An MVP is the simplest form of a product. In most cases, it is designed to lure in early adopters or your first customers. Minimum viable products are like beta versions of a video game. They contain all the features to get beta testers hooked.

For those who are unfamiliar, beta testers are people who test the game. They are given the privilege to be the first ones to play it before it's released to the market. The games are either given free or discounted to beta testers.

In exchange, game developers expect those testers to provide feedback. The feedback is expected to help them fix any issue found in the game. This, in turn raises the game's quality for the market.

Taking advantage of an MVP makes it easier for businesses. Startups in particular tend to use MVPs to find a profitable product they can use now and later in the future.

It is also less costly since they will be getting refined data from reliable sources. These sources are the beta testers. They are reliable since they have a large amount of interest towards the products.

And they don't care if the product is incomplete. They recognize the potential. They are willing to endure any concerns or flaws of the product just to have a shot at it.

They would even shell out money even if it's bare. And they don't care if the only features the provided are the minimum. They also love the fact that they can be considered the pioneers or called the early adopters/beta testers.

MVPs attract getting reliable feedback. It also saves the business from the cost of hiring R&D people or analysts. It also poses minimal risks. The numbers of early adopters are few after all.

Compared to waiting to perfect a product, launching it in full production once assumed it's ready for the market, learning later that it will flop in the market, and receiving tons of complaints from customers, letting a small number of people hate you for an unpolished product is a small price to pay.

The Early Adopters

As you might have already perceived, the early adopters are the key for MVPs to work. Since lean startup and analytics rely on MVPs to succeed, early adopters become immensely crucial if you want your business to succeed.

Due to that, you should prioritize the hunt for early adopters after the first build development cycle.

Also, take note that aside from being reliable sources of feedback, early adopters are also more forgiving compared to regular customers. They also tend to provide more feedback since they are proven to be already interested in the product you give them.

Lastly, taking advantage of them allows you to avoid developing or creating the wrong product for your target customers.

MVPs' Other Purposes

Here are the other purposes of minimum viable products aside from using them to achieve the perfect product with minimal risk and higher success rate:

1. It makes it faster and easier for the businesses to learn about the strengths and weaknesses of a new product.
2. It's easier and faster to test a prototype product with minimal resources used.
3. It prevents wasting time in adding more features and bloating the product.
4. Feedback generated from the MVP can be used on other products.
5. The MVP can also become a base for another product even if it fails.
6. It gauges the skill and power of the product development team or the startup itself. It tests if the actual company and its target goals is viable,
7. Aside from being a good marketing material for early adopters, word of the products and bawdiness' existence can easily get around the neighborhood.

MVP as Prototypes and Visions

Despite using the word minimum, there's no standard when it comes to the actual minimum features or cost to be used on an MVP. It's up to the organization and its resources on what the actual minimum is.

Because of that, it's much easier to refer to MVP as a product prototype. It's easier to understand, and it's much more of a familiar term.

Since MVPs are basically product prototypes, the main test for the product isn't to know the features that should be applied on it. Instead, the test is to know if the product is viable for the business to create and sell.

Despite being regarded as prototypes, you should treat MVPs as products. It's just a vision that you sell to visionaries and not customers. What comes out of it is the actual product you would sell to customers. Most often than not, MVPs are used as marketing materials.

Minimum Viable Service and Collective Minimum Viable Product

For you startup, creating an MVP allows you to focus on one single product that you will rely on. You might have some doubts on how it will work, especially if you have a retail store that serves multiple products and you can't exactly improve the products you are selling. But MVP isn't limited to only products.

You can also apply lean startup and analytics on services. Also, you can treat all of your products into one and call it your MVP. For example, if you want to run a liquor store, you can treat all the liquors you have as one product.

You can do that by collectively treating them as your Minimum Viable Service. Your liquor store will start with the minimum viable products like a single brand of the most popular beer, spirit, and wine.

As you go with your business, you will surely encounter people looking for certain brands and liquor. You can take note of their requests and just stock up on those brands that they mentioned.

Instead of treating a single product as your MVP, you're going to treat your whole stock as a single minimum viable service.

Takeaway

A business running lean would always start with a minimum viable product or service. Instead of selling or providing multiple products or collections of products, you start with the ones with the highest chance of satisfying customers and providing you with profit.

As your business grows and you follow lean analytics, you can turn that minimum viable product as the perfect product. Thanks to the build, measure, and learn cycle, your product can progress into something more profitable, which would then also help your business improve.

You should also remember that aside from running lean and minimizing risks, your MVP can serve other purposes.

On another note, you must also make sure that you have early adopters. These people are the ones that will help you jumpstart your business and assist you in attaining your perfect product or service.

And when you deal with your MVP and early adopters, always remind yourself that your MVP is not a product, but a vision you're selling to them. It only becomes a product if your early adopters accept it as such.

Now that you have a full idea on the importance and positive effects of minimum viable products, lean startup, lean analysis, and a data-driven mindset to your business, the next step is to know what their disadvantages are, the oppositions' opinions about them, and how to circumvent those disadvantages and flaws.

Chapter 4

The Opposition and Words of the Wise

"Perfectionism is a disease. Procrastination is a disease. ACTION is the cure."

—Richie Norton

There is one big flaw in lean startup and analytics. It is the tendency to put all the work into the entrepreneur. It's true that the methodology and approach reduces a lot of the required resources to run a business. However, in turn, the entrepreneur needs to work twice as much.

On the other hand, proponents defend that going lean isn't about the money. It isn't about preventing quality of life improvements in the business. It's not about not hiring employees. They say that running lean means working with customers solely. It's designed to work like that, instead of pushing efforts on different directions.

Detractors also mention about the methodology being too product centric. They argue that having the best product shouldn't be the only goal of a business.

Simplifying a business to the point that it only revolves around its product can be a huge pitfall. A business isn't all about making and selling. There are other faces an entrepreneur must consider when operating. A few of them are marketing, logistics, accounting, and even legal.

Nonetheless, you could have already identified that the methodology has addressed this issue. Most of the points from the opposition have been already addressed.

Against Minimum Viable Product

Minimum Viable Product has been split into multiple types. This is to avoid the tendency of a business to rely and focus too much on one product. Second, proponents have already gone preaching to make metric flexible.

It's supposed to be dynamic, according to the ever-changing needs of their businesses.

However, followers of lean analytics should know that MVP is not always the solution. It is not the only way to grow your business. This is especially true if you're in the latter stages of your business' life. Producing or releasing a lackluster product can be detrimental. An MVP with your recognizable business name on it can backfire on you.

More established businesses have been adopting lean startup methodologies. And they're not doing any good to the entrepreneurship community. MVP should be reserved to startups. There are other forms of products like MVP, but are well suited to bigger companies.

Also, even if you're a startup, you can actually get away from using MVP and its risks. The key is to use the MVP of your competitors. Yes, that sounds awful, but that's business.

Don't risk your name by releasing a product on its weakest state. You can actually get the data you need without an MVP. That method is to check out your competition's MVPs.

Google and Facebook didn't slowly climb their way up to success by pioneering a product line from an MVP. They skipped the build and measure cycles, and started on the learn cycle first.

The competitors they had were AOL/Yahoo and Multiply/Friendster respectively. The two companies did the measure and build cycles for their competitors' MVPs. They didn't battle directly with MVP vs. MVP. They immediately created better and robust versions of their competitors' products.

Against the Metric

Another point that the opposition makes is the one metric that matters. It's true that it's nice to only check one metric alone to gauge the current condition of a company. However, it's a pipe dream. A business, especially as it grows, is a complex mechanism.

You just can't measure it with one metric alone. You can't synthesize metrics into one single metric that can tell you everything. A business is dynamic. Its needs change every time. One metric will not be able to provide such accurate insight on the current state of a business.

Some people and experts believe that an MVP can actually provide more harm than benefits to a company or a startup. AN MVP creates a risk. That risk is when a competitor decides to copy the MVP and get a head start on developing the actual product.

Also, it can be said that the negative feedback can hurt the company. Plus, early adopters who have no idea about the concept of MVP can become detractors.

They may think that the almost featureless product is the actual product. And they would rather find another which is already completed and feature rich.

Most entrepreneurs believe that the metric should be complex. But it should be also simplified, effective, but creative. No. It doesn't have to be like that. And those characteristics are too oxymoronic.

The metric should be a measure of your progress. It shouldn't be creative or flashy. You should focus on functionality over form. If the number of sales gives you an idea if you're doing well, then use it. Don't create calculations or synthesize a lot of data points just to say you have the perfect metric. That's not the point of your business.

How to Avoid Making Mistakes with Lean Analytics

Entrepreneurs are everywhere and one too many. Don't be lax just because you're running lean. Never forget that doing lean startup and analytics isn't a surefire method to be successful. The two are a methodology and approach in business. They help a startup stand their ground despite the lack of financial power.

You should avoid copying how today's billionaires become successful. You don't need to drop out from college or to start your company in a garage.

Don't be a pseudo-visionary. Don't lead your business with weird and unheard-of business tactics.

Always remind yourself that entrepreneurship is mostly about management. Changes and innovations don't happen frequently in the industry. This is the truth regardless of trends and dynamisms. Before you try something new, be sure that you already have a solid foundation.

Also, don't ever think that a business is just about its products and selling it. It's true that lean startup preaches about focusing on products and customers. However, it doesn't mean that you can forget about the other technicalities of running a business.

Startups are not just about developing creating, and selling the perfect product. A startup is also created to identify or discover if a certain line of business is viable. It also tests if the entrepreneur does really have what it takes to run a business. That's why lean startup and analysis is heavily favored by the modern entrepreneur.

In addition, a startup business is an organization that you need to manage in order to be successful. Many techniques and methodologies have been developed. These techniques allow beginners to manage their startups in a more effective way. Be sure not to only learn about lean. You should also know about other methodologies and approaches in business.

Never skip the boring stuff. As an entrepreneur, you should always be accountable. You should learn how to measure your progress and successes. You should know how to make goals. You also need to know where and what you need to prioritize.

Lastly, it always boils down to: build or turn ideas to products. Measure how your customers respond to your ideas or products. Learn if you can continue creating and selling the product or if you need to stop and develop a new one.

Regardless of methodologies, the simple build, measure, and learn development cycle is present. Even if you don't like lean startup or analytics, you shouldn't disregard this form of development cycle.

Takeaway

The key takeaway here is that lean startup and analytics are not perfect. They have flaws, and they can't be treated as a meal ticket to success. And for you to take full advantage of it, you must embrace some of its flaws.

Firstly, expect that it would be difficult. Running a lean business is simple, but it's taxing. You're sacrificing many conveniences to run. Use as little resources as you can, but don't expect profit large enough to sustain the business.

Second, center around your business on your product and customers. Remember that if those two fail or disappear, you're already a goner. If the inflow of your customers grinds to a halt, immediately focus on getting them back. The same with your product. If your product isn't selling, improve that product or replace it with something much better.

Third, minimum viable product is controversial. It sounds good on paper, but it can bring in some problems. This is especially true if you keep on using one even at the latter stages of your business life.

Remember that MVP is effective during the early stages of your business. As much as possible, you should only have one. When you have perfected your product, you should change your business methods and practices.

Fourth, never forget that your metric changes together with your current business goals. It can't be stressed enough. Be sure to be always aware with the data you gather for your metric, too.

Just to remind you, the metric is good and all. What always goes wrong with it is how entrepreneurs use it and interpret its importance.

Fifth, you can follow everything in this book, but you can still make mistakes. Lean startups and analytics don't save entrepreneurs if they make a mess. They're only guides and roadmaps to make your startup survive. The early stages of a business are tough. You need to follow the guide to make it easier for your emotional and cognitive health. Starting a business without any concrete idea on what you need to do or what's going on can make you crazy, you know.

Lastly, you're already at the end of this book. Congratulations in advance. What's left for you to do now is check out the last part, which will nicely wrap everything up. If you can, it might be good for you to have a good review of the previous chapters. Just to be sure that you got everything right.

Conclusion

Here's a curve ball for you: data is the oil of the 21st century. It is what makes people billionaires. The era of coal mining and software development to enrich oneself is over. Acquiring, processing, and analyzing data is the most profitable business now.

Just look at Amazon, Facebook, and Google. The biggest element in their businesses that they have in common is data acquisition. Every day, their businesses harvest information online.

Aside from gaining financial success, data can be used for political power. Just think about the recent election shenanigans. People believe that companies that have control over data have the capability to influence the country's democracy.

A good example of the usage of data for political power is the Cambridge Analytica case. People allege that they have harvested personal information from voters through Facebook.

They processed the data they gathered, and then developed an AI that can predict a person's future decisions. It sounds like a story ripped from a science fiction book, but it's real. And you can observe it. Just log in to your Facebook account.

Try messaging a friend and mention a brand or product in your chat. Close the chat box, and refresh your timeline. Look at the advertisement on the side of the page. There's a 90% chance that you'll see the product or brand you mentioned on the ad that's placed there.

That's how powerful data is. There's no reason you shouldn't take advantage of its power. You can do that with apps and tools that are overly available to everyone.

Lean analytics is an approach that has become a "must do" for every startup ever since it was conceived. It will be difficult for any entrepreneur to work half ass. It is important to establish lean startup without lean analytics.

Success is now measurable by just flicking your fingers on a smartphone. Progress can be easily monitored by reviewing a digital spreadsheet on your laptop. And data can be gathered by a static website you made months before. You can gather data with it without you speaking any words to any customer.

Technology has made starting a business as easy as playing a computer game. However, it doesn't change the fact that you'll still need real money to start a business. And it's the biggest hindrance of them all when you're new.

Nonetheless, by playing it a bit safe, focusing on the most important parts of the business, minimizing risks, and using data to help you with your decisions, you'll be able to hold your ground and achieve success.

Anyway, just to close this book off on a high note, here's a quick rundown of what you need to do to get started with lean startup and analytics.

Create a goal for your business. It's the first step after you start your operations.

Second, pick the metric that you want to use to measure the progress of your business towards the goal you set. Don't overcomplicate it. Just make sure that it can really measure your progress.

Third, create plans on how you can improve the numbers of your metric. Test the plans out and see which is the most effective. Measure the effectiveness of the plans or actions.

Fourth, choose the most effective method. Discard or save the rest for later. Exhaust the most effective plan you have. Once it doesn't bring you towards your goal, reevaluate if the current business goal is still relevant.

Lastly, repeat the whole process all over again.

Do the same with your product. It doesn't matter if you call it your prototype, first product, or minimum viable product. The goal here is process its improvements through lean analytics. The main goal is to improve it until you can build a stable business around it.

As a follow up, always remember the five major benefits of lean startup and analytics.

1. Decisions are heavily based on data instead of an executive's gut feeling.

2. Development of products and services is faster.

3. Improvements done to existing products and services are faster. Products and services are flexible and will always change for the better.

4. High quality feedback from stakeholders and consumers is easily attainable.

5. Improved customer perception and company reputation.

Going back to what I promised, the discussions and examples in this book demonstrate the huge potential of lean startup and analytics in your business.

It's true that more workload is coming your way if you follow the steps indicated in this book. However, the reward on doing the steps is that you can go about your business knowing what direction you are going.

I've been like you. In my first business, I was so lost on what's going on. I questioned myself everyday if I can get through every month with my business. In the end, I didn't. Because I had no idea on what the hell was going on with my startup.

But, unlike me, you have the proper knowledge on how to get through that. If you want to avoid getting stuck with a business loan for a business that already failed, then just follow the advice listed here.

The steps make sense for those who have limited resources or for those who just want to have a solid foundation for their business without the huge risks.

Unlike traditional methods on building business, lean startup and analytics let you start faster with minimal restrictions on your budget. In exchange, you will have a relatively small business that functions as if it's a medium sized one.

And at this point, I believe every word you need to hear or read has been laid out. This book will be always at your disposal any time you need to refresh what you have learned today. I wish you well and good luck to you and your business.

Book #3

Lean Enterprise

The Essential Step-by-Step Guide to Building a Lean Business with Six Sigma, Kanban, and 5S Methodologies

PART ONE

The Principles Behind Lean Thinking

"Improvement usually means doing something that we have never done before."

—Shigeo Shingo

Introduction: What Do We Mean by "Lean Enterprise"?

"The difference between market takers and market makers isn't product innovation, it's business model innovation."

—Vala Afshar

What sets apart the companies that have stood the test of time from those that failed to take off? Well, aside from learning how to polish their branding, they continuously work on improving their human capital and management systems — changing accordingly with the times, and adjusting their strategies as they seem fit.

In contrast, brands that were never heard of again weren't able to plant a firm footing in the industry. It's mainly because each step in their workflow had issues that they weren't able to solve. It most likely didn't occur all at once, though. More often than not, a failed business' downfall started with a seemingly harmless misstep — until the rest of their system followed.

No matter how seemingly good a product or a service may be, it will only remain relevant to the market that it's supposed to serve if the whole work process is meticulously addressed. This is especially necessary during the

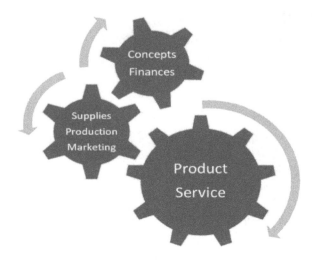

beginning phases of building a business. The key is to lay down everything such that they will move in sync, so that when one part starts working, the rest will simply go with the right flow

Figure 1. *Simplified analogy of the relationships between work processes and a company's desired output*

The supposed workflow of any organization can be compared to a group of gears working in unison to move an entire machine. Figure 1 is just an ultra-simplified version of how products and services — or more generally, outputs — are related to all the steps that come before it. So long as the gears are constantly well-oiled and nothing gets caught in them, the machine will move and operate as it should.

However, when faulty components start slowing down the movement of the smaller cogwheels, every part of the process becomes inefficient. Ultimately, the biggest cogwheel will be affected, and no output will be delivered according to the company's set standards — if any had been set at all.

This is why all parts of a process must be constantly assessed and measured. Otherwise, improvement will almost always be impossible, and moving towards the next goals will just remain a pipedream.

Thus, if you don't get your act together within the company, you're bound to offer people a bunch of products that aren't serving any real purpose for them. This may also damage your relationships with investors and suppliers. All it takes is another careless mistake and your reputation will now be forever tainted.

Successful businesses are going to have none of that. They know exactly how to get things done by using the most effective processes that they have applied through the years. Otherwise, they wouldn't be able to keep their gears rolling at the speed they want to. The question is, are they going through their workflow in the most cost-efficient and most resourceful way possible?

Lean Company, Lean Manufacturing, and Lean Enterprise

It's one thing to know how to get the job done. It's another thing to know how to get it done outstandingly. But it's a whole other level to know how to deliver high-quality outputs using the least amount of wastes and resources. Given the complexity of planning and production, it's normal to wonder whether it's possible that simple waste elimination can lead to the best products and services.

This is where the concept of lean thinking comes in. At its core, lean thinking focuses on how to come up with better methods of utilizing financial and human capital. Its ultimate goal is to provide maximum benefits not just to loyal and potential customers, but also to society as a whole.

This system attempts to operate on the idea that if each individual or group in the entire system can identify and eliminate the biggest wastes in their tasks, then all of them — as a whole — will be able to produce more valuable outputs using far less expenses. Not only will this drive an organization to its golden age, but it will also develop its employees' overall competence and confidence in themselves.

Lean thinking is the basis for all efficiency-driven mechanisms that are practiced in companies, manufacturing or productions, and even enterprises. But what does it really mean when every aspect of an organization is "lean"?

The following items illustrate the general idea of how lean enterprises are built:

- **Step 1: Building a Lean Company**

This is a company that follows lean thinking methodologies when it comes to production. Each step of the process has been aligned with the rest of the workflow to give way to a smooth and continuous cycle. Goals are typically addressed by creating a team that is composed of experts from various departments (cross-functional team).

- **Step 2: Employing Lean Manufacturing**

Also called "lean production", this involves a series of systematic methods for eliminating wastes and hurdles within production processes. It carefully assesses the wastes caused by uneven workloads, evens them out, and minimizes the chances of overburdening staff to improve output value and overall costs. A lean company abides by a number of lean manufacturing principles to enhance the workflow — beginning from the conceptualization phase, distribution, and even beyond.

- **Step 3: Establishing a Lean Enterprise**

This can be regarded as the ultimate product of all the offshoots of lean thinking. The lean enterprise is a grand collaboration among a number of companies — all of which are working to perfect a product or service that all of them will benefit from. The caveat, however, is that it can be tough for a lean company to reach its full potential if it's working with companies that aren't following lean methodologies.

Lean Thinking and Lean Behaviors

For lean thinking to make it to the enterprise level, it needs to be perfected on a personal level first. If individuals can make their tasks more efficient, these seemingly minute improvements are bound to translate to enterprise-wide successes.

However, members must also learn how to trade extreme individualism for team effort. It is inevitable that certain members or teams may have legitimate needs that are in conflict with other components of the system. A strong sense of cooperation then becomes necessary, which can only be achieved when all individuals agree to expand their roles in the name of a company or an enterprise's ultimate goal.

Members of cross-functional teams are usually trained to become more well-rounded. For example, full allegiance to their original function (e.g. marketing, financing, engineering, design, production) isn't encouraged in a lean environment. Team-oriented thinking and behaviors are needed to ensure that no phase in the workflow will ever end up being stuck.

This is why it's necessary for members of cross-functional teams to accept, right from the beginning, that they will need to pursue an offshoot of their original career path to succeed

as an employee of a lean company. Instead of performing their original function, they now work together with other experts to establish new value-adding processes or best practices for the roles that people like them play in an organization.

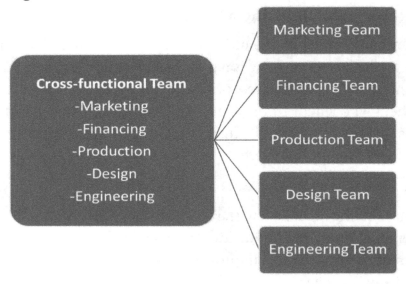

Figure 2. *Individuals from specialized backgrounds form a cross-functional team to develop better processes for the teams that perform the tasks involved in the workflow*

Figure 2 illustrates how the members of a cross-functional team work with each other to develop a grand system that will sync team roles for maximum efficiency. They will look into the various roadblocks that get caught up between tasks performed by different teams. Once they come up with a viable solution, they will then meet with the respective teams so they can start implementing the new and improved system.

Now, when these roles are translated to the lean enterprise, member companies will need to establish new behavioral standards that will help regulate behaviors and activities involved in the enterprise workflow.

What's important is that companies focus on what they're really good at to become a reliable member of the enterprise.

Lean as the Key to Productivity

In order for a lean enterprise to succeed, member companies need to refine their existing models to become more adept at doing more tasks using less resources. The problem is, while companies work towards eliminating wastes in their processes, this may cause stress in their employees, who fear that they might eventually be laid off from their jobs due to redundancy. Hence, companies need to explore and exhaust all of their options when it comes to job preservation as they work towards becoming lean.

Becoming a lean company may take years before you notice the fruits of all your efforts. Of course, when you have more wastes to eliminate, you also need more time to straighten out your workflow. This book will give you an overview of what you need to go through, plus the tools that can help you accomplish this huge task.

The lean models of business may be the key to building a company — and eventually an enterprise — that will generate the workflow efficiency that you've always wanted. If you're looking for ways to improve how business is done within your company, gradually shifting to lean thinking will not only help you increase your overall productivity, but also provide your employees with their much-needed career growth.

Chapter 1: How Lean Businesses are Built

"Every job is a self-portrait of the person who did it.

Autograph your work with excellence."

—Jessica Guidobono

In order to understand how to build a lean enterprise, it's important to learn how lean businesses are built first. Lean thinking within a company is often considered the foundation of pursuing lean practices, no matter what level you may be at. After all, it would be difficult to translate certain practices to bigger scales if you can't make it work at the lowest levels.

Lean thinking is known to enhance your workflow's speed and agility. Generally, it helps you become adaptable and competent enough to continue providing customer value in a world where people's needs are constantly changing.

Figure 3. *A general illustration of how lean thinking works*

The 7 Principles of Lean Thinking

Lean thinking primarily started as a required practice in Toyota's manufacturing floor. The term "lean thinking" was first coined by James Womack and Daniel Jones in their book, *Lean Thinking: Banish Waste and Create Wealth in Your Corporation.*

All of their insights were a result of their comprehensive study of the Toyota Production System (TPS). They noticed that Toyota focused on creating system frameworks that makes manufacturing a lot more value-adding and efficient. Most lean strategies that you'll come across can be traced back to the wide success of the TPS. It remains the primary reference where most lean manufacturing methods are based.

Any business that is trying to get into the lean mindset will need to integrate the following principles into their processes:

• **Eliminating Wastes**

Wastes found within the knowledge workflow are usually linked to the management and to the people doing the work, and not exactly on the production floor. Examples of wastes involved in the knowledge work are:

- <u>Context Switching:</u> This occurs when people need to switch from one tool or platform to the other just to complete a single task. This may involve opening a ton of programs or apps all at once.

It usually requires a certain order to accomplish so it's prone to confusion. In a way, it overlaps with multitasking since your attention is scattered across various tasks.

- <u>Poor Appropriation of Tools:</u> Sometimes, slow completion time can mainly be blamed on inappropriate tools. Oftentimes, when employees are forced to use a tool that certainly isn't the best for the job, the production flow doesn't move as quickly as it should.

- <u>Inefficiency of Information Systems:</u> This is related to the previous point. If the workflow relies heavily on information systems, yet company reports say that these systems aren't helping like they're supposed to, you can't expect that things will be accomplished as planned.

It's even worse when user feedback isn't integrated into the design — either before the system was launched or after a system overhaul had been made.

- <u>Ineffective Communication Among Teams:</u> The phrase "communication is key" isn't emphasized in many contexts for nothing. The lack of open communication and transparency is often the cause of many delays during the production process.

- <u>Lack of Viable Market:</u> Any factor in your product that your customer wouldn't be willing to pay for is ultimately considered a waste in the whole workflow. What's the use of something if nobody wants it?

- **Creating Knowledge**

For companies to become a truly lean business, knowledge and learning must be integrated into the organization. When employees are constantly given the chance to learn the industry's best practices from experts, not only can they add more value to the work they do, but they also learn how to be valuable in other ways. This is typically done by:

- Having retrospectives

- Cross-training employees

- Holding regular discussions about employees' work processes

When a company values knowledge creation, they will be able to perform their tasks with more value at a much faster rate. This is a way for them to constantly update their skills and competencies.

- **Integrating Quality**

A company that envisions long-term growth needs to utilize systems that are as error-free as possible. Lean companies usually do this by automating tasks that are repetitive, mentally uninteresting, and prone to human error.

As a result, employees can pour their time and focus on skills that actually engage them mentally. This allows them to devote themselves fully to the pursuit of both personal and company growth.

- **Delivering on Time**

Lean thinking is primarily driven by the idea that focus is the root of all high-quality outputs. When your work environment isn't conducive enough to maintain an uncluttered mind, this slows your work down. Top-quality work is hard to produce when an employee is constantly distracted.

Lean systems always have steady workflows. This means that everything is delivered and accomplished on a consistent, predictable basis. A bad workflow, on the other hand, is always unpredictable because of unsustainable and unreliable work habits.

Lean teams are always refining their workflows to optimize value at every level. They do this by greatly limiting their WIPs (works in progress) and providing a good work environment so nothing gets stuck in the workload traffic. Multitasking is prohibited because it only prevents people from finishing tasks on time.

- **Deferring Commitment**

Careful planning is necessary to accomplish long-term goals. In lean thinking, however, it is discouraged to plan for a product's release way out in advance. This prevents having stocks that may only end up being useless.

Instead, it recommends that you decide to pursue something at the last responsible moment — during the time when you've thoroughly considered all the factors that would help you come up with the best decision possible.

This goes back to the main goal of all lean systems: eliminating wastes.

Deferring commitment helps you decide more smartly by going over the data and reports that accurately reflect the current market situation. This prevents you from pursuing seemingly innovative projects that don't really translate into an urgent or even viable market need in reality.

- **Respecting People**

The root of a lean system's success all boils down to one basic thing: respect.

First, the concept of lean was born out of a desire to respect the customer's needs and preferences. Second, lean systems are able to thrive because their employees are well-respected by their superiors. They are provided with environments that encourage them to perform at their best.

On an individual level, respect generally entails maintaining kindness and courtesy to everyone that you're working with — whether it's your superiors, your colleagues, your employees, or your customers. Respect is also often shown through:

- Providing safe environments for idea sharing

- Encouraging employees to develop themselves in whatever way they wish

- Trusting employees' decision-making processes

Respect goes a long way in lean systems because trust is required to maintain good workflow. After all, building good relationships is the key to creating a stable system that produces high-value outputs.

- **Optimizing the Whole Organization**

All decisions in a lean company must be made relative to the whole organization. For instance, decisions to optimize processes must not only involve one team — it must involve everybody else.

Naturally, an improvement in one component can already be enough to see significant differences in the workflow. However, to become truly lean means to address all possible sources of waste.

Building a lean enterprise all starts with creating a lean business. The next step would be to find others who also share the same lean ideas as you do. Maintaining collaborations among companies can already be difficult enough since each member will have their own goals and agendas. However, if all of you can work towards operating under the same lean system, then overall work and production is going to be a breeze.

The 5 Principles of Lean Manufacturing

Many businesses are beginning to switch to lean thinking and lean manufacturing to develop the kinds of products that have a good chance of penetrating the global market. Aside from consistently meeting customer demands, it also enables them to earn more profits and enhance product quality with less cost.

Lean thinking gave way to the five lean manufacturing principles that have greatly improved the workflow of many successful companies today. These are often considered

as key factors in improving overall efficiency in the workplace.

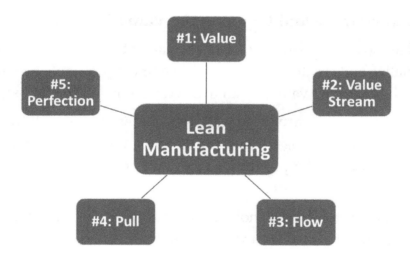

Figure 4. *How lean manufacturing moves from one phase to the next*

- **Defining Value**

The first step of lean manufacturing begins with learning what exactly the customer values in a particular product or service. This will help a business determine how much a customer is willing to pay for what, which then allows them to set a reasonable target price. After which, the cost of manufacturing the product will then be defined.

To properly establish value in a lean system, it is vital to learn about the market's recognized and latent needs.

While some customers may already know what they want exactly, others may not be aware that there might be a product or service out there that they actually want or need. Or perhaps, they know they need a particular something, but cannot express what it's supposed to be.

That's where market research comes in. This is typically done through interviews, demographic assessment, web analytics, user testing, surveys, etc.

By defining what your customers really want, you get to create something of great value — not just a product that seems innovative in theory. This also helps you understand your customers' purchasing power, as well as the way in which they want this product to be delivered to them.

- **Determining and Planning the Value Stream**

The value stream consists of all the activities that allow you to conceptualize and create the most useful yet most profitable product that matches the customer values that have been defined in the first step.

This is the product's journey from the raw materials stage all the way to the customer usage stage. The stream even includes the customer's eventual disposal of the product, which paves the way for considerable upgrades in the next release.

Naturally, activities that do not provide value at the end of the value stream (customer) are regarded as wastes. These wastes can be subdivided into two types: necessary waste (e.g. quality control) and pure waste (e.g. supplier delays).

The latter should be completely eliminated, while the former should be continuously perfected so they don't get in the way of the value stream. Otherwise, they'd only delay the rest of the process.

- **Creating Flow**

A river will always make its way to the ocean eventually, provided that nothing stops the water in its tracks. However, a significant amount of debris in one part of the river system may cause the water to be trapped and unable to follow its natural path.

This is exactly what waste does in a value stream. It interrupts the natural flow of the production process, causing delays that might start out small. Eventually, however, it might end up becoming a massive setback that prevents everything from moving further forward.

That said, a company must take their time to fully understand their flow systems to eliminate wastes effectively and completely. The concept of flow in lean manufacturing is all about creating a series of steps that are in sync with each other — one that hardly ever gets interrupted.

- **Setting Pull**

One of the most significant wastes involved in manufacturing is inventory. To solve this, a pull-based system must be established. This system aims to minimize inventories and works in progress as much as possible. Relevant materials should always be available to maintain the company's flow.

Instead of creating products way ahead of schedule based only on market forecasts, a pull-based system encourages you to begin working on something only when a customer expresses the need for it. Thus, you'll only begin production at the moment of need, and only in the quantities requested.

This allows you to develop the most efficient way to assemble a product, as you need to deliver your promise within a reasonable timeframe.

- **Pursuing Perfection**

The first four principles of lean manufacturing are all about identifying and reducing wastes as much as possible. This last principle is the crucial point that holds all lean thinking concepts together. Perfection based on company standards helps deliver products in the best state possible to the end user.

Although a perfect product can never technically exist, pursuing perfection is what inspires companies to continue serving their customers to the best of their abilities.

This is what ultimately sets them apart from the competition. After all, if small mistakes can be removed from the value stream every single day, there will come a time when errors will be close to non-existent.

The shift towards lean thinking may not exactly be an easy task, especially if you've just realized that you have major roadblocks in all the steps of your value stream. But when you've identified what exactly your problem areas are, you've already taken the first step in creating a more efficient business. Applying the principles of lean thinking and lean manufacturing gives you a more competitive edge, simply because you've addressed all of your wastes.

Takeaway:

•	Lean thinking becomes possible when an organization consistently works on waste elimination, knowledge creation, quality integration, timely deliveries, smart commitments, respect, and overall process optimization.

•	Lean manufacturing helps you focus on what truly creates value for your customer. By eliminating all the pure wastes in the value stream, you can create a smooth and steady flow that will allow you to pursue perfection.

Chapter 2: The Primary Wastes of Lean Systems

"If you define the problem correctly, you almost have the solution."

—Steve Jobs

Every industry abides by their own sets of best practices. Lean thinking practices, on the other hand, seem to be valuable in every type of business context. After all, it does get rid of significant setbacks that prevent processes from properly moving forward.

But how exactly do lean systems eliminate their wastes and problems? How does it ensure that every person within the value stream are working only as necessary, and using components only in the needed amounts? How is it able to maintain that kind of focus as the tasks flow down the value stream?

The Toyota Production System (TPS)

In Chapter 1, we mentioned in passing that the Toyota Production System (TPS) is the precursor of all lean manufacturing methods. In this section, we will further elaborate on the concepts that have turned the TPS into a timeless lean thinking reference — something that has been extremely useful for many businesses today.

Just-in-Time (JIT) and Jidoka

The overall success of the TPS stands on two conceptual pillars: just-in-time and jidoka. This approach was created by Taiichi Ohno, an industrial engineer who is considered the father of TPS. It aimed to solve 3 key issues that are often encountered in the value stream: inconsistency (muri), overburden (mura), and waste (muda). Improvements in the production line are usually achieved by:

• Eliminating inconsistency in the value stream by automating repetitive tasks, thereby smoothening the flow all the way down to the final output.

• Minimizing overburdens or company-wide stress as a result of removing inconsistencies (i.e. far less errors flowing into the value stream).

• Improving stress levels among employees and managers, which significantly reduces the wastes that have to be cleaned up later on.

The just-in-time thinking operates on the principle that businesses should produce only the parts and outputs that they need, only on the moment that they need it, and only in the quantities that they need. Hence, even when products aren't assembled ahead of time, a lean business will still be able to put it all together in a timely, "just-in-time" manner. This is usually how the process goes:

• Upon receiving an order, the first phase of the production line is prompted to start the production process.

• There must be enough stocks of all the needed parts in the assembly line. It must be no more or no less than what has actually been ordered. This ensures that the product can be put together as efficiently as possible.

• All the parts that have been used in assembling one product are replaced. Only the same number of parts should be retrieved to prevent overstocking.

- As for manufactured parts, the production line must only make the particular parts that have been retrieved. This makes them prepared for the next production cycle once a product has been ordered again.

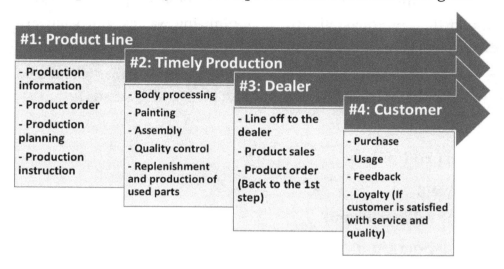

Figure 5. *A simplified chart of how just-in-time and jidoka play out in Toyota*

To ensure that the JIT system moves smoothly, quality control must be applied. This is achieved with the help of jidoka, which means "automation with a human touch". It involves a machine that stops on its own once the normal production cycle is completed, or when it detects a defect in a product. This reduces wastes or "muda", since it prevents the production from creating more defective items.

Only those that have passed quality control will be able to proceed to the next steps in the value stream. Since a particular machine automatically stops as soon as an issue arises, the human operator can continue working using another functional machine. Then, they can assess the root cause of the first machine's problem.

A single human operator can manage multiple machines, increasing the company's overall productivity. This doesn't only make it easier to identify problems, but it also minimizes delays by allowing the workflow to proceed as planned.

DOWNTIME: The 8 Deadly Wastes of Lean Systems

Manufacturing wastes come in various forms. We already know in theory that the lean manufacturing framework is all about keeping your value stream and final products aligned by minimizing wastes. But what are wastes, exactly? How do they play out in the real world?

So far, the TPS has identified 8 deadly wastes of lean systems. This can be easily remembered by the acronym DOWNTIME, which stands for:

- **Defects**
- **Overproduction**
- **Waiting**
- **Non-utilized Talent**
- **Transportation**
- **Inventory**
- **Motion**
- **Excess Processing**

- **Figure 6**. *The lack of standards is usually the root cause of all manufacturing defects*

1. Defects

A defect refers to any mistake that needs additional effort, money, resources, or time to rectify. In non-lean productions, defects typically halt the flow of the value stream because of a component that needs to be completely remade.

The truth is, all wastes can never be fully eliminated. However, if you can work on eliminating defects, the rest of the lean wastes will follow suit. This can usually be accomplished by standardizing all aspects of the production process and applying stricter quality controls at every point of the value stream.

2. Overproduction

This is often the result of not following the pull-based or JIT-jidoka systems. As we have learned, lean systems try to minimize wastes by producing and assembling parts only when they are needed. Overproduction can get the value stream stuck when the flow ends up in a bottleneck. This is generally caused by:

- Just-in-case production as opposed to just-in-time production

- Producing based on uninformed forecasts

- Changes in product design and engineering

- Long production and assembly times

- Unassessed customer needs

- Ineffective automation processes

To solve issues with overproduction, it's important to focus on what the customer really cares about, and then develop the most straightforward value stream. This ensures that none of the company's efforts will ever be put to waste.

3. Waiting

This happens when there's been a hold-up somewhere in the value stream. For instance, everything may have to be stopped because of machine breakdowns, lack of complete supplies, lack of approval from higher-ups, or overwhelmed staff. All of these may happen due to:

- Insufficient or unreliable staff (and managers)

- Staff absences

- Uneven workloads

- Unexpected downtimes

- Poor communication and processing

Just like overproduction, this waste is typically due to process bottlenecks. One way of solving this is by having enough staff so that the workload is evenly distributed at these points.

Although you may think that having a smaller staff can help you save money from salaries, it may actually incur even more expenses. This is because waiting and delays cost more money than simply paying a few more people to do the job well.

4. Non-utilized Talent

This wasn't part of the TPS' original list of lean wastes, but this has become quite a common occurrence in many modern businesses. This happens when a company fails to utilize their staff in the best way possible. This is often seen through:

- Poor communication among departments

- Poor management

- Insufficient staff training

- Lack of cooperation

- Inefficient workflow at the admin level

- Mismatch between an employee's skills and their given tasks

Improper utilization of staff's skills and talents may not seem like a big deal, but its bad effects over the long-term is usually made apparent when the whole company fails to reach its goals within their scheduled timeframes. It's also one of the main reasons why there is a resounding lack of employee engagement within a company. On the other hand, businesses usually thrive once they begin to give employees the recognition that they deserve.

5. Transportation

This doesn't only refer to actual transportation by a vehicle from one place to the next. Transportation is a general term that covers any process that involves getting something from Point A to Point B — even if the task is purely digital in nature. For instance, sending memos via e-mail can already be considered as "transport". Oftentimes, transportation wastes are results of:

• Wasteful steps in the value stream

• Workflow that is out of sync

• Poorly-designed processes and systems

• Bad office layouts and/or poor planning of office locations

The longer it takes for a product to get where it's supposed to, the higher the transportation costs will be. Not only does this waste time, but it also makes the product more prone to deterioration and damage. Transportation wastes can be eliminated by simplifying workflows, improving layouts, or simply shortening the physical distances between steps.

6. Inventory

More often than not, inventories are necessities for a business — especially for one that is highly in demand. Production lines will need raw materials and manufactured parts that are value-adding to the final product.

The retrieval processes for these materials need to be well-documented in order to spot any errors more conveniently. Additionally, having enough stock will allow you to be more adaptable when it comes to following through with the customer's needs.

The thing is, inventory can sometimes be the source of problems in lean systems. This is usually illustrated using the ship metaphor.

Figure 7. *How inventory hides a ton of company problems*

As Figure 7 shows, your company moves as a ship in an ocean called "inventory". As long as the ocean you're moving in is at a safe water level, your ship will be able to go to wherever it wishes. However, what you don't know is that there are problems lurking beneath the surface — as represented by the rocks.

Just because you're able to move as usual, it doesn't mean that problems aren't there. In fact, it may only take a slight shift in water level before your ship finally hits one of those rocks. Examples of issues that are hidden by inventory are:

• Poor documentation and management

• Incompetent monitoring systems

• Unclear communication

• Lack of foresight

- Defective deliveries

- Unreliable suppliers

- Inconsistent manufacturing speeds

- Untrained or mismatched staff

Still going by the metaphor, this means that you need to dive deep into your inventories to figure out whether rocks are just waiting for their turn to bust through your ship. Once these issues have been detected, you must do whatever it takes to eliminate those rocks so you can steer your ship in any direction — without worrying about the water level.

7. Motion

Wastes relating to motion are quite similar to transportation wastes. This involves non-value adding steps that are covered by machines or employees. In contrast with transportation wastes, motion wastes are found in any unnecessary movement within the value stream. Generally, motion is affected by:

- Bad workstation or shop layouts

- Badly designed processes

- Bottleneck in workstations caused by shared tools

- Poor staff training

Eliminating motion wastes can be as simple as making the movement between workstations more convenient. More often than not, the reason why people aren't driven to do what they have to do is because the layout and circumstances make doing the task utterly inconvenient and difficult.

8. Excess Processing

While lean systems are all about providing quality, sometimes even quality controls can be over the top. Customers will only need a few key things, and constantly checking for something that goes beyond that only adds to waste. That's because you're investing time and resources in certain things when the customers have zero interest in what you're trying to offer.

Quality controls are necessary but only if they actually help in the value stream. All attempts at quality control must be designed to serve only what the customer considers important. You may have good intentions with your unsolicited updates, but unless the customer wants it, that will largely just go unappreciated.

In order for your business to go lean, you must first discover the factors that produce the most wastes in your current value stream. You can't just shift to a new system without knowing what's wrong with the current one in the first place.

Once these problems have been identified, it then becomes so much easier to conceptualize solutions that can eliminate them completely. Then, when every part of the process is free of waste, you'd soon be able to see that your company had that much potential all along.

Takeaway:

• The Toyota Production System started out as a practice for eliminating 3 key issues in the production line: inconsistency (muri), overburden (mura), and waste (muda). It is the main precursor of all the lean thinking and manufacturing systems that we know of today.

• DOWNTIME is the main roadblock of all lean systems. Getting rid of the waste from these components gives your work processes a lot more room to flow to where it should go.

Chapter 3: The Major Benefits of Going Lean

"The product that wins is the one that bridges customers to the future, not the one that requires a giant leap."

—Aaron Levie

Becoming lean as an individual can make a big difference in your tasks as an employee. When you apply its concepts consistently enough, they're bound to affect your life's other aspects positively. Over time, you'll find that you're able to process decisions in a more systematic way. If lean concepts can have such a profound effect on a personal level, you can just imagine the possibilities if you scale the leanness all the way to an enterprise.

Shifting to Lean: What's in It for You?

Lean thinking encourages people to apply doable changes in small increments. The ultimate goal is to speed up all the workflows within a system without compromising product or service quality. Lean is certainly not a quick fix for eliminating company wastes. It involves being in a long-term commitment with continuous growth and improvement.

Even if a particular lean technique has been proven effective by many companies, changes certainly didn't happen within a few months of applying the methods. It usually takes far longer than that for anything significant to be noticeable. Of course, it's also understandable how people may feel discouraged to stick with the new methods if the benefits aren't that obvious. To help you stay lean when you're tempted to think that it doesn't work, here's a list of its short-term to long-term benefits:

Short-term Benefits

• Improved Management: Even though problems will still come up every now and then, lean makes the work environment more convenient to deal with if you're a manager. With better task standards in place, it will be easier for you to pinpoint anything that's disrupting the flow of the value stream. Most of the time, you will be able to figure out that something isn't quite right just by looking at an area's set-up or layout.

•   <u>Improved Efficiency and Productivity:</u> As a result of standardizing every piece of the workflow, it becomes automatic for employees to know what exactly they need to do — and when they need to do it. It reduces a lot of redundancy and overlaps that stem from task confusion. It also ensures that they are doing their work correctly every single time.

They no longer have to constantly ask whether a particular task is under their responsibility. They can just focus on their own task list without worrying about anything else.

•   <u>Safer and More Convenient Layouts:</u> Since literal wastes will be decluttered, turning lean gives your company more space to move around. This will instantly make task movements a lot more convenient. Additionally, it will provide your staff a safer space for working when the layout is reorganized to eliminate hazards.

•   <u>Involvement from the Whole Company:</u> Lean is something that isn't applied only to one team or department. When a company decides to go lean, every level of the hierarchy is involved — from those on the top all the way to the ones on the bottom. After all, lean systems depend on the cooperation of everyone involved.

Medium and Long-term Benefits

•   <u>Improved Cash Flow:</u> Once you get rid of **DOWNTIME**, you can now focus your energy on ensuring that the value-adding steps of your value stream flows as smoothly as possible. In the absence of roadblocks, workflow bottlenecks, and delays, not only will you be able to deliver products in a just-in-time manner, but you'll also improve the cash flow within your company.

•   <u>Customer Satisfaction and Loyalty:</u> Customer satisfaction is one of the most immediate results of applying lean, so they become more likely to trust your brand again in the future. If you keep on doing what works, you're bound to gain their loyalty in the long run.

- <u>Employee Satisfaction and Loyalty:</u> While lean systems are mainly focused on the desires of the customer, it also promotes better mood and morale among employees. The changes may be met with resistance at first, but once they see that it takes them far less time to complete tasks compared to before, they'll become more open to the overall idea of lean.

Additionally, since lean is all about constant improvement and collaborations, they tend to feel better about themselves because they're part of a team that actually cares about others. Lean systems give them a safe space to voice out their concerns and provide suggestions for further improvement.

- <u>Marketability for Collaboration:</u> What makes something marketable? In terms of companies, marketable companies are usually the unproblematic ones. You need to be *that* company if you wish to be a part of a lean enterprise. After all, lean is all about efficiency, and you need to be an efficient team player to ensure that you don't disrupt the flow of the entire system.

Lean is not merely an exercise in cost-cutting. It is more of a long-term opportunity for consistent growth. Once you have smoothed out your lean processes within the company, you will eventually become the preferred suppliers of particular products and services.

That's because your consistency and standards translate well to your products — something that lets both customers and collaborators know that you're a company that they can trust.

What are the Challenges?

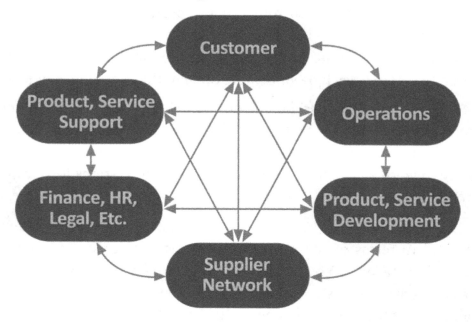

Figure 8. *Various relationships within a lean enterprise*

Lean thinking all sounds good in theory, and it can be exciting to continue applying it once you've seen how great it can be in practice. However, as Figure 8 shows, the tasks between teams or entities cannot always be as conveniently executed as getting from Point A to Point B in a clean, straight line. Their involvement with each other goes back and forth, which emphasizes how every component must be free of wastes to ensure a smooth flow.

Of course, shifting to lean has its own set of issues and challenges. Like any other form of change, you should resist hoping that it would do its "magic" in just a few weeks or months.

Technically speaking, when every factor is ironed out right from the beginning, it can be possible to have everything sorted out in just a short time. But that only applies when the scenario is ideal. Experience will tell you that situations are rarely ever ideal, especially when transitions are concerned.

Here are some issues that you might have to deal with on your way to lean:

- **Cultural Resistance**

This may be the biggest hurdle that you have to get through when transitioning from wasteful to lean. When a status quo has already been set, most people are resistant to any change in the company culture. That's usually a result of staying in their comfort zones for long enough. They feel that change is unnecessary since they already like the current workflow.

To gradually ease the workforce into the lean system, training (or retraining) people must be prioritized. Here's what you need to clarify with them:

- What are the changes that you'll be implementing?

- Why are you implementing them?

- How are they going to benefit from these changes?

- How will it benefit the whole company?

Although all four of these are important considerations, they're likely going to be most concerned about the third point, as this involves their role in the company. However, if you can clearly explain the good things about these changes, then people will be more inclined to accept it.

- **Costs and Upkeep**

On a personal level, there are cases in which you'll need to spend money today to be able to profit or save more money in the future.

Going lean requires the same thing. Eliminating wastes will need money, because going for the long-term fix requires money. Eventually, however, the money you spent will eventually go back to you in the form of increased profits from minimized defects.

And, just like your home needs yearly maintenance, lean also requires upkeep. Proper planning and execution will ensure that you won't have to worry about running out of certain parts or having outdated systems.

- **Talent Gaps**

Since lean processes may now require updated technologies, companies that are going lean must bridge the talent gap. This means that they may have to let go of general-labor employees in favor of those who have licenses and certifications to operate lean system equipment. These employees are adept not only at handling these systems, but they are also capable of performing maintenance, inspections, repairs, and designs.

- **Technological Hurdles**

One of the initial costs involved in lean is investing in newer software and technology. Since lean encourages automation in almost every area, it is crucial that you choose the system that doesn't keep you stuck in your old ways. Not all systems are created equal, so you must go through your choices carefully to ensure that you ultimately get the one that is reliable enough to sustain your lean methods.

Implementing lean will not be as straightforward as it seems to be. While lean is there to make processes a lot simpler, going against the usual grain might complicate things at first. This is especially difficult when you already have a set system among your various teams. After all, when you already know how to communicate with other members in a certain way, it does take effort to change all of that into a process that might be the total opposite of what everyone is used to.

The most effective companies and enterprises know how to mobilize the entire workforce to create the best products or services for their customers. Lean thinking can help you do just that, because you'll no longer be caught up in problem-solving all the time. Your focus can now shift towards your company's biggest asset, which are your employees' talents.

Takeaway:

- Lean thinking is beneficial from the personal level all the way up to the enterprise level. The short-term gains typically involve a more efficient and less stressful workflow on a daily basis, while long-term gains are all about multifactorial company growth.

- Shifting to lean can be a challenging endeavor, especially when you're met with all sorts of resistance. The biggest problem, perhaps, is the resistance from your own workforce due to ingrained company culture. Fortunately, it only takes a bit of planning and foresight to get past these hurdles.

PART TWO

Tools for Building Lean Systems

"However beautiful the strategy, you should occasionally look at the results."
—Winston Churchill

Chapter 4: The (Lean) Six Sigma Methodology for Continuous Improvement

"Continuous improvement is better than delayed perfection."

—Mark Twain

All businesses have components that they can improve on. If you have never thoroughly assessed your processes before, it can indeed be difficult to determine which areas are ripe for improvement. It therefore becomes essential to streamline your workflows first so it's easier to identify where the process bottlenecks are.

Lean, Six Sigma, and Lean Six Sigma

The first part of this book focuses on the most important lean concepts that can transform your business into a more efficient manufacturing machine. In this chapter, we will discuss another tool that seeks to eliminate waste: Six Sigma.

Lean and Six Sigma are waste elimination systems that are both popular in manufacturing. In essence, they share the same end goal of process efficiency — they just have different approaches in getting things done. One of their key differences is their waste identification methods. Lean identifies wastes by examining the company's 8 Deadly Wastes (DOWNTIME). Meanwhile, Six Sigma does this by using the DMAIC (Define, Measure, Analyze, Improve, Control) method.

Lean vs. Six Sigma

Lean primarily focuses on eliminating steps that don't add any value to the final product. Value is regarded as anything that customers appreciate enough to actually pay for. For instance, motion or movement isn't really something that customers would willingly pay for when they get their product. One of the goals of lean is to limit such wastes as much as possible, as they aren't really value-adding.

Six Sigma, on the other hand, relies on data to solve problems within work processes. It puts a heavy emphasis on customer satisfaction by minimizing product defects. At its core, Six Sigma aims for a 99.99996% defect-free rate. You can expect a Six Sigma workflow to only have 3.4 defects or less out of a million outputs. Defects are any factor in the product that doesn't satisfy customer expectations.

As you may notice, both lean and Six Sigma care about what the customer ultimately wants. The focus of their approach is what mainly sets them apart. Lean works toward increasing the flow (or reducing traffic) within the value stream, while Six Sigma chases consistency in their processes and outputs.

Essentially, here's how lean and Six Sigma go about eliminating wastes:

• Lean lowers total production time and limits the use of resources to ultimately maximize customer value.

• Six Sigma aims for product perfection through reduced variation to ultimately reduce costs and improve customer perception.

Lean Six Sigma: Waste Elimination Tools Combined

Here's where it gets exciting. What if both of these systems are combined? What if you use lean principles to make your tasks flow as efficiently as possible, and then use the Six Sigma system to create processes that are consistent across the board?

This is where Lean Six Sigma comes in. Lean is a system that goes for defect detection, while Six Sigma goes for defect reduction. Combined, Lean Six Sigma brings you defect prevention — a methodology that prioritizes both the product quality and customer satisfaction by reducing wastes, production cycles, and product variations, all while standardizing work processes and flow.

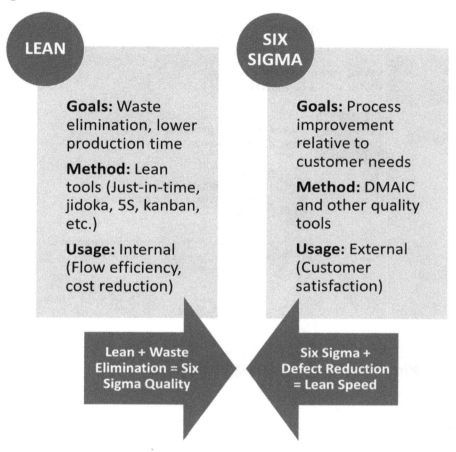

Figure 10. *How lean and Six Sigma complement each other*

In a nutshell, Lean Six Sigma is a system that not only improves flow and efficiency, but also enhances the quality of the whole process. As shown in Figure 10, lean and Six Sigma are two similar approaches that work really well when used together.

This is because lean's emphasis on reducing waste supports Six Sigma's focus on quality, thereby eliminating most opportunities to have defects. By the same vein, Six Sigma's value for the highest quality supports lean's goals on process efficiency, as consistency plus the absence of reworks leads to faster cycle times.

The DMAIC Roadmap

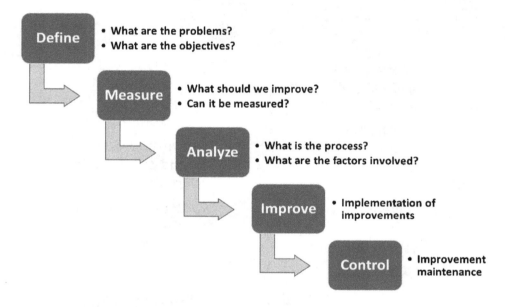

Figure 11. *The problem-solving process of Six Sigma*

Earlier, we mentioned that Six Sigma identifies and eliminates wastes by using the DMAIC method. This is a five-step framework that aims to reorganize current work processes such that every task produces a consistent output. Here's how a Six Sigma project typically starts:

• **Define**: This stage explores particular problems that can be worked on plus the objectives behind solving these problems. The following items are outlined and discussed in detail:

- Problem statement and objectives

- Project scope

- Required resources plus timeline

- Projected benefits

• **Measure**: This is the data-gathering stage. The different variables involved in work processes are measured, and data is collected afterwards. From here, baselines or standards are set. This will be used to compare performance metrics across time periods. The capability of the newer processes will then be measured accordingly.

• **Analyze**: This is where root-cause analysis takes place. The goal is to identify all the root causes of a particular defect in the product or in the process. This will help determine an appropriate solution that really addresses the problem.

• **Improve**: Once the root causes of the problems have been identified, the next step is to come up with solutions for improvement. This involves the conceptualization and testing of various solutions through experiments and simulation studies. Prototypes and beta versions are made to determine how feasible they are for short-term and long-term implementation.

• **Control**: After testing various solutions, their performances are documented in detail. Control systems are then installed to record their rates of improvement. Additionally, response plans are waiting should there be a failure in a particular solution.

Control charts show how each solution performs relative to the others. The process undergoes standardization, while the development of work instructions ensures that the process maintains consistency. The actual benefits of the project are then compared to its initial projected benefits. Ultimately, this stage is all about maintaining process gains.

While lean alone or Six Sigma alone can improve business workflows, an integrated approach like Lean Six Sigma may be better at helping you reap the full benefits of having a zero-waste process.

The lean portion usually takes care of removing wastes, while Six Sigma further polishes it by minimizing the variations of processes. It's all about continuously improving the organization's performance by eliminating errors that delay the most important tasks in the value stream.

Who Will Gain from Lean Six Sigma?

When applied correctly, Lean Six Sigma will clean up the messes of your business' entire workflow. As a result, it creates a bigger infrastructure for various processes, thereby allowing tasks to move without getting caught up in a bottleneck.

Of course, the benefits of Lean Six Sigma aren't limited to the company's owners or managers. It also extends to the following groups:

• **Employees**: When cultural resistance has been overcome, employees become more accepting of the upcoming company changes. As a result of the renewed openness to change, Lean Six Sigma is bound to improve your employees' job performance.

Consequently, the goal for continuous improvement means that they'll constantly undergo training to keep their skills and knowledge updated. This can be fulfilling even on a personal level.

• **Customers**: When efficiency and defect reduction are combined, customers will always get products that really improve their lives.

• **Suppliers**: Variations and defects usually come from raw materials. Lean Six Sigma can help suppliers determine the root cause of these variations and work on eliminating their occurrences in the future. This lowers the overall costs of creating the materials.

• **Stockholders**: Consistency in materials, products, and workflows can significantly reduce the costs needed for reworks, capitals, storage capacities, and staffing.

Just like lean, Six Sigma and Lean Six Sigma are effective tools in minimizing the need for additional resources. It operates on the premise that high standards can be achieved by maintaining the consistency of products and processes. Diversity is typically celebrated, but in Six Sigma, the lower the variation, the better.

Takeaway:

•   Lean and Six Sigma are systems that aim to improve workflow through waste elimination and variation reduction. Though different in their approach, they share the same ultimate goal of making processes efficient and producing the best products for their customers. Lean Six Sigma integrates these two systems to optimize every facet of the value stream.

•   The DMAIC roadmap is what fuels the Six Sigma problem-solving process. It seeks to define a problem and works on it until a maintainable solution with good improvement potential has been found.

•   Managers and company owners aren't the only ones who are going to benefit from Lean Six Sigma. Other groups that will get to experience its good effects include employees, customers, suppliers, and stockholders.

Chapter 5: The Kanban System for Backlog Reduction

"How does a project get to be a year late? One day at a time."

—Frederick Brooks

Most of us have gotten stressed at one point because of delayed projects. Such issues are usually blamed on a person's lack of time management skills. While that is definitely a logical cause of delays, sometimes the inability to manage time isn't really the problem. It's more of the inability to minimize works in progress (WIPs).

This is similar when you have multiple tabs open all at once. Even if you actually know the order in which to get to them, the right sequence will eventually be lost on you. This is how workplace wastes usually start out. When employees are always switching tasks, they never stay at one task long enough to actually progress to the next step.

As a result, most of them will always be "busy", yet they are rarely every productive. In such cases, applying the Kanban system may just be what you need to eliminate employee unproductivity and backlogs once and for all.

Kanban: The Original Scheduling System for Lean Manufacturing

Kanban means "card" or "signboard" in Japanese. It first came into existence as the scheduling system used by the Toyota Production System to properly execute their just-in-time product workflows.

Because the production line relies on customer demand, they needed a system that could help them visualize the entire flow across the value stream. Hence, they used actual cards to signify which tasks are already done, and which ones are still awaiting completion. This ensured that no one was doing too much at any one point.

The Core Principles of Kanban

Kanban's primary focus is to ensure that everyone's tasks are accomplished on schedule and that no backlogs will cause a significant impediment in the workflow. The following principles highlight how Kanban succeeds as a lean tool:

- **Workflow Visualization**

If you really want to see how every checkpoint in the value stream is related with each other, a Kanban board will show you how tasks move between stages. By pulling and moving cards from the "In Progress" column to the "Finished" column, employees can find it a lot easier to recognize which tasks should be prioritized, and which should already be delivered.

This is usually done using an actual board that's subdivided into columns, with tasks written on cards. It can also be a digital version, using a customized program or app.

- **WIP Reduction**

As mentioned in Chapter 1, context switching is usually one of the biggest sources of waste. When an employee or a whole team's focus shifts at the middle of their current tasks, it typically harms the whole workflow. Kanban reduces the WIPs allowed in every stage so employees can work on tasks only when the Kanban board says they're free to do so.

- **Flow Management**

Kanban is mainly fueled by its goal of making workflows as smooth and as trouble-free as possible. By revealing the whole process in visual form, it becomes easier for managers to see how the process can be sped up in a sustainable manner.

Instead of keeping employees busy, Kanban allows the manager's focus to shift to the workflow and figure out how tasks can move through the value stream at a faster rate.

- **Feedback Loops**

Regular updates are also scheduled to keep everyone in the loop. These short meetings are generally done in front of the Kanban board to let everyone know what their tasks are, together with those tasks' current status.

Feedback loops put everyone in the same page. Additionally, operations reviews, service reviews, and risk reviews are also conducted at regular intervals to further encourage process improvement.

Integrating Kanban into the Workplace

A Kanban board that is filled with employees' necessary tasks is one of the simplest solutions you can apply if you want to know where your bottlenecks usually lie. The effort to do this change is also simple enough to overcome any resistance. Overall, Kanban simplifies the route your tasks are going to take.

Kanban boards usually come in 3 to 5 columns. The 3-columned ones are usually labeled with "Requested", "In Progress", and "Finished". The 5-columned ones have the "In Progress" column subdivided into three parts: "Working", "Waiting", and "Review". Depending on what your organization needs, your Kanban board can be as simple or as complex as you need it to be.

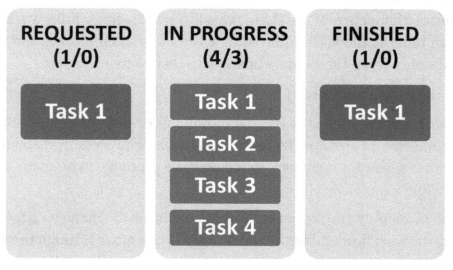

Figure 12. *A 3-column Kanban board showing a bottleneck at the "In Progress" stage*

Since Kanban is a highly visual system, it immediately reveals what's delaying the entire work process. In Figure 12, we can see that Column 2 has more tasks than what is recommended. Hence, managers and employees can work together to find ways on how these cases can be minimized — especially when it's happening too often.

Fortunately, Kanban is flexible and versatile enough to be integrated into your current work system without causing a company culture shock. The changes can be small enough that it wouldn't even take extreme efforts to sustain. It may not be the cure-all for your workflow problems, but it can at least encourage people to take the necessary steps to improve how tasks are done and delivered.

Takeaway:

• Kanban, a Japanese term which means "card" or "signboard", was first used as a tool in TPS to help Toyota employees visualize the tasks that should flow down the production line.

• Kanban is all about getting things done and removing things from your current workload. Its tactic for doing so is by limiting WIPs as much as possible so no one gets stuck at a particular checkpoint. This also ensures that employees devote their attention only to what's on their plate, instead of constantly switching to other tasks.

Chapter 6: The 5S Process for Workspace Organization

"A clean warehouse means employees can move around more quickly and get things done easier. It's just common sense."

—Lee House

Lean Six Sigma and Kanban are tools that improve work process efficiency by eliminating wastes and applying necessary changes to the current value stream. Both of them tend to be more mental in nature — meaning, the changes usually come from a gradual shift in people's understanding of company-specific workflows. Given that, can wastes be eliminated in ways other than changing the mindset of the whole workforce?

Workspaces and Process Efficiency

Apparently, applying physical changes to your current office setup can also improve your workflow significantly. We're not just talking about eliminating transport and motion wastes, in which layouts are modified to simplify the movement between processes. We're also talking about putting everything in their rightful place.

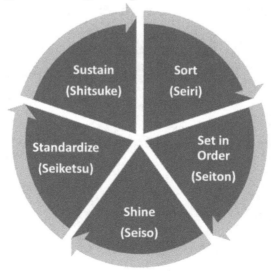

Figure 13. *The 5S cycle for systematic neatness in the workplace*

This is exactly what the 5S process is for. Each S in the cycle aims to organize workspaces such that all tasks can be performed safely and efficiently. It operates on the idea that if the workplace is kept clean and things are where they should be, it will be easier for employees to accomplish their tasks without wasting their time on non-value adding steps or exposing themselves to safety hazards.

Like Kanban, just-in-time, and jidoka, 5S is a concept that started out as a tool at the Toyota production floor. In fact, 5S is regarded as a foundational component of the Toyota Production System because it helped keep the workplace neat and highly organized. This methodology was put in place because they knew how difficult it was to produce consistent results when a place is utterly messy.

Mistakes, delays, and accidents are probably not immediately blamed on all the clutter in the workplace. However, if you really think about it, all the mess usually prevents people from focusing on their jobs. Consequently, this only impedes the flow and it's only a matter of time before everyone gets stuck on the same spot.

Hence, to ensure the functionality of a workspace, the 5S can be used as a standard for maintaining order and structure. The terms were originally in Japanese, but close equivalents are used for the English translation. Here's what they stand for:

- **Sort (Seiri / Tidiness)**

The first stage involves the examination of all the tools and equipment that are currently present in the area. The goal is to determine which of them should stay and which of them should be removed to free up some space. At the end of this process, only the necessary tools should be left behind. Thus, it's worth asking:

- What's the purpose of this particular item?

- Who's using it?

- When was the last time it was used?

- How often do people use it?

- Is it really a necessity in this workspace?

The best people to ask regarding the items' value would be the people who are actually working in that area. For items that have been tagged as "unnecessary", these may be given away to another department, recycled, sold, thrown away, or put into the storage.

- **Set in Order (Seiton / Orderliness)**

Now that you've set which tools or equipment will remain, you can now proceed to organizing items based on what reduces motion wastes the most. The key is to remember the statement, "A place for everything; everything in its place."

This means that things shouldn't just be grouped together in a logical manner, but they should also be placed in a logical location. For instance, if an item is used frequently, it should be located in a place where it's easy to pull out.

- **Shine (Seiso / Cleanliness)**

Of course, keeping an area clean and organized requires work. Although it sounds very trivial, general cleaning is important enough to actually be involved as a crucial step in this process.

This stage emphasizes the regular cleaning of work areas, which includes putting items in their storage, sweeping, mopping, wiping, etc. This also includes regular equipment maintenance. Cleanliness ensures that problems don't go hidden by clutter, while maintenance prolongs the lifespan of your tools and equipment.

- **Standardize (Seiketsu / Standardization)**

In order to know which strategies are really working for you, detailed documentation must be conducted. This helps you establish standards that serve as an instant reference for how 5S can be maintained in your company.

Oftentimes the workplace instantly transforms when you've completed the first three stages of 5S. Making the changes permanent is usually the next challenge. To turn the new habits into a lifestyle, standards must be put in place. These can be in the form of setting schedules or assigning routines. Standards ensure that all your efforts towards order will not go to waste.

- ### Sustain (Shitsuke / Discipline)

When the cleanup process has finally been standardized, you must then do the necessary work to maintain your new routines and update them as the situation deems fit. This final stage is all about keeping 5S going with the help of the entire workforce — from the managers to the employees.

The goal is to make 5S a long-term commitment, and not just a short-term solution for workflow efficiency. When people are disciplined enough to stick with 5S, it usually yields remarkable improvements.

Although 5S is relatively budget-friendly, its full effectivity still relies on your available resources. At the very least, it will involve expenses during the cleaning process. Additionally, you will need to train your employees regularly and acquire supplies such as labeling, shelving, floor markings, etc. to sustain the new practice.

In theory, the 5S methodology is very similar to a general house cleaning. In the workplace, however, there is this added consideration of whether item placements help in any way with movement and employee convenience. The general consensus is, the more convenient it is for everyone to get what they really need, the better.

Of course, starting the whole process can be daunting at first, especially if your workspaces haven't been neat for quite some time. Fortunately, implementing 5S can start small, and you only need to assign a few individuals — or one team at a time — to begin the process. A training module is highly recommended to show the full benefits of 5S over the long term.

Ultimately, the 5S methodology believes that a clean workspace is a productive workspace. If people never have to waste time looking for things ever again, then a general cleanup is indeed a great investment.

Takeaway:

The 5S stands for sort (seiri), set in order (seiton), shine (seiso), standardize (seiketsu), and sustain (shitsuke). This methodology encourages everyone in the workplace to keep a neat environment to boost productivity and enhance safety.

Conclusion: Greatness is Possible in the Absence of Wastes

"To be competitive, we have to look for every opportunity to improve efficiencies and productivity while increasing quality. Lean manufacturing principles have improved every aspect of our processes."

—Cynthia Fanning

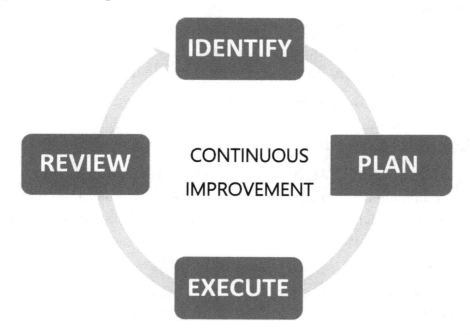

Figure 14. *How lean is implemented using the continuous improvement cycle*

Wastes are the main adversaries of long-term productivity and cost-effectiveness in any organization. This is where lean thinking comes in. Lean is a methodology that aims to eliminate wastes at every part of the value stream. So far, lean has identified 8 Deadly Wastes, which can be remembered by the acronym DOWNTIME. It stands for:

• **Defects**

• **Overproduction**

- **Waiting**
- **Non-utilized Talent**
- **Transport**
- **Inventory**
- **Motion**
- **Excess Processing**

In the lean context, wastes are defined as anything that doesn't add value to the company's end product. This refers to extra efforts that don't make a particular item any more valuable to its end user. Hence, additional labor or materials spent on fixing defects is considered waste.

Eliminating these wastes involves a thorough assessment of your work processes plus the application of various lean tools. Some of the lean methodologies that we discussed in this book include:

- **Just-in-Time (JIT)**: A set-up where every component can be pulled conveniently when there is customer demand. Instead of assembling products way ahead of time, hoping that the market wants it, just-in-time kickstarts a process only when customers ask for the product themselves.

Since efficiency is already a part of the mix, the company can deliver the product "just in time" even if they didn't have one assembled in the storage.

- **Jidoka**: Also known as "automation with a human touch", it involves the management of multiple machines that detect and prevent defects. This is because a machine automatically stops its operations when the process is completed or when a defective item has been produced. This prevents the whole system from producing any more defective materials, thereby saving time and costs.

- **Lean Six Sigma**: Lean and Six Sigma are methodologies that both specialize in waste elimination, they just have different approaches for doing so. While lean focuses on creating a smoother workflow, Six Sigma aims for production that is 99.99996% error-free.

Combined, Lean Six Sigma is a great tool for addressing both workflow quality and product perfection.

• **Kanban**: Kanban is a highly visual scheduling system used at the Toyota production floor. It consists of task cards that are pulled and transferred according to where they are in the value stream.

Because it's visual, it makes it a lot easier to detect where the process bottlenecks usually are. Kanban is one of the easiest changes that you can apply when you are thinking of shifting to lean, as it doesn't require a high-degree of commitment to maintain.

• **The 5S Process**: Neatness and cleanliness are the forefronts of the 5S methodology. It operates on the idea that if everything is where they should be, it's bound to save on a lot of costs, time, and resources.

True enough, a lot of waste comes from a simple inconvenience in workspace layout and item placements. 5S solves this right at the core and provides an environment that allows everyone to work without worrying where things are supposed to be.

It can be quite overwhelming to apply the lean tools that you've learned all at once. Surely, your intentions for a better, more efficient workflow may be met with resistance if you attempt to apply massive changes that are the total opposite of your current systems. However, by taking little steps and laying out its benefits in a clear manner, it will be easier for you to get everyone on board.

Wastes can be insidious, and you may not even realize how much your current processes are plagued with them. But if you decide to start small now, you'll definitely see huge benefits if you stick with it for at least a few months.

Lean concepts are generally best applied on a personal level first. When you're managing people that are already lean within themselves, it will become so much easier to apply it as a company-wide culture. And, in becoming a lean company, you can then put yourself out there and work with other lean companies to build a lean enterprise.

Book #4

Lean Startup

How to Apply the Lean Startup Methodology to Create, Innovate, and Accelerate Successful Businesses

Introduction

This book *"Lean Startup: How to Apply the Lean Startup Methodology to Innovate, Accelerate, and Create Successful Businesses"* is a foundational must-read for entrepreneurs. It contains helpful tips on how to create successful businesses using the lean startup methodology. It aims to teach entrepreneurs, both new and seasoned, business innovations fit for the twenty-first century.

Most entrepreneurs fail because they can't follow through with ideas that produce successful and sustainable results. However, the contents of this book will teach entrepreneurs, aspiring entrepreneurs, and even those who are just curious about the whole idea of entrepreneurship. Among these is how to avoid mistakes that can break their business, as well as how to employ validated learning to make their business.

It contains innovative steps, as well as strategies, to help entrepreneurs create and manage their own startup while leveraging on the successes and failures of other entrepreneurs before them. Think of this book as a cookbook for entrepreneurship and management.

Thanks for purchasing this book, I hope you enjoy it!

SECTION 1: Create

Have you ever been in a situation where you have everything down pat in your mind, but these all scatter in all directions as soon as you try to implement them? Well, I have, and believe me, it's not funny. That's why I decided to divide this book into three sections – Create, Innovate, and Accelerate.

In this first section, "Create", I will try to show you everything I know about entrepreneurship and entrepreneurial management. Here, I will identify what an entrepreneur is, what he is made of, and what entrepreneurial management means. I will also try to share some learnings that will determine whether a business is progressing towards its goals or if a bit of science is necessary to make it more sustainable.

Chapter 1: What Makes an Entrepreneur?

Let's start off by defining what an entrepreneur is. In the simplest of explanations, an entrepreneur is someone who is brave enough to set up a business and actually take responsibility for it. That includes welcoming the risks that come with starting a business, embracing those risks, and managing them.

I should know, because I am an entrepreneur, too. I've had years of experience in the field of entrepreneurship, and as such, I can confidently say that over the years, I have learned how to be insightful when it comes to opportunities and threats that are ever-present in this field. Moreover, I have learned how to acclimate, so to speak, with regards to the volatile business and financial climates.

What, though, of new entrepreneurs? Given the fact that they are barely starting, it's safe to say they lack the experience necessary to brave the storm. Yes, they may be risk takers who know how to calculate risks by being level-headed and using good judgment. Nevertheless, there are times when safety guarantees just don't cut it and sure wins are beyond attainable. Believe me when I say these are unavoidable. I have been there, and I have done that. What did I do then? I trusted my gut feelings and decided to brave it and tread on dangerous grounds.

This early, you're probably thinking, "Did this guy even succeed seeing as how he made asinine decisions?" Well, I hope I am not raining on your parade when I say, "I did! I succeeded." However, it was not without difficulties and plenty of uncertainties. Because I chose to be an entrepreneur, I had to be a swift decision-maker who is generally confident with his choices.

Along the way, I learned how to take sides once I've analyzed what is at stake or once I am convinced of the rewards awaiting me despite the risks I had to take. I surmised that I am no fence-sitter, but instead, I can act and decide quickly as long as I have analyzed things and have deduced that positive results will outweigh the risks.

Yes, I don't pretty much believe in luck nor do I believe that I was destined to be a successful entrepreneur from the get-go. Rather, I believe in hard work. I believe that when you create a business from the ground up, you need to plan and predict possible outcomes instead of leaving things to chance. There is no room for compulsiveness when you're an entrepreneur because chances are you will find it difficult to control your ideas, so much so that parts of your life that are separate from your business are disrupted (Farbrot, 2014).

If you truly want to succeed as an entrepreneur, you need to realize, just as I did, that there is no substitute for hard work. In a startup business, which is pretty much what new entrepreneurs have in their hands, you need to follow a grinding work schedule that allows you to be all over several places at one time. "Huh," you're probably thinking, "does this mean I need to clone myself?" Well, wait right there. There's no need to be *that* creative just yet. I just mean you need to embrace the mindset where you never back out of a commitment no matter how overwhelming it looks. In addition, you need to be willing to jump with both feet into a particularly scary situation when the need arises.

What Is an Entrepreneur Made of?

Here's a fact: any sound economy depends on its entrepreneurs as its strength of character. In the United States alone, it has been reported that 62% of billionaires living there are self-made, which means they, too, started from scratch like you and me. Do you want to be one of the 582 million (give or take) entrepreneurs all over the world? I bet you do. You wouldn't want to be a statistic. Neither will you want to add to the 22.5% of startup entrepreneurs who fail within their first year (Vojinovic, 2019). Given that, you need to understand just what an entrepreneur is made of.

As an entrepreneur, you need to be properly motivated to create a business from scratch. You must also be resolutely determined to complement that motivation with perseverance, self-belief, and swift decision-making. Why are these important? Keep in mind that entrepreneurship is volatile. There is bound to be an onslaught of challenges, unforeseen occurrences, and unpredictable changes that can affect you and the organization you are trying to build. Unless you are willing to make sacrifices here and there, don't expect your business to take off the ground.

You have probably heard of people who don't even have college degrees yet were able to launch successful businesses. A classic example is Richard Branson, the man behind the Virgin Group of companies – Virgin Atlantic Airways, Virgin Mobile, Virgin Records, and Virgin Galactic. Although he has a real-time net worth of $4 billion, he dropped out of high school at the age of 16 because dyslexia made it impossible for him to perform well in school (Entreprenoria, 2016). Do you wonder how he was able to make it, eventually landing a spot in the top 500 billionaires in Forbes' list?

Branson fought through everything with sheer determination backed up by creativity and innovation. The title of this book emphasizes just how important being innovative and creative is when it comes to starting a business. A packed resume or a long list of school accomplishments is not the basis of business acumen. Just because you don't have a college degree doesn't mean you cannot make it big in the world of business. A college degree, countless medals, and overflowing achievements are just trappings meant to put you in a box. Be brave enough to get out of that box and assert your self-confidence and self-reliance.

That's because when it comes to starting a business, you don't have anything else to cling to but your own intrinsic value. That and the things you will learn in this book are what you can use to start a business using an innovative methodology. You don't even have to be a certain age in order to start a business.

Achieving Success as a Young Business Entrepreneur

Age is just a number. That's a statement that many of today's young business entrepreneurs seem to be telling us because of their tremendous success. Take it from Mark Zuckerberg, founder of Facebook, who launched the social network in his dormitory room during his college days. In fact, Zuckerberg admitted that when he started the site when he was 19, he didn't have a clear idea about the business.

Obviously, he eventually figured out how to run a company along the way and he is now considered as one of the wealthiest individuals of our time. Of course, there are some lesson we can all learn from Zuckerberg and other successful young business entrepreneurs.

- **Knowledge**

Naturally, knowledge comes first when we talk about the formula of success. Thankfully, you don't have to be an expert in your chosen field before you can begin with your business. There are countless sources for anyone eager to boost their knowledge.

Attending trainings and short courses can be an option. Other than that, reading books and browsing the internet can be valuable. Knowledge is literally at your fingertips so grab every chance to learn if you hope to hit it big.

- **Tools**

The tools you will need are highly dependent on the specific industry you aim to penetrate. For instance, getting the right machines and supplies is necessary if you are establishing a bakeshop. The same can be said regardless of what business you want to pursue.

Think of your equipment as an investment because that's what they really are. However, it's always wise to ask around before spending money. Consulting with experienced entrepreneurs can work for your advantage since it will help you avoid the same mistakes that they've done in the past.

Another tip is to keep your eyes peeled for the latest technology. Staying ahead of your competition is often necessary if you want to stand out in the crowd. As always, do some research first and honestly evaluate if some advanced tools are really needed and if you can afford them.

- **Determination**

Whether you like it or not, discouragement is part of the game - and the only way to win is to stay determined. Many young business entrepreneurs of our day can attest to that. You can't expect to be the exemption!

Hard work and discipline are key elements you need to implement perhaps especially during trying times. There are risks to take and sacrifices to be made in every step. Having the right attitude is one of the secrets effective entrepreneurs use, so don't lose focus and stay on your track.

"One of the secrets," you're probably wondering. "So there's more?" Well, these are not secret-secrets actually, if there's such a thing. I am pretty sure lots of entrepreneurs have stumbled upon these secrets time and again. The fact that I will be sharing some of the secrets I applied to my business is proof that these are not tightly-guarded secrets. These are free to anyone who wants to take them. And since we are on the subject of entrepreneurship, let me go all out and share these not-so-secret secrets to you.

Secrets of a Successful Business Entrepreneur

Establishing a business may be simple but we do not doubt that every entrepreneur can say that achieving success is entirely another matter. Of course, not all businesses hit their target and some eventually encounter failure even after just a few months in the industry. Is there any magic formula that assures victory in the endeavor?

Successful business entrepreneurs will probably tell you that there are no secret tricks – just essential ethics that need to be observed at all times. Read on as I share with you a few trade "secrets" that will lead your enterprise to greater heights.

- **Dream Big**

It may sound every cliché but dreaming big is an essential step towards success. One quotation perfectly sums it up by saying "To be without dreams is to be without hope and to be without hope is to be without purpose."

The exact same mindset applies when it comes to the business world. Having clear goals and working on achieving them one at a time is a worthwhile pursuit for every business owner.

Best-selling author Stephen Covey (The 7 Habits of Highly Effective People) describes the process as beginning "with an end in mind." Visualizing what you want your business to be in five years, for instance, makes the entire struggle worthwhile.

- **Consider Your Strengths**

Focusing on your strong points is always more effective than dwelling on your faults. Although handling a business can help you overcome several weaknesses along the way, you need to be passionate in what you do and that's where your strength will play a crucial role.

If you're a good marketer, then use that to your advantage to be a successful business entrepreneur. On the other hand, there's nothing wrong with hiring people if you're not too inclined when it comes to accounting tasks or maintaining a website.

- **Plan, Plan, Plan**

Having a plan gives you direction and writing them down gives you the chance to review them constantly. That way, you will be able to tell whether you are progressing or not. Adjustments may be needed as you proceed, so make it a point to set some time for planning.

Keep in mind that failing to plan is the same thing as planning to fail. That's something you'd want to avoid if you're serious about becoming a successful business entrepreneur.

- **Be Willing to Work Hard**

A common misconception among those dreaming about having a business is that it's easy and they don't have to work hard anymore. This is a wrong notion you may want to avoid. You'll be surprised at how hard you will need to work as a business owner. A frequent experience among start-up entrepreneurs is to work even beyond their regular schedule. If you apply all the pointers we've mentioned here, then we're sure things will be a lot easier in no time.

Since we've got that down pat already, it's time to transition into the meat of this book, which is the innovative methodology I have been babbling about from the get-go. However, before we get to that, let us first try to understand what entrepreneurial management is and why it matters when it comes to applying the aforementioned methodology.

Understanding Entrepreneurial Management

The thrust of building a business is building an institution, an organization of sorts. It's impossible to start something of a certain magnitude without considering how you'll be managing it. This is the part of starting a business that many entrepreneurs find confusing. To them, using the words entrepreneurship and management in a single context is directly oppositional. Why is that?

Think of it this way: you build a business because you want to make it on your own. The idea of working for someone else, having a manager hovering behind you, no longer appeals to you. So why in the world should you implement management practices in your business, right? Such can only stunt the business' growth. Moreover, if you have a few employees helping you run the business, you fear that implementing management practices will only encourage bureaucracy and suffocate their creativity, as well as yours.

That may be possible if we're talking about general management. The thing is, we're not. General management will not cut it as far as entrepreneurship is concerned. As I have learned in my journey as an entrepreneur, a special kind of managerial discipline is necessary when it comes to entrepreneurship. This type of management will allow entrepreneurs like you and me to harness each and every opportunity thrown our way. It is known as entrepreneurial management.

It is typically a fusion of entrepreneurial knowledge and management practices. On one hand, entrepreneurial knowledge is that which determines the skills, concepts, and mindset that a person desiring to start a business employs in an effort to grow the business. On the other hand, implementation of management practices aims to address vital

217

management issues that a business entrepreneur faces (Price, 2011). These management issues basically relate to the following:

- A business' mission and values statement that explains what the startup is about

- Its goals and objectives, which determine the direction to which the business should go

- The business' growth strategy, which shows how the business will get to its "destination"

- The people and resources working together for the business to help it get to its destination

- An entrepreneur's organizational capabilities that establishes what structure is necessary to build and run the business

- The business' financing strategy, which decides how much money the business needs and when it is needed

- Its vision of success, which is extremely important if an entrepreneur desires to recognize his business' destination immediately

Obviously, building a business is so much easier if the right kind of management practices is enforced. In the next chapter, we will see how entrepreneurial management fares when the innovative methodology mentioned previously comes to the fore.

Key Takeaways from Chapter 1

- An entrepreneur is someone who sets up a business and takes responsibility for it.

- An entrepreneur is a risk-taker who trusts his gut feelings and is brave enough to tread on dangerous grounds.

- An entrepreneur is not compulsive. Instead, he believes in hard work.

- Entrepreneurs are any sound economy's strength of character.

- Proper motivation is necessary to build a business from the ground up.

- Not all successful entrepreneurs earned college degrees.

- An entrepreneur needs to be innovative and creative to break out of a mold and start a business.

- When it comes to business, an entrepreneur has his intrinsic value to rely on.

- Age doesn't matter when it comes to starting a business.

- There are not-so-secret secrets to becoming a successful entrepreneur.

- You can't build a startup without implementing management practices.

The right kind of management practice for startups and businesses is entrepreneurial management, which fuses entrepreneurial knowledge and management practices together.

Section 2: Innovate

In the previous section, I have already gone through the nitty-gritty of entrepreneurship. I have also mentioned several times about an innovative methodology that aims to make the most of entrepreneurial management.

In the section, "Innovate", I will try to introduce a particular methodology in the hopes of making important changes to a new business. I will also briefly discuss the difference between a startup and a business (small, medium, big, whichever floats your boat), as well as why implementing the said methodology is crucial. I don't want to preempt the proceeding chapters, but I feel it somewhat of a disservice if I don't put a label to said methodology.

So I am going out on a limb here to tell you that next few chapters you'll read will focus on the LEAN STARTUP METHODOLOGY. I will try to discuss it in detail, making sure all bases are covered so you will not have a hard time implementing it in your startup.

Chapter 2: Getting to Know the Lean Startup Methodology

Theodore Roosevelt, the twenty-sixth president of the United States who served from 1901 to 1909, once said, "Nothing worth having comes easy." That can't be truer when it comes to building a startup, and I can attest to that.

During the planning stages of my business, I was focused on how fast it can make profit and bring a return on investment and how much "richer" my bank account will be. I prematurely gauged the success of my business by how much money it will rake in for me. I failed to realize that there will be potholes and bumps along the way, and mind you, there were plenty of them.

Only after one scalding mistake after another did I understand that you can't look through rose-colored glasses when starting a business. You have to be strong enough to take whatever comes with it – pain, failures, and disappointments included. It was foolish of me to think I can relish the positives and avoid the negatives altogether. It was only after I sat down and started analyzing things did I realize that before ultimately reaching success, I will need to weather the storm first.

And weather the storm I did, but not after taking the time to fully and truly understand that I needed something to guide me, see me through the entire journey. That something turned out to be the lean startup methodology, which, for all intents and purposes, can be considered the brainchild of Eric Ries, entrepreneur, blogger, and author of the book "The Lean Startup: How Today's Entrepreneurs Use Continuous Innovation to Create Radically Successful Businesses".

In the book, Ries gamely shares that this innovative method traces its roots to the lean manufacturing revolution that was developed by two Japanese men working for Toyota (Ries, 2011, p. 28). I will not go into the nitty-gritty of the book, but I will try to explain the lean startup methodology as best as I can based on how I understand it. I am quite

221

confident I can explain it; after all, I have applied it in my business and have seen how beneficial it is.

Unmasking Lean Startup Methodology

At this point, you're probably looking at the lean startup method in the same way you will a recipe – a list of ingredients right there, step-by-step procedures right here, and finally, the finished dish. However, recipes can be tweaked to suit your palate. You can tone down the taste of a dish or make it even more savory depending on your mood. That isn't the case with the lean startup. There are no tweaks to this method. If you do it right, then this methodology will definitely be the perfect model to use for building a startup.

Lean startup is a system specifically introduced by Ries to entrepreneurs who have expressed their desire to create businesses. And just to be clear, a startup is different from a [small, medium, or big] business. Yes, that is a point of confusion among entrepreneurs; they think the two are one and the same. It's important that you know the differences between the two since such knowledge can influence your decision when it comes to actually starting your business.

One of the starkest differences between a startup and a small business (we're here using the term small business loosely) is that the former is meant to be ***temporary*** while the latter, depending on how foolproof your business plan, is virtually ***evergreen***. Another difference is the motivating force behind the business – a startup is founded with the intent to disturb the market with a business model that's scalable and has an impact on the market while a small business is founded by someone who wants to be the boss of himself, someone who wants to secure an established presence among his competition (Pope, 2019).

Funding source for a startup and a small business differs, too. Initially, both may be funded by the entrepreneur's own money or a loan from a financial institution. Nevertheless, once a startup takes off the ground and becomes successful, further funding is secured typically from a venture capitalist. Moreover, because a startup is usually identified with tech companies, it's a tad riskier to create than a small business.

That is not to say, though, that small businesses are better than startups. In fact, there are common pitfalls associated with small businesses, specifically as regards marketing strategies, as you will read next.

The Common Pitfalls of Small Business Marketing

Marketing is considered by many as one of the most important investments for any small business. Without it, your target customers may never know about you, your products or services offered, or why buying from you is a better decision than buying from your competition. As a result, your products or services go unnoticed. Marketing is a broad discipline and entrepreneurs must be able to overcome the pitfalls of small business marketing in order for your business to succeed.

Consider this a bonus section that will outline and discuss some of the most common pitfalls of small business marketing. This particular section will definitely provide you with useful insights that can help improve your marketing strategies and methods. That way, whether you're starting a small business or you're more likely to brave your way into a startup, you will know what you should and shouldn't do if you want a successful business that follows the lean startup methodology.

1. Defining Target Markets

Who do you plan to target? Where can you find them? This thing may seem like a very basic matter, but the groundwork of your marketing efforts actually starts here. If you want to achieve marketing success, you need to have a clear concept of who your target market will be. Create a brief narrative or profile of your target customer. Jot it down and polish it; collaborate with your team; figure out what your target client uses as its buying criteria. Defining who your ideal customer is will help you put everything in order and customize your marketing efforts based on their needs and wants.

2. Creating a Marketing Plan

Every small-scale entrepreneur must have a marketing plan to support their business goals. If developing a marketing plan is a challenge, there are plenty of resources on the Internet that can provide you with marketing plan templates. To give you an idea of what you should include in your plan, download some of these templates and use them as a guide. Be sure to keep it short and limit it to three pages if you can. If you can afford it, get a marketing specialist who can help you develop the plan.

3. Finding Resources for Marketing

One of the most common pitfalls of small business marketing is the cost of advertising, but small businesses cannot afford not to invest the time and money into this thing. Buying a full-page Saturday newspaper ad or NBA TV commercials is usually not a financial dilemma for large-scale businesses. However, such costs are obviously a predicament for many small businesses. To overcome this, spend some time studying and exploring what you can achieve with the low-cost marketing methods that are now available to small businesses.

4. Getting Referrals

Most small business entrepreneurs will probably agree that referrals are an important asset to their business. Even so, many remain cautious when openly asking for referrals. If you want to grow your business, be sure to let your existing customers, as well as your network of contacts, come to the realization that their referrals are a great help to your business. Try to make referrals an integral part of your marketing strategies so you can expand your reach and widen your customer base.

5. Increasing Sales Conversions

If you are faced with this common pitfall of small business marketing, try to look again at your marketing message. Deal with this challenge by making sure that you make a relevant and attractive offer to your intended customers. Before running a marketing campaign, test it first and then refine it. Small businesses cannot afford to only invest on advertisements that build image or brand. You can develop and promote your company image while causing increased sales by providing an offer to motivate your target customers to take action within a specific period of time. In general, your promotional campaign should focus on eliciting a response from your target customers that translates into sales while building your brand at the same time.

Whatever industry you are in, it is very likely that you would encounter one or more of the common pitfalls of small business marketing. Fortunately, there are ways to overcome this dilemma. All you have to do is explore your options and be creative in your marketing methods.

Now that you know the difference between the two, as well as the common pitfalls associated with marketing a small business, let's go back to the discussion on hand – the lean startup methodology. As the name of this innovative method implies, it was founded with startup entrepreneurs at the forefront of Ries' mind. Why do I say so?

We've mentioned earlier that a startup is riskier to create than a small business. Risk is the epitome of a startup because you are practically venturing into the unknown. Some of you have probably done it. I have done it. I have left a stable job just so I can start my own business without even considering what will become of me in case things don't go according to plan.

The risk factor of startup businesses is what prompted the idea of the lean startup. Its founder wanted to lend companies of all sizes a hand, so to speak, to help them navigate through rough waters and lower the risk factors through three things – minimum viable products or MVPs, painstaking experimentation, and full commitment to learning (McGowan, 2017). In a nutshell, the lean startup methodology centers on the creation of a sustainable business where minimal time and money is wasted.

Think of it this way: you spend an obscene amount of money trying to come up with products that you think the consuming public will love, **"*you think*"** being the operative words. Did you even stop to think if the products you're creating can solve a particular problem or address a pressing situation? You probably didn't, and guess what? You're more than likely to fail. Scratch that. YOU WILL FAIL.

Harsh words, right? However, I'm speaking the truth, and that is something that Ries' realized as well.

Earlier, I said that Ries' concept of the lean startup method was developed because of two Japanese men who worked for Toyota – Taiichi Ohno and Shigeo Shingo. Observing how these two worked, Ries' saw how the entire process of building Japanese cars worked – waste is reduced and eliminated, if at all, in order to release the cars at the lowest cost and without sacrificing the high value of the cars. Through his observation, Ries' was able to visualize a system that can likewise be applied by entrepreneurs.

Understanding the Lean Startup Methodology

If you read through the introduction of Section 1 of this book (and I am sure you did), then you probably remembered my mentioning that a bit of science is necessary to guarantee a sustainable business. That scientific element is actually the lean startup methodology, which can be construed as a scientific approach as far as creating and managing a business goes. At the cusp of it is ensuring that customers get the products or services they paid for in no time.

For all intents and purposes, the lean startup methodology is like a diagram that teaches entrepreneurs how to navigate through a new business – how to steer it to the right direction, when to turn, and when to keep up with the current pace to reach the destination. More than that, however, this innovative methodology aims to teach entrepreneurs how they can grow a business by going "full steam ahead". The lean startup particularly works for businesses where product development is a major catalyst to sustaining the business.

Remember how in the previous subheading I mentioned that some new entrepreneurs fail in product development because they create products that they think people want? They don't take into consideration the actual needs and wants of consumers, so they spend copious amount of time, energy, and money to "perfect" products without giving consumers a chance to give their two cents.

Finally, when the products bomb, they immediately blame other factors – poor marketing, wrong concept, et cetera, et cetera. What they failed to realize is they never asked potential consumers if the products they're conceptualizing are interesting. I am not saying each manufactured product should be given the green light by consumers. I am basically explaining that when it comes to product development, the voice of consumers matter *a lot*, and unfortunately, that's something many entrepreneurs overlook.

Nevertheless, through the implementation of the lean startup methodology, entrepreneurs who are in the planning stages of product development are persuaded to raise questions along the way – from the time the initial ideas are set forth up to the point where design choices are made, or additional features are given consideration.

Such questioning is considered an important process of the lean startup methodology since it allows entrepreneurs to potentially come up with their MVPs. In turn, the MVPs need to be shown to a few chosen test customers who will then decide if the products need further improvements or whatnot. Do you see how beneficial such testing is?

An Alternative to the Business Plan

You can think of the lean startup methodology as an alternative to a business plan. If you are not convinced that your plan is sound, you have the option to run a business based on the lean startup approach. It can work like a prototype that can test if your concepts or strategies can work in an actual business. A lean or small operation can still cost you some investment, but it will not cost you much in case your strategies do not work. Yet, with a lean operation, the business stands a good chance of surviving.

If successful and as this prototype grows, you will still need a good plan to support your bigger operation in order to know how much more funds you will need to accommodate growth, to help you compete better, and to stay focused on your set goals.

Whether you opt for a plan or a prototype, remember that for your business to survive and succeed you need to know what will make your business tick, which ones will be your competitors, what your common products are going to be, and what benefits you can offer your customers. Being unique is important. After sales, customer service seals relationships. Understanding competition can give you the edge in the market.

The Build-Measure-Learn Concept

As an entrepreneur, the abovementioned process will prevent you from manufacturing thousands of products, which are not foolproof, from the get-go. Instead, you'll only be manufacturing a few products for the test customers; thus, you save time and money from production. You may not see the difference it makes immediately, but the feedback you'll get from the first set of test customers will help you see what works, what doesn't, and where to go from there. Only when the products are proven highly marketable will actual production take place. It's a win-win.

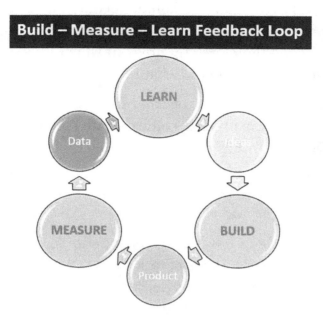

And that, ladies and gentlemen, is the crux of the lean startup methodology. It is hinged on the "build, measure, learn" model that Ries came up with, and that model is meant to be followed repeatedly until such time that the MVPs become actual offerings that can sustain a business. More importantly, the repeated cycle of that build-measure-learn model leads to innovation, which is the main thrust of the second section of this book.

It All Winds down to Innovation

How does innovation fit into all these? Just think. By adhering to the build-measure-learn model, the feedback you get from test customers will allow you to turn from one product idea or niche to another in the hopes of coming up with an even better product. It is risky, yes, but that's the whole concept of a startup; it's all about the risks you need to take. Otherwise, you'll never know what works and what doesn't.

Believe me when I say to innovate my business was the furthest thing from my mind back then. I figured, "Why should I meddle with something that is already working?" However, after applying the lean startup methodology, I realized there are still areas in which I can significantly improve the quality and reliability of what I offer consumers.

Indeed, even if I already had a structured idea, there was no harm in tapping into my creativity in order to come up with better ways to test my products. What worked can stay put, but I deduced that I can always come up with a new and improved version that my loyal customer base will certainly take notice of. In addition, even if I had minimal resources, I was able to innovate.

Here is a classic example of how the build-measure-learn model can be applied to a business. Let's say you're a fitness enthusiast and have decided to launch a healthy meal prep delivery service. Initially, your goal is to target busy, single people in their 20s in urban areas. You figured these 20-somethings are always on the go and are busy making their mark as yuppies and food prep may be furthest from their minds.

However, since there is no hard and fast rule regarding who can and cannot order from your delivery service, even those outside your target age group have started ordering, too. In fact, your healthy meal preps have a ***better market*** among 30-something new moms who live in affluent suburbs. Will you stick to your original target market? Perhaps. Nevertheless, you can always add more delivery schedules, as well as types of healthy foods to prepare that addresses the nutritional needs of new moms who may be nursing. Eventually, you may start prepping healthy meals for these new moms' husbands and other children.

Obviously, you didn't stick to a one-track game plan. You changed its course based on what the needs of the consuming public were. That is how lean startup's build-measure-learn model works.

That's the central concept of the lean startup method. That is not to say, though, that things get easier from there. When I took on the build-measure-learn model, I honestly thought I had it down pat. Boy was I wrong! It took me a while to realize that it was a research-intensive process. In fact, I had to tap into the humble storehouse of knowledge I built while I was still in school to recall the six parts of the scientific method!

See what I did there? I have been saying that the lean startup methodology is scientific in its own right, and I will tell you why. I'm sure you still remember those six key elements that characterize the scientific method:

- Questions
- Hypotheses
- Experiments
- Observations
- Analyses
- Conclusions

Relating the abovementioned to the lean startup method, I mentioned previously that questioning (questions) is an important process of lean startup since it paves the way for entrepreneurs to come up with their MVPs (hypothesis). Then, once the products are ready, these are sent out to test customers (experiment). The test customers' feedback (observation) will help entrepreneurs tweak the products (analysis). Once the products have been improved, these are deemed marketable (conclusion).

It is an on-going cycle, one that can weigh you down emotionally especially when feedback from test customers comes in. Imagine the sheer agony of putting your products out there before these are even deemed marketable and embracing whatever feedback the test customers give. They can give you sugar-coated feedback, or they can blatantly brutal; it doesn't matter. You need to be tough enough to take in everything they have to say about the products and find the strength to implement it.

So, yes, the lean startup methodology isn't all sunshine and rainbows. Nevertheless, if you apply it well and do it properly, it can help you create a business that actually, sincerely caters to the needs of its consumer base.

And when customers are satisfied, you can expect repeat business. Hence, you are able to grow and sustain your business, which is the idea behind your entrepreneurship.

Key Takeaways from Chapter 2

- Starting a business isn't all sunshine and rainbows. There is bound to be mishaps, and you need to be prepared for those.

- The lean startup methodology can't be tweaked. You need to follow through on that model to build a business.

- The lean startup method is perfect for startup entrepreneurs who live and breathe risks.

- Simply put, the lean startup methodology focuses on creating a sustainable business that wastes very little time and money.

- The lean startup method is built around the build-measure-learn concept.

- Adhering to the build-measure-learn concept allows for innovation of products and services.

- The six key elements of the scientific method can be applied when you follow the lean startup methodology.

- Innovation makes for a sustainable business.

We have skimmed the surface of the lean startup methodology in this chapter. In the next one, I will explain the five principles upon which this innovative methodology is anchored. Hopefully, at the end of the chapter, I will have shared with you several takeaways that can prove to be gold nuggets of helpful learnings as you build your business.

Chapter 3: Five Principles behind the Lean Startup Methodology

Believe it or not, the lean startup methodology has had its fair share of criticisms, both constructive and destructive. For instance, some people said it's already an easy enough process; thus, oversimplifying it seemed redundant. So many blogs have been written about the subject claiming the lean startup is already simple – all of its basic elements are there to explore – so why make it simpler?

Well, dissatisfaction is, perhaps, human nature. It's impossible to please everybody. Here's the thing, though: inasmuch as the lean startup may seem simple, it's one heck of a complex system. ***You think you know*** what to do with it, but once you're actually doing it, you'll realize its intricacy.

Moreover, just as it is with any other system, you can't just window-shop for the parts you "like", choose those, and leave the rest behind. No. It's impossible to make a system work without tapping on all its parts to work seamlessly together. And that's what makes the lean startup multifaceted.

Like I have said earlier, it's a research-intensive process. You can't downplay the importance of research since it will gauge whether or not you're up for the challenge. If, during the course of research, you realize you're not cut out for the lean startup method, you're free to consider a different approach. At least, you haven't expended much time, effort, energy, and money yet since you're still on the research phase. On the other hand, if you think you can take on the challenge, by all means, go!

Perhaps understanding the five principles on which the lean startup is hinged will help you see if it's something you can work with. That's what I did, and that's why I can freely talk about the methodology in this book. I'm not saying I'm an expert at this method, but I try to apply what I learn (after all, it's a continuous process). And that's what I want you to do, too.

The Lean Startup Principles

Principle is defined as a fundamental truth serving as the cornerstone of a particular system of belief or reasoning. With that said, it's only right to assume that the lean startup methodology is founded on a set of fundamental truths that govern how it works. In this part of the book, I will try to expound on those five principles that are behind the lean startup methodology (The Lean Startup, n.d.).

1. ***Entrepreneurs are everywhere.*** Unlike regular employees who are cooped up in their offices from nine to five, entrepreneurs (self-made people, if you will) are found just about everywhere. You can create a startup from your garage or your bedroom (or dorm room like Mark Zuckerberg). That's the beauty of entrepreneurship: it, in itself, is a human institution from which innovative products and services can be created regardless if conditions are uncertain. With entrepreneurs being everywhere, it goes without saying that the lean startup method will work anywhere, regardless of the size of a business or which sector of the industry it belongs to.

2. ***Entrepreneurship is management.*** Just because it's a self-made business doesn't mean management practices can't be applied. Like I have discussed in the early goings of this book, there is such a thing as entrepreneurial management. It's a type of management specifically geared towards entrepreneurship. Keep in mind that entrepreneurship is a human institution, not a product or service, and an institution cannot function fully unless capable hands are managing it.

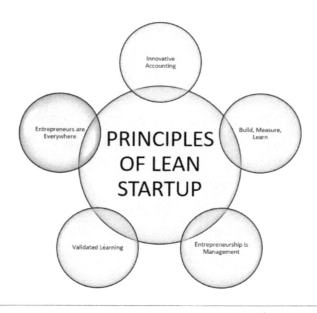

3. ***Validated learning.*** You don't create a business with the sole purpose of making money or being at your customers' beck and call. Heck, you don't even create it, so you'll have an excuse to make products or formulate services. You start a business with the aim of learning how to make it sustainable. Remember how I said the six parts of the scientific method applies to the lean startup method? Well, the experiment part applies when you need to validate your learnings scientifically to see whether these work. It's a continuous process.

4. ***Build-Measure-Learn.*** Ah, if it isn't our favorite concept. Seriously, though, this three-step concept is basically what makes the lean startup methodology tick. Overall, the primary activity of a startup business, as you can see in the illustration in Chapter 2, is to formulate ideas, turn these ideas into viable products (build), see how customers react to the products (measure), and use customers' feedback to see whether you need to go to a new direction or continue until the product becomes marketable (learn). It's an on-going loop intended to accelerate the growth of a business.

5. ***Innovation accounting.*** In the lean startup method, it's important to measure certain metrics like how much progress you're making, how milestones should be set up, and which task should be prioritized. Implementing entrepreneurial management whole making sure these metrics are met can be difficult. Hence, innovation accounting is necessary. This novel type of accounting is specifically designed for startup businesses. Its use is the only way you can figure out if you are, indeed, making progress or if your efforts are for naught. This particular principle of the lean startup focuses on numbers that are pivotal for the growth of your business like engagement and customer acquisition cost.

Are you now fully convinced that you should try the lean startup methodology for your business? If you're still having second thoughts, then perhaps this next segment will tickle your fancy even more.

Is Adapting the Lean Startup Methodology Necessary?

I have been giving you the 411 about the lean startup methodology almost from the get-go, but I am quite sure you're still adamant about giving it a try. After all, it's the fate of your business at stake here. One wrong move and everything you have worked and been working hard for can go down the drain.

Of course, I can always convince you that ***it did work*** for me. However, what works for one will not always work for another, right? That's why I still want to share some reasons why I think you should adapt the lean startup in your business. In fact, these reasons will work whether yours is a new business or already an established organization.

1. Regardless if you're a startup or an existing business, you are bound to create new products or services. Hence, you will potentially be reaching new markets. Adapting the lean startup methodology will help your business decrease cycle time, gather customer feedback faster, and reduce waste.

2. There will be new processes you will want to employ in your business, processes that will certainly have a bearing on your customer base. So you want to ensure the best results by deploying a customer-validated process. Through the lean startup, you will get continuous feedback and validation.

3. You may already have a five-year projection in place. In a volatile environment, that five-year plan may not succeed. Nevertheless, adapting the lean startup will bring in the agility and speed you need so you can adapt in an ever-changing environment. It will certainly help you go a long way.

4. Adapting the lean startup methodology will help you foster innovation in your business minus the wasted money.

5. With the lean startup backing you up every step of the way, you will not be overly concerned about the success and adaption rates of the new digitized system you are planning to deploy.

Keep in mind that two of the main purposes of this methodology are: to make your business competitive in such a cutthroat environment and drive growth. In a nutshell, here are some benefits of adapting the method:

- Throughout the course of adapting the process, you stay focused on your goals and you get clear **visibility** of which direction you plan on going.

- The process gives you a heads up when it's time to make necessary changes to the strategies you are currently using. As a result, you spend **less time, effort, and money**.

- By the time your product or service is deemed marketable, you will have already **established a customer base**. This includes the test customers you reached out to during the build-measure-learn phase.

- The process/es you will create using the lean startup will already have been **tried and tested**.

The lean startup method is focused on five key points:

- Speed
- Flexibility
- Innovation
- Customer focus
- Elimination of uncertainties

Key Takeaways from Chapter 3

- The lean startup methodology may seem simple, but it's an intricate web of complexities that you need to carefully study.
- It's a multifaceted process that is research-intensive.
- There are five principles, fundamental truths, which govern the implementation of the lean startup method.
- There are at least five reasons why it is imperative to adapt the lean startup methodology in any business (whether startup or already established).
- There are four key benefits to adapting the lean startup.
- The lean startup method if focused on five key points – speed, flexibility, innovation, customer satisfaction, and eliminate uncertainties.

This section of the book really laid bare the ins and outs of the lean startup methodology. So far, I have provided you insight on how to create a business using the build-measure-learn model. I have also helped you see how the lean startup can help make innovations to your business.

At this point, we are heading on to the third section of the book, which will discuss how the lean startup methodology figures inasmuch as the acceleration of your business is concerned.

Section 3: Accelerate

To accelerate literally means to gain speed. In the just-concluded chapter, I made mention of the fact that one of the reasons why the lean startup method works for most businesses is it allows for speed, especially when it comes to dealing with unwarranted circumstances.

In the third section, "Accelerate", we will see how adapting the lean startup method can boost the speed in which a business grows. Along the way, we will also discuss how acceleration, as it relates to this awesome methodology, factors in with other aspects of a business.

Chapter 4: Grow Your Business with Maximum Acceleration

Are you guys still with me? I really hope so, because I am positive the learnings you'll get from this book will be extremely beneficial for your business. We have been going back and forth about the subject of lean startup methodology (as is to be expected since it is what the book's all about). And so far, we have pooled together three key takeaways about lean startup – it teaches you how to drive a startup, it teaches you when you need to pivot or turn to another direction, and it teaches you when to continue going.

These key takeaways have a common goal in mind – to help you, the entrepreneur, to grow your business with maximum acceleration. And as we have been discussing from the get-go, the main thrust of the lean startup method is for entrepreneurs like you and me to embrace a principled approach when it comes to product development. Why do you think so?

Well, history will show that there are far too many failed startups and a trail of broken hearts after it. These startups failed because while they spent a considerable amount of time perfecting what they think is an awesome product, they didn't take one important factor into consideration – customers' feedback. In their excitement to build a product they think will rake in thousands in revenue, they disregarded the feelings of customers, so to speak, and never bothered asking them if the product was interesting or not.

Only when the customers state voicing their dissatisfaction, their indifference towards the product, will entrepreneurs realize they made a mistake. However, it may be too late already.

The lean startup methodology aims to eliminate that one-track mindset of entrepreneurs. I will boldly tell you that if you want to succeed, stop thinking about yourself and start thinking about your prospective customers. If you start putting the interests of your customers ahead of anything else, you will accelerate the growth of your business in no time.

The last thing you want is to have uncertainties when running your business. The lean startup approach helps you eliminate such. How? By building or creating a product that you will let test customers sample and by absorbing the feedbacks you'll get from these customers, you will avoid second-guessing. With a prototype, you will not be wasting as much money as you will if you marketed a product that people will not buy. With a prototype, you'll get to find out what works, what doesn't, and what changes or tweaks you need to make.

By applying these changes, you will come up with a product that is not only marketable but also one that already has an established customer base. That's because the same test customers will more than likely buy the product knowing that their two cents were taken into consideration during product development.

Acceleration Is Easy-Peasy

If there is one universal truth that's common in some business owners, it is that over time, lethargy creeps in and gets the better of them. When that happens, everyone, from the business owner to his smallest employee loses the enthusiasm that has been the driving force from the get-go. Once this enthusiasm is lost, everything is bound to start crumbling down, which can lead to the demise of the business.

If it isn't lethargy that will lead to the untimely death of a business, then, it most likely will be bureaucracy. That means the business owner will strictly and precisely define rules and procedures that each and every one in the company needs to follow to a T. Such type of authority can stunt the growth of a business since no one else except the business owner has the freedom to explore things that can lead to the improvement of the business.

As a startup business owner, you will want to avoid lethargy and bureaucracy at all cost. Yes, both are not the end-all and be-all of a business. With the right driving force, you can make your business succeed and never lose the agility or speed it had from the start. In fact, if you apply the lean startup approach to your business, you will be able to sustain and maintain its agility and speed, not to mention its disposition to learning new approaches and methodologies. Most importantly, you will find it easier to cultivate a work environment that embraces unorthodox thinking; thus, there is more room for growth and innovation.

And for a business that dreams of scaling in the fastest amount of time possible, applying the lean startup method can serve to accelerate the business. How? Well, the lean startup approach encourages the practice of doing things in small batches. Ries explains this in his book in which he used the example of Japanese carmaker Toyota and its car production technique post-World War II. Apparently, American carmakers were then mass-producing their automobiles using extremely huge batch sizes that demanded huge amounts of money. These Americans figured mass-producing the cars will bring down the cost of each part and make the cars inexpensive. Moreover, the cars will be totally uniform.

However, since the car market for the Japanese was way smaller, they had to take on a different approach to their car production. Ohno and Shingo, mentioned in an earlier chapter, innovated Toyota's car-making methodology by using general-purpose machines that were much smaller and able to produce small batches of different parts in one go. These two Japanese reconfigured each machine to meet the "by batch" demand. As a result, Toyota manufactured cars in small batches.

Do you think the smaller batch approach slowed down the car-production of Toyota? On the contrary, Toyota was able to produce different product varieties at a much faster pace. The company was able to address the smaller demands of its fragmented market while keeping in step with its mass-producing competition. Toyota kept to this system of production while increasing the size of its market, and by 2008, it became the largest carmaker ***in the world*** (Ries, 2011, p. 182).

Now you're probably thinking, "What does Toyota's example have to do with my business? Mine is dramatically smaller." That may be true. However, if you apply the same system to your business, you will be leaving a smaller room for second-guessing. Envision this scenario: you produce a product in big batches only to realize only a couple of your customers actually want it. Think of the time, energy, and money you will have wasted trying to build the product that only two people loved. If you produced in small batches, though, even if only two people supported the product, you will not have wasted as much time, effort, and money.

Sticking to the abovementioned system will eventually lead to sustainable growth. Here, I use the term sustainable growth specifically in the context of a startup business applying the lean startup methodology. A business using this method is practically accelerating its growth potential since the system makes accelerated production feasible. And do you know the possibilities of such?

When a business is able to produce more quality products in a short amount of time, return on investment is faster. Not only that. Keep in mind that your production is now based on the build-measure-learn model, which means customer feedback is at the forefront. From this point on, your succeeding productions will already be based on the feedback you received from test customers. Then, when the product has reached its marketable status, your test customers will be the first ones to buy it. Since the product is now made according to their "specifications", customer satisfaction is guaranteed. And when customers are satisfied, you can expect an onslaught of new customers.

Yes, your past customers' behavior affects the influx of new customers, which translates to sustainable growth. In what ways?

- When customers are satisfied with a product, they are bound to tell others about it. Containing their enthusiasm will be futile, and once they start telling their friends and family about it, the curiosity of these people will move them to try the product themselves.

- When customers use a product, awareness of the product is imminent. Everytime the product is used, other people are knowingly or unknowingly exposed to it and may be influenced to buy it.

- A business may pay its customers to advertise the product through their social media pages or blogs. Payment will usually come from revenues that sales from these customers generated. They become influencers in their own right and are more than likely to entice others to try the product out.

- A product may be designed for repeated purchases. An example of this is a grooming subscription box for men. Such product is released monthly, and since the box contains different products each month, men will buy it every month.

The abovementioned catalysts of sustainable growth are all made possible through accelerated production.

Key Takeaways from Chapter 4

- The principled approach of lean startup helps you grow your business with maximum acceleration.

- Many startups fail because they disregard the feelings of customers.

- Customer dissatisfaction often moves business owners to do some serious self-examination to see in which areas they can improve.

- The lean startup methodology will help business entrepreneurs focus on improving customer satisfaction.

- Lethargy and bureaucracy can lead to the untimely death of a startup.

- Sticking to the lean startup methodology can lead to a startup's sustainable growth.

- Past customers' behaviors can be catalysts for sustainable growth.

I have just finished sharing what I know about accelerating a business through the lean startup methodology. In the next chapter, I will be talking about the lean startup technology in action.

Chapter 5: The Lean Startup Technology in Action

We are nearing the end of this book, and I am pretty sure your curiosity has been piqued greatly about the lean startup technology, and rightfully so. After all, we have discussed many ways in which it can maximize the accelerated growth of your business. In this section, I will talk about the lean startup methodology as you observe it *in action*.

One specific area I will talk about in relation to lean startup is how you can efficiently manage your employees using the methodology (Sheth, 2019). It's a vital approach that ensures continuous progress for your business. Nevertheless, you need to anticipate that trials and errors will be part of the process since you will need to continue experimenting, testing, and investigating whatever it is your offering, whether products or services, repeatedly as these develop.

You will notice the stark difference between a business that follows the lean startup methodology and a traditional startup. A traditional startup follows a methodological process that is built on long-term vision, strategy, and plans. On the other hand, a business following the lean startup will expedite the processes by going through the steps I have discussed in the previous sections of this book. Another difference is that information about the products or services will be kept to a minimum few – employees, investors, and test customers – until such time that the offerings are deemed marketable, keeping in mind that the entire process is done in stealth mode.

By now you're probably wondering, "What do all these have to do with effective employee management?" The answer is quite simple, actually. The more streamlined process offers managers a chance to discern whether or not there are some inefficiencies with the current processes. Thus, they can correct or change whatever needs correction and only deliver to customers what they deserve – value for money.

Bonds Strengthened Because of Lean

Another example of the lean startup technology in action is the development of a strong A-team. Because the build-measure-learn process is put in effect, the right people are hired and put in the right place. As a result, each one is given tasks based on the skills they possess, as well as their adaptability to the lean startup methodology. As your business grows, you can transition your first batch of employees, you're A-team, as brand marketers. This time, their job will be to talk about your business to others. This will result in a chain reaction of sorts in which brand awareness is raised without you having to invest money. In turn, this awareness will start raking in revenue and improve the confidence of your employees.

Once their confidence level is improved, they can go ahead and train a fresh group of employees with the same vision they had when they started with you. This unified faith in the vision and mission of your business is crucial because as much as possible, you want to have people working collectively for you to help you reach your main goal.

How to Get Started with an Effective Lean Startup A-Team

Here's the thing: a business' A-team doesn't just fall automatically down from the sky. In fact, one of the key elements in forming an A-team for your business using the lean startup approach is to hire people based only on the open positions. If there are no open positions in the business, then don't hire people. That is the best way to keep the business efficient. Moreover, because the lean startup methodology is somewhat of an unorthodox approach to starting a business, another vital element to forming your A-team is to choose people who will fit ideally to the lean startup culture you are trying to cultivate.

Then, you will want to entice these employees comprising your A-team to stay with your company by offering them something tangible. Knowing what an employee can bring to the table to add a unique value to your business can help you determine what sort of "incentive" you'll offer them.

Some businesses that follow the lean startup methodology offer employee stock ownership plan (ESOP) to their employees. An ESOP is a benefit plan, an equity, in which employees are given ownership interest in a business (Ganti, 2019). The ESOP, as mentioned earlier, will be based on a distinctive skill that an employee can offer to make the business better.

Why should you, the business owner, go through such great lengths to keep your current roster of employees that comprise your business' A-team? Well, most of those employees left the security that corporate jobs offer just to join a new business. It is such a huge leap of faith, one that requires you to make them see that the big risk they took was not for nothing. They will have something to gain out of their big move. On the flipside, you need to make sure the incentives you will offer the employees will not, in any way, impede with business activities. You need to ensure the company stays protected and that every business activity is always carried out in a professional manner.

If you decide to give your employees ESOP, you need to ensure you're doing it properly. There needs to be a structure you will follow to make sure the process flows smoothly. Perhaps a good way to decide how much an employee will get is to have a pre-determined range of equity stake. This percentage will be paid over and above the salary that an employee receives. Here's a model you can follow:

- Rank-and-File Employees and Junior Managers – 0.2 to 0.33%
- Managers and Senior Lead Managers – 0.33 to 0.66%
- Directors – 0.4 to 1.25%
- Product Development Leads and Engineers – 0.5 to 1%
- Independent Board Members – 1%
- Vice Presidents – 1 to 2%
- Chief Operating Officer (COO) – 2 to 5%
- Chief Executive Officer (CEO) – 5 to 10%

As you can see, the bracket range above includes everyone, from the rank-and-file employees to the business founder(s). Keep in mind that the above is just a model you can use in your own business. There is no hard and fast rule as far as range brackets go. You will decide on the best compensation; thus, it's vital that you fully understand the types of ESOPs you can offer to employees.

A flexible schedule is yet another thing you can offer employees. Believe it or not, there are people who work best during daytime and there are those who work best after the sun has set. If that is the case with your current roster of employees, then by all means, yield to the schedule that allows them to function in their fullest potential and efficiency.

Really now, if you want to keep your top employees happy, you need to learn how to be flexible especially when it comes to their work hours. Applying the lean startup methodology in your business will allow your employees to either work together in teams following a rotational schedule or anytime that is convenient to them. If you will opt for the flexible schedule, then you may want to consider allowing some of your employees to work from home, too.

Another way to allow for flexibility in a lean startup "environment" is to veer away from setting hours for team members. Try giving project-based work that follows a specific timeline. This means there is only a set number of hours they have to get the job done.

Indeed, the lean startup methodology can do wonders to improve the efficiency of employees. Nevertheless, it will all depend on how "understanding" of their circumstances you are as an employer. If you're unyielding, then the growth of the business will be stunted no matter how hard you try to implement the lean startup approach.

The whole idea of adopting a lean startup culture in a business is to help it improve continuously. If you will not be open to changes, continuous improvements in your business, no matter if these are big or small, will be impossible. Remember, a business that applies the lean startup approach revolves around change.

Just make sure everyone of your employees, from the lowest to highest rung of the ladder, is aware when changes are implemented. It doesn't matter what the changes are about. The changes are meant to benefit not only the business as a whole but also each and every one of your employees. Hence, you need to make them aware of the changes if you want them to be on the same page as you are during the implementation period.

Every one of the people comprising a "lean startup team" must be moving in the same direction. That is the key to the successful implementation of the lean startup methodology. Employee's commitment, whether you're the CEO or a rank-and-filer, is necessary since the whole idea of the lean startup is everyone having a shared purpose to foster a culture of improvement in a business.

Key Takeaways from Chapter 5

- The lean startup approach can help you manage your employees efficiently.

- Following the lean startup methodology in a business can help managers discern if there are inefficiencies with the current processes and be able to remedy these right away.

- The bond between your business' elite employees and those in the lower rung of the ladder becomes stronger because of the lean startup approach.

- One way to get started with the lean startup application is by giving deserving employees some sort of "incentive".

- Flexibility in their work schedule is one way to improve the efficiency of employees.

- If you want to efficiently manage your employees using the lean startup approach, you need to learn how to "yield" to changes.

- A business adopting the lean startup methodology centers on continuous small improvements for the betterment of the business.

- Every one of the employees, from the highest to the lowest rank, must be on the same page for the continuous improvement of the business adopting the lean startup approach.

I have probably covered everything there is to discuss about the lean startup methodology and why using it in a business is advantageous. In the final chapter of this book, I will try to summarize everything we have come to know about the lean startup methodology to make it even easier for you to apply it in your business.

Chapter 6: Summarizing the Key Points of the Lean Startup Methodology

Applying the lean startup methodology in a business (whether it's a typical business setup or a startup) significantly changes its landscape. And the ensuing effect will depend on how yours adapt to the process. It certainly isn't a one-size-fits-all kind of thing, and that's why it's called a methodology in the first place. There is a system in place that you will need to follow, otherwise, your efforts may be for naught.

Thus far, we have discussed in detail how the lean startup methodology works. Nevertheless, with the amount of information we covered, you may be overwhelmed at this point. That is why I have decided to summarize the key points of the lean startup methodology to make it easier for you to apply it in your business.

In a nutshell, the lean startup approach is all about finding out what it is your customers want right away (or perhaps as soon as you decide to start a business). It is also about adapting to the needs of your customers through continuous testing and feedback-gathering without wasting any of your financial investments.

I divided this book into three sections CREATE, INNOVATE, and ACCELERATE.

In the first section, I endeavored to explain what entrepreneurship is all about and why entrepreneurial management matters especially in a new business. In the second section, I discussed the lean startup methodology in detail and explained why using this methodology in your business will be for its best interests. Finally, in the third section, I showed you how adapting the lean startup method can boost the growth of your business.

Key Takeaways from the Entire Book

- The lean startup methodology is all about creating or developing products or services that customers actually want.

- This innovative methodology aims to do away with wasted time, effort, and money by making sure products or services only come out for actual consumption or use once these are deemed marketable. Otherwise, the products or services will go through a special cycle.

- The leans startup methodology's groundwork is the build-measure-learn process. This means after producing something, you take the time to measure how it will fare with your target customers by going through a testing period. This testing period will let you know whether or not the products or services you offer need further enhancements or improvements.

- The only time actual products or services are launched or released to the public is after these have gone through a series of continuous improvements. That ensures no money or time was wasted in the actual production.

- The build-measure-learn system helps you see whether you should stick to the initial direction you planned to take or whether you should go on an entirely new direction. This is referred to as pivoting. Deciding when to pivot may be difficult, but if you don't want to fail in your endeavors, then you need to be open to the possibility of pivoting or turning to a new path.

- The lean startup approach is proven effective because of five principles that govern how it works. These same principles are what you need to apply in your business if you want it to succeed and especially when you apply the lean startup methodology.

- Accelerating the growth of your business is possible when you adopt the lean startup methodology.

- The lean startup method can also be used to efficiently manage your employees.

These are just some of the important points from this book. Hopefully, as you plan your business, the knowledge gleaned from this book can help you journey on the right path towards success. After all, that's the reason I came up with this book – to help you succeed by applying the lean startup methodology, just as I did.

Conclusion

I'd like to thank you and congratulate you for transiting my lines from start to finish.

I hope this book was able to help you to start a business that is destined to succeed from the very start. The purpose of this book is to reduce the number of failed businesses since these could have been prevented in the first place if only a system were in place.

The next step is to apply the proven steps to make your business succeed and grow around the lean startup methodology. Don't be another statistic. Be different from the rest. Work towards the success of your business by learning, adopting, and embracing the lean startup culture.

I wish you the best of luck!

Greg Caldwell

Book #5

Agile Project Management

The Complete Guide for Beginners to Scrum, Agile Project Management, and Software Development

Introduction

There are a lot of questions that revolve around the fields of project and software development. Is this programming language better than the others? Should we allow others to do the testing or should we do it ourselves? What bugs must one deal with in every phase of the development process? And so on and so forth.

But the most pressing question that managers often have to deal with is this: Can things be done at a faster and more effective pace? As someone who has been managing projects for years now, I could tell that you that is not technical and inherent problems that anyone involved in a project gets the most worked up about.

Coding issues? Let someone who knows the language deal with it? Bugs and glitches? A tester can find and identify them through their work? The software engine not compatible with the program? Perhaps replacing it with one that does will do the trick.

It is on the things that revolve outside of the work of teams that give managers the most problems. The constant need to coordinate teams, the dealing with deadlines, inter-team communication issues, and the logistics of human resources and technical skills. These are the things that keep everyone involved in a project awake at night; metaphorically and literally speaking.

And if that was not enough, you would have to deal with pressure from the higher-ups who may or may not know how the development process goes but insists on having things done in one way. Worse is if they insist on seeing results within a ludicrously short period of time or, without a notice, change goals and deadlines which your team has to adapt to ASAP.

More often than not, it is in finding a balance between being speedy and producing the desired results where managers often find the most pressing of challenges at during the project development process. Without a doubt, having to make sure everybody is one the same page in meeting goals while also making sure that the end product kind of works is a rather difficult task for most managers and leads.

But what if I were to tell you that there is a way to make things faster and more convenient? And not only does it make things easier for you, it allows you to produce the desired results in time or earlier. This is where Agile Project Management comes into play and might save you and your team from a lot of pressure, stress, and frustration in the development process.

What is the Agile Project Management methodology, exactly?

Without giving away too much (since you'll be reading about it for the entire book), the agile methodology is merely adopting a management style that is adaptive to whatever happens in the middle of a project without losing sight of the need to finish whatever was started in the soonest time possible.

What you have to understand is that a project is like clockwork. If you want things to run as smoothly as possible, you must make sure that everything not only functions but that said functions ultimately contribute to the attainment of a goal.

It's easy to bring in the best resources for a project, it's an entirely different thing to make sure everything is in sync and working towards a common goal. And not only should everything be working together but should remain so as you and your team have to address any changes and adjustments made to the plan.

Of course, you will learn how Agile came to be and why it would be an ideal strategy to implement in your project. And when you learn why it works, you should be able to identify the different strategies that you can use to make the methodology compatible with your group's current layout.

As with a lot of management methodologies, Agile is not a one-trick pony. As a matter of fact, it is so lenient that it allows you to implement the method through 4 different frameworks: Scrum, X, Kanban, and Lean. In this book, you will learn how each principle can be implemented, what makes them different from one another, and which is best according to your current project.

However, talking about implementing these changes would not be enough if your team itself is not willing to embrace the changes. As such, you would also learn how your team handles changes in the middle of the development process and what you can do to make the transition more comfortable for them.

You would also learn what motivates entire teams to complete common goals and, alternatively, what hinders them from reaching the same or impede others from contributing to it. It is by understanding how a team thinks as a group and individually would you be able to help them become more effective in implementing the methodologies that you are about to learn.

Such implementations, in turn, allowed the project leads to yield tremendous results from their projects. By learning how these methodologies have been implemented in the past, you may be able to identify how you can implement the same in your project or build on their successes by doing something even better.

But of course, we'd have to address the elephant in the room: can this methodology work for your project? The answer is always a yes. The beauty with Agile is that, for all its seemingly technical nature, is actually a rather simple process to follow.

The methodology helps you by breaking down the more complex aspects of your project and make your team focus on the most pressing of tasks and problems. This way, you and your team can deliver value to clients and eliminate a lot of waste on your development processes on a regular basis.

Just do remember that the success Agile Project Management methodology is reliant on how well you implement it on your project. As such, it is best that you learn as much of it in the simplest and most straightforward of terms possible. And this is where this book would into play.

If you have no further questions, let us head on and master the art of implementing the Agile Project Management methodology.

Chapter I: The Basics of Agile Project Management

What is Agile Project Management, Exactly?

This might be the first question that will pop up in your head and it is best that we answer it first. The most basic definition of APM is that is a methodology in which work is completed and delivered in short cycles (sometimes called sprints) and tweaked over time. This is done with the goal of providing value through increasing performance results as well as improving the structure of the project plan. This has similar features as most project planning and management methods in which the entire project is divided into smaller tasks.

The goal of the methodology is to simply cut out the cost by doing away with the trial-and-error strategy used by many project managers. By using a more cautious and yet proactive approach to project, one should be able to get better results from it.

Sounds straightforward, right? If you are still wondering what the style is, it would be better if we compare it to other methodologies.

The Flaws of the Classic Method

The classic project management method is simply the methodology that every manager typically uses as a default. It can differ from one manager to another but it mostly manifests the same flaws in each project. They are the following:

A. Too Much Time on the Planning Phase

A major flaw with the classic project management method is that you are planning the entire project up front. This means that you would spend more time finding the resources, evaluating costs, and assigning tasks and schedules for your team to follow.

The problem here is that a major portion of the time you spent for planning your strategy can be used more productively like actually executing the plans. And the long time spent on planning also leaves the method open for another flaw which is...

B. Plans Become Inflexible Eventually

When you spend too much time on planning, you become dead-set on implementing it no matter what. A lot of managers do this because they don't want to waste all that mental energy they have spent creating the plan.

However, this does mean that the plan does not account for changes in the middle of the process. There will always be a chance that new deadlines have to be met which, in turn, requires for the acquisition of new resources, the reshuffling of teams, and evaluation of new costs. This means that you can easily shoot over the budget and make the development process even more chaotic than necessary.

C. Treating the Team as Mere Resources

During planning, miscalculations can occur. Tasks or even entire projects could get underestimated. This would usually result in changes in schedule and resource allocations.

If you are not careful in this phase, you are inadvertently giving the impression that your team is expendable. Worse, you could just attribute failure in implementation of the changes over the team. This can increase animosity between teams and team members which ultimately impedes everybody from achieving shared goals.

What Makes Agile Project Management Different

More often than not, it is preferred that you use any other methodology instead of the standard method. This is where Agile Project Management comes into play and it has a few characteristics that instantly set it apart from the standard method.

1. **It is Segmented by Design**

The agile methodology is comprised of several "iterations" that last about 4 weeks. This can help managers in the sense that it makes evaluation all the easier to perform on a regular basis.

Also, the subdividing of the larger project into several iterations can psychologically help managers and team members focus on develop specific parts of the project. If one part of the project has to be done in a later iteration, then there is no need to worry about completing its sub-goals; just yet.

2. **It is Based on Time Periods**

In as much as projects in the agile method are divided into segments, each segment itself has a fixed time period. As was stated, each iteration can last up to a month and this cannot be modified down the line if the team agrees to such conditions.

With their efforts focused on one part of the project for a short period of time, the agile method can help teams become more productive and generate observable results within each iteration. And this is even if there are changes brought about by outside forces during each cycle.

3. **It is Easy to Understand, even for Non-Tech Folk**

One of the problem areas in project management is actually in communicating progress to clients, shareholders, and other people who might not have a good grasp on the more technical aspects of your work. In some methodologies, progress is either rarely communicated on a regular basis as they are long-term in nature. Basically, there is nothing to report regularly as overall goals take a while to be achieved.

And if some goals are short term, they are communicated in a manner that is highly technical and confusing. All the clients see are pretty graphs and numbers. Nothing about it seems to inspire their minds or give them the assurance that everything is running according to the plan.

Since the agile method runs on iterations, clients and the powers-that-be in your company can be certain of regular reports regarding the progress of a project. And not only will the reports be regular, they are presented in a manner that is easy to understand. This should give the clients an impression of what is going on and what to expect next.

The Principles of the Agile Method

So, what makes the Agile methodology work? The truth is that the method is guided by 12 principles that help managers implement the method properly and get the results they expected from the project or more.

And the best part about these principles? They are actually quite easy to remember. They are as follows:

1. **"Our highest priority is to satisfy the customer through early and continuous delivery of valuable software (or whatever else you deliver)".**

In the agile method, the focus is always on providing clients with updates on the progress of software. With this method, it is so easy for anyone to see that there have been progresses made in the project and that such progresses are observable. Through regular reports at the end of each iteration, a client can get an idea as to how a project is ultimately going to look and feel like once it is completed.

The method also takes into consideration any input that the client gives. After all, the software should be the ultimate expression of what the client has envisioned. Anything less than that is never acceptable.

2. **"Welcome changing requirements, even late in development. Agile processes harness change for the customer's competitive advantage."**

Unlike other methods which balk at the idea of constant changes, the agile method embraces it to the fullest. For the agile method, change is but a mere opportunity that can enhance the project and help the team complete it in the soonest time possible.

This is something noteworthy as changes can occur even in the later stages of the development process. And such changes can be frustrating as they can drastically change the buildup of the end product. With the agile method, you can anticipate for such changes and build the software in a manner that makes it compatible to the same if they were to pop up in each iteration.

3. **"Deliver projects frequently, from a couple of weeks to a couple of months, with a preference for the shorter timescale."**

This might sound contradictory to what has been said but it is vital to the success of the agile method that you stick to the development cycles. Even if you finish early and have a working product to present to the client, don't rush things through but instead, allow for reworks and testing until the cycle is complete.

Changes might happen in the middle of the process but a manager must be able to keep their team focused on what needs to be done and produce results within each time period. This way, progress can be seen either in small steps or big leaps forward.

4. **"Coordinating team members must work together daily throughout the project."**

The stakeholders of the company must also know of whatever is happening in the project. As such, your team and the higher-ups must have an open and transparent line of communication so that concerns at both sides are aired out and addressed efficiently.

On the manager's part, they should know exactly when shareholders and upper management would like some changes made in the project. This way, they can communicate the same to their team as quickly as possible and adjust the work accordingly.

5. "Build projects around motivated individuals. Give them the environment and support they need and trust them to get the job done."

All the best equipment and a good team setup would not matter if your team is not made up of highly motivated people. In fact, the agile method is highly dependent on the ability of people to maintain a motivated mindset when at work.

This can be a rather tall order since change, by nature, can be discouraging. Some of your team members might even feel frustrated by the lack of consistency when it comes to the overall plan.

This is where you as a manager would play a crucial role in as you can rally your troops to do what they do best but also diplomatically tell them to make some course corrections. The more efficient you are in helping your team stay motivate but accepting of changes, the faster you can finish your projects and in good quality to boot.

6. "Face-to-face conversation is the most efficient and effective method of conveying information to and within different teams."

The stream of information within your team and outside should not only remain open. It should also be simple. The line of communication in agile project management must be so straight that there is only one source, one messenger at a time, and receivers at every team and level.

With this, you can make sure that information you receive from the higher-ups and clients are the most accurate so you can quickly relay the same to your team. This also works in reverse if your team wants to inform outside people of what is going in the project.

In practice, they should relay the information to their leader who is going to relay it to you and you will then report the same to your superiors. The simpler the line of communication is, fewer chances there will be of crucial information being lost in translation and never acted on.

7. "The final product is the primary measure of progress."

How could you tell if your team is making progress under the method? The answer is if the end product for each iteration works. This is why you should push your team to produce something functional at the end of each iteration for the clients and shareholders to test for themselves.

However, you have to be careful that you do not rush things through. It is often a mistake that managers make to overwork their team just to produce something decent to present in the next report. If possible, just give them a compelling reminder to get things done and tested before the iteration ends.

Also, make sure that the product gradually changes in each iteration. If it was functional in the first, then make sure it is enhanced in the next. Do this until the product is in its best possible version upon the completion of all iterations.

8. "Agile processes promote sustainable development. All stakeholders should be able to maintain a constant pace indefinitely."

The workflow of your project should not be mired by periods of inactivity. Every iteration should focus on one aspect of the project so that milestones could be met at the end of every cycle.

The momentum of your team in every project must be so strong that you do not stop building on what has been achieved so far. In other methods, there are periods during which things stop as people wait for the necessary resources. To avoid this, set up milestones and deadlines for your team that are easy to meet but produce observable results.

9. "Continuous attention to technical excellence and good design enhances agility."

This might be basic but the software you are producing should be designed with functionality in mind. Combine this with the agile project management method and your team should be able to produce something functional at the end of each cycle.

However, you must also build on the functionality. If it works in the first time, then it must work in the next instance that you would present the same product to clients and shareholders. This constant improvement on the functionality and design of the product should give the impression to outside elements that your team is working on something that is eventually going to be great upon release.

10.   "Simplicity—the art of maximizing the amount of work not done—is essential."

The core essence of the Agile Project Management method is that you don't waste time. And there is nothing more time-wasting than needless elaboration. Make sure that you get the basics of the product's design first before you complicate things with new features and functionalities.

Aside from the product, this also applies to the culture of the team as well. Every task that you assign to them must be met with the corresponding amount of effort depending on the urgency of the task. In essence, do not make the team work harder if not necessary but make sure that they greet every new task with the same amount of zeal and drive.

11. "The best architectures, requirements, and designs emerge from self-organizing teams."

In the agile method, constant supervision or (as I would like to call it) excessive hand-holding is never recommended. Your team must possess the initiative to get things done at the right time without you having to tell them constantly how to do their jobs.

The reason for this is that in-company politics and bureaucracy can get in the way of finishing things on time. If your team can solve problems without raising an alarm to the higher-ups, just let them be so that they can get the project done in the soonest time possible.

12. **"At regular intervals, the team reflects on how to become more effective, then tunes and adjusts its behavior accordingly."**

One element of the agile method is the ability to adapt to new conditions. This means that a team must regularly consider how they can improve on their work. As such, you as the manager must conduct regular meetings to discuss the team's performance in every iteration.

Where did the team excel at? Where was it lacking? Such things can be answered by looking at the end result for each cycle. Once problems are identified, all that is left to do is to address such and do better in the next cycle.

These principles are best if everybody knows about them and, to an extent, is constantly reminded about them. Post these principles in the workplace as much as you can so people can get the reminder that they need and produce the best possible results out of their work.

How is the Agile Method Done?

The Agile Project Method, regardless of what principle you will use, is always focused on dividing the entire workload into smaller sections. By doing this, a manager instantly makes their project more attainable with set milestones in each section.

In essence, a manager makes the project easier to complete by giving each section its defined set of supplementary goals and objects. With this, it is easier to identify what needs to be developed further or what must be looked back at a later phase of the development process.

After each cycle, the team will then have a meeting with you, the upper management, the shareholders, and the clients. There, progresses will be presented and the product given a demonstration (if possible). An exchange of ideas is also possible as stakeholders can critique the progress and the team can air out concerns that the upper management can address.

The biggest benefit with the agile method is that any problem that arises is addressed and corrected before things get out of hand. It also makes sure that everybody is on the same page and communications remain as transparent as possible.

Project Roles

Teams under the agile method, regardless of their chosen strategy, should always work like gears on a machine. Everyone should know the role they play in the project and what they can contribute to its success.

As such, it is important that managers outline each key role that team members and outside persons can play in the development process. Regardless of how you name the roles for your team, they should at least follow the sequence like the one below.

A. The Product Owner

This is the person who is in charge with communicating information between the clients, the stakeholders, and the team developing the product. To be a product owner, a person must be knowledgeable of the product as well as the vision and needs of the clients.

Also, they are required to work with the development team on a daily basis so that they are on track with the time period for each iteration. If it is not a dead giveaway already, this role will be assigned to managers or, to put it more bluntly, you.

B. The Development Team

This is the group assigned for creating the product from the ground up. Since the development process is a long and arduous one that takes up multiple phases and requires different sub-processes, it is advisable that you divide the team even further into sub groups.

For instance, one team can serve as the main designing group, the others will work on the programming, the others will work as bug and glitch fixers, and the others can fulfill other supplementary roles such as designers, code engineers, and testers.

Regardless of how you divide the teams, it is necessary that you make sure that everyone is hands-on in the project. This prevents anyone from excusing themselves if things don't go as planned or, alternatively, make sure everyone is able to celebrate on every success achieved.

C. The Scrum Master

Also known as the Project Facilitator, the Scrum Master plays a huge role in supporting the development team. In essence, they serve as a liaison between the team and the company's administration, eliminating potential roadblocks in the communication system so that information and other resources flow freely in between groups.

To be a Scrum master, one must have a strong understanding of the concept of servant leadership. They are the ones that work closely with the development team and will report to outside groups as to what the team has achieved so far.

D. Stakeholders and Upper Management

Although not directly involved in the development process, these individuals can still provide valuable input for the team to consider. They might have a perspective on the product that the team did not look into but would ultimately help in improving it.

As such, the goal in working with these people is to maintain a communication that is honest, transparent, and open. Development teams should not feel intimidated by the higher-ups in relaying their concerns and the higher-ups, in turn, would not feel left out of the development process.

This is why regular meetings are necessary in making sure everyone within the team and outside knows what the other is doing. This also helps in addressing issues between groups which should help in speeding up the development process.

E. The Mentor

The Mentor is simply someone who already has an experience in implementing the agile method in previous projects. It is their role to provide tips when needed and guide everybody else through the implementation phase.

Although mentors are not directly involved in the development of the software, they are still invaluable as their tips in applying the principles would ultimately affect the quality of the end product. Due to nature of the Mentor's role, you can have someone from outside the team and even outside the company fill in this position. A consultant is most recommended for the role although there is no stopping you from seeking advice from other executives and managers.

Inherent Flaws

With all of these said and done, is the Agile Project Management method a perfect strategy? Sadly, the answer is No. It is not for every project or for every management style out there as it possesses two inherent flaws.

1. It is Easy to Lose Track

By breaking down a project into several smaller sections, you actually run the risk of losing sight of the overall goal. Instead of one goal that everybody must do their best in order to meet, you have now multiple vital goals that must be met but may not automatically contribute to the larger goal.

As such, due to this flaw, it is rather important that you get everyone involved during meetings. Stakeholders should be able to present their vision, upper management provide the guidance, and the development teams given the chance to air out their concerns.

The point here is that everyone should be able to provide a perspective to the project that is focused on meeting the larger goals. If at least one person knows that the project can stray off the path or has strayed off, then the chances of a major course correction later on may be minimized.

This is why it is also necessary that you make it a habit to regularly call for meetings. Perhaps everyone can get so engrossed in their short-term goals that they forget that they are supposed to align their work to ultimately contribute to the larger project goals. Through regular meetings, everyone can get in touch with everybody and make sure everyone is working to meet common goals.

2. **It is Heavily Dependent on Quick Decision Making**

Due to the adaptive nature of the method, Agile Project Management requires leaders that are quick to think of their feet. This means that you should be able to improve if conditions change in one way or another during the implementation without losing momentum for the team.

The agile method requires you to make decisions that would greatly affect the project later on and you have to make that decision ASAP. If you are the one that tends to linger on the decision making process, then perhaps the Agile Method is a bit too fast for you.

However, you can counteract this by decentralizing the decision making process and sharing it with your team. Perhaps they can come up with a beneficial decision at a rate faster than you can. In addition, this helps in bolstering their trust with the management and ownership with the project. They more they feel that they have a say in the decision-making process, the more motivated they will be in making the agile method sustainable.

Chapter II: The Agile Process

There are two things that should be achieved with the agile project management methodology: shorter production cycles (without sacrificing quality, of course) and more frequent product releases. By having shorter development iterations, a team should be able to react to changes from outside sources more effectively.

As was stated before, there is more than one way to do the Agile method. Scrum and Kanban, for example, feature fairly different work structures from the others. However, each agile methodology follows the basic process which is as follows:

1. Project Planning

Like with any method, you should make the team understand the end goal of the project before starting it. Here, you will explain to them the potential value that succeeding in the project will bring for the team and the company and how it should be achieved.

You may set up a scope for the project here but do not make it unchangeable. The whole premise of the agile method is to adapt to changes that may happen in the middle of the development process. As such, you should avoid getting your team stuck on achieving goals through a static work frame.

2. Creating the Product Roadmap

A roadmap maybe a buzzword for tech guys right now but it is a rather simple yet vital concept to software development. To put it simply, it is a breakdown of what features will make up the final product.

What makes it crucial to the development process as the roadmap tells your team what to focus on in each phase. Also, at this point, you will set up the product backlog which will list all the features and deliverables that will be included in the final product. When you plan for iterations in the future, your team can refer to this backlog to identify what to focus on.

3. Planning Releases

In traditional project management methodologies, there is only one implementation date that comes after the entire project has been developed. However, in the agile method, your project will have a shorter development cycle with features released at their ends.

Before you start the project, you should make a high-level plan for feature releases. And when beginning a new cycle, you shall revisit and re-assess the release plan for those new features.

A high-level plan is basically one that provides a manager's view of the project in its entirety. It's not just a detailed plan where all the tasks required for project completion are indicated. A high level plan includes information on what needs to be done, who is supposed to do the task that needs to be done, how it is done, and when things are expected to be done. This plan is developed with the goal of making sure that progress can be tracked over time.

4. Planning Cycles

Before starting each cycle or iteration, the shareholders need to plan with your team on what shall be accomplished in each segment. Of course, this will also include how such things shall be achieved and how much of a task load should each member of the development carry.

At this point of the process, it is important that you make sure that the load is shared evenly amongst members. This way, they can efficiently accomplish each of their assigned tasks per iteration.

Also, you will need to document your workflow visually. This is to make the task assignment process as transparent as possible to your team and to prevent bottlenecking from occurring when implementing the schedule.

5. Regular (Ideally Daily) Meetings and Correspondence

In order to make your teams accomplish their tasks more efficiently in each cycle, or assess what needs to be improved on, you have to make a habit out of holding short meetings every day. During these meetings, every member will be given the chance to talk briefly as to what they have accomplished for that day and will they be working on in the next.

But it is important that you **keep this meetings short**. Spend no more than 15 minutes in talking with your team as these meetings are not meant for extensive problem solving or chances to talk about things that everybody else has already settled or know of. In fact, you can even do these meetings standing up.

6. Cycle Reviews and Retrospectives

At the end of each iteration, the team will hold two major meetings. In the first major meeting, you will do a cycle review with the client and the shareholders to present to them what has been achieved. And not only are you going to present a sustainable feature, you are going to show to these people a working product.

This is a rather important meeting as it bolsters the communication lines between your team, the shareholders, and the clients as well as allowing them to give an input which could help in the next iterations.

The second major meeting is the Cycle Retrospective. Here, you and the shareholders will discuss the things that went well during that cycle, what didn't, and whether the work load may have been too heavy or too small for the team. Of course, this meeting will also focus on identifying recurring problems that should be dealt with in the next few iterations, if any.

If you and your team is relatively new to the whole agile project management concept, it is important that you do not skip on these meetings. These meeting would help you determine the task load that your team can handle in each iteration as well as the most effective length for each.

What is the Agile Mindset?

In order to properly implement this methodology, it is important that you and your team have to change your mindset. To do this, you must adopt some values that are necessary for the success of the methodology:

- **Client Satisfaction is at the Top**

The needs of the client must be put first. As such, you must make it a goal to regularly produce content that is functional and of good quality in a timely manner.

When you present progress to a client, they must be able to test it for themselves and come to the conclusion that it is good. They must also be given the chance to air out their concerns and input for the project while also being assured that their concerns are duly noted and will be applied to the best of your abilities.

- **Adaptiveness and Improvisation**

Changes can happen at any time during the process. Even last-minute changes can occur which would ultimately affect the quality of the product. Despite this, you and your team must be accepting of change in any form it takes and adjust your efforts to meet the new goals and conditions.

For leaders, this comes with the extra requirements of being fast enough to act on sudden changes and make important decisions as quickly as possible. The less they mull over what to do next, the more responsive the team will be in addressing sudden shifts in project conditions and goals.

- **Fast Development Cycle**

The ultimate goal of the agile method is to optimize your time. In essence, you and your team should make it a point not to waste time by focusing on the most important goals for each iteration.

Of course, this should mean that each stage of iteration of the development process should be as short as possible. However, you must be always ready to show results and the progress you have made when clients, shareholders, and management would demand of them in the end of each iteration.

If you have noticed, these three qualities basically summarize the Agile Project Management methodology. They are not exactly written in stone but, as the method itself states, this is the best strategy that you can use to adapt to changes instantly without losing sight of the overall goal.

Also, if certain aspects of your methodology do not work out as planned, you can always make improvements until you see the desired results.

All in all, with the methodology, you should produce three things: a good product, a timely delivery of the same, and a really satisfied client.

Chapter III: Skills, Software, and Organizational Hurdles

A key component in implementing the agile methodology in your project is learning how you can do it. After all, a method is just as good as the tools and implements it offers at your disposal.

Fortunately for you, the agile method is not just about a fancy system of getting things done fast. In fact, you are all the better for the system if you identify what you can do and what you can use to implement the method in your own team.

What are the Key Agile Skills?

Aside from the agile methodology being dependent on the tools that you use, it is also dependent on the people implementing it. Project managers like you should possess certain qualities to make the method effective and sustainable.

A. Ability to Prioritize

At a glance, every task that could be involved in a project seems to be essential. Although this might be true, a project manager knows how tasks are to cut out so that everybody could focus on what is important now.

The project under the methodology, after all, is going to be divided into various iterations. This means that some tasks are not yet important until their corresponding phase arises or, due to the segmentation of the work, are deemed redundant. Your ability to identify what work matters and what is unnecessary will then be crucial for this method.

B. Calm Under Pressure

A project manager using the agile method should have the ability to keep calm under pressure and make crucial decisions even under tremendous stress.

You have to remember that changes are meant to be uncomfortable. Once everybody has settled into a pace or have mentally prepared themselves to do one thing, the last thing that they want to hear is that the rules have changed.

As a project manager, you should be able to handle changes, even last-minute ones, and adjust the work of your team accordingly. In this aspect, you might even have to develop your diplomacy skills to deal with the eventual dissent coming from your team.

C. Coaching Skills

One of the key principles of the agile method is to have a motivated team. The problem with motivation is that it does not exactly last long on its own. You as a leader should be able to keep your team motivated enough to finish each iteration of the development process. You should give them the assurance that everything is still according to plan and, if they are not, you are there to help them transition to the new status quo.

And aside from motivating your team, you should also be able to enhance their skills and guide them through their work without heavy hand-holding. In essence, your leadership should make sure that your team's skillsets and abilities are not the same at the end of an iteration. The more dynamic and expansive the team's combined skillsets are, the more capable it will be in handling challenges that might pop up in the process.

D. Organizational Skills

As a leader, it is your goal to make sure that everyone is doing their share of the entire workload. Aside from prioritizing what needs to be done, you need to be able to remind everyone of deadlines for each iteration.

A major flaw with the agile method, after all, is that it is easy to lose track of the overall goal especially if the iterations are long and numerous. It is your role, then, as a leader to remind everyone that everything that they do must not only contribute to the success of that iteration but to the overall project.

E. Quick Thinking

The ability to make important decisions is a major highlight in the agile method. Project managers then should be able to make rapid changes when the need arise without losing the momentum they have already built for the team.

This means that you should be able to drop strategies at a moment's notice no matter how strongly you feel for that tactic. You must understand that changes are there for a reason and you have to respond by making the necessary adjustments to your schedule. And keep in mind that some decisions have some time limit to them. If you take too long in mulling over your thoughts, you might lose valuable opportunities which results in some periods of inactivity for the rest of the team.

F. Adaptability

Accepting change should start from the leadership. As such, you should be the first to welcome the prospect of changing conditions in the development process.

When you are the first to adapt, you are actually helping the team adapt to the changes as well. This should reduce confusion in the implementation process while also preventing a further breakdown of communications.

But being adaptable is not going to help you if you relay the need for change as quickly as possible. You have to make your team understand why there is a need for changes and demonstrate to them that such changes do not negatively affect the entire iteration but, instead, would enhance the quality of their work.

Management Software

Anyone who wishes to use the Agile Method should also find the corresponding software for it. These programs come with features and systems that make implementation of the agile process possible and, in some cases, easier. Here are some of the Agile-optimized software that you could use for your project.

1. **Planbox**

One of the most important parts of the agile method cycle is what are called burndown charts (more on this later on). Planbox is a program that can track down these charts so everybody in the team has an accurate idea as to how far (or near) the team is in achieving a certain goal.

The program also integrates features like customer feedback, bug reports, fixes, and other user-generated content that can help you improve on your end product. It also comes with evaluation tools that should make your periodical reviews and retrospective more comprehensive.

Lastly, the program comes with an advanced reporting system that allows you to easily review the status of problem areas in each iteration. And the best part is that Planbox is absolutely free in the market right now.

2. **LeanKit**

If you are attempting to implement the Kanban variant of the agile method, then this program is the most suitable for you. One of the major features of this program is a live reporting feature where users can post work items and have the same addressed in real time.

This is ideal if your team is not physically together in one workplace. Perhaps you have remote teams working in other areas which makes daily meetings near impossible. But with LeanKit, in-team correspondence is easier which should make sure that everyone involved in the project is on the same page.

Aside from a live posting and reporting system, LeanKit is also optimized for cross-team platforms and is great for keeping track of dependencies. The program can also be made compatible for Scrum work frames.

The entire program can cost you in between $20.00 and $30.00 per month.

3. **Jira**

Built from the ground up for the Agile methodology, Jira is often considered to be one of the more dependable project management operating systems out there. It has a rather robust set of features that could help you track, monitor, and even communicate with the rest of your teams through each iteration of the process.

The only major flaw with Jira is that it can be intimidating for newcomers to the agile methodology. It can be complex to use at times and the act of merely setting it up for your workplace will require the help of an experienced developer.

Aside from this, Jira can be expensive. The solutions it offers and the services offered by the team can set up any company by at least thousands of dollars every year. If you are part of a small tech startup, then Jira might not be the best solution for you. Just yet.

Despite these flaws, Jira is rather excellent when it comes to tracking and addressing bugs, and inter-team correspondence. It also has various custom fields that allow you to make the program fit the specifications of your current projects.

4. GIthub Project Management

This program's main selling point is that it is the largest hosted GIt-based server in the market right now. So, you may ask, what does that do for your agile project management method? The answer is that the server allows all your developers to store all code done in projects that have been already finished.

This means that you don't have to rework code you've already done for new projects which can cut the development time by a considerable degree. And the best part is that it can record edits done in real time which means that work can continue where it was left in case of emergencies.

One of the great features of the GIthub program is that it can integrate many other tools for different people involved in the project. There is a panel dedicated to developers, another for product owners, another for project managers, and so on and so forth. Your development team can even set up a private communication channel or a public one dedicated to improving code.

The end result is that your team will always have access to the best versions of codes that they have already worked with which should keep work momentum at a high. Pricing for this management program starts free with a $21.00 per user monthly subscription fee if you want access to more features.

5. Clickup

If you have been looking for the most ideal agile management program, then Clickup might be the answer for you. A core feature within Clickup is a feature-driven management program that allows teams to get on top of what needs to be done per iteration while making sure that their efforts contribute to the larger end goal.

Clickup gives users the ability to see an overview of tasks that were completed, yet to be completed, works in progress, and dependencies. With this, you can at the very least prevent tasks from bottlenecking your entire team.

Some of the other features provided by the program include the ability to create epics and set up story points, analyze iteration progress in real time, give users access to custom templates and statuses for process management, time tracking, and other tools that could help in daily meetings.

The best part with Clickup is that it has a Free Forever plan. What this means is that you can get a hold of a copy of the system for absolutely free. However, for access to even more comprehensive features as well as maintenance costs, the program will ask for a $9.00 per month subscription fee for every person that will use the program.

Identifying Organizational Problems

In order for the agile method to work, the entire team must adhere to its principles. This is why the biggest challenge that you would face in implementing the system in your organization is the organization itself. As a matter of fact, there are a number of inherent problems that could impede you from fully enjoying from the agile method if not properly addressed.

A. The Culture

Not every company and team culture out there supports or is even compatible with the agile method. And even if your team is immediately on board to the process, there is the chance that the higher-ups are not so welcoming of it.

This is where a lot of diplomacy should come into play as you have to convince the people that you directly report to that there are benefits to be had from the agile system in order to support it. You have to see things from their perspective in order to do this.

Perhaps the management feels that they are giving away too much independence to your development team and are afraid that this would disrupt internal communications. Or perhaps they have mere misconceptions about the methodology.

Whatever the case, you can actually do a lot on your part to dispel their fears about the system so they would support your project across the different iterations.

B. Unclear Understanding of The System's Impact

In order to get the best results from the agile method, it is not enough that you just implement the systems and tools at your disposal. More often than not, blindly following the principles without reconciling it with the company's goals can result in you wasting time, effort, and money.

Aligning the system with the company's goals and values will still matter as this helps the rest of the company understand why you have to do your project in different iterations. If your team and the rest of the company understands how the Agile method can positively affect the entire organization, you can be certain that the system becomes sustainable in the long run.

C. A Tendency to Rush

One fatal flaw of the agile method is that it taps into man's annoying tendency to rush things through. In the hopes of getting things done fast and in massive quantities, the brain tends to overlook key details.

This results in teams getting focused on getting things done ASAP while missing the most simple and manageable aspects of the development process. This can lead to serious repercussions later on as problems set up in previous iterations can pop up in later ones.

As such, project managers must find a way to keep everyone focus while maintaining the pace of work. In essence, you serve as the first and last line of defense against your team becoming reckless in the development process.

D. Limited Resources

Although agile is quickly becoming popular across the market now, it also means that resources for project managers are still limited now. It can be rather hard to find good talent that can help you implement the method in your team.

However, that does not mean that implementing the system on your own is not entirely impossible. You can start without any mentor for your team and then just look for one once everything has been put in place. And even if you do not find consultants and mentors in your area, you can still make your team generate the best possible results. All that is needed is for you to get the basics of the methodology right.

Chapter IV: The Agile Software Development Process

There is actually no single methodology out there that can work for every project. However, there is no doubt that many development teams and companies are slowly doing away with the more predictive and restrictive methodologies like Waterfall and embracing something more adaptive like Agile.

In fact, you might be surprised that methodologies like Agile were born primarily out of a frustration on how things were used to be done back then. By giving the team much more control over how things are done and for how long, the theory is that the end product will be a far more comprehensive software while still staying true to the client's original vision.

With that, you can easily understand that the Agile process will follow a considerably different development path than conventional and traditional methodologies.

How Development was Done Before

So what was the development process in methodologies like, say, Waterfall? What would be discussed in the next few paragraphs might be elementary to long-time developers. However, it is still necessary that we make a distinction over predictive methodologies over adaptive ones.

The conventional software development process will involve six phases which are as follows:

1. Planning

Obviously, every development process starts with you laying down the specifications of the project. Here, the flow of work will be identified and segmented into smaller and more manageable parts.

The functionalities of each segment and element will also be identified as well as the schedule for each phase of the project. Lastly, workload will be identified here as well as the roles that each member of the development team would perform.

2. Analysis

This part will involve the identifying of goals as well as setting the scope for the entire project. This is a far more detailed process than the planning phase as each stage of the project will be scrutinized.

A major focus on this phase is identifying the allocation of resources for each part of the project. What is the budget for each phase? What are the tools and programs needed? Is there a need to outsource work or hire entirely new people for the job (even temporarily)? These questions need to be sufficiently answered at this part of the process.

Of course, this process will also involve identifying potential issues that might pop up in the middle of the project. In turn, this allows managers to come up with solutions to prevent such from happening.

3. Design

Once planning and analysis have been completed, the team can move on to designing the product. This is a purely conceptual phase as you and your team would visualize what the project looks like by setting up its framework.

Here, the standards for each phase of the project will be established. As such, the team knows what they have to do in order to produce the desired software while also eliminating flaws.

4. Development and Implementation

This is the phase where the product is actually being built. Depending on the chosen methodology, this phase will involve multiple processes which include code writing and the implementation of programming tools and languages.

Once the software is developed, the implementation process kicks in where it goes through various studies and experimentations to see if it, at the very least, functions without crashing.

5. Testing

Once the basic structure of the software is finished, it will then go through a series of tests. Here, the goal is to identify bugs and glitches embedded into the code through the development process and then to fix them.

Like the development process, this is a rather extensive phase as the program has to be scrutinized in all of its aspects and functions to see if it is fit for mass production and distribution.

The most important aspect to be tackled here is determining whether or not the product meets the criteria set in the initial phases of the project. In some cases, the overall layout of your program would be changed in order to address inherent flaws.

6. Maintenance

Prior to mass production, the team should then systematically scour the code for any bugs or glitches that were not identified and addressed in the previous phases.

This part also includes updates that would be introduced way after the product has been released. Patches to the code to address issues or enhance the functionality of the base product.

Flaws in the Conventional Method

Almost all predictive methodologies follow the sequence as laid out above. However, some methods like Waterfall would like to add a few more steps in between such as Research and Feedback.

Whatever the case, predictive methodologies tend to follow a strict sequence in order to create a product that works. However, that does not mean that it is applicable in all cases.

As a matter of fact, there are flaws inherent to these methodologies which may make them inapplicable to your project or, better yet, inferior to other more adaptive methodologies.

1. Restrictive Nature

At a glance, predictive methodologies are so rigid that you have no other option but to follow the plan as was established in the earlier phases. Of course, this means that you are not exactly responsive to changes as they occur in the middle of the project.

In the end, you will produce something that might meet the criteria of the project but does not take into consideration developments that newly occurred. In short, the product might be good if made in restrictive methods but it could have been better.

2. Late Testing

These methods often put the testing process late in the project. This means that the identifying and fixing of bugs is not as comprehensive as you would like them to be. After all, if everything has a set deadline and follows set protocols, you are merely finding and fixing surface-level problems; not inherent, program-breaking ones.

This is where adaptive methods are superior as the testing phase is evenly spread out across all iterations. Simply put, you are correcting your mistakes as you are building the base product.

3. Client Feedback Not Impactful

In most restrictive methodologies, client feedback is often ignored. And if they do acknowledge client feedback, these do not have much of an impact in the development process.

For instance, a client might want to add something to the product during the Feedback and Testing portion. Depending on how big that change is, it may be ultimately ignored so as not to change the structure of the product or haphazardly applied that it ultimately ruins the quality of the software.

4. High Risk

Since these methodologies are so rigid in their application, you run the risk of not addressing major problems in the coding or add enhancing features until it is too late.

Also, there is a chance that you would have to deal with constant crunch periods as deadlines for each phase are tightly set one after another. As a result, the workload of your team increases along with the pace of work. As such, you run the risk of bottlenecking your project to the point that that end product is haphazardly completed.

The Agile Process Cycle

The process of implementing the agile method differs from one strategy to another. However, they all follow roughly the same sequence, which is:

1. **Conceptualization** – Here, the product is being visualized and designed. The framework for the project will be set up and segmented which helps in prioritizing what needs to be done. Issues like the allocation of resources and the distribution of workload will also be tackled here.

2. **Inception** – Once the project has been conceptualized, the manager must then focus on building the team (if it does not exist yet, of course). Here, the roles of each team member will be identified while the initial workloads and requirements will be designated to them.

3. **Iteration and Construction** – The most extensive part of the project, this process involves the teams going through each "sprint" or iteration as they build the product. The goal here is to present something that meets the criteria established in each iteration to upper management, shareholders, and the client.

   Since the agile method is iterative by nature, it is necessary that the team goes through each of the set iterations and finish them according to the set time. At the same time, the product that they are building on must grow and develop to meet new standards and other last-minute changes per cycle.

4. **Release** – Once the base product is ready, it will undergo further Quality Assurance checks. This is where major bugs are fixed while the overall layout and user experience of the product will be revamped or enhanced.

   This process will also internal and external testing, documentation of what has been fixed, and the final release of the iteration into mass production.

5. **Production** – At this phase, the developers should provide ongoing support for the software. This includes further testing and maintenance as well as the introduction of patches to the code, if need be.

   This should serve as an extra "cycle" to the process where the product is enhanced even if it has already passed the mass distribution phase. Your team can even build on the product's base features by adding more while keeping the code as functional as possible.

6. **Retirement** – Eventually, that product will reach the end of its lifespan, which lasts a year or a few after release. At this phase, the team should initiate some end of product life activities like notifying users of what is to come next and preparing them to migrate to the new product.

The sequence above presents the entire life cycle of products made using the agile model. In fact, there can be more than one agile-centric projects occurring in the same company or multiple iterations being logged in on different product lines. Better yet, the model allows a company to cater to different customers, internal or external, with their own range of needs that need to be met.

The Iteration Workflow

The agile process is dominating by cycles and iterations. Each segment of the project that is completed will actually build on the end product. In essence, with the agile method, you not only have a functional program in each iteration but also supporting features, documentation, and a code that can be used for future projects.

Iterations usually last between 2 weeks and a full month with a fixed period for completion. Since it is time-bound, the process is meant to be methodical and the scope is limited to what must be done in each iteration.

It is not uncommon for a project to have 3 to 10 iterations, depending on its size and type. Each iteration will also follow its own workflow, which can be visualized as follows:

A. **Requirements** – Here, the specifications of the iteration will be set. These must be based on the backlog for the product, the backlog for each cycle, and the feedback of customers and shareholders, if any.

B. **Development** – At this phase, the team develops or builds upon the software based on the goals set for that segment.

C. **Testing** – This phase will include Quality Assurance tests, internal and external training, and documentation of what has been improved or developed.

D. **Delivery** – Once the product is functional, it will then be integrated to make it cohesive. After this, the iteration of the product will then be sent for mass production.

E. **Feedback** – Once it is in the market, the development team will then monitor how the software is being received by the end users. Are there major flaws that need addressing? What bugs did the team miss but the customers noticed? Is there are a way to improve on the user experience? These questions can be answered at this point of the cycle.

Once the feedback phase is completed, the cycle begins anew with the team conceptualizing on what needs to be done next for the new iteration. The beauty of the method is that you can come up with a better product or an entirely new offshoot in a short period of time.

What are Product Backlogs?

The most basic definition of product backlogs is that they are a list of features that can be added to an existing software created in a previous iteration. And aside from new features, backlogs can include infrastructure changes, bug fixes, and other activities that is necessary to deliver a specific outcome in a current iteration.

In other words, a product backlog answers this question:

"What can we do to make this software Better?"

Aside from the project manager, the product backlog functions as an authoritative source of what needs to be done per iteration. This means that if a task, a feature, or a fix is not on the backlog, then the development team should not even think about investing an iota of effort in performing such a task.

However, the presence of a task on a backlog does not give the assurance that the same can be delivered exactly at the end of that iteration. It only presents the team with an option on how to deliver something that was already promised at the start of the project. It is not a mandatory task that you and your team should commit to.

For example, you and your team might be working on a videogame like, say, a massive multiplayer online role-playing game (or an MMORPG for the sake of convenience). Perhaps your product backlog would include the following:

- Increase item and weapon drops

- Expand on existing world maps

- Add new maps

- Balance skills and classes players discovered to be over-powered

- Fix game-crashing bug on Zones X3 and F10

- Improve chat-based communications

- Introduce Player vs. Player mode

Now, at a glance, you can determine for yourself which of the items must be added ASAP and what could be put off for the next few iterations. The point is that the backlog gives your team an idea as to what should be improved in the next iterations so the overall product is better.

The best part about product backlogs is that you can add on them the more the product is expanded on. The addition of new features to a software gives rise to new opportunities and problems.

However, do rein in your team a bit when it comes to finishing the backlog. There is no rule that your team should clear off that backlog in each iteration. In fact, some of the items in that backlog can be introduced as entirely new features in the next project, depending on the situation.

Burndowns

Arguably, the thing that you have to deal with the most in any project is time. To be specific, you have to make sure that the progress your team is making is sufficient enough to cover the entire time period for that iteration.

And there is this fact that people outside of the development team that want you to finish your tasks *yesterday*. Their intention, after all, is always this: get things done and fast.

As such, it is the job of project managers to understand that time is an element that they must proficiently control in every project that they take. The better data they have when it comes to time in relation to the work that needs to be done, the better a manager can make sure that their team sticks to the approved schedule.

This is where a burndown chart comes into play as it tells how much needs to be done and how much of time has been consumed by the team so far. A burndown chart is simply a graphical representation of how quickly your team is working through a customer's project.

How each agile tool comes up with a burndown chart varies but it often draws information from "stories", detailed descriptions of features of a program as provided by an end-user or the project manager.

So, how do You Read It?

Burndown charts are actually rather simple graphs. The amount of work remaining is always shown on a vertical axis while the time that has elapsed since the start and the projected end of an iteration is drawn horizontally.

The X-axis, the one that represents the timeline is always at a straight line since the period is set. However, the y-axis representing the work that has been done or needs to be completed might fluctuate from day to day. As such, you only need to read the graph from left to right.

But, of course, the more pressing question that you might have with the chart is "what is the ideal burndown trend?" To answer that question, you have to look for certain elements in your reading.

- **Ideal Work Remaining** – The ideal trend for this part should be a straight line connecting from the starting point to the current one. This is a telltale sign that each task has been sufficiently performed and there are no goals that have been untouched as of that iteration.

  Also, at the end point, the y-axis line should cross with the x-axis. This indicates that no work is left undone.

- **Actual Work Remaining** – But, of course, it is not exactly easy to pull off a flat line when it comes to graphs. Changes in your work plan can cause some shifts in that graph, resulting in spikes of activity in every point of the chart.

  So how are you going to make this work? The best actual trend in this situation is for the actual work line to never go above the ideal work line. If the actual work line does go above the ideal, it is an indication that more work is left undone than originally planned. To put it simply, your team is way behind schedule.

But if the actual work line is below the ideal, then it tells you that your team is actually finishing their tasks on time or, better yet, you are completing the iteration way ahead of the schedule.

To Summarize

So far, we have been discussing how the agile methodology is different from other development methods in relation to how it works and what you need in order to pull it off properly. The point is that you can yield considerable results in your team using this method provided that you get the basics of it right and be constantly proactive when it comes to sudden changes in the project's plan every iteration.

However, there is more than one way to implement the methodology on your project. For the next few chapters, we shall go about how the Agile Method can be carried out by your team through its different frameworks.

Chapter V: The Basics of Scrum

It is important that we talk about the framework that is closely related to the Agile Project Management Method: *Scrum*.

What is Scrum exactly and how do you implement it in your projects? If you have been in the development business for quite a while, you might have heard of this term. You might even have heard it used interchangeably with Agile.

But make no mistake, Agile and Scrum are two different things altogether. Agile is the methodology. Scrum, on the other hand, is the framework wherein that methodology can be implemented.

What Makes Scrum Different?

As its own standalone agile framework, there are a lot of things that make Scrum rather distinct from its siblings.

For starters, time in Scrum is divided into periods called "sprints". They last in between 2 to 4 weeks and, at the end of each sprint, a demonstration of the product as it has been built or improved on will be provided to the client, the upper management, and the shareholders.

At a glance, Scrum is the methodology that is the most at home in teams that already adopt a mindset focused on product development. However, that is not to say that it can't be made to be compatible with other teams, especially those that are relatively new to the entire agile process.

This is not the only way that Scrum is fundamentally different. Here, there are no projects with definite start and finish dates, giving the development full rein as to when they would present a product at the end of the iteration.

Another difference is the hierarchy of management. In Scrum, there is no singular project manager. In fact, there is no project manager necessary to tell people what to do, when to do it, and when it must be submitted.

Instead, in Scrum, the team decides when to deliver improvements to a product over a period with which they are most comfortable. As such, Scrum has the most decentralized decision-making body amongst all project management methodologies right now, even among Agile-based variants.

Lastly, Scrum is not that particular with upfront planning. In this framework, teams can adjust their work according the feedback of clients and shareholders while keeping the pace that they have set for that sprint.

The Principles of Scrum

As with other project management methodologies, Scrum's framework is based on several foundational concepts. If you want to succeed in implementing this framework, then you should adhere to the following principles.

A. **Self-Organization** – The team should never think that they are doing this project because someone is telling them so. To come up with a product that they can identify with, they should have some sense of autonomy over how to do things and what to include.

To put it in other words, a project tends to be more successful if the people making it identify themselves with it more. This includes being free to determine who does what and when things should be delivered.

B. **Delivering Value** – Teams should be focused on delivering value for each iteration. So what does value look like under the Scrum framework? The most basic answer to that is an improved product.

Simply put, the product should have expanded and grown by leaps and bounds for every iteration it goes through. If it was mediocre and basic in the first iteration, then it should be better and expansive in the next, and more comprehensive in the succeeding sprints.

C. **Collaboration** – Cross functionality is a major concern that needs to be addressed under this framework. Essentially, they should be able to assist their own team members in identifying problems and then finding solutions around them.

It is important that each team member knows what they can contribute to the entire effort and what role they must play in the overall project. Also, they must be able to motivate others in completing tasks on time or, better yet, way ahead of the schedule.

D. **Time** – Sprints are meant to be short bursts of activity that allow teams to produce something within the time period. As such, the leader must find a balance in keeping the team focused on getting the job done on time without pressuring them to meet a deadline.

The point here is that the team should be fast and efficient in their work but without adopting a deadline-focused mindset in the project.

E. **Iteration and Improvement** – The team must make it a point to improve on the product in every iteration. When they ship it, they have to wait on the feedback. And, depending on the feedback they received, they will plan their next sprint so as to enhance the product even further. Rinse and repeat.

Why Should You Use It?

What is the point of using this framework, if there is any? The truth is that the Scrum does offer some benefits for those that implement it. They are the following:

Better Team Morale – Ownership over a project is what separates a Scrum team from other development teams. Since they have a say in how things are done, then they have more a personal stake in the project's success.

Thus, a scrum developer go out of their way to contribute to the entire effort to the best of their abilities. To put it simply, if they have a say in what the team's success should look like, they are more empowered. And an empowered team tends to bring in more than 100% of their effort every day.

Fewer Risks – Conventional project management will involve a lot of heavy-handed planning at the start of the project. This is basically the time when everybody else knows the least of what they are going to build.

As such, planning in this stage is rather risky as teams have to figure out what the end goal is. And then there is the fact that changes in technology can happen mid-process which increases the chances of teams having to do the project all over again.

In Scrum, however, the team can interact with customers and shareholders more efficiently at every stage of the development process, especially the earlier ones. As a direct result, the chances of the product being a poor fit for the market where it is to be distribute and it being negatively affected by sudden shifts in technology are at least minimized.

A Better Product – A key feature in Scrum is the ability to ship out a working product in a short period of time. By shortening product cycles, the team can get hold of customer feedback at a faster pace. In fact, you can get the input that you need as soon as they are created in real time.

Thus, you have a system that allows you to improve on what has been shipped on a constant basis. This way, your team creates an ultimate expression of the client's vision faster and more efficient than in any other development frameworks.

3-4-5

All these talks of Scrum can look complicated, but it is actually rather simple to follow. In fact, you can break the framework even further into a set of 3 roles, 4 "artifacts", and 5 events.

All in all, these elements form a structure that is responsive to feedback and is more than able to go to toe with an increasingly unpredictable trend in development in recent years. It sounds simple, right? And it can be made even simpler.

1. 3 Roles

The Scrum Framework only utilizes 3 roles for the entire project which are as follows:

A. The Scrum Master – The scrum framework might do away with the project leader or manager but it does need a coach. This is where the scrum master comes into play as they facilitate the implementation of the process.

The role of the scrum master is rather straightforward. They are primarily there to remove potential impediments in the flow of information and resources and make sure that everyone is working according to the pace they have agreed to at the start of the project. They are not there to tell everybody what to do but to make sure that they are doing what they have agreed to perform.

Another role that the scrum master performs is ensuring that the work of the team remains uninterrupted. This means that they also act as liaison for the team with upper management, shareholders, and stakeholders while also acting as a "lightning rod" in case disputes arise. By dealing with outside interruptions, the scrum master makes sure that the team can focus on delivering on their promises in every iteration.

B. The Product Owner – This person serves as the proxy of the client to the team. He is the one primarily responsible for conveying the vision of the client to the team to guide them on what to do for each iteration.

AS such, the product owner sets the standards for the project by prioritizing the product backlog (one of the artifacts of the Scrum method), preparing the criteria for acceptance, and approving of items at the end-of-cycle review.

The product owner is not someone that needs to be tech-savvy in order to be effective in this role. However, they do need to have a good grasp of what customers perceive to be acceptable in a product. They also should have an understanding of the competition, trends in the market, and other outside elements that could affect the overall reception of the product.

In essence, the product owner is there to remind everyone involve that the vision must be upheld first and foremost. This should guide the developers in determining how to adapt to sudden changes in the market and what must be done in the next few iterations.

C. The Scrum Team – The team is the one primarily responsible for, well, developing the product through every iteration it goes through. For software projects, a team would usually include engineers, architects, programmers, quality assurance experts, testers, and programmers.

In each sprint, the scrum team is responsible for identifying the kind of goals they must accomplish from the artifacts and choose the method of which they are to meet the goals. They also have full autonomy over how things are done in each cycle but would still have to rely on the guidance of the scrum master and product owner.

2. 4 Artifacts

The Scrum framework is dependent on several artifacts that dictates the specifications of the project. Combined, these artifacts tell the project team what needs to be done, where it goes, who handles on the team, and when.

A. **The Product Backlog** – This is a list of prioritized deliverables that should be implemented as part of the project or a specific iteration. This artifact is important for decision-making sessions as they help the team understand what needs to be done or what might become important in the future.

In other words, the product backlog helps in ensuring the team works on the most critical features of the product. This includes fixing bugs, adding new features, and other work that is important to the overall quality of the product.

B. **Product Backlog Items** – What, then, makes up a product backlog? There are actually a wide array of Product Backlog items (PBIs) to choose from. In the realm of software development, however, they are all classified in 4 groups.

The first two groups consists of elements that are easily observed by end users. These are Features and Bugs and it is the role of the development team to improve on the former while minimizing the latter.

The other two, however, are more technical in nature. Thus, they are things that are too complex or invisible to the end user but would nonetheless affect their overall perception of the product.

These two classes are Technical Debt and Spikes (information gathered from research that is not code).

PBIs are usually written in what is called a "Story" form. Thus, it could look something like this:

"As a (Insert User here), I want (Insert useful action here) so that (Insert value here) can be achieved".

C. **Sprint Backlog** – This backlog contains work that the team must do now or as part of the 2-4 week sprint. Sprint Backlogs are usually formed during meetings and do not change at all for the duration of the sprint. They also dictate how the team is performing as far as the Burndown chart is concerned.

Sprint backlogs are usually user stories that the team has committed to meeting during that iteration. However, it could also include some issues shared with the product backlog such as fixing bugs, adding features, and restructuring the product.

Unlike the product backlog, which is merely a list of what the user wants, the sprint backlog is a bit more technical. It breaks down what the team must focus on for that sprint and details how the stories can be implemented on a technical level. The Scrum master will refer to this backlog in guiding the rest of the team through the sprint.

D. **Increment** – This is simply the sum of all the PBIs that have been completed during a sprint. Simply put, it determines if the team is one step closer to achieving the overall vision of the client.

Ideally, at the end of each sprint, the increment placed on each PBI must be "done". This indicates that all tasks set for that cycle have been successfully met and there is no work to be carried over in the next period.

But how can you tell that something is "done"? For software developers, completion simply means that that feature is usable and efficiently implemented into the code of the product. The scrum master, product owner, and the team will then refer to the increment in presenting to outside individuals what has been done so far in achieving the overall goals of the project.

3. 5 Events

The scrum framework has several defined events throughout each project. These events, in turn, combine to give the team the focus they need on providing value to the clients across every iteration. The sequence of events under the scrum framework, then, are as follows:

A. **Sprint Planning** – At the beginning of each sprint, the team convenes for a meeting. Here, the team, master, and owner plan what needs to be done for the upcoming cycle.

It usually starts with the product owner presenting the top priority PBIs and ends with the team committing to a sprint backlog. It is important, however, that the team chooses the items that they are most confident of completing by the end of that sprint.

B. **The Sprint and The Standup** – the sprint is simply the time-fixed period where the team goes about completing the tasks they have agreed to. But, of course, there is a chance that the team might get behind due to some changes or, worse, a lack of supervision.

This is where the **Daily Standup** becomes important. As the name implies, this is a meeting held every day where the scrum master tells the team what to prioritize for that day or for the week. And also as the name would imply, you could do this meeting standing up so keep the meetings short. This way, everybody can get the reminders that they need and get back to work immediately.

C. **The Sprint Review**

Once the sprint is ending, the scrum master will call for another meeting. Here, he presents the results of what has been achieved to shareholders and the client (if the latter is available, of course). Ideally, the Sprint Review is where a tangible product must be presented in the form of a demo of an actual working version. This is how the team should showcase what they have achieved for that sprint and to demonstrate that the acceptance criteria that has been set in the start of the sprint has been met.

D. **The Sprint Retrospective**

Also held at the end of the sprint, this is where the master, owner, and team evaluate several key issues in the current sprint. These include:

- What happened in the current sprint?
- What challenges did each team faced?
- How efficient was the team in achieving the sprint goals?
- What can be improved in the next sprint?
- What should be included as PBIs in the next sprint?

At this retrospective, the development team should focus primarily on what they can do to improve as a group. This means that they ought to put their focus on the things that they have direct control over with like the handling of workloads, scheduling, and the flow of information between persons and sub-teams.

Anything that they cannot handle like corporate policies, client concerns, and pressure from upper management is best left for the Scrum Master and Product Owner.

Chapter VI: Extreme Programming Part I: The Basics

In practice, the Agile Methodology is highly applicable in all sorts of projects; not just those that involve coding and programming. If you have a project that involves something that needs to be developed prior to mass production, then you can use various Agile frameworks to guide your production and development process. This is irrespective of the fact if that end product has to be made on a work bench or a desktop computer.

However, the Agile was designed primarily for software development and this all the more apparent with its software-focused variant, Extreme Programming (or XP for short). XP is an Agile framework whose core purpose is to improve the quality of the software as well as the work process of which the development team is to adhere to. And if the process and the end product is improved, then needs of the customer are satisfied or more.

Core Principles

Extreme Programming is a framework by nature. As such, its success is utterly dependent on its implementers adhering to 5 basic values which are as follows:

A. Communication – The XP framework demands that the development team maintains an open, transparent, and effective channel of communication within each other and with people outside. The exchange of ideas, concerns, and other crucial information must be so clear and direct so as to minimize confusion and waste of time.

B. Simplicity – Reduction of waste is a strong focus in the XP framework. This, in turn, can only be possible if the team adopts a system that is straightforward and a software design that focuses on the basics. This way, the team can put all their efforts into creating important features, addressing the most pressing of issues, and creating a product that is easy to produce, monitor, and maintain.

C. **Feedback** – There is no doubt that feedback is integral to creating a good product. However, the XP framework takes things a bit further and demands that feedback be not only constantly given but also immediately acted on. This will help the team quickly identify where they can improve on and make important changes to their development practices.

D. **Respect** – The XP framework understands that each person in the team plays a crucial role in the success of the project. Thus, their personal needs have to be respected and the members must bond with each other both at a professional and personal level. A more cohesive team will be able to achieve the project's goals quickly and more efficiently.

E. **Courage** – The XP framework encourages everyone involved to be courageous. And by courage, the framework needs everyone to speak out when they feel something is not working or something might negatively affect the quality of the product and the efficiency of the development process. Alternatively, they must be courageous enough to face criticism or feedback of their work and improve on their methodologies accordingly.

When is it Applicable?

Due to the unique nature of the framework, XP is not exactly applicable for all types of projects out there. The general characteristics, principles, and practices promoted by this framework is best appreciated in projects that revolve around or deal with the following:

- **Changing Software Requirements**

  Software development processes were meant to be short because technology changes at a blistering pace especially in recent years. The Videogame Duke Nuke Forever, for example, was announced somewhere in the mid-1990s but was released in 2011.

Aside from the usual development problems and corporate issues involved, one major element that impeded the game's release was the changing of technology especially with graphics processors. In fact, the game had to be overhauled by no less than 3 times in a span of a decade as graphics engines and corresponding hardware developed quickly especially during the early 2000s.

Moreover, despite all of the efforts and money pooled into the project, the end result was disappointing to many as the conflicting engines and design philosophies ultimately lead to a jumbled mess of a game.

- **Time-Related Risks in Using New Technology**

If a project were to capitalize on a new piece of technology, then it goes without saying that the product needs to be released while that technology is still relevant.

Longer development times run the risk of certain technologies being incorporated in the software being replaced by ones that are more efficient. This means that if such shift were to happen mid-development, then the team has to do everything all over again. This constant doing-over can cause a lot of time to be wasted as well as production delays. Ultimately, the end product released is but a compromised version of what the client intended in the first place.

- **Small Development Team**

The XP framework was designed to take advantage of smaller development teams. A small development team means that communication lines are smaller, more direct, and easier to manage. It also means that issues get addressed quickly while feedback is near-instantaneous.

This even works across multiple subgroups so as long as they are co-located or are working in the same vicinity.

- **Autonomous Program**

The technology that should be used in the project must allow for automated unit and functional tests. This is because the team should be given the chance to fully focus their efforts on developing the software or improving on existing ones.

Automated tests do speed up the testing and maintaining phase which shortens an already short development period. If incorporated right, the team should have no problems moving from one phase of the project to another.

What's the Advantage of XP?

So what should you expect if you are to apply the XP framework in your projects? The answer to that could be different from one project head to another. However, let us just say that XP is something that is not definite in the advantages that it offers to its users.

What it does offer, however, is the chance to do away with some of software development's more infuriating issues, which include the following:

A. **Slipped Schedules** – With a focus on shorter development schedules, XP allows a project team to deliver something tangible and of value to customers on a regular basis. This also means that they can get to finish tasks on time without overexerting themselves.

B. **Cancelled Projects** – Ultimately, it is client dissatisfaction that kills projects. Whether something gets delayed for several times or the client itself is disappointed with the end result (or a bit of both), there is a high probability that elements in the development process will result in the entire project being canned or put on hold. Either way, everybody wasted their time for something that won't see the light of day.

C. **Change-Induced Costs** – In the XP process, ongoing and extensive testing makes sure that changes are implemented into the program without compromising its base functionality. A running and working system always ensures that changes are accommodated and given enough time and attention at in order to be properly incorporated into the main code.

And the best part is that the team can adjust their work accordingly without losing momentum.

D. Production and Delivery Defects – Constant testing and integration will expose flaws and bugs in the design which the team can then address to the best of their abilities. With these tests, the structure of the code is thoroughly cleaned which means that the team can now shift their focus on "enhancing" the product post-launch instead of "fixing" what is inherently wrong with it that users have to discover for themselves.

E. Misunderstandings – More often than not, projects result in failure because of a failure of communication. It is either that the customer was never given the chance to constantly communicate or, if they do, the developers never fully understood what the latter wanted out of the project.

By making the customer an actual part of the team, communication is now direct and clearer. If the exchange of ideas and information is faster and more transparent, the end product will be a more accurate reflection of the customer's vision and intention for the project.

F. Business Changes – Change is always inevitable but they are often detrimental to the team. After all, there is nothing more damaging to the morale of the entire group than to tell them to start everything over again.

In the XP framework, not only is your team more open towards change. They can also be more anticipative of it. This means that they conduct their work in a manner that allows them shift gears in the instance that they need to do so. And while doing this, the team must never lose sight of the goal which is to complete the vision of the customer to the best of their abilities.

G. Constant Staff Turnover – As a result of delays, technical issues, and interpersonal conflicts, a team's roster can change frequently which affects the quality of the end product. The XP framework puts a strong focus on team collaboration and communication with external people.

On paper, this should promote transparency and goodwill with everyone involved in the project. If everyone identifies with the project and has a strong sense of ownership over it, they can contribute 100% of their effort in completing the project.

XP in Practice

Aside from values and principles, the XP framework is dependent on you adopting new practices. These practices, in fact, were made to be interconnected with each other through the framework provided by XP. They are the following:

1. **The Planning Game** – XP addresses two key questions in software development: what must be done before a due date and what needs to be done next? The emphasis, then, is on directing the project instead of predicting what needs to be done and how long. As such, the Planning Game can be done in two strategies.

   A. **Release Planning** – Here, the customer presents the desired feature to programmers who, in turn, estimate how it should be done and how difficult each feature is to incorporate. With cost estimates at hand and with knowledge of how important each feature is, the Customer essentially laws out the project. All that the development team has to do is to follow the specifications and produce the desired results to the best of their ability.

   However, release plans may change and those project estimates are never definite. Even if the initial release plan is manageable, the XP team must revise the plan regularly to fit in changing development conditions.

   B. **Iteration Planning** – In this strategy, the team is given direction of what needs to be done every two weeks. Essentially, the project is divided into what we now know as "iterations".

   As this is the more Agile-ready strategy, developers are given the option to determine for themselves what needs to be done for every iteration and commit to completing the same within that time period. The point here is that they must be able to produce something functional at the end of that period.

But what should you and your team talk about when doing planning sessions? Here are a few issues that need to be tackled by the business and management people in the team.

Scope – How much of a problem must be solved in order for the system to be better? The upper management, customer, and the coach are in the position to determine whether or not enough effort has been done to address issues and where the team should focus on next.

Priority – With all the tasks that need to be done, which ones need to be completed first? Yes, the team ultimately decides what they want to do with each task but it is the leaders who should determine what stories are ultimately important to the end product.

Release Composition – How much (or how little) needs to be done before the business improves with the software than without it? This is something that a leader can only determine as a developer's intuition as to how the business is going to benefit from the completion of the project is not as accurate as that of a management-trained person.

Date of Releases – When should the end products be released to the public? And if they are released on that date, would their presence be welcomed in the market or even have a huge impact on it?

The overall impression of the public to the software upon release is something that managers and project heads are more capable of identifying than developers and software technicians.

These are management related issues but what about the more technical stuff? Your development team can also discuss issues that it can handle such as:

Estimates – How long will a feature take to be implemented? This is something that developers can determine based on their combined skill sets and expertise.

Consequence – There are some strategic management decisions that can only be made if the management folk are fully aware of some technical consequences that could arise from such. If strategy A were to be used, what would happen next? And if B was used, what detriment would it serve to the company?

The development people need to explain this to management so they can make better informed decisions in behalf of the entire project.

Process – What is the organization of the team for this project? What is the workload for each member? The team must be a perfect fit not only for the specifications of the project but also the culture for which they are to operate under.

The reason for this is that the end product will reflect the overall cohesion of the team. If the team functions well, then the software should have a stable structure with all of its promised features properly implemented.

Schedule – Within a planned released, what stories should be included? The developers should have the freedom to schedule the most labor intensive and riskiest segments first so as to reduce the overall risk for the entire project.

Of course, this in-team set of priorities must be reconciled with the business's overall priorities for the project. If done so, this reduces the chance of important features being dropped just to meet deadlines.

At a glance, you should realize that the planning process should be a joint collaborative effort by the development team, the business persons like upper management, and the customer.

2. **Small Releases** – In XP, teams do small releases in two different ways. First, the team releases running and tested software to the customer in every iteration. The customer can use this software for

any purpose that they have in mind. The goal in this strategy is to give the user something tangible and useful for every iteration.

The second option is to release something to end users as frequently as possible. This means that an initial product is released and the team continues to build (and fix) that product over a period of time.

3. **Metaphor** – Teams following the Extreme Programming framework must develop a common vision of how the program should look and function which is the "Metaphor". The best definition of this metaphor is that it is an accurate description of what the end product would be like after extensive development has been done on it.

   This metaphor, as the name would imply, does not need to be technical. It can be poetic or it can be dramatic as the framers would like. The point here is that the metaphor is an expression of the vision of the entire team which points them to a general direction when starting a project.

4. **Simple Design** – The XP framework puts a lot of focus on software with a design that is simple but is adequate. The project starts with something simple and, with further programming and testing, ends up with something that is still simple.

   As such, the Team must keep the design suited for those conditions. Needless elaboration is a waste of motion which complicates the value of the product.

   However, designing is not a one-time affair in XP. It always occurs in the project to meet new needs and address current technological shifts. Also, there are dedicated design phases in each iteration. With this, the software changes for the better in each cycle but stays true to the notion of simplicity.

5. **Testing** – XP is largely focused on feedback which can only be acquired through constant testing. Good XP teams practice what is called as "Test-Driven Development" where they work in short development cycles, add a test run, and make things work.

However, there is a difference between setting up a good test and running it. Your team must do test runs correctly once they release new code to the repository. Also, you have to make sure that the test covers 100% of the new code. This should provide the feedback of which your team relies in determining what needs to be done later on.

6. **Refactoring** – Also known as Design Improvement, this practice focuses on delivering value to the customers in every iteration. To accomplish this over the entire project, your team must abide by the Refactoring process, which focuses on improving several key issues of the design.

First, the team must detect and remove duplication all over the code, which is a telltale sign of poor software design. After this, the team must then work in improving the cohesion of the entire code and ensuring nothing is fundamentally broken.

On practice, this allows the team to start with a good and simple software design and build on that in every iteration. This reduces the chances of the team having to start from scratch in every cycle, streamlining the development process even further.

7. **Pair Programming** – All production in the XP framework is built by two programmers who work at the same code at the same time. This should ensure that the code is reviewed, tested, and implemented by two different people who understand how it works line by line.

The act of letting two people what one can do on their own might sound impractical but programming seems to be the deviation of the norm. Research has shown that paired programmers produce code that is more functional and easier to implement than singular programmers. To put it simply: Two heads are better than one.

Aside from resulting in better code, pair programming also helps in communicating information to the team in a more efficient manner. When working on a shifting basis, every pair involved in the development process can get to learn what the others have been working on and where they specialize in.

The more a programmer learns from their peers, the more valuable they become to the team. In essence, Pair programming helps your team evolve as a self-sufficient group without having to add new talent every cycle.

8. **Collective Ownership** – On an XP project, any pair of programmers can improve on the code on their shift. This means that the code itself gets the benefit of being attended to by many people, which reduces defects and improves its overall quality.

   There is also another, more important, benefit. When everyone has ownership of the code, they are more invested in making it work. Singular ownership of a code can result in features being replaced or written over when a new programmer replaces the old one. The result is that the code becomes too complex or, if functional, a major deviation of the customer's initial vision.

   Of course, Collective Ownership can make people work blindly on a code without fully understanding what it must do. This can be easily avoided through tests and constant communication. This way, improvements are delivered when they are requested and everybody on the team share the same knowledge on how to complete the product for each iteration.

9. **Continuous Iteration** – The XP framework is all about optimizing work. In other methodologies, daily builds are seen as irrelevant or, in some cases, weak. But the XP method understands that daily builds are not only integral to producing good product but can be done multiple time in a day.

   To understand what this means, think of the software development process as building a car. Each team might work on some part of the vehicle like one team focuses on the engine and transmission while the others focus on the electronics, interior, and fuel intake. All of their work is necessary to the completion of the product but there is still the challenge of making everything cohesive during the actual process of assembling the car. Some parts might be well made but don't fit the overall design. Some might fit the overall design but could negatively impact the overall functionality.

Software integration faces the same problem. Your team might find that some lines of the code are not compatible with each other or, worse, create bugs in the system. Of course, errors in the system means that your team has to work double the time in fixing them while delivering on the software on the promised date.

With continuous integration, your team can correct on its mistakes as they are made as you make sure that each part complements one another as they are being developed.

This way, the overall software is cohesive and major, program-crashing errors are eliminated before the software gets mass produced. After all, it is easier (and less stressful) to fix problems while the project has not yet been shipped.

10.   **The 40 Hour Work Week** – The XP framework directly addresses one of the major criticisms of software development: it's reliance on Crunch Times. What we know as Crunch Times are basically periods in the development process where people have to invest more time in delivering the promised features on a due date.

The XP framework recognizes that crunch times are not only unnecessary, they are detrimental to the health, sanity, and overall wellbeing of the developers. The team must commit to delivering the features on time but they must not over-extend themselves.

In essence, they must give100% of their effort for 8 hours and 5 days of the week. Nothing less and nothing more. This could be done by distributing the tasks over several iterations and making the team prioritize on what needs to be done for that specific iteration.

This way, value is provided in every cycle and your team members are not left severely exhausted at the end of each segment.

11. **The On-Site Customer** – The team using the XP framework must coordinate their efforts with a representative of the client as closely as possible. This "on-site customer" gives the team an impression of what the end client wants from the project.

Also, they are the tones that primarily test the product at the end of each iteration. Here, they can provide feedback which gives the team an idea as to what to do and improve on the software in the next iteration.

12. **Coding Standard** – IF people work on the code by pairs, how is the XP framework going to ensure its cohesiveness at the end of each iteration? This is done by making the team follow a common coding standard.

Basically, the team must adhere to a set list of principles and specifications when working on the code. These principles and specifications are, in turn, based on the information provided to them by the on-site customer.

By adhering to the standard, the development team can create code written as if only one person has been working on them. The specifics of the standard are not exactly important here. What is more important is that the end code, all of the parts that comprise it, would look familiar in support of the notion of collective code ownership.

Chapter VII: Extreme Programing Part 2: Unifying Practices

Over the years, those that use the XP framework discovered that the 12 practices above often complement one another. For example, a Common Standard in the code helps in reinforcing the idea that everyone has ownership of the end product as a collective. Or the 40-hour work week helps developers prioritize what is important instead of spreading themselves too thin, complementing the practices of simple design, small releases, and refactoring.

But there is always risks entailed in implementing these practices, risks that would otherwise derail the entire project. To eliminate such risks, you must find a way to unify ALL XP Practices and, to do that, there are a few tips that you can keep in mind:

1. **Mind the Team Buildup**

Teams should be comprised of cross-functional subgroups made up of different people with different sets of skills. With this, the team members can complete each other in accomplishing a specific goal for each iteration.

2. **Sit Together**

Most people would agree that conversations done on a face basis are the best form of communication for projects. As such, teams should find a time where they could sit together (or stand) without barriers to direct communication.

3. **Make the Workspace Informative**

The workspace must be arranged in a way that teams can directly work or communicate with one another. If the exchange of ideas and information is unimpeded on a practical scale, the project can be done at a faster pace.

4. **Keep the Work Energized**

Everyone working on the team must be focused on the work at hand, which means that they must be mentally and physically healthy at all times. As such, they should not be overworked by abiding the 40 hour work week schedule. Also, a person must support the need to protect the mental and physical wellbeing of other members.

Roles

Although Extreme Programming is not that strict in making your team adhere to a specific combination of practices, it does not also exactly establish roles for your team to fill in during the development process. That being said, however, there are certain positions which have popped up across XP teams in different projects. You are not required to follow these roles for your team, mind you, but they should give you an idea as to what task must be done by who in the project.

1. The Customer

This person is responsible for making all the decisions regarding the project. In fact, they are the ones to determine what to do with issues such as:

- What should the end product do?

- What features should be included in it?

- How would the team know that a product is finished? What are the acceptance criteria?

- How much should the team spend? What is the available funding?

- What should the team do for the next iteration?

A customer in the XP framework is required to be actively engaged with the development of the product since they are essentially part of the core team. Of course, there is no law out there that says you can't have more than ONE Customer for every project. Your team can benefit greatly from multiple perspectives so as long as there is a clear direction of what needs to be done.

2. The Developer

Since the XP framework is not particular with role definitions, everyone who is directly involved in building the product is going to be called a

"Developer". This does not matter if they are tasked with building the code, testing it, or doing bug fixes.

Developers under the XP framework are the ones primarily responsible for realizing the vision of the Customer. And since every project requires a different set of skills, and because the XP method is reliant on cross-functional team support, those who made the framework felt there was no particular need to lay out the different roles that a developer should take in the project.

What is only necessary is that the skills and expertise they have can complement what others have, resulting in a more cohesive team for the project.

3. The Tracker

Some XP teams find it necessary to include a tracker in their lineup. More often than not, these are the developers who would devote an extra bit of their time every week to fill in this role. The primary purpose of the tracker is to track the metrics relevant to the project and make sure that the team is completing their work on time.

They are also responsible for identifying where the team should improve on in the next iteration. As was stated, this role is not required for your team in every project you take. A tracker is only needed if your team finds it necessary to have someone monitor how everyone is doing in their respective tasks.

4. The Coach

And since we are assuming that this is your first time applying the XP method to your projects, you would need some veteran to guide you through the process. This where the Coach comes into play and he is usually someone who is outside of the team but definitely knows how XP works. As such, it is his role to guide you and your team through the framework and make sure that you are optimizing it on your project.

It is necessary for a Coach to have first-hand experience in handling XP projects. This way, they can guide you through and help the team avoid common mistakes in the framework, some of which they might have personally encountered or have committed in their own experiences.

As was established, the XP framework is not too fussy in you defining roles for the team. Your team lineup might be quite different from the others but would fit the specifics of the project. The point is that you must make sure that each person plays a crucial role in translating a client's vision into a working, bug-free software.

What are the XP Activities?

Regardless of the tasks your team has agreed to per iteration of the XP process, the framework would still require you to do 4 main tasks which forms the entire XP development process. They are the following:

Designing – A good code always starts with a good design. The design is what guides the project through and helps the developers identify what must be included in the project in order to meet customer goals.

When designing a product, the team must make sure that it adheres to the notion of simplicity. The design itself must allow for straightforward coding as unnecessary embellishments only complicate things, leading to more bugs and errors in the final product.

In order to prevent design-based issues, the developers must create a design structure that helps organize logic through its system. Simply put, the flow of information and the interconnection of multiple lines of code must be simple enough that end users can get the hang out of using the product once it is mass-produced and shipped.

A good design also avoids the problem of dependencies in the system. This is where changes made on one code or feature will affect the functionality of the others. If possible, the code structure must allow for a single line of code to be isolated when necessary and its changes do not affect the stability of the rest of the system.

Coding – To those that swear on the effectiveness of XP, the most vital component of the process of developing the software is building the code. Coding is important for laying the groundwork for the transition from a mere idea to a working product.

Here, the development team will go about building the code in pairs. The framework demands that the code must not only be simple and straightforward but shares a unified design regardless of who is currently working on it. The sharing of feedback and addressing of issues is also necessary when integrating the work of the respective programmer pairs into a functional system.

Testing – If a few tests can eliminate flaws in the system, then constant testing can do a lot in cleaning up the entire program and optimizing it. Unit tests must be performed in order to assess which features are working (or not) according to the specifications set.

Acceptance testing is also necessary to make sure that the developers understand the requirements of the project and, in turn, find ways to meet the same with their work.

Developers must also write automated tests to speed this process up without sacrificing accuracy. If all goes well, then the primary code can be regarded as working and complete.

The point here is that every line of code included in the system must be tested and determined to be optimized before moving on to other features.

Listening – This is not exactly a technical process but it is nonetheless necessary in the completion of the project. The development team and manager must take the time to have a sit down with the customer and other individuals to discuss the progress of the project.

Here, they are to listen to whatever concern these people might have especially the ones that delve with the performance of the project. Perhaps there is a perspective here that the team has not yet tapped into or a potential problem that they did not take notice of.

Whatever the case, the customer, shareholder, and upper management have a voice that needs to be heard if the team were to create something that meets their expectations.

The XP Lifecycle

The XP framework espouses the concept of simplicity which is not only limited to the design of the software. This can also be seen in the process and, ultimately, the lifecycle of the project.

First, you must describe the desired results of the project by having the customers define a set of stories. As these stories are being developed, the team estimates the size and requirements for each story.

This estimate along with the relative benefit estimated by the customer will give the team an indication of the relative value of the story. This allows the customer to determine the sequence of stories in the development process according to their priority.

But do keep in mind that not all stories are not easy to estimate which means that they take a bit more time to apply to the system. Of course, there is the chance that they don't fully understand all the technical considerations and specifications it involves. So what is the team supposed to do with them?

In the middle of the development process, they can introduce a "spike" where they can focus on that particular story or feature. Spikes are short, time-boxed time frames that are set aside for the team to do research on something that they don't fully understand.

If you have to put a spike, however, place it in between iterations. This way, your team does not have to drop everything that they have to do just to learn something new.

Once the stories have been settled, the team can then start on creating a release plan based on what they feel is reasonable for the project. This release plan details what stories should be tackled on a specific time period or what is to be released. This way, the team settles on what needs to be done first and then next and next after that. And so on and so forth. This is then where the concept of Weekly cycles would become important as they help the team stay focused on the tasks at hand. Simply put, the stories must be broken down into tasks for each week. This in turn gives each team member a clear set of what needs to be done for a day or for the entire week, depending on the size of a particular task.

At the end of each week, the team will then do a progress report and review what has been achieved. At this point, the customer has full say on whether or not to continue on the project. If sufficient value has been provided by way of a functioning feature or a revamp of the entire program, the customer can then decide if they want to add more to the end product.

This process goes on and on until the product is ready for mass production. Once the final phase of the development process is reached, the team can then declare the project to be over and move on to a new one.

Chapter VIII: Lean

There are many goals that could be achieved if you are seriously considering applying an agile methodology in your projects. However, if there are one thing agile project managers could agree on what is one of the more important goals to be achieved with the method, it would be an increase in Productivity?

What does productivity look like? That would be different for every development team and project manager. For some, productivity is reflected in a change in inventory management. For others, it is the increase of output while the input is lessened or maximized.

And then for some, productivity is the elimination of waste in the production and development process. And if eliminating waste is an issue that is close to your heart, this is where the Lean methodology would play an important role in your project.

What's the Lean Project Management Method?

Lean is a management philosophy created by Toyota Production System. It is something that has been implemented in Japan for decades now, but it was only in the 1980s when the rest of the world took notice of it.

Simply put, a lot of western companies noticed that their Japanese counterparts were slowly outperforming them. How could a country whose production facilities were leveled by a war just a few decades ago not only rebuild itself but managed to outpace western countries?

Whatever the answer was to that question, there was no doubt that the West tried to copy what made Japan successful at that time by emulating the TPS. They called it by many names like World Class Manufacturing and Continuous Flow Manufacturing, but it was still the Lean methodology at its core.

Lean's popularity soared even further amongst manufacturers in 1988 when somebody named John Krafick wrote the article "Triumph of the Lean Production System". It was just supposed to be a thesis for his Master's Degree at MIT Sloan but it eventually became the basis for further research and a by-word for manufacturing companies.

As a testament to its high applicability, Lean today is not only limited for manufacturing ventures. It can be used for other fields like Education, Construction, Information Technology, Software Development, and other industries.

Benefits

The Lean system does offer a number of advantages to you if you apply it on your projects properly. These include:

A. **Better Customer Service** – The lean method puts a great emphasis on delivering value. By giving exactly what the customer needs, then the manufacturer should be able to provide for a better customer experience.

B. **Improved Productivity** – Productivity in the Lean method is all about improving the output of the manufacturing process. However, it also involves increasing the value provided by each product while also eliminating factors that reduce its overall efficiency in the production process.

C. **Quality** – The Lean method is particular about setting up quality checks. This should reduce defects in the products as well as the need to have them reworked.

D. **Innovation** – Through a series of brainstorming sessions and implementation of creative ideas, the product is enhanced by a considerable degree.

E. **Waste Reduction** – The lean method addresses several key production issues such as inefficient use of space, production of unnecessary physical waste, and optimizing the logistics of key resources.

F. **Better Lead Times** – The team should be able to respond to changes in the project's requirements and reduce delays.

G. **Better Inventory Management** – In the lean method, the team should reduce the amounts of Works in Progresses (WIPs) in its inventory. This should prevent bottlenecking which can further lead to delays.

Why Obsess with Waste?

As you might have noticed by now, the Lean method is rather focused on eliminating waste. But why the strong obsession with it? The reason for this is that Waste can take on many forms. For manufacturing projects, they manifest through unnecessary motion, copious amounts of unneeded byproducts and refuse, and unused materials.

Waste is easy to observe in projects where the processes and end product are tangible (or easily observable). But what about projects whose processes are not seen because they are all relegated in a computer? What kind of waste can you imagine from something like, say, developing software?

The truth is that Lean acknowledges all kinds of waste, not just physical ones. Lean would describe waste as anything that the customer would not pay for and would definitely not agree to be created through the project. To put it in other words, waste is something that exists because of a production but does not add any sort of value to the end product.

The Lean project management calls waste as "Muda" which is Japanese for "trash" or "useless". By identifying the Mudas in your project development process, you can optimize on your team's every moment that is related to producing something for that project.

What are the Mudas of Lean?

It's true that Lean is designed to address various production-related problems for every project. In fact, how Lean works for you is going to be different from other project managers.

But if you do want to know how Lean could be effective to your project, it is best that we go back to the source of it: Toyota. What prompted the company to develop Lean in the first place? During the 1970s, Toyota faced a number of challenges when they were streamlining their production line. The Lean method calls these challenges as "Areas of Waste"

  A. Transport – A production line may move things that are not necessary for that phase of the process.

B. Inventory – How does the facility organize its materials? Can a person there tell components apart from finished products? How about the storage of raw materials and waste products?

C. Motion – Every motion that a production facility makes must be optimized. Any procedure that generates a lot of motion without contributing a lot to the development process should be eliminated. This includes unnecessary steps in the process or redundant procedures.

D. Waiting – Usually a problem with collaborative efforts, waiting is simply the act of one team having to wait for another to complete their part of the process before they can begin theirs. This also includes delays in the delivery of materials necessary to start or continue the production cycle. Long waiting times are considered waste as they leave several parts of the production process inactive.

E. Overproduction – Oftentimes, production facilities create more than what is needed. Their quality notwithstanding, an overproduced batch can take up unnecessary space in the inventory.

F. Over processing – This occurs when you devote more resources to a part of the development process than what the standards have required.

G. Defects – This is perhaps the most telling that your production system has flaws. It can be caused by a lack of quality inspection or assurance, substandard materials, or outdated processes in the production cycle.

H. Underutilized Skills – Exclusive to the Six Sigma method, this type of waste is primarily associated with the knowledge and skills pool that you have set up for that project. It can be arising from your team's skills being inadequate for the task or that you as a manager are not tapping into their full potential for the entire project. This usually happens when you hire people that are overqualified for the job or place them in positions where they cannot fully display their abilities.

What are the Types of Lean Project Management?

Perhaps unlike its other project management siblings, the Lean methodology can be further broken down into 3 sub-types.

1. Kanban

Without giving much away of the process (since it will have a separate chapter dedicated to it), here's the quick rundown of this methodology:

Kanban is a process that is named after the Japanese word for "card". This means that Kanban is a more visual variant of the Lean system as it puts heavy emphasis on making the team communicate more clearly either verbally or non-verbally. The end goal, of course, is to make sure that everybody is on the same page.

Another major feature in Kanban is that it categorizes task queues so as to reduce wastage in the development process while increasing the product's value. Tasks here can be categorized under "Doing", "To Do", and "Done" or other similar terms. Of course, Kanban is a system that can be optimized using Kanban-ready software.

2. Lean Six Sigma

The more statistics-heavy approach to Lean, Lean Six Sigma is designed to remove 3.4 defect Parts Per Million (PPM) in the production process. Lean Six Sigma does this by identifying root causes inherent in project management with a strong focus on eliminating waste in time and resources.

Lean Six Sigma is broken down into 5 phases, which gives rise to its alternative name, **DMEDI.**

- **Define** – Here the goals and the scope of the project are identified along with the value needed by the client.

- **Measure** – How is success achieved in the project? What does it look like? Here, the team sets and quantifies the metrics of which success can be achieved for the project.

- **Explore** — Can things be done more efficiently or is the current production layout adequate? The team should identify different strategies for achieving key points of the project here.

- **Develop** — The team must then come up with a highly applicable yet fool-proof project plan. This can be done by assessing the requirements of the project and the overall budget for it.

- **Implement** — The team then starts the project while adhering to the specifications laid out in the project plan.

Six Sigma is a methodology that works best if you use certain tools. If you do opt to use this version of the Lean Methodology, you best equip your team with the following skills and strategies.

A. **Value Stream Mapping** — What does the project look like in various phases of the production cycle? This has to be visualized by the entire team so they know what to do for each phase.

B. **Research** — The team must be able to rely on outside sources such as customer feedback and focus groups in resolving recurring issues in their development process.

C. **Root Cause Analysis** — It is easy to point to something as the major factor in the occurrence of a problem. But is it really? Root Cause Analysis helps the team understand the underlying issues that plague their development process as well as its symptoms.

D. **Charts** — Visual media like Gantt Charts, Bar Charts, and Statistical Progress Control Charts help the team in understanding how they are faring in a particular phase of the process.

3. The Deming Cycle

This method is based on the Kaizen tools of lean project management and popularized by W. Edwards. The methodology is defined by four phases abbreviated as PDCA.

A. **Plan** — The problem must be identified and analyzed.

B. Do – Solutions must be developed and designed to address that problem.

C. Check – Upon implementing the solution, the team must then monitor their progress. If improvements are necessary, the team must make them as soon as possible.

D. Act – The team will then execute the plans as revised.

The Deming Cycle is actually useful when taking on recurring projects.

For instance, you could start by organizing an impact analysis during the Planning phase. Then, you could follow on this by assessing what worked and didn't in the previous processes while also determining if things were bottlenecking there.

Then, in the Do phase, your team would be attempting to identify solutions to certain problems.

In the Check phase, you can monitor the quality of the solutions as well as their effectiveness in addressing the problem.

Finally, in the Act phase, you could make some improvements on the solution. On paper, this allows you to improve on the quality of the project whenever the production cycle begins anew.

Apart from the manufacturing process, the Deming Cycle is also useful in Software development with its iterative nature as well as construction. In fact, this method is highly applicable in projects with a tiered or systematic production cycle.

Implementation

In order to implement the lean management process, you have to know first the Toyota principles. Use them as a point of reference or inspiration as they form the cornerstone of this agile philosophy.

To summarize, here are the principles.
1. Develop plans based on long-term thinking (as opposed to short term financial goals)

The people that form part of your team should have a sense of purpose to achieve their goals. A good motivation creates a clear vision wherein your team can align themselves to the goals that were set up for the project.

As such, it is your job to identify gaps or waste in the project management and development process. The team's ability to learn from the mistakes of past iterations will ultimately determine the success of the current one and in all projects to come.

After all, there are more worthwhile pursuits in a project than a Return of Investment and short-term profit.

2. Highlight Problem Areas by Creating a Continuous Process Flow

Your team should not focus on improving the project one task at a time. You should focus on improving the entire project management process as a whole

This principle must never be forgotten if your team comprises more than 10 persons. A constant need to innovate the process will also be necessary in improving the development cycle.

3. Use "Pull" Systems to Remove Overproduction

How would your team know when to stop producing or shipping products to a client? For starters, the client would tell you to stop. However, there are also other cues that you can use to stop overproducing and overprocessing.

You should keep the communications between the client, the team, the shareholders, and the management as direct and transparent as possible. You can also use software like Trello to sync your work with the needs of the client and the set production schedule.

4. Divide the Workload Evenly

Do remember that each of your member has a defined role to play in the project. If they feel overburdened or can't catch a break due to the schedule, the quality of their work dips.

As a project manager, you should prioritize quality over quantity. Make sure each team member has enough of a time to focus on part of the project at a time. Assign tasks on each person based on the overall workload that they can handle per development cycle.

5. Create a Culture of Fixing Problems

All members of the development team should have a say on implementing solutions. In turn, they should not feel afraid to voice out their concerns or even alert everybody else on a potential quality issue.

This also means that you and your team should be open to feedback either from within the group or outside.

6. Maintain Consistency of Tasks for Continuous Improvement and Employee Engagement

Project managers must create a standardized process through maintaining quality control checklists and making sure that everybody follows standard operating procedures. Without standards or parameters wherein success can be achieved, your team can't do its job properly and the project's quality won't be improved.

7. Focus on Reliable and Tested Technology to Improve Project Management

As was identified a few paragraphs ago, your team's success under the Kanban variant of the lean management process depends on you using the recommended tools and strategies.

8. Empower Leaders and the Team

Your team must have a constant drive to innovate and this won't be possible unless you set up a command structure where people see leaders and senior members as mentors, not just people to take orders from.
In addition, the team members should be exposed to the latest training and tools that could help them carry their work more efficiently. When people feel that they can grow and improve under the team, the team will

become more innovative which helps in keeping the lean method sustainable.

9. Make a Decision Based on Consensus

There are times when projects do not meet the client's expectations. However, you can avoid this from happening by following these parameters:

- You Have to Know What is Going On

- Determine the Root Cause of Each Problem that Surfaced

- Consider all the Alternatives presented to the Team

- Create a Consensus on the Resolution

- Communicate the decision using tools and strategies that are efficient

10. Create a Learning-Based Organization through Constant Reflection and Improvement

The last thing that you would want for your team to become is Stagnant. The environment on which the team works on should be conducive enough for constant learning and personal development.

This also means that your team must take the time to discuss what has been done so far in each segment of the project. This would provide everybody the opportunity to find out where they are doing great and where they're lacking. Consequently, this helps them create solutions that address the former.

The point is that your team should not possess the same quality of skills and tools after the completion of every development cycle. Instead, it should be better and more efficient with each project that it completes. The more a team grows and evolves, the better suited it is in completing projects on time.

Lean and Agile

In the field of software development, there is a strong tendency to confuse Lean with the Agile methodology. The truth is that they are actually separate philosophies. Lean is its own thing and is in no way a variant of Agile like Scrum or XP.

But here's the thing, though: they share many similarities which is why you can't fault people for thinking the two are related. In fact, they share almost the same set of qualities which include:

- Adopting a culture where the employee does not burden all the blame which increases buy-in in the Lean method and efficiency in the Agile methods.

- The need for a strong facilitator, not a manager, to ensure that the project stays on track with the schedule everybody has agreed to following.

- Eliminating actions that are wasteful or redundant, replacing them with ones that are efficient and straightforward.

- The act of streamlining processes to ensure that promises are delivered on time.

So what makes them different from one another? For starters, lean is more extensive than agile. It focuses on making the process as efficient and waste-free as possible while also delivering benefits that would be felt across several more projects in the future. Agile, on the other hand, is simply a method to ensure that whatever the customer has envisioned for the project will be translated to something tangible in every iteration.

In addition, lean is best applied across large numbers of people, through multiple groups, or with a large organization. Its overall goal is to encourage efficiency among people while also improving the performance of different related systems. Agile, alternatively, focuses on streamlining the decision making process for specific projects and teams. It is not meant to be applied for works and elements outside of a particular endeavor.

Chapter IX: Kanban

The premise of Kanban is rather simple: by limiting what your team has to do, the group becomes more productive. And when you think about just how much time is lost because everybody is aiming to do so many things at once, you will see why Kanban's premise is attractive.

Kanban is not as widely accepted during the early years of the Agile Software Development movement. This has something to do with the fact that it is a relatively newer (or technically speaking, more recently known) work management methodology. But there is a chance that Kanban might just be the better alternative if you feel that Scrum is restrictive in its design.

How did Kanban Came to Be?

Although Kanban as a methodology has only been recently accepted, the kanban (note the emphasis on the lower case k) concept itself has been around since the mid-20th century. Kanban is a Japanese term that translates to "visuals" or "card".

Like the Lean method, Kanban was developed by Toyota during the 1940s and was partly inspired by Japanese grocery stores. The reason for this is that Japanese stores, unlike their western counterparts, do not overstock. Instead, they store only what is needed or in demand by people and would signal their suppliers only if they need more.

Thus, Toyota came up with this system of using kanban in their production facilities. These visual aids would signal the rest of the production line that some parts are needed or to stop supplying them with materials for now.

Kanban eventually formed part of a movement in Japan called Just in Time. Under this philosophy, Japanese companies only produced and shipped what was needed. By not making more than what's needed, these companies were able to conserve a lot of their resources. And if you consider what Japan had to go through for the mid-1900s, such a system was greatly effective.

Waste and Eliminating It

Upon hearing the word waste, you would immediately think of all those unwanted byproducts in your manufacturing or development process. In essence, waste for you is the things that you produced that nobody would pay for.

But waste in the Kanban method is actually more comprehensive a concept. To explain this, here's a scenario:

Supposed that you run a car manufacturing facility and one of your teams is assigned with making and installing tires. Would it make sense for them to create 1000 tires while a client just ordered 5 cars? No, it doesn't.

Or how about if you are a software engineer and you have an entire group dedicated to adding features to a software. Do they start their work even if the designing team has yet to come up with a concept? No, they don't.

But it would make sense for either team to start working on what they were assigned at the moment that they are given the signal. So, for the car facility, perhaps someone in the production line puts up a Kanban signaling the tire people to start producing tires.

Or, for the software team, somebody puts up a signal saying that the concept has been verified and that the main developers have started building on the primary code. The point is that you can avoid a lot of waste in your production process if people only worked on what is required on that moment for that specific phase of the project.

Of course, you don't have to learn intricate hand signals or put up actual visual aids in your production line in order to implement Kanban properly. Instead, signals are emanated from looking at the overall Work in Progress at any given moment.

So, in a Kanban management program, you might want to signal your feature builder team that the main code is ready. You might put the task on a column that says "Code Ready". This gives the signal to everybody else that you are about to pull a new task and place them on the workload. By focusing on what is important for that moment, Kanban should help in minimizing waste in your entire production process.

The WIP Limit

Unlike other methodologies that use timeboxes and deadlines to dictate what needs to be done, like in Scrum, Kanban uses something that is called as Work in Progress (WIP) Limit.

WIP limits are, as the name implies, constraints on the amount of items that an individual, a team, or an entire organization is actively working on.

The general rule in setting WIP limits is that they should be slightly constraining. A good starting point is the number of team members working on the project plus the number 1.

Say, there are 10 team members who are working on a specific e-commerce website development project, and the tasks that can be completed for the entire undertaking number in the hundreds, albeit with some tasks requiring only a few hours and others requiring weeks and massive effort. At any given time, the entire team should be working on only 11 tasks. The project manager would just have to make decisions as to which ones are urgent depending on time-sensitivity and the cost of delays.

These tasks are presented in a visual manner through a tool called a board in which tasks are presented in a chart grouped according to status (e.g. Developing, Ready, Testing, Deployed, etc).

If a team goes beyond that limit, waste would be part of the system. And when that happens, that limit becomes a formalized part of the Kanban production process.

The beauty of WIP limits is that they are actually more flexible than schedules, perhaps even more flexible than what Scrum uses. They can vary from one person or team to another and from one phase of the project to another.

So say, a sub team for your project composed of 4 people have a WIP limit of 20 on their Doing column on the Kanban program. This means that each person would be attending to 5 tasks for that phase.

However, the limit of work being reviewed might be different from what was set. This depends greatly on how long this piece of the project needs to be finished and how many people are being allocated to it.

As such, you as the project manager should constantly monitor the WIP limit for each team in each part of the project to ensure that work is done according to the specified quantity. Nobody exceeds and nobody falls short.

What are the Pillars of Kanban?

The WIP Limit might be the heart of Kanban but the methodology still relies on some core principles. In order to successfully implement Kanban, you have to adhere to the following:

1. Visualize the Workflow

Kanban is primarily a visualization method as it helps you see the flow of work with your team. And a key tool here is the Kanban Board where the entire process can be presented in a highly visual form.

However, you should not be so deadest in following the board as the metrics for success can change mid-process. The visualization is only there to remind you and your team what to do now and what to prepare for next.

2. Limit the WIP

The WIP is simply the number of items that your team should work on at any given time. A limit must be set here so that your team does not exhaust itself in one phase, leaving no energy for the other parts of the process.

There are a number of benefits to be had from limiting your WIPs per person which are the following:

- Work Gets done Faster

- Feedback is Acquired Faster

- You deliver more value to the customer in every step of the process

- You minimize the switching of context

- You can anticipate bottlenecks and prevent them from happening

- You don't leave too much work unfinished in the next parts of the project

So what is the ideal WIP Limit then? There is actually no set formula as each team or person has their own limit depending on their skills. Just make sure that every person in the team is doing enough tasks in the project.

3. Measure the Flow and Manage

A Kanban team must always put the WIP first and foremost. To do that, they have to focus on three artefacts:

A. The Kanban Board as it helps them see what tasks need to be done and to prevent bottlenecking. B.

B. Work metrics like lead time, cycle time, throughputs, and queues which help them analyze the flow of work and resources.

C. Project retrospectives to make necessary improvements in the process and remove critical flaws and constraints.

4. Make Process Policies Explicit

Depending on how you make your Kanban board (more on this later on), you will notice some interesting entries which take the form of "rules" for each stage of the work process.

These rules are made when teams identify places where they need to improve on the process. If a flaw is discovered, then the rule should be like "Avoid doing X so that this Flaw Y can be prevented" or something to that effect.

Rules help in removing the more ambiguous elements of the work process while making sure that everybody understands the conditions that they agreed to follow. The less a worker has to interpret something in the workflow, the fewer mistakes they will make.

5. Use Models to Recognize Improvement Opportunities

This goes without saying but you should always communicate progress to your team. This comes in the form of charts and graphs that help people understand what has been achieved and what remains to be done.

By visual presentations, your team can quickly put two different elements together and understand how the quality of one part of the project will affect the rest. With this, they can implement improvements where necessary without having to be told to do so.

Unlike Scrum, Kanban is not that particular in defining how work must be done or managed. It does not even require you to do regular meetings with the team or set up unique roles that persons have to fill in.

The methodology will assume that you and everybody in the project is operating under a notion of project management but you want to improve on it. In short, you already have a system in place already but you feel that you want to take things a bit further.

This means that Kanban is rather easy to implement as you only need to build on what has worked for your team up to that point. There is no need to redo your entire management process and philosophy from scratch just to do Kanban right.

Kanban is also a methodology that is ready to adapt to sudden shifts in the work environment. No two teams in the Kanban method, even if they belong to the same mother group, will implement the system in the same way.

This should make sense as bottlenecks are different from one team or another. The workload of one team might be heavy for another and what strategy one team thinks is effective in addressing an issue might be ineffective for another.

In essence, the core message of Kanban is this: development teams should think for themselves even if they use the same tools and systems. You and your team are always permitted to use Kanban, modify it to fit your project's specifications, and develop a process that is unique to your group.

With this, Kanban should help your team develop a unique value to your clients, streamline the allocation of resources and skills for each project, and manage the risks that might arise from your production process.

Scrum vs. Kanban

More often than not, Kanban is seen as a direct answer to Scrum. To an extent, you could even see it as an alternative. As such, it is of no surprise that some teams would like to move from Scrum to Kanban.

So what makes Scrum different from Kanban and vice versa? Here are a few points.

A. **Cadence** – Scrum projects are usually divided into segments or "sprints". This means that it is a purely iterative production system with each sprint being a self-contained cycle that still correlates with the others.

Kanban, on the other hand, presents a continuous workflow. There is only one Work in Progress but and the team makes sure that they ultimately deliver the composite parts that make up that end product at the end of each phase.

B. **Release Methodology** – Due to its iterative nature, Scrum makes sure that the team offers something functional and tangible at the end of each iteration. This means that they have to present a working product to the client in every Iteration Review.

In Kanban, the cycles are not so defined but the team still aims to deliver something in set periods. Better yet, they have full discretion as to when and how they are going to deliver value to the client in every phase of the project.

C. **Project Roles** – In Scrum, there is the Product Owner, the Scrum Master, and the Development Team. They all collaborate with each other to ensure that the product is improved in every iteration.

In Kanban, there is no defined roles. In fact, the method assumes that you already have a defined system for the project as it focuses more on delivery under that system as opposed to replacing the structure entirely.

D. **Key Metrics** – A major defining metric in Scrum is Speed. Goals have to be achieved on time or before it and value must be given to clients at the end of every cycle as set.

For Kanban, the metric is Cycle Time. Simply put, everybody must follow the sequence as set during the planning phase, doing work only when it is necessary.

E. **Change Philosophy** – Although welcoming to Change, Scrum still insists on teams doing their job of completing the goal. This means that change is still viewed as something adversarial that the team has to adjust to.

In Kanban, it fully embraces change. Metrics and goals can shift in the middle of the project and it is the team's goal to make sure that their work would completely adjust to the new conditions.

F. **Core Principle** – Scrum is a variant of Agile which makes it ideal for close-knight groups working on individual projects. Kanban, on the other hand, is a derivative of Lean which means that it is to be applied on an organizational basis.

Implementing Kanban

Transitioning into a Kanban system is not actually that hard. As was stated, Kanban is already content with whatever system you are currently employing and build on that.

But it does demand for you to follow a sequence so that your team can embrace its principles. Here's how.

1. Start from Where You Are

It is a common misconception in Kanban that you have to re-do everything from scratch to transition to the method. However, Kanban is not requiring you to adhere to some new artifacts or events.

It only asks that you start with what you have now. What are your existing roles and processes? What is only necessary in Kanban is that you follow set procedures but strive to improve them according to their guidelines while also taking ownership over the development process.

2. Set a Kanban Workshop

Kanban is relatively straightforward but don't be fooled by it. It is actually that demanding and would demand a lot of discipline from your team in order to implement it properly.

This is why a workshop must be held before implementing the system. Here, the team can get acquainted with Kanban's principles and how to make it compatible with the current production processes and philosophies.

3. Coming up with a Kanban Board

Now that you have understood the Kanban principles, it is time to build on your board. To do that, you must first understand what a Kanban Board does for your team.

- The Board follows a three-stage flow of work. In other words, all tasks are to be classified as either To Do, Doing, or Done.

- The board is not a ticketing system. The completion of one task does not open the others. Instead, it simply visualizes how each task is interrelated to one another.

- The To Do column serves as your project backlog. It should be prioritized in order of Importance. In practice, this means that the most pressing of tasks need to be placed higher in the list. The more of a priority an item is, the better its quality should be.

  However, do not spend too much time planning things further in the backlog. This is because priorities can change depending on outside conditions. Plan just in time.

- The Doing List is where top priority items from the To Do list are to be placed when their schedule is up. As these are the things that your team is currently working on, it is best that you limit the WIP Limit at this stage. The lower the limit, the fewer backlogs there will be, eliminating bottlenecks.

- The Done List is where items you have completed will be moved to next. The goal here is to get valuable work flowing through your team as quickly as possible. This means that an item must move from To Do, Doing, and Done in the littlest amount of time possible.

So what does your Kanban Board look like? If you want to keep it simple, the board should be comprised of nothing but three columns: One for To Do, another for Doing, and another for Done. That's it.

The point here is that the board should be straightforward to help your team see what needs to be done next and what has been done for that time period. You could also use digital Kanban Boards provided by Kanban-compliant software. They are easy to build and would adjust their data in real time as tasks are completed.

Just keep in mind that this table is just the first iteration of the board. It will change over time as you explore Kanban more. So, just keep things simple for now.

4. Hold Retrospectives Regularly

Once your Kanban system has been set up, the next challenge to face involves making incremental changes to the process. After all, Kanban is only good if you can commit to improving on your current layout.

This is where a Retrospective comes in but you might be surprised that Kanban's retrospectives are not exactly compatible with the ones that Agile uses. This is because the Agile retrospectives are not exactly fine-tuned towards looking at metrics or even consider experimentation.

So how should you do a Kanban retrospective? There is no definite process, but you could take a look at the following aspects.

A. **Open** – Here, you should do a quick check-in activity to start the process and engage with the team.

B. **Last Improvement** – You should review the last experiment or activity that the team has performed. What did everybody learn here? What should be retained? What should be discarded in the next phase?

C. **Kanban Board and Other Metrics** – Review the workflow done by your team. What does the data show you on what needs to be done? As for the things that have been done, were they performed adequately or on-time?

D. **Generate Insights** – You have to discuss with your team on what challenges they were facing in that part of the development process. What were the constraints that dragged them the most? Alternatively, what aspects of the process did help the team out the best?

E. **Next Improvement** – Once key issues are identified, you and your team should agree on an experiment aimed to directly address that problem. Use a hypothesis-based format like this: "We believe that (Improvement) will result in (Outcome) while also addressing (Problem). We know we have succeeded when (Metric) is achieved.

F. Close – To end the retrospective, summarize what has been discussed and reiterate what the team needs to do next.

Alternative Step 4. Replenishing the Kanban Queue

So Kanban is not exactly that particular with review and retrospectives. What's your best replacement for such then? Your team can use something called a Queue Replenishment Meeting. These meetings are designed to refocus the team's efforts in prioritizing the work backlog i.e. the "To Do" portion of the board.

These meetings must happen at regular intervals, but they don't have to be done that often that they take valuable time from your team. Time, mind you, that could have otherwise been spent on making the system work.

For example, if you release new content every week, the queue replenishment meeting can be done once a month. Whatever timing and frequency you choose for these meetings, you have to always make sure that it is consistent.

This is because a steady cadence for queue replenishment meetings reduces costs for calling and holding the meeting while also providing certainty and reliability with the development team's relationship with the rest of the company. As such, and if possible, have some of the people higher up and involved in decision making join with the team in these meetings.

These people more often than not can provide more contextual detail and a perspective that your team might have yet to tap into. But always keep in mind that the goal in these meetings is to produce a Backlog from which the team can work with confidently and to the best of their abilities.

And with this, you are ready to implement Kanban on to your project.

Chapter IX: Making Kanban Work for You

If you do choose to use Kanban as your Agile methodology, you have to remember that the whole premise of the framework is to change little of your existing system; if it could be helped. Also, you should have mapped out how things go from Point A to Point Z before you even think about improving the system.

If you do that right, you should at least make your team and system compatible with Kanban. That is but the first part of the challenge, the next part would actually involve you making the most out of what Kanban has to offer. And here's how:

Always Focus on Quality

First and foremost, your team should commit to providing the highest possible quality in the work. Quality is a rather subjective term, mind you, as what one team considers to be of good quality is different from another. And that is even if both teams are working on the same department.

As a rule of thumb in Kanban, however, quality should always be this: the product or component being produced must be at its best possible form before you move on to the next phase of the project. This means that your development team should minimize the team it spends correcting defects by avoiding in making them in the first place.

This does hold true to the goal of Kanban of doing work when it is only necessary. For example, you don't need to allot tasks to fixing bugs and glitches in your software if you already have an optimized system of quality assurance set for it in previous phases.

The more accurate your team is in conducting its work, the less movement it makes or wastes. This in turn maximizes the time allotted for that part of the project.

Reduce Works in Progress

More often than not, quality is assured if the Work In Progress Limit is lower. As such, this step must be implemented in tandem with the one above.

The reason for this is quite simple: if a particular member of your team has a lower WIP limit, then they have fewer tasks to accomplish. This means that they can devote more of the allotted time in refining the quality of their output in each tasks.

So, in practice, a person with only 3 tasks per segment of the project has a better chance of providing 3 quality outputs. Conversely, a person tasked with 7 tasks per cycle has a lower chance of producing 7 quality outputs.

Now, what is an adequate WIP limit is different from person to person. There is no hard and fast rule as to how much your team members have to individually tackle for that project. As such, you only have to make sure that the WIP Limit for each person of your team reflects their current skills and capabilities.

Deliver as Often as Possible

Similar to its Agile brethren, Kanban is best if you can constantly deliver something tangible and valuable to clients at the end of each set phase of the product. Yes, you are building just one product for the entire project but, at the very least, your team should show progress at each set segment. For example, you might show a working Alpha Model of the software a few months after the start, then a more enhanced Beta Model by 4 more months. And, finally, a few months before the due date for mass production, your code should be stable and the features you included are functional.

To put it simply, you and your team should deliver on what you promised (and more) in every period that you have agreed to present something to upper management and shareholders.

So why be consistent in the delivery of features and a working code? Not only is this something expected from professionals but it does build trust between the team, the upper management, and the client.

Also, it helps the client get an impression of what the end product would look like once the development process is complete. Perhaps they want some changes or enhancements to be done which helps the team adjust their work accordingly for the next phases. And this makes for a perfect segue into the next tip which is...

Find a Balance between Demand and Output

More often than not, it is at accepting new tasks that your team is going to find a lot of challenges at in the Kanban process. So how can you still provide quality if there is more work to be done while the deadline has not been pushed for even a day late?

More often than not, you will find yourself having to find a way where quality can still be provided even if the WIP limits of everybody else has to be increased. And, of course, you'd rather not risk encountering a bottleneck in the later stages of the development process.

This is where Slack comes in which are short bursts of extreme activity in your production and development process. Keep the slacks short as possible so you don't overextend your team while they still deal with the new tasks in the To Do list. In short, Slacks are the best way for you to balance the demand with the promised output under the Kanban process.

Prioritize, Prioritize, Prioritize

When there is no unpredictability in your team, prioritization does not matter. But, we all know that even the best planned projects have to deal with a certain degree of unpredictability. Not everything is going to be implemented as planned.

So what can a project manager can do to balance things through the project. The answer is in prioritization and your Kanban board will be your primary source of information here.

When new tasks are added into the To Do list, priorities can change. Suddenly, what was topmost priority a few days ago is irrelevant today. It is your duty as the project head, then, to constantly monitor the influx of new tasks and how their presence in the To Do list would affect the ones at the Doing and Done list.

This is also an effective means of preventing bottlenecking in your tasks. If certain new requests come through, they might render upcoming tasks unnecessary to perform. As such, there is a strong chance that new customer demands might not affect the respective WIP limits of your team or, better yet, reduce it.

Attack Sources of Variability

More often than not, you have to deal with variability in your projects as it is the one that can increase WIP limits tremendously while lengthening development cycles. Of course, variability and unpredictability is unavoidable in projects. It only becomes alarming if you have more instances of variability in your project than normal. This often means that your team has actually lost control over how the project should be done.

To avoid this, you must set a distinction over what elements you can control and cannot in the project. If possible, you should have more controllable aspects of the project than those that are variable or unpredictable. This is a telltale sign that your team is actually adaptive to sudden changes in the project, not an entire slave to it.

And when the team does reach a high level of maturity in the Agile philosophy, you can start experimenting with process policies. Which ones need to change so that you and your team can be more adaptive? Are your process policies now hindering you from maintaining agility in the project management process? You can try out different strategies at this point but just make sure that you still produce the expected quality of content even as you are trying out new things.

Conclusion

Learning of all these different Agile methodologies is all well and good. However, we still have yet to answer the most important question of all:

Which one's right for my project?

To answer that question, it is best that we briefly go through what we have learned over the course of this book.

Scrum

As the most popular agile model out there, this is the best strategy that you should use if you want full control over the incremental changes in your projects. With sprints that can go in between 1 week to 1 month, the short development cycles ensure that your team is frequently delivering on the software and features you have promised to a client.

And aside from control, Scrum is ideal for those that are used to (or want to) decentralizing their internal decision-making process. A shared responsibility and voice under the Scrum procedure allows every developer to take full ownership over the entire project. And if they feel that they have a say on what goes next, your team will most definitely go all out in ensuring that tasks are done on time.

Here's a brief breakdown on what responsibilities that each member of the development team should abide by:

- The product owner creates the vision and handles the business and political aspects of the project.

- The Scrum master directs and facilitates the development process, making sure that each team member brings out the best possible results from their work. They are tasked with the more managerial aspects of the process such as eliminating obstacles, organizing meetings, and monitoring the progress done on each iteration.

- The Development team focuses on the more technical aspects of the project such as the building of the code, adding the features, performing quality assurance, and post-launch support.

If your team consists of no more than 15 people per project and wants to remain independent from outside interferences during the project, then the Scrum methodology is your best option.

Extreme Programming

Out of all the Agile methodologies out there, XP is the one most ideal for any project that involves software development. It has a short iteration of 1 to 3 weeks with a strong focus between the constant collaboration between the developers, the upper management, and the development team.

It adheres to principles such as a simplistic design, seamless and transparent communications, constant feedback, and following a well-defined set of coding standards. As such, XP is ideal for projects that span multiple iterations and are inherently complex in nature like, well, software development. It is also the best option if plan-based methodologies are not working for you.

Lean and Kanban

Although not exactly Agile methodologies themselves, Lean and Kanban are related to Agile in the sense that they also focus on streamlining the development process. Where Agile focuses on keeping things short, Lean focuses on keeping things efficient. In essence, no movement should be wasted and the output should only be made when it is truly necessary.

A major focus on Lean, especially the Kanban variant, is the need to continuously improve and deliver without straining the team. In fact, it follows three basic values, which are:

- Visualizing tasks within the context of other tasks and priorities.

- Minimizing the Work in Progress Limits to produce output of better quality in each task.

- Improving the Workflow currently employed by the team instead of outright replacing it.

This methodology is ideal if your project has no limitation on size or team makeup. Also, this might be the best methodology if the specifications of the project require constant output without a defined deadline.

To put things simply, there is no superior methodology in Agile that is applicable for all types of projects. Each method has its own strengths (and weaknesses) that you should be mindful of in order to bring out the best possible results.

However, do keep in mind that the end goal of Agile is always the same: Make teams deliver on their promises frequently, collaborate with stakeholders and upper management constantly, and do adjustments and changes to the overall project strategy whenever the need for such arises.

And this does give rise to another question:

Will Agile Work for my Project?

The short answer is yes. You have to remember that software development has greatly changed in the past few years. The overall dynamic climate of the industry means that any methodology that is dead-set on its own philosophies and strategies would not prosper under the current conditions.

In fact, the rate of failure has relatively increased in recent years. More projects are getting delayed as the base code of most products have become more complicated to keep stabilized. Things like higher development costs, poor planning, and an ever-expanding scope of competition can also affect the development process which results in inferior products.

As such, you are better off using a methodology that is flexible enough for change but is efficient enough to get things done on time and with minimal changes to the overall cost. And that is something that the Agile methodology is quite good at.

And aside from streamlining the development process, the Agile method is ideal in improving how your team interacts with other persons involved in the project. From the higher ups who make key decisions for the project to the client whose vision the team must translate into a tangible product, there are multiple overlapping relationships that are integral to the success of a project.

The agile methodologies can put equal emphasis on human interactions just as much as it does with tools and processes. Furthermore, it focuses on getting things done despite uncertainties rather than following protocols and other constraining systems.

Ultimately, the Agile method is a framework that is best for people that understands that unpredictability is a naturally occurring that must be met with the proper response while not losing sight of what must be eventually achieved through the process. And if that description fits you and your team to a degree, then going Agile might just be the best possible decision you could ever make.

And that concludes this book. Thank you for reaching it this far. Now, you should have a good grasp of what Agile is and how to implement it on your projects. All that is left to do is to act on your plans and see the results for yourself.

Good Luck!

Book #6

Scrum Mastery

The Essential Guide to Scrum and Agile Project Management

Introduction

Scrum was created over two decades ago in 1995 as a more reliable and faster way to develop software in the tech industry. At that time, there was a clamor for an alternative to the Waterfall method, where software is created in stages following rigid rules. Project managers call the shots and make the big decisions. The autocratic leadership eliminates the opportunity to get valuable input from the people who are actually building the software.

Projects moved painfully slow because the team cannot move on to the next stage until the current stage is not completed. No one moved until every item in the checklist was ticked. As a result, delays in release became a normal occurrence. Instead of just being an anomaly, it became the norm.

With an inflexible method like the Waterfall, project management became a conundrum to project managers and organizations. How can a method with step-by-step plans and Gantt charts be so problematic? One would think that with all the tools and resources made available to the team, the projects would be completed on time and on budget. Unfortunately, most software development firms fail to deliver on time. Projects were notoriously over budget as well.

Why the sudden fall from grace for the Waterfall method? The sequential one-direction process had worked rather well on simple straightforward projects. But the business landscape has changed over the years. Software development and IT projects have evolved and became more complex. Customers demand more features that developers cannot deliver. It's not for the lack of talent or skill, but because there are massive impediments brought on by an archaic method. There was no flexibility and wiggle room for developers to work their magic.

Aside from the actual coding and programming, software developers were pretty much just waiting for instructions from project managers. If they are not coding and testing, they are waiting for other team members to finish their part of the work. It's not slacking or being lazy, it's just how things worked then.

Scrum was invented by Sutherland to address the faults and limitations of the Waterfall method. It was a radical change because Scrum was everything Waterfall was not. It was adaptive and has self-correcting mechanisms that address the issues of wrong product delivery.

Early adopters of the new method experienced a spike in productivity. Products or iterations of the products are being delivered on time and best of all, they were delivering something that brings value to the customers. It didn't take long for Silicon Valley to adopt the framework in managing their complex software and hardware projects.

Being part of a software development team in a time when IT companies are gradually transitioning to Scrum means knowing firsthand how difficult the process can be due to the sheer amount of unlearning required. With a drastically new way of doing, not everyone is convinced that it was the way to go. But when the benefits outweigh the inconveniences, people start to see the light. Scrum quickly became the standard in the IT project management sphere.

Although Scrum became the darling in the tech world, it was virtually unknown to other industries. Having worked as a consultant for a non-tech company, it became apparent to me that not many businesses outside of Silicon Valley knew that such a project management framework exists. This is quite ironic considering that Scrum's origins can be traced back to Toyota's production system, a non-IT company.

When Scrum was applied to processes in non-tech companies, they experienced the same improvements and successes that tech companies were talking about. It shows that Scrum can be applied to any industry and it will have the same positive results. It has transformed and is continuing to transform how companies plan and execute projects in virtually every industry imaginable.

But as they say, Scrum is easy to learn but hard to master. This is because some of those who try to master it still clings on to obsolete methods, creating hybrid methods that don't always work as anticipated.

Scrum can be overwhelming for someone who is used to the Waterfall method because the structure and principles are radically different. Mastering Scrum requires embracing the Agile principles that the Scrum framework is based on. Learning a new system means understanding the problems, flaws, and shortcomings of the old system. This is because if people turn a blind eye to the faults of the old system, old habits will remain. These old and inefficient work habits can creep into the new system, making it difficult to learn and master.

This book is written in a way that will help the reader understand why there is a need to switch to Scrum. It explains the problems of traditional methods so that it can help the reader better understand the new system. If they don't acknowledge the inefficiencies, inadequacies, and wastefulness of old methods, they will have a hard time learning and mastering Scrum.

Chapters are arranged in a way that shows the progression of Scrum. It introduces concepts as they relate to a specific process in the Scrum framework so that it's much easier to comprehend. Some real-world examples are discussed to show how companies are integrating Scrum in their work processes and reaping the benefits.

This book explains how projects are prioritized, how development teams are utilized, how mistakes and errors are rectified, and how projects are monitored and released. It also explains the Scrum mindset that needs to be developed in order to succeed in delivering high value to customers.

One would think that it would be easy to transition to Scrum if there's proof that it works better than traditional methods. There is a reason giant tech companies like Apple, Google, and IBM are using Scrum framework in their own processes—it just works.

Organizations must buy in to Scrum fully or not at all. This book will help you to know the problems of faulty methods, acquire new concepts, learn real-world case studies, and apply Scrum concepts to your industry.

Chapter 1 Problems with Traditional Methods

*"There's a better way to do it–find it." – **Thomas Edison***

Software development teams face a range of problems with varying levels of difficulty. To better understand the impact of the Scrum framework on software development projects, take the case of a hypothetical software engineering group tasked to create a fully functional hardware and software system. It's a complex project that required the services of multiple software and hardware engineers. The project team utilized the Waterfall Software Engineering Model.

Problem 1: Rigid Methods

The Waterfall method (and other Jurassic procedures for that matter), follows what's called a *phased approach*. The first phase is to analyze the requirements to understand what the client wanted to get done and delivered.

The team proceeded with the next phases where the requirements were implemented, tested, verified, and maintained in software production environments until the team reached the end of the software engineering lifecycle.

No matter how competent the team members are, their software project failed. It's not because of the lack of skills or resources, but because of the extremely rigid sequential chain of different phases that the team had to adhere to. They could not move on to the next phase until the phase before it is completed.

This poses a problem because if one phase is delayed, subsequent phases are delayed as well. This effectively overshoots the timeline. This is not only frustrating to the team, but it is extremely time-consuming and costly.

The project timeline is set from the start based on the requirements of the project. The project manager takes into account anticipated problems that the project could face. But the reality is that it's just not possible to anticipate all the possible setbacks while you're still in the earliest phase of the project.

Because there is strict adherence to the requirements, the team treats the requirements as complete and infallible. But that's not how projects work in the real world. The more realistic expectation is that requirements change throughout the project.

Why does it change? Keep in mind that the requirements were identified by the client and the development team's job is to implement them. It's possible that there is an inaccurate gathering of requirements. But more importantly, the requirements don't articulate the needs of the client.

About 60% of the initial requirements of complex projects tend to change over time for the simple reason that the changes were not foreseen during the requirement gathering.

The implementation of unnecessary requirements cost the team time, effort, and money, which could have been used for other undertakings that provide better value to the client.

The grave mistake is treating the different project phases as separate stages when they are working together in parallel with each other. Although the Waterfall method is not effective and efficient for complex projects, it can be used to implement straightforward projects with lower risks.

Before the Scrum framework was introduced, the team's work process is bureaucratic, inefficient, overly complex, and unproductive. But more than that, employee morale drops and people are less committed to the overall organizational mission. The whole organization suffers and it takes time to get employees to engage and commit for the next projects.

Problem 2: Organizational Demands of Leadership & Silo Mentality

Before Scrum, the focus is on meeting the demands of the organizational leadership. Teams must comply and deliver the product on a fixed deadline. There is strict monitoring of the progress of the project based on the phases.

Leaders penalize team members who go off-track, not because they are incompetent, but because there were unforeseen events that hindered the members from progressing to the next phase.

There is a huge expectation (and pressure) for the team members to fix the emerging problems before the scheduled delivery date. This brings out the larger problem of independent silos.

People who are tasked to work for the same project come from different teams and don't even know each other by their names. For instance, the software testing team is totally independent of the software engineering team. So, each team doesn't know what the other is doing.

What's the implication of these separate silos? It means that project managers borrow people and resources from these silos, making the arrangement temporary. So these temporary teams are dissolved when the project is completed and members move on to their next tasks and assignment.

There is little to no commitment on the part of these temporary teams because they were just chosen for their skills for one project. And because there's no mechanism in place for these silos to learn from their mistakes, they're bound to repeat the same errors. They are not compelled to commit to the business to improve the bottom line. They don't feel that they have a stake in the success of the company.

Problem 3: Change Management

With the Waterfall method, project managers and team members treat error handling as an exception rather than a natural part of the process. They view impediments, errors, and changes as unnatural things that should not have happened in the first place.

Unforeseen changes or errors in the software project lead to costly delays that affect everything. Because the delays impede the team from delivering the product at the set deadline, the project fails. Teams then look for someone to blame for the failure. This results in finger-pointing and unfair accusations. It creates chaotic working dynamics not conducive for projects to succeed.

Problem 4: Autocratic Decisions

Management styles vary depending on company leadership and culture. Mainstream leadership tends to operate the traditional way and have leaders who make autocratic decisions. This means that decisions are solely in the hands of the leader and don't take into consideration the combined intelligence of the teams.

Those who are doing the actual work have little say on the decision-making progress and they are often overruled over the course of the software engineering lifecycle. Decisions are shifted away from teams and work centers, and more towards managers who are not directly involved in the nitty-gritty of software development.

As a result, it becomes very difficult for the hardworking team to decide on matters that require immediate attention. Mission-critical decisions have to come from the top. Even if the leaders are highly competent, not being in the work center could lead to uninformed decisions and not well-thought-out judgments.

But the worst part of autocratic decisions is that employees feel that they are undervalued and ignored. It completely stops them from thinking of creative and innovative means to solve problems. Constantly being overruled also results in the collapse of employee morale, which in turn can lead to many other problems down the line.

Autocratic decisions discourage teams from sharing their inputs when they are needed the most. Teams tend to disengage because they expect to be shot down. As a result, the people whose contributions and decisions are needed are discouraged to engage.

These problems continue to persist because companies maintain a leadership that favors autocratic decision-making over democratic ones. However, many companies are changing the way they work and starting to adopt a more inclusive method where the team's combined intelligence, technical skills, and inputs carry more weight than the decision of a person who is indirectly involved in software development.

Key Takeaways

- The traditional Waterfall method of project management no longer works in the ever-changing business landscape.

- Traditional methods are rigid, autocratic, bureaucratic, inefficient, and unproductive.

The next chapter discusses Agile Management and the principles that became the foundation of the Scrum framework.

Chapter 2 But First, Agile Management

"Changing practices is one thing; changing minds is quite another"

—Mike Cohn

Agile Manifesto

Scrum has fully embedded the Agile Manifesto values in its framework, that's why the terms Scrum and Agile Scrum mean the same thing. They both refer to the Scrum software engineering process.

The core principles and the underlying philosophy of Scrum is deeply rooted in the Agile Manifesto values which focus on the following:

- Individuals and team member interactions over tools and rigid processes
- Working software or product over comprehensive documentation
- Collaboration with customers and clients over contract negotiations
- Responding to changes over sticking to plans

These values are favored by Agile Scrum over traditional software development principles because they serve the stakeholders better and create value for them. They also elevate and enhance the software engineering profession as a whole, regardless of roles and career levels.

Self-Organization

In the traditional software development process, there is a project manager who calls the shot. The purpose is to organize and lead the team to complete a project. But in Scrum, there is no manager or team leader who tells members what to do. There is a strong focus on self-organization wherein members decide among themselves what tasks they have to implement and execute in order to deliver the goals of a Sprint.

It may sound like a chaotic way of doing things because there's no designated leader who ensures that everyone is working and doing their jobs. People coming from the traditional way of doing things may struggle just a little bit to adjust to a more consensus way of working.

Evidently, there is a learning phase for everyone. During this phase, team members will get accustomed to Scrum elements like Sprint Backlog, Daily Scrum meetings, and Sprint Burndown Chart. Once these things are integrated into their work process, they can get into the swing of things and will find that the Scrum framework makes much more sense from a software development standpoint.

Although there is no leader to speak of, each team has a qualified and certified Scrum Master to support the team every step of the way. Scrum Masters know Scrum like the back of their hands and they make sure that team members are on the same page.

It may seem like a tall task to expect everyone to agree to a decision, but if team members adhere to the core values of Scrum, they'll find that working together despite conflicting opinions is possible. Compliance and trust in the joint decision-making process are the hallmarks of self-organization.

Inspect and Adapt

Two concepts that separate Scrum from other software development and delivery frameworks are *inspect* and *adapt*. They are easy to comprehend but difficult to master and properly implement because there would be resistance and friction at first. Add the fact that team members are not yet used to the Scrum process.

To understand these two concepts better, it's necessary to look at how the traditional process works. With a project manager overseeing the project, there is the risk of not being able to foresee problems that can affect the project significantly. Worse, the team is not equipped to adapt to the changes because they are focused on rigid plans.

With the inspect-and-adapt mentality, team members follow a standard operating procedure to help them adjust their courses of action while they are running the project and not when the project has already been delivered.

Toyota's Improvement Kata was born out of the need to continuously improve the production process and move from the current situation to a new situation. It makes people work more efficiently and help achieve the desired results. This culture of continuous learning and improvement applies so well in manufacturing, but it works just as efficiently in software development and delivery.

Scrum's Inspect and Adapt has four steps that can lead to efficiency.

Step 1: Inspect. With their current technical know-how, resources, and capabilities, the team inspects that backlogs and determines how the project is coming along based on certain criteria and requirements. Inspect happens during review and retrospective meetings.

Step 2: Adapt. Based on the information from the Inspect stage, the team members, in consensus, determines the direction and forecast (vision) of the next steps of the project with a clear strategy on how to implement and execute the vision. Adapt happens during planning and backlog refinement meetings.

Step 3: Learn. There is always a lesson to learn from the process. The team keeps a log of the things that work and things that don't work. Being aware of these things allows the team members to improve their work or become more efficient in how they complete their specific tasks. Learning happens even during the work process.

Step 4: Restart. The team starts over from the first step and repeats as long as necessary within the given Sprint time frame (30 days or less).

Agile Principles

Agile does not stop at the core values; it expands on those values and defines twelve Agile principles that serve as a guide for software development teams. The Scrum framework adheres to these principles.

1. Deliver the product early or deliver smaller working sections of the product.

2. Ask for feedback from the client, customers, and stakeholders and make the necessary changes even if the project is at the home stretch. Customer satisfaction is the main goal.

3. Deliver working prototypes or versions of the product at regular intervals to the client or customers so that they know how the project is coming along and they can provide feedback and input to enhance the product.

4. Developers and people from the business side of the operations should work together over the course of the project.

5. The development team must be given all the support they need to ensure that they can get the job done as per the requirements.

6. Hold regular meetings where critical information and issues can be conveyed clearly, systematically, and effectively.

7. Measure the project's progress by the working prototypes or early versions of the product.

8. Developers and stakeholders of the project must maintain a constant pace throughout the project's lifecycle.

9. The team must start with a good design and use attention to detail to enhance the product and the process.

10. No matter how complex the product is, the process must be kept simple. Unnecessary steps or bureaucracy must be removed from the process.

11. Self-organizing teams work more efficiently. They are able to filter all the inputs and choose those that provide the best designs and architecture.

12. The team must reflect on what they have to do to become more effective. They must be flexible and open to adjusting their behavior and process to achieve a common goal.

Even if the tools, techniques, and resources change, these Agile principles do not change. While the principles are straightforward, it does not mean that they are easy to implement. It still depends on the team how they would apply these principles to their current project.

It's normal for some team members to be resistant to these principles, especially if they have been doing things the traditional way. But then again, the people in the team must commit to the Scrum values, otherwise, the project would not go smoothly.

Adhering to the principles doesn't mean there will be no challenges and problems along the way. It just means that the team can make adjustments and rectify the errors without jeopardizing the entire project.

Platinum Principles

The Agile Manifesto and the twelve Agile Principles are the basis of the modern agile development methods, to which the Scrum framework is built upon. There are three additional principles added to augment the original principles to capture the contemporary agile thinking that evolved over the years. These are additional guiding principles to help teams transition to agile project management with Scrum as the framework.

- Eliminate formality.

Formality is not efficient and prolongs processes. It's better to be straight to the point when conveying your message to other members. For instance, there's no need to create a PowerPoint presentation when you can easily post a note on the board for everyone to see.

Compare the time it takes to create that presentation with the time it takes to write down a note on a sticky note pad and you'll see the inefficiency of formality. If messages are communicated directly, immediately, and informally, you more likely to get a quick response and you can get back to your work without any fanfare.

When formality is eliminated, the team will evolve and create a Scrum culture of no-nonsense approach to tackling a project.

- Think and act like a team.

If you ever watched a basketball game where a team plays like a team, you can tell early on that the team has a higher chance of winning than a team that focuses on isolation play.

In corporate America, people tend to be competitive with their peers. The cutthroat business culture is making employees act like everything is a competition. This is because they want to stand out, get the promotion, and advance their respective careers.

In Scrum, the success or failure of the project is heavily reliant on the team dynamics. By aligning the team to the Scrum values, it can create a culture of participation, engagement, and collective ownership.

This is why there is no Project Manager to captain the ship. The focus is on how the team can deliver high-quality products to make customers happy and satisfied.

When fancy titles are eliminated, it's telling everyone on the team that no one owns any area of development. No one is singled out for his or her contribution or skills; it's always looked at as a team effort.

- Visualize.

Writing things down isn't bad, but pictures, graphs, and diagrams work better when conveying complex instructions or messages. Scrum Team members are more likely to understand concepts better when these are presented visually.

Even in social media platforms, text with photos pique the interest of people and they tend to engage more. This is no different in the Scrum setup. Sending information visually is encouraged to supplement the text content. It doesn't have to be intricate graphs or charts; a simple hand-sketched diagram on a notepad would do. As long as the message is communicated in a way that is easy to understand, aesthetics is not a priority.

Key Takeaways

- The underlying philosophy and principles of Scrum are deeply rooted in the Agile Manifesto

- The twelve Agile principles serve as a guide for software development teams.

- Three additional guiding principles capture the contemporary agile thinking that can help organizations transition to Agile with Scrum as the framework.

The next chapter gets into the nitty-gritty of Scrum and explains the values and framework in detail.

Chapter 3 Scrummage

"Question whether there are any ways to improve how you're doing, what you're doing, any ways of doing it better and faster, and what might be keeping you from doing that."—Jeff Sutherland

Why Scrum?

Scrum got its name from the rugby term *"scrummage"* which is a method of restarting a play after a stoppage. In a game of rugby, players from opposing teams are packed close together like in a huddle to attempt to gain possession of the ball. It emphasizes the importance of working as a team to achieve a goal. In complex product development, teams are given challenging objectives and tasks that can only be achieved through teamwork.

Scrum came into existence to address the shortcomings of the traditional Waterfall method. Project managers stood by Waterfall's linear sequential process because it is quite straightforward and easy to manage. But as projects became larger and more complex, the cracks of the Waterfall method began to show. It soon became apparent that Waterfall was too rigid and project managers were having a tough time integrating changes that they didn't anticipate.

With the traditional way of doing things, project teams are able to complete the deliverables within 18 to 24 months, as expected. What then is the problem? The problem is that they were delivering the wrong products with the wrong features and capabilities, leaving clients unhappy and unsatisfied.

You might wonder why a project could fail spectacularly even when all requirements were met. You see, as teams go through the process of gathering all the requirements and delivering them within the deadline (say, in 24 months), the world around them had changed drastically that what could have worked in the first six months no longer worked after 24 months. The Waterfall method was too rigid that it didn't have room for constant and frequent inspection to see if the product is still relevant to the times.

So, in 1995, Ken Schwaber and Jeff Sutherland presented the Scrum framework and offered an alternative approach to handling complex projects. More than that, it addressed the inadequacy and limitations of the Waterfall method. By delivering small things in small increments and in short periods of time, it not only allows teams to develop the right products, but they are also able to sustain these complex products.

Scrum was born out of the need to take into account the constantly changing requirements. Instead of having a predictive process where you generate the same output following the pre-determined steps, you are doing frequent inspection and adaptation as the work proceeds. By factoring in real-world scenarios and accepting that unpredictability exists, you can have a much more accurate picture of the tasks at hand.

What happens is that the situation dictates the type of process to apply in order for the product to adapt to changes. It's all about getting products to the market and supporting it through its overall lifecycle.

Although Scrum is best used for software development, it can also be used for:

- Research
- Hardware
- Government
- Process development and marketing
- Managing organizational operations
- Marketing

Scrum Values

It's easy for Scrum teams to go into disarray when problems arise; more so if they don't follow a set of values to keep them upright. A firm grasp of the Scrum values is necessary for the team to succeed and thrive with the Scrum framework. If team members subscribe to these values, they can get things done and deliver a product that would satisfy not just the customers but all the other stakeholders.

For Scrum to work, everyone must work together and adhere to the following values:

Courage

Team members need to have the courage to deal with problems and issues that can come up at any time. They must feel empowered to take action to fix even the toughest problems.

There will come a point where the team would face seemingly insurmountable challenges. Team members may even feel unhappy with the Scrum ecosystem—at least initially—which may affect the overall dynamics of the team.

Teams will face tough situations wherein they will be forced to make hard decisions. But if team members buy in on the Scrum values, they will decide and act courageously in times of difficulty. It's the commitment to stay courageous that makes teams succeed no matter how difficult the tasks are.

Focus

It's important that team members are focused on the goals set out for them to ensure that everyone is on the same page. When team members lose focus, it could lead to friction and disagreement.

To ensure that everyone in the team has a laser focus on the project like their lives depended on it, they must be clear on two things:

- Identification of correct task or work

If team members are able to identify the necessary tasks to deliver the Sprint goal, then they are more committed to completing the project. The task and the skill set should match. If members know the things expected of them, they will work to the best of their abilities to deliver the best product that will satisfy the clients and stakeholders.

- Prioritization

Projects can be overly complex with different moving parts requiring different levels of prioritization. The team must then decide which tasks are more important. With prioritization, the team can operate like clockwork.

Fortunately, the Scrum framework has several built-in rituals and events to identify and prioritize user stories and tasks.

> ➤ ***Scrum Grooming.*** This is also known as Backlog Refinement Meeting. This meeting is solely focused on prioritizing the Product Backlog and nothing else. It prepares members before they go to their Sprint Planning Meeting.

> ➤ ***Sprint Planning Meeting.*** In this meeting, team members identify and realize the correct order of work and see the work dependencies in order to complete and deliver user stories.

> ➤ ***Sprint Review Meeting.*** This is where feedback from stakeholders shows what things work and what don't work. It prompts the team where to re-channel their resources to have more successful Sprint reviews in the future until the next iteration of the product is released.

> ➤ ***Sprint Retrospective Meeting.*** In this meeting, team members identify certain aspects of their software engineering processes that need to be improved.

Commitment

Every Scrum team member must personally commit to achieving the goals of the team. Without commitment, members will lack in contribution and engagement. It's quite difficult for people to commit to something if they have no clear understanding of the bigger picture.

In the realm of Scrum, commitment is synonymous with obsession. To be successful in business and life, you should become obsessed with your goals. It's no different from software engineering goals. If team members don't have that kind of commitment, it would be easy for the team to stumble and fall even at the slightest impediment.

When teams "malfunction" from the lack of dedication and commitment, the team will start making excuses for the failure. The team will begin to create justifications to legitimize the failure.

In the Scrum framework, there must be no room for excuses. If team members are totally committed and dedicated to the project, it becomes a lot easier to solve problems and provide value to clients.

Respect

Every team member has different skill sets that can contribute to the team's success. Respecting each other's different skills and capabilities can go a long way in managing expectations and team performance.

Every member of the Scrum team should respect one another regardless of age, gender, race, experience, or level of competence. There is a tendency for people who are more experienced with Scrum to invalidate or dismiss the contribution of less experienced members. If there is respect, such a case would have been allowed to happen.

Openness

Part of being transparent is being open to all the work and challenges with performing and completing the project. Team members must be honest and direct when they interact with fellow members and stakeholders.

When these values are instilled in Scrum team members, you are taking the element of surprise out of the equation. With Scrum, there should never be a surprise because everyone knows what everyone else is doing. No one is trying to hide anything because there are regular inspection and adaptation. If anyone is trying to hide something in the execution of the process, Scrum will find it because there is transparency.

The kind of openness required in the Scrum framework is the willingness of every team member to be transparent. Errors and mistakes are less than optimal outcomes, but with transparency, they can be rectified at the earliest and could improve the overall productivity of the team and the quality of the work. Doing so would have a positive impact on the achievement of the goals and the overall mission of the Scrum team.

The Framework

It is important to remember that Scrum is **_not_** a methodology. A methodology tells you exactly how you're going to work and the exact steps you're going to follow. These steps don't often change because they are pre-determined.

Scrum is an empirical process that allows you to consistently and continuously inspect and adapt to changing situations. It enables you to improve and enhance your process team by team and group by group.

You'll find a lot of difficulties if you try to assemble a team and force them to work in a certain way. This is because teams work differently. What you need to establish is transparency wherein one team knows what the other teams are doing, making sure that teams are constantly inspecting and adapting.

What Scrum does is implement the empirical process.

- **Transparency** – Everyone in the team knows what's going on

- **Adaptation** – Teams change tactical direction depending on the situation

- **Inspection** – Look at what teams do and how they do it

There is a dynamic process where teams are allowed to change based on the learning and based on the new knowledge brought on by different situations. The process evolves through constant inspection.

To simplify, the entire process revolves around these three things:

1. What the team is doing
2. How teams are doing it
3. What teams need to change to get to where they want to be

The Scrum framework is not as complex as it looks. Everything looks complicated when you're still starting with a new process, but Scrum is really a simple framework that's easy to understand and implement, however, mastering it is difficult because the team is constantly inspecting and adapting.

But before you master Scrum, you have to start at the very beginning and that's to understand the elements of the Scrum framework—from sprint planning to delivery.

The Scrum framework lets team members know what their responsibilities are. It allows them to inspect and evaluate every element in the cycle and introduce new elements when they receive feedback. It's a very dynamic framework to ensure that the product is relevant and the right one for the stakeholders.

Scrum operates in a 3-3-5 framework:

- Three Artifacts
    - ✓ Product Backlog
    - ✓ Sprint Backlog
    - ✓ Product Increment

- Three Roles
  - ✓ Product Owner
  - ✓ Scrum Master
  - ✓ Development Team

- Five Events
  - ✓ Product Backlog Refinement
  - ✓ Sprint Planning
  - ✓ Daily Scrum
  - ✓ Sprint Review
  - ✓ Sprint Retrospective

The Scrum Team and Governance

Product Owner

The job of the product owner is to maximize the value of the product and manage the product backlog. It's also part of the job to work with different stakeholders, whether internal or external.

The product owner is ultimately responsible and accountable for the product. There is only one product owner, but it doesn't mean he or she works alone. In fact, the product owner engages with different stakeholders to get important pieces of information to help deliver value back out to stakeholders and end users.

The primary responsibilities of the product owner are to:

- Maximize the value of the product
- Manage the product backlog
- Decide on what product and when to release it

- Act as a representative of stakeholders and customers to the Development Team

Scrum Master

The job of the Scrum Master is to ensure that the team understands what they are doing and that they are working well together. He or she is the person who removes any impediments that the team may encounter.

Team members need guidance and support when it comes to understanding the Scrum framework, values, practices, and rules. The Scrum Master must be able to help members make sense of the Scrum guide so that they adhere to the framework.

Contrary to popular belief, the Scrum Master is not the Project Manager. He or she guides the Scrum team members as they're working to self-organize. They cut impediments and ensure that everything that the team needs is there to deliver the products.

The primary responsibilities of the Scrum Master are to:

- Help team members understand the Scrum framework as defined in the Scrum Guide

- Provide support and ensure that the resources needed by the team are available

- Cut impediments to create a working environment where the Development Team can deliver and succeed

Development Team

The job of the Development Team is to get things done and deliver the right product. Members of the team have specific expertise and specialization to self-organize and work in a series of sprints.

Team members create and develop the product and ensure that they meet the goals of the project based on the requirements and make the necessary adjustments. They engage and collaborate with the Product Owner to ensure that they are doing things right.

The primary responsibilities of the Development Team are to:

- Create the product and the product increment
- Self-organize itself and its work process
- Work and operate in a series of Sprints to get the job done
- Collaborate with the Product Owner to ensure that the team is working towards maximizing value

Stakeholders

Stakeholders are internal or external entities that have a stake in the project and are impacted by the actions of the Scrum Team through the product or increments they deliver.

- Internal stakeholders are from within the company that could be from any department, division, or branch. They could be from sales, marketing, human resources, or legal.
- External stakeholders could be the end-users, customers, or investors.

Benefits of Scrum

If done correctly, the Scrum framework can have the following positive effects to the team and the company:

- Better product quality that meets or exceeds client expectations
- More frequent code deployments (which means visitors to a site or users of the software or app can use the product and benefit from it through bug fixes, added features, or upgrades)

- Faster lead time from committing to the project all the way through to code deployment

- Lower change failure rate

- Reduced costs of deployments

- Improved employee motivation

- Improved organizational performance as a result of faster delivery of better or superior product

- Improved overall productivity

- Improved market penetration, increased market share, and higher profitability

Companies that utilize the Scrum framework find themselves able to adapt to the ever-changing requirements of clients and stakeholders with less chaos and confusion. They know that they're creating a product that will remain relevant even if there are sudden changes in requirements. It's a win-win situation for the Scrum Team and the stakeholders.

Key Takeaways

- As projects became larger and more complex, the flaws of traditional methods of managing projects are exposed.

- Ken Schwaber and Jeff Sutherland presented the Scrum framework as an alternative approach to handling complex projects.

- Scrum will only work if teams work together and adhere to the Scrum values of Courage, Focus, Commitment, Respect, and Openness.

- Scrum implements the empirical process of transparency, adaptation, and inspection.

- Scrum operates in a 3-3-5 framework where there are 3 Artifacts, 3 Roles, and 5 Events.

- If the Scrum framework is implemented correctly, the organization stands to gain tremendous benefits that can have a positive effect on productivity and profitability.

The next chapter discusses the three important roles that make up the Scrum Team and details their responsibilities and functions.

Chapter 4 The Big Three

*"If you focus on the strength of the team, you will begin to find work as a positive challenge." – **Salil Jha***

The Product Owner

The Product Owner does not own the product in the literal sense, but he or she represents the clients, customers, and other stakeholders. Only one person is designated as the Product Owner, not a group of people calling the shots. The focus is on delivering the right product to the customers. Maximizing value is always a priority to meet or exceed project requirements.

Not to be confused with a Project Manager, the Product Owner takes care of the business side of things—return on investment, prioritization, requirements. But more than that, the Project Owner ensures that technical and business priorities are aligned with each other. This is critical because it ensures that the product being developed is what the client needs.

Main Responsibilities of the Product Owner

- Identifies the goals and vision for the product
- Writes the vision statement
- Creates and maintains the Scrum Team Roadmap which contains the scope of the product and the relevant product backlog
- Takes ownership and responsibility of the product backlog
- Makes critical decisions concerning prioritizations and trade-offs
- Accepts and compiles feedback and adds them to the product backlog by level of priority
- Sets Sprint Goals and Release Goals
- Determines the product backlog that will go into the next Sprint

- Ensure that all product backlogs are visible to all Scrum team members

- Takes care the business side of the project and balances the business risk and the return on investment

- Makes himself/herself available to the development team throughout the working day to ensure that the team has a direct line of communication

- Accepts or rejects work results throughout the daily Sprint

- Decides which product increments are releasable or not

- Manages the expectations of customers and stakeholders

Evidently, the Product Owner plays a central role within the Scrum framework. The role not only unifies the product with the project management tasks and activities, but it also seamlessly integrates development and delivery.

Everything that the Scrum Team does is closely monitored by the Product Owner so that he or she can effectively coordinate their activities over the course of the project's lifecycle.

Given the enormous responsibility, the Product Owner can delegate some activities but the accountability remains with him or her.

Managing the Product Backlog

The Product Owner is the only person permitted to own the contents of the product backlog—from creation to maintenance to prioritization. He or she ensures that all members of the Scrum team comprehend the user stories in the product backlog and implements them accordingly.

To manage the product backlog, the Product Owner has to:

- Create and maintain the user stories in the product backlog

- Describe and explain the user stories in a clear and precise manner

- Prioritize user stories and align them with the business goals so that the team can fulfill the requirements of the product

- Ensure that everyone in the team understands the user stories in the product backlog so that they can implement them over the course of the Sprint

The Product Owner is not someone who tells everybody what they ought to do. What he or she can do is to clarify the objective and prioritize requirements. Part of the job is to minimize distractions so as to set an environment that is conducive for the development team to thrive and work efficiently with little to no supervision.

Since the Product Owner decides which requirements to pursue, he or she can also guide the team when they can shift from those requirements and move on to the next.

What the Product Owner can't do is tell the development team how much of the project they can do because there are different variables affecting that part of the task that only the development team can handle better than anyone else. All the Product Owner can do is to let them know what project they should work on based on priority.

A Product Owner is the main point of contact of team members whenever they need clarifications on the objectives and requirements. The Product Owner does not impose on team members how the work should be done, he or she only ensures that the work is done.

With the help of the Scrum Master, the Product Owner aims to create an environment where distractions to the team are minimized. Together, they deflect any business noise that could affect the development team. They are there to ensure that the development team does not have to deal with any business-related distractions.

It's important to note here that any member of the development team can contact and communicate with the stakeholders or other individuals outside of the team if they need clarifications on something they are working on. Keep in mind that Scrum eliminates bureaucracy so this kind of interaction is allowed.

Managing the Release of Product

Every project team aims to deliver a quality product that provides value to customers. A Product Owner ensures that the team accomplishes the project goals. To do so, he or she has to create and maintain a release plan. The release plan helps the Product Owner decide on product deliveries, end-user functionalities, and the order they need to be delivered.

To have all the needed data and information for the release plan, the Product Owner has to collaborate with the team members on a regular basis. This is a way to further enhance, fine-tune, and prioritize, as well as estimate user stories.

Aside from the development aspect of the project, the Product Owner also manages budgets and costs. So, it's really a challenging role that requires balancing the business aspect and the development side of the project.

Why Product Owners Prefer Scrum Framework Over Rigid Management Methods

- They are able to align the functions of the business and the development teams.

- They are able to forecast cost more accurately because there is daily progress.

- They know that at the end of every Sprint, there is a fully functioning and shippable product ready to go.

- They can get customer feedback continuously from the beginning to the end.

- They are able to know the return on investment at the end of every Sprint because there is a functional product being delivered.

- They know that with the flexible setup of the Scrum framework, the entire Scrum team can adapt to the ever-changing business needs and incorporate new requirements or rectify errors as soon as they are discovered.

The Scrum Master

If you think the role of the Scrum Master is as intimidating as it sounds, perhaps you have every reason to think that way. The role of the Scrum Master is to ensure that everyone in the team adheres to the Scrum framework. He or she coaches the team to develop norms and standards that comply with Scrum.

The primary responsibilities of the Scrum Master are to:

- Ensure that the Scrum framework is implemented in the business and development team ecosystem

- Coach the Scrum team as they adjust to processes and act towards the fulfillment of the project

- Make sure that the team members understand the Scrum values and commit to these values

- Ensure that the Scrum Product Owner and the Scrum Team are working together as efficiently as possible with each other

- Eliminate impediments to the continuity of work

- Shield the Scrum from outside interruptions and external interference so that the team is not distracted and could work in peace

You may have noticed that there may be an overlap in the responsibilities between the Project Owner and the Scrum Master but only in terms of eliminating interruptions, distractions, and interferences. In that aspect, they perform a similar role. But to understand the delineation of roles, think of it this way—the Product Owner directs the team while the Scrum Master enables the team to work towards a common goal. In that sense, you'll be able to tell one from the other.

The Scrum Master is well-versed in the Scrum framework and is considered an expert in all things Scrum. But it doesn't mean that's the only thing he's good at. He or she must also possess people skills. Diplomacy and exceptional communication skills are necessary to talk to a diverse group of people who make up the Scrum team. In return, the team must respect the Scrum Master and trust that he or she can help the team resolve difficult problems.

Ideally, the Scrum Master should be chosen by the team, but in practice, the management decides who the Scrum Master should be. It's important that the Scrum Master works with one team full-time. Although it's possible that a Scrum Master can work on multiple teams, it is not recommended because the focus would be split between teams, which could result in issues down the line.

What the Scrum Master is not

There are many misconceptions and false notions about what the Scrum Master actually does. Perhaps the term "Master" makes people assume that the role is that of an infallible guru that has all the answers to all software development problems. Of course, no such superhuman exists.

To better understand the role of a Scrum Master, it's necessary to dispel the myths about Scrum Masters.

- ***The Scrum Master is not above the team.*** Many people tend to think that a Scrum Master's role is similar to a Project Manager who lords over the team. This can't be further from the truth. Keep in mind that there is no "boss" in the Scrum Team, but there is one person held accountable for the project or product and that's the Product Owner. In a self-managed team, there is no one person who has a higher position or rank. So in that sense, the Scrum Master is not above the team.

- ***The Scrum Master's suggestions and ideas are not always accepted.*** Being the expert in Scrum does not make the person's suggestions Gospel truths. The team will take them into consideration but ultimately, the team will implement the idea that is best for the project even if it doesn't come from the Scrum Master.

- ***The Scrum Master is less important than the Product Owner.*** For some reason, people are comparing and gauging each role's importance to determine which one is better or carries more weight. To set the record straight, both roles are extremely important to the success of the team. They have completely different functions that comparing them is pointless.

Self-managed teams that thrive under the Scrum framework have a high level of maturity, are committed to the goals, have respect for one another, and work with a proactive mindset, which somehow appears to dilute the responsibilities of the Scrum Master. But keep in mind that not all teams will start out as efficient as a well-oiled machine, hence the need for a Scrum Master.

The Scrum Master helps the team members understand the common objectives so that they can create a solid plan to achieve them. As a facilitator, the Scrum Master:

- Remains neutral and don't favor one side over the other
- Encourages members to do their best thinking and practices
- Promotes collaboration, engagement, and synergy
- Provides charismatic authority

Some developers see Scrum Masters as guardians because they protect the team from superficial events or activities that are not necessary. They minimize the business noise that distracts and derails the flow of work.

The Development Team

The development team is comprised of individuals who are capable of creating a shippable increment to the product. They can be software engineers, programmers, testers, marketers, analysts, and other key personnel depending on what the product is. Whatever the case, the development team is supported by the Product Owner and the Scrum Master.

Members of the development team implement the requirements of the software and they make a joint decision on how to deliver the best possible product increment during the Sprint.

These bunch of high-performers, as a solid team, have the following characteristics:

- Autonomous

- Self-organized

- Small

- Full-time

- Cross-functional

- Work in the same room (not in separate silos)

The team dynamics in Scrum moves away from the traditional practice of waiting for tasks to be given to members of the team. Instead, the team volunteers to own the tasks. The members are empowered to work for a common goal. There's a sense of pride and team spirit in taking on a project that they consider their own.

Again, keep in mind that a Scrum Team does not start as a well-oiled machine. In the beginning, it may be chaotic and without a clear direction. After all, they are an assembly of individuals with different skills and expertise.

With the help of the Scrum Master, a more cohesive team is developed. The more they learn about what Scrum is all about, they start to embody the principles of transparency, inspection, and adaptability. They develop the ability to utilize efficient processes, communicate better with one another, and take ownership of the project.

Size and Proximity

The Development Team can have a maximum of ten dedicated and full-time members. It is just the right size to enable the team to become independent and self-organized. Bigger teams can lead to more elaborate and complicated processes that can be inefficient and costly.

Collaboration is a key factor in a cross-functional team. With a small team, members can bring up an idea from start to finish in less time. This is because the inputs and discussions can be much more focused.

Proximity in Scrum is also an important consideration when choosing members of the Development Team. Keep in mind that this cross-functional team consists of people with complementary skills. If they work from different locations, communication is most likely done through email or chat. What's the problem with this kind of setup? It causes delays and adds more unnecessary processes, which defeats the purpose of Agile Scrum.

The solution is to put everyone in one big room where they could work closely together, literally. This kind of setup encourages open communication and quick response. Working in the same room eliminates writing an email for things that can be done verbally. The waiting time for a response is drastically reduced.

Being in the same room is also conducive for spontaneous exchange of ideas. Sometimes, spur-of-the-moment ideas can help with finding solutions to problems. There's no need to call meetings frequently when members are in close proximity to one another.

The benefits of a small-sized co-located team are:

- Face-to-face communication allow members to better understand the messages conveyed because they can hear the tone of voice, see the facial expressions, and understand concepts when illustrated on whiteboards and sticky notes.

- Team members can receive an immediate response with their inquiries.

- Everyone knows and understands what everyone is working on.

- There are fewer errors, defects, or wasted effort because there are fewer misunderstandings in the workflow or process.

- There are cost savings when unnecessary processes are eliminated.

There may be extraordinary circumstances that may require the company to outsource the work. In this case, it is suggested that a local product owner is hired for the job to work directly with the outsourced co-located Scrum Team.

Key Takeaways

- The three main roles that make up the Scrum Team are: the Product Owner, the Scrum Master, and the Development Team.

- Different sets of responsibilities for the roles create unique team dynamics conducive for success.

The next chapter introduces the Scrum Artifacts and explains the elements that make Scrum unique in the execution and implementation of a project.

Chapter 5 Scrum Artifacts

"Greatness can't be imposed; it has to come from within. But it does live within all of us" – ***Jeff Sutherland***

Scrum Artifacts are elements that provide key information that the team and stakeholders need to be aware of in order to understand the product under development, the activities that need to be done, and the processes involved in the project.

1. Product Backlog

The Product Backlog is an ordered list of requirements needed in the product. It serves as a collection point for feedback received from the customer, stakeholders, and the Development Team. It is in a constant state of flux. So, new items are added to the list as they become available. It's managed by the Product Owner.

Here are some examples of valid Product Backlog Items (PBIs):

- o Feature Definitions
- o Constraints
- o Behaviors
- o User Actions or User Stories
- o Bugs and Defects
- o Use Cases
- o Desirements
- o Non-Functional Requirements

The team is not limited to working with these product backlogs nor are they restrained by specific items. There's nowhere in the Scrum Guide that says this is how the team will define the backlog items. It also does not indicate which ones to use. The rule of thumb is to use what's right for the team based on clear acceptance criteria.

As Scrum is all about inspecting and adapting, the team is free to use the backlog items that they are more comfortable with. They can use cases or a combination of PBIs. Ultimately, it will depend on how the team defines its process within Scrum.

Despite that, a Product Backlog Item has to meet the following specifications:

- o It must be a transparent unit that is deliverable.
- o Everybody in the team can see the item, discuss it, and decide how to work on it singularly or in combination with other items.
- o It must have clear criteria for successful completion.
- o It can reference other artifacts.
- o It may be completed within a single Sprint in combination with a few other Product Backlog Items. Oftentimes, items are broken down into smaller pieces to allow the team to work on them more efficiently and effectively.

It is the job of the Product Owner to maximize the value of the product over time. To do this, he or she makes sure that the most important items in the list appear towards the top.

Prioritization is quite straightforward under normal circumstances, but it can get complicated when a high-value item depends on a lower value item. So, it's important for the Product Owner to push lower value items on top of the priority list if they are part of a high-value item.

Prioritization is key in organizing the Product Backlog, but the reality is that priorities can change at any time. What was important or valuable yesterday may not be so today or tomorrow. What's more, new items arrive all the time and can be slotted in at almost any point, even towards the top of the list if the item merits it and if it is sufficiently refined.

Items in the Product Backlog are not always refined though. In fact, when a new item comes up, it's usually fuzzy and vague. Low-priority items normally don't undergo refinement, especially if they're at the bottom of the list. Top priority items, on the other hand, need to be refined and clearly defined.

The refinement process is an ongoing activity for the Product Owner and the Development Team. They work together on the item and iron out the details until they can be clearly understood by the team.

Product Backlog Refinement includes adding details and estimates. More importantly, it sets order to the items in the Product Backlog. While refining is pretty straightforward, it's the estimates that may take time to have a concession. The point of estimates is to select the amount of work for a specific Sprint. Being in a well-refined state is a consequence and a condition of their elevated status or prioritization.

What then happens to other items in the list that are not well-refined? The items at the bottom (or low-priority) are not target for refinement for the simple reason that they will not move up to the top of the list and may not be developed. The teams will not waste time refining them if the chance of them being developed is slim to none.

Understanding User Stories

User stories are written as a way of describing what the Scrum Team should build and deliver to the client. These stories are held in the Product Backlog and are used to help the team prioritize the work by value—from the highest value to the lowest.

Self-organized teams find ways to organize their work in a way that follows Agile values and principles. Before creating user stories, however, the following must be kept in mind:

- A working product or software is the primary measure of progress.
- The highest priority is to satisfy the customer through early and continuous delivery of valuable software.
- Simplicity is essential.

User stories must tell compelling stories about the value to your customers. For instance, on the product or software you are building, the story should focus on the ***Who, What, and Why***. <u>Don't</u> include the *How*.

When writing a good user story, put yourself in the mind of the customer and think of the value that they could derive from the product. The value is what they expect when they use the product. For example, a customer wants a system that's fully functional and stable. These two requirements are what the customer will get out of the product.

Knowing your users or customers can give insights into what they want in a product. To do this, you must create rich personas that are good representations of customers. This will help the team understand the different types of customers, their priorities, and their situations.

Sometimes a user story would have multiple benefits for multiple customers. For example, an e-commerce site can benefit a customer by finding products to buy through the search functionality of the site. Another user can benefit by finding retailers in the hope of doing business with them in the future.

Writing user stories from the perspective of the user can help build the necessary parts to create value for the user. In turn, this likely means you will have to start building some of the database, but only the pieces needed to allow for the completion of each user story. When user stories are clear, the development team can focus on providing real business value to customers.

Building the application the way the user thinks about value minimizes the risk of delivering a product with the wrong features and functionalities. As user stories become much clearer, a rework may be necessary, but if you think about it, its cost is marginal compared to the perks it brings in delivering business value in the shortest possible time.

2. Sprint Backlog

This is where all the activities the Scrum Team needs to do is held. The team pulls information from the Product Backlog into the Sprint Backlog. It holds all the work for the specific Sprint goal. This is managed by the Development Team.

What can you expect in a Sprint Backlog?

o The selected Product Backlog Items for the Sprint, which the Dev Team owns in collaboration with the Product Owner.

o A list of tasks based on the Sprint goal. These tasks aim to deliver the Product Backlog.

o At least one high-priority process improvement. This was added in the Scrum guide to ensure that the team can make improvements and enhancements.

Items brought into the Sprint Backlog are forecast to be delivered, so it does not necessarily mean that the team must commit to delivering them. It would still depend on many other factors. This is where the flexibility factor of the Scrum framework comes in. Things can change during the Sprint so the Product Owner can make a decision to push through with that item or not.

3. Product Increment

Increments are working additions to the product. Every product in the Sprint must be a fully working piece of product that is potentially releasable. The increment can be made up of many releases. There's no limit to how many releases can be made in a day. The team can release as many as necessary throughout the Sprint as long they make sense and are allowed and approved by the Product Owner.

Increment is essentially the sum of all the product backlog items in a particular Sprint. It must meet the following specifications:

- o The increment must be usable and fully functional.

- o It must be potentially releasable. It doesn't have to be released when it is done; it can be made up of several releases throughout the Sprint time frame.

- o It can be made up of items delivered throughout the Sprint.

- o It must be done. This is based on the team's definition of "done". There must be a clear definition of what it's going to take for the increment to be complete. Typically, if all of the criteria are met, the increment can be considered complete and done.

Key Takeaways

- Scrum artifacts replace the formal and rigid documentation that traditional methods use.

- Scrum artifacts are dynamic, changeable, and easy to share and manage.

The next chapter discusses the main event that make Scrum happen. This covers the planning stages, the implementation, the actual Sprint, the Daily Scrum, the review, and the retrospective.

Chapter 6 Scrum Events

"Rituals bring people together, allowing them to focus on what is important and to acknowledge significant events or accomplishments."—**Luis Gonçalves**

Officially, there are five Scrum Events specified in the Scrum Guide, but it's necessary to include Scrum Grooming as a prerequisite to Sprint Planning. Each event has a specific purpose for the Scrum Team.

1. Scrum Grooming (Product Backlog Refinement)

This is the process of refining, estimating, and ordering items within the Product Backlog. Although this is not an official event in the Scrum Guide, the development team may spend 10% of their capacity supporting backlog refinement. It's just good practice for items to undergo backlog refinement before introducing them at Sprint Planning.

Holding a backlog refinement event a few days in advance of Sprint Planning can help the team discover issues and problems, and they'll have enough time to do more research before the Sprint.

The Product Owner can show the team a proposed list of Product Backlog items for refinement hours before the Scrum Grooming event. This way, the team can have a look at user stories and anticipate issues.

During this event, the whole team gathers together and starts discussing the highest-ranked backlog item. It will help tremendously if the items are on index cards or sticky notes posted on walls or whiteboards. Keep the discussion going until items meet the Definition of Ready.

When all items have been refined, the Product Owner or the Scrum Master can conclude the event and move on to Sprint Planning.

2. Sprint Planning

This is where the team looks at the Product Backlog and creates a forecast of what can be done within the Sprint time frame specified by the team.

This is a critical point in the process because it sets the Sprint Goal and ensures that everything that the team does ties back to the goal.

The entire Scrum team attends this Sprint Planning so that team members will have a clear idea of what it is they are going to deliver. This is also the time to ask the Product Owner about the criteria, requirements, and specifications of the product. It's an opportunity for the members to come together to make a forecast without being too ambitious or ambiguous.

The Sprint Goal is an objective that must be met during the Sprint. It helps keep everyone focused throughout the implementation of the backlog items. With this kind of setup, the team is given enough flexibility in delivering the Increment.

It's important to remember that the Sprint Goal is fixed throughout the Sprint, but the framework allows members a little more wiggle room for the implementation of the Product Backlog Items. The team is not going to say that they will deliver exactly the set of features as presented in the Product Backlog Items because these are just forecast. What the team will do is to ensure that whatever features they are able to create and implement must be tied back to the Sprint Goal.

3. Sprint

The Sprint is essentially a container for all the activities and events of the Scrum. A Sprint duration runs for 30 days or less. It starts with Sprint Planning and ends with the Sprint Retrospective. It cannot last for more than 30 days because anything beyond that time frame and the team members start to lose focus. Then, feature creep starts to rear its ugly head.

The idea here is that you don't have to deliver the whole product in 30 days. You only need to deliver some value within that time frame. If the team can't deliver some value in that 30-day window, it's time to rethink what the team is trying to deliver. It also doesn't mean that you have to use all 30 days to deliver value. There are teams that do one-week Sprints or two-week Sprints and they are able to deliver increments without any problems.

- o Sprint is the container of all Scrum events, activities, and everything in between.

- o The Scrum Team focuses on developing activities to deliver value within the specified time frame.

- o A Sprint starts with Sprint Planning and culminates with Sprint Retrospective.

- o A Sprint must be done in 30 days or less to enable regular feedback and prevent feature creep or excessive addition of features.

Sprint Burndown Chart

The Sprint Burndown Chart is the visualization of the team's progress within the Sprint. It is a way for the Product Owner and the Scrum Team to monitor how the Sprint is going—and to check whether the team can accomplish the Sprint goal on time.

The graphical representation of the outstanding work vis-a-vis time is useful in predicting when the Sprint can be completed. A burndown chart is a must-have tool for the following reasons:

- Monitoring the project scope creep

- Keeping the Scrum Team on schedule

- Comparing the team's planned work against the actual work

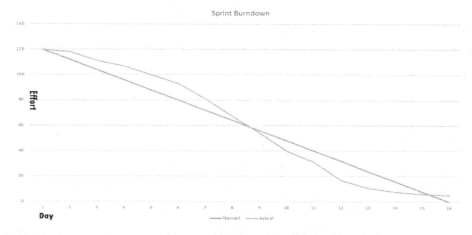

Figure 1*. An Example of a Sprint Burndown Chart Comparing Planned Work vs. Actual Work*

The burndown chart is also a gauge of how well (or how badly) the team is making estimates or anticipating unforeseen impediments. It can help the Product Owner and the Scrum Master figure out what's causing the team to slow down, making sure all impediments are removed to keep the team working at full speed.

4. Daily Scrum

This is a 15-minute daily meeting wherein the team looks and inspects its daily progress. Doing so allows the team to make changes and updates to the daily plan. Daily Scrum is not a status meeting. It is an opportunity for the Development Team to inspect the progress and adapt towards achieving the Sprint Goal.

It finds answers to the following questions:

- o   Is the team moving towards the Sprint Goal?
- o   Does the team need to re-plan?
- o   What are the things the team needs to work on to achieve the goal?
- o   Does the team need help?
- o   What critical issues need to be addressed immediately?
- o   What impediments have team members identified?

If there is a need to re-plan, the team can create a plan for the next 24 hours. Holding short meetings daily optimizes not just team collaboration but team performance as well.

It's also worth mentioning that team members shouldn't wait for the Daily Scrum to bring up issues and problems. The point is to report issues as they happen and not let them go unaddressed or unreported.

A Daily Scrum is necessary to share commitments, identify impediments, stay focused, increase collaboration, and maintain situational awareness.

5. Sprint Review

This is the event where the team reviews the product or increment with the stakeholders and updates the Product Backlog as necessary. Here, stakeholders can be external customers, end users, the marketing or sales department, or any group that has a stake in the project.

Stakeholders are provided a demo of the product and they are encouraged to provide feedback, criticisms, comments, reactions, or opinions for the sake of improvement. Based on the insights of the stakeholders, the Product Backlog is updated to incorporate all valuable and sensible feedback.

Sprint Review is a two-way communication process that takes into account the stakeholders' inputs. The Scrum Team, in turn, adapts by making changes in the Sprint Planning for the next Sprint.

Getting feedback is critical because it is a way to build products and features that customers actually want. What the team wants doesn't always match what the customer wants. If a team insists on delivering a product based on what the team wants, they are not delivering value to the customers. So, feedback is necessary and must be sought from stakeholders.

Sprint Review is not about selling a product. It is about communication between the team and the customers to ensure that the product being created is providing value to the end users.

Definition of Done

In the Scrum framework, Definition of Done (DoD) defines when a product or software feature is considered complete. If it meets the required quality standard set by DoD, then the product is done. This includes all the expected outcomes in design, coding, testing, validations, documentation, and non-functional requirements.

DoDs are categorized by user stories and tasks. While the DoDs of user stories focus on functional and non-functional requirements as set out in the product backlog, DoDs of tasks focus on activities from the Scrum Team members.

The Scrum Product Owner and the Scrum Team jointly define the user stories and the tasks incrementally throughout the development process—and rightfully so.

The operative word here is *incrementally*. This means that the development process allows the team to adjust their actions when the need arises. They do so in a controlled manner so that there is no added risk or costs to the project. It also prevents jeopardizing previous work or delaying the project unnecessarily.

Because the Scrum Team builds a shippable product increment at the end of each Sprint, they can discuss these with the Scum Product Owner and the stakeholders and get feedback that can be incorporated to the next steps of the project. A working product is created and if there are functionalities that need to be added, removed, or enhanced, the team will address them on the next steps.

This kind of flexibility eases not just the software development process but the operational processes as well. It optimizes the use of all the available resources and minimizes waste.

Release Planning

Release planning takes place either as part of the Sprint Review or during preparation for the subsequent Sprint.

The main goal of the Scrum Team is to provide value to customers as quickly and as efficiently as possible while keeping the development work aligned with the needs of the business. To ensure this happens, Release Planning is done. It's an opportunity for the company's vision and product roadmap to be in the same space as the people who are designated to implement it.

This sub-event helps the Development Team plan how they will execute the activities in the roadmap. It helps the team successfully work toward delivering value

There may be some confusion on the term *release*. It could mean the release of the completed product to the customer. In Scrum context, release refers to a Timebox that the team is planning for a certain time period. It specifies the goals and deliverables that the team must achieve.

The team might deliver at the end of the Timebox or spread out throughout the timeline. Essentially, release planning refers to different release cadence:

- Release after multiple Sprints
- Release every Sprint
- Release every feature

Release Planning is an opportunity for the team to make a commitment to the completion of the highest-ranked product backlog item for the upcoming Timebox. It also gives the team a chance to synchronize objectives and understand their work better.

To get started with the Release Planning meeting, you need to begin with the highest-ranked product backlog. This is the responsibility of the Product Owner in advance of the meeting. He or she works with the stakeholders and the Development Team to write user stories and rank the items in the backlog that can be successfully delivered. You also need a vision and roadmap that reflect the market and the objectives of the organizations.

A successful Release Planning meeting must align with the plans as specified with the roadmap. The meeting kicks off with the team's vision and roadmap so everyone is on the same page about the overall goal of the product.

The team then reviews the architecture and important technical information in order to understand the technology baseline for the release. A release name and theme are determined to help the team coalesce around a goal while providing focus for reviewing the user stories.

A review of the team's velocity is conducted as well as a review of the iteration schedule for this release. This lets members understand how much work will be in the release and how to best distribute it across its iterations.

It's also important for the team to review the items in their backlog against the DoD to know how much time and resources the team can commit to completing the work. The estimates need to be based on a shared definition of what it means to be done.

The point of the release planning meeting is for the Product Owner to present the highest-ranked user stories in the backlog, which should be the Scrum Team's focus in the next release.

The team reviews user stories and provides estimates typically in the form of story points. Any story that is too big to be completed in a single iteration needs to be broken down into smaller user stories so that it can be distributed appropriately during this process.

The acceptance criteria must be validated by the team so that everyone is clear on the work that needs to be done for the distribution of stories across all the iterations. If release has been completed, the team should look back and identify any issues concerning dependencies and assumptions that have come up during the meeting.

A release planning done well accomplishes more than just the plan itself. The team develops a clear understanding of the work so that they could build the most valuable product increment. The two-day planning session is a time investment worth taking to get the team on a regular release cadence and makes Sprint Planning a little less chaotic.

6. Sprint Retrospective

A Sprint Retrospective is one of the five mandatory events of Scrum. Like all other events, it is an opportunity to empirically manage some aspects of Scrum. Empiricism refers to transparency, inspection, and adaptation. This is where the team members come together and talk about what happened and discuss what worked and what didn't. It evaluates the previous Sprint and makes necessary adjustments and improvements for the next Sprint.

The intent of a Sprint Retrospective process is to encourage the Scrum Team members to pause and reflect on their interactions with one another and with the stakeholders. They inspect how effective these interactions are and then identify specific actionable improvements that they are going to make as a way of adapting their interactions in the next Sprint.

Sprint Retrospective is done after every Sprint Review. Only members of the Scrum Team should participate in this meeting. No external stakeholders are invited. This is because it is supposed to be a safe place for the team to discuss both the successes and the failures of the Sprint.

This is about inspecting how the Scrum Team works as a team and how it adapts to changes. Based on the discussion, the team identifies actionable improvements for the next Sprint. These are hard conversations and discussions that make some people uncomfortable and vulnerable (because who wants to talk about their weaknesses, right?). This is where the Scrum Values come in. The commitment, openness, and respect among members are in full display.

The retrospective should take place after the Sprint Review for the current Sprint and then before Sprint Planning for the next Sprint. The duration is set at a maximum of three hours for a 30-day Sprint and then proportionately shorter for smaller sprints.

The Scrum Master participates as a peer and facilitates the meeting to ensure that the discussion does not go off-track.

Format

The flow of the retrospective starts with the Scrum Team discussing how the previous Sprint went—identifying things that went really well and ranking them. One of the most important agenda items for this event is to ask whether the team learned something that might help improve the quality of future increments.

Some of the things that could have gone better, especially when it comes to delivering high-quality valuable shippable increments to stakeholders, are also discussed. It's a means of identifying what the team might try to do differently in the next Sprint. To do this, the team can evaluate performance based on the DoD.

Then, the team can start looking at the interactions from different lenses. For instance, one lens could be about relationships and interactions with each other. Another lens could be tools or development practices and processes.

After talking about this, they can shift to adaptation. This is where the Scrum team organizes and identifies at least one actionable improvement that they are going to take in the next Sprint as a result of the retrospective. This step is necessary because if thoughts and ideas are not converted into adaptation or action, the retrospective may be useless. So, transparency and inspection are important for empirical management.

Participants must use this opportunity at least once every Sprint to talk about improvements so they can be implemented at any day at any time during the Sprint.

Key Takeaways

- Scrum Events cover the planning stage, implementation, review, and retrospection.

- Each event has a specific purpose and it moves the workflow along in a rapid and consistent manner.

- The events give the team the opportunity to inspect, adapt, and correct, and learn.

The next chapter shows a typical Scrum scenario to illustrate how a team uses the Scrum framework to create a product. It also lists down some real-world examples of companies that embraced Scrum and succeeded.

Chapter 7 Scrum in Action

"Thriving in today's marketplace frequently depends on making a transformation to become more agile." —*Scott M. Graffius*

Typical Scrum Scenario

To better understand the 3-3-5 Scrum framework, here's a project scenario that will give you an idea how Scrum works in the real world.

Traditional Method:

The goal of the company is to create a web-based trading platform. Six months prior to adopting the Scrum framework, the company had the lofty goal of completing the project and delivering all the big features of the trading platform in six months.

During those six months, the team struggled with the project because there was a lot of going back and forth on what features to change and what needs to be added or removed. The team was hell-bent on delivering the complete product based on the requirements and specifications without a proper feedback mechanism.

As a result, they ran into different kinds of problems and they attempt to fix things on the fly. Ultimately, they completed the web platform but they soon realized that they delivered the wrong product. The platform was functional but it didn't have the right features and benefits.

With Scrum Framework:

Sprint 1 – Day 0

In the Sprint Planning meeting, the Scrum Product Owner presents the stakeholder requirements and the backlog items to the Scrum team. The items should be arranged from highest to lowest priority.

The team tackles the matter of whether they have the required skills, technical know-how, and enough capacity and resources to complete the project. They then commit to complete user actions or user stories 1, 2, 5, 6, 8, and 9. They decided that items 3 4, and 7 cannot be realized in Sprint 1 because some resources and technical infrastructure are not yet set in place.

After the meeting, the Scrum Master rounds up the team to get their inputs on how the items, particularly those they have committed to do, are going to be carried out. Based on the details, the tasks are listed down and placed on the Sprint task board so that the team can see it. Every member of the Scrum Team picks a task which they will handle.

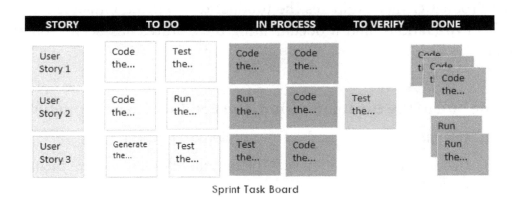

Sprint Task Board

Figure 2. *An Example of a Generic Sprint Task Board*

Sprint 1 – Day 1

The team holds their Daily Scrum Meeting in the morning to give updates on what have been done so far. The team also updates the remaining hours. Members of the team share any impediments to completing their tasks. As it turns out, one team member needs a license for the software he is using. He could not proceed without it.

The Scrum Master asks if there are other problems hindering the progress of the projects and says he'll handle them. In 15 minutes, the meeting is over. The Scrum Master orders the required licenses for the team members that need them.

Sprint 1 – Day 2

The team assembles in the morning for the Daily Scrum meeting. One team member opens up to the Scrum Product Owner about having trouble understanding a process in one of the user actions. The Product Owner explains to him the details and then he figures what he had to do to implement the action.

Sprint 1 – Day 28

On the last day, the Scrum Master invites the entire team for the Sprint Review Meeting. In 30 days, the team has managed to build a working trading platform that users can start to use.

The Product Owner evaluates the product to see if the implementation meets expectations, and if documenting the features has been properly done.

At the end of the Review Session, the Product Owner concludes:

- o User stories 1, 2, 5, and 6 are completed as expected.
- o User story 8 could not be completed; therefore, it was not included in the implementation.
- o Story 9 needs more tweaking before it can be implemented.

In the afternoon, the team gathers for the Sprint Retrospective Meeting. They discussed the things that went well as well as those that didn't. They identified the things that can be improved.

The consensus was that there was some confusion about the overall platform architecture. The Scrum Product Owner then invites the person who designed the platform to explain the details so that everyone is on the same page.

Sprint 2 – Day 1

The Product Owner adds items to the Product Backlog based on customer feedback. He also added items that will address the shortcomings of User story 9. Taking into consideration the findings from the Retrospective Meeting, the team commits to the new user stories. With the Scrum Master serving as key facilitator, the team begins the second Sprint.

This is, of course, the simplified version of the workings of Scrum. It is quite systematic but it's by no means linear nor rigid. There's always room for discussion and correction.

You may have noticed from the example that the entire product was not delivered after 30 days. The Product Owner decided that only four of the six user actions can be implemented and delivered. Even then, the team was able to deliver a working trading platform with enough features to make the site functional. Other aspects of the site (Increments) will be implemented in the next Sprints.

The triangle of project management consists of three project success elements of time, budget, and quality. With Scrum, quality is not optional, it is mandatory. The Scrum Team works with clients in mind and strives to deliver the best possible product that can be built jointly.

Scrum in the Real World

The combination of Agile and Scrum has gained popularity among big software development companies as well as governments and banks. Here's how they achieved tremendous success by adopting Scrum in their large-scale projects:

Adobe

o To compete with Apple's Final Cut Pro, Adobe adopted an Agile mindset in 2008 for its Adobe Premiere Pro video editor. The first release using Scrum was Premiere Pro CS5, which delivered a substantial improvement in product quality and overall market perception.

Amazon

o The online retail giant has been using Agile practices since 1999. Scrum became widely used across business units since 2004.

o Scrum implementation in Amazon starts at the ground level. The system is decentralized and designed to let development teams deliver high-quality software.

o Amazon eliminated the silo approach so that developers can deploy codes to any of the servers. This enables them to innovate and deploy faster with little to no impediments or restrictions.

Google

o Gmail was developed using the Scrum framework.

o Multiple Scrum Teams work in synchronized Sprints on various tasks—compose functionality, spellcheck functionality, and search functionality.

o The Gmail integration team then integrates everything into the Email module.

Spotify

o How does a European startup company with a current valuation of $4 billion compete with and outperform Google, Apple, and Amazon in the digital music service space? Spotify adopted an Agile approach to running its business.

o Spotify recruited leading Agile trainers to take on the Scrum Master roles.

o The company organizes teams from all over the world into clusters known as squads. Each squad is treated as an individual startup. Squads are each given a piece of a product that is completely theirs. So, they are able to change, upgrade, and deploy constantly without affecting other products.

IBM

o The tech giant has adopted Agile Scrum in its business operations by focusing on three areas of change (People, Process, Tools). As a result, IBM experienced improvement in their metrics.

o IBM created its proprietary management software called IBM Rational Team Concert which has Agile development integration.

Australia and New Zealand Bank (ANZ)

o In 2018, Australia's third-largest bank adopted an Agile approach using Sprint. The large-scale transition to Agile resulted in new leadership and greater efficiency. The bank handles the same level of workload with 30% less employees.

FBI Sentinel Project

o In 2006, the FBI green-lit the Sentinel project aimed at digitizing case records and automating related processes. The budget was $451 million. It was expected to be deployed to 30,000 FBI agents and personnel by December 2009.

o By August 2010, the FBI had spent $405 million but only managed to deliver functionality for two of four phases using the Waterfall method. It was a failure.

o In 2010, the project was restarted using Scrum framework.

o By 2011, the Sentinel Project was completed for $30 million.

Key Takeaways

• A typical Scrum scenario can work in a 3-3-5 Scrum framework.

• Big companies use Scrum and Agile framework to complete large-scale projects with a high level of success.

Conclusion

Traditional models of software development focus on work efficiency over value. Although they may have worked wonders for decades, the cracks in the obsolete processes have been exposed. With rigid methods and a bureaucratic approach to development, projects go over budget and over schedule. Worst of all, the products may be outdated by the time they are released to the customer.

When such an unfortunate thing happens, the product is considered a failure. Even if the product looks great or has some promising features, all that won't matter if the final product doesn't provide value to the customers and the stakeholders.

A solution to all these project management woes is Scrum. Not only does Scrum reveal the shortcomings of traditional software development practices, but it also shows the potential of the framework to accelerate the productivity of the team as well as improve the quality of products to meet or exceed customer expectations.

Scrum's unique approach to project management allows the people involved in the project to correct errors as soon as they turn up and not after the product is released to the end users.

With the Agile framework as its cornerstone, Scrum allows a flexible workflow that focuses on creating a product that provides value at every iteration. This means that every time a version of the product is released, there is a substantial benefit for the end users.

Without a leader that tends to monopolize decision-making, the team is given free rein to choose the best possible solution to deliver the best product. Guided by the Product Owner and the Scrum Master, the team is able to make the right decisions because the system allows them to.

A self-organizing Development Team does the work during Sprint which can run from a week to four weeks. During the 15-minute Daily Scrum, the progress is monitored and inspected. This is an opportunity to find out what's working and what's not, and the team will act accordingly. This enables the Development Team to work together to deliver value once a day, ultimately making it much easier to finish the product.

Through the Sprint Review, the team is given the opportunity to interact with the stakeholders where they inspect the Sprint results together. This is followed by the Sprint Retrospective where they assess their work and suggest plans for improvement.

Organizations that use the Scrum framework in their project management and work processes derive a tremendous amount of benefits, whether tangible or intangible.

Better Product Quality

Scrum employs inspection and testing. When a Sprint is initiated, the team works on a particular product backlog item and the testing happens right there and then. This ensures that whatever work item is being created, it passes the quality based on the requirements.

Increased Time to Market

When it comes to creating a product, every company wants to be the first to release a new feature or a new iteration of the product in the market. It makes perfect sense to do so when there are many competitors in the market. With Scrum, a product (or a version of it) can be released into the market before another company does. Because of the many feedback mechanisms in place, the product becomes shippable at the quickest time possible.

Increased Return on Investment

As a result of the fast delivery of a high-quality product in the market, sales follow just as quickly. Because work is done with less time, effort, and cost, the return on investment is higher. The efficiency of Scrum enables the team to minimize errors and at the same time, reduces the risk of delivering the wrong product to the end users.

Higher Customer Satisfaction

Scrum allows the Development Team and the stakeholders to come together during the Sprint Review. This enables a steady stream of feedback about the product. The stakeholders' involvement in the process allows the team to deliver a product that fulfills the requirements. If there are features in the product that don't add value or do not match the requirements, the team can adapt and make the necessary changes. The team works with customer requirements in mind.

Higher Team Morale

With Scrum, teams are self-organized and efficient. There is a sense of ownership and responsibility. Members are committed to the project and they generally have a sense of appreciation and respect towards one another. Their involvement in the decision-making and design process gives them a sense of pride in their work. It boosts their morale and it benefits the organization tremendously.

Increased Interaction with Stakeholders

The Sprint Review enables the Development Team to have direct access to the stakeholders—clients, customers, end users, or internal customers. The increased interaction creates a harmonious relationship that fosters transparency and openness. The more comfortable they become, the easier it is to discuss problems and find solutions.

Increased Collaboration and Ownership

The work processes under the Scrum framework encourage collaboration and engagement. This creates an environment that is conducive for people to thrive and excel in their work. It also encourages transparency so the entire team knows what's going on. There are no surprises or inexplicable events that could derail the progress of the team.

Reduced Risk

Because there is constant inspecting and adapting during Sprints, the team is able to do some mid-course corrections to fix errors. It prevents finding critical issues very late in the development of the product. This kind of monitoring reduces the risk of delivering a product with the wrong features or poor functionalities. The risk of failing is greatly reduced because every step is taken to avoid disappointing the customers and the end users.

All in all, Scrum provides an empirical foundation that enables teams to deliver products or iterations more frequently with higher value and better outcomes to customers. If you want to transform your organization to create higher-value products and make customers happy, you must adopt the Scum framework into the work processes of your project management or software development teams.

Book #7

Kanban

How to Visualize Work and Maximize Efficiency and Output with Kanban, Lean Thinking, Scrum, and Agile

Introduction

If you're looking to find a way to get maximum work efficiency, you're going to find a tool that can help you do exactly that through this book. This book will guide you on how to use Kanban and other work visualization tools in order to help you and your team boost your productivity.

It's a struggle to stay focused especially if the workload accumulates quicker than you can finish whatever you are currently handling. Not only that, it can become even more stressful when someone cannot finish the task they are working on because their skills do not match what they're doing, or that they're unmotivated.

Sometimes, it's the skills mismatch that causes the loss of motivation. When these things happen, expectations coming from the higher-ups and customers or clients are not met. Everyone becomes unhappy and the company loses resources. This is a far too common scenario.

I remember working with colleagues on several projects at once, thinking that multitasking helps finish the tasks at a faster pace. However, it became too stressful and somewhere in the middle of working those projects, the progress slowed down significantly and the quality of the output did not meet the demands of the clients. It cost us precious time, money, and potential clients since we were not able to accommodate new projects since we were still working on some projects.

There were also cases in which I worked on team projects, where each of the members is assigned specific tasks, and that the progress and results of each task are dependent on each other. Working on team projects required each and everyone in the team to have a full grasp of the progress of every aspect of the project. It was difficult especially since it's not easy to point out problems in the project due to everyone being busy on their specific tasks. It led to problems occurring later on during the project duration and it was too late to do something about the problems.

That's why I developed this book. I want you to know that there are tools out there that you can use.

With this book, you will be given techniques on effective visualization of the work. Not only that, but this book will also provide ideas on how to achieve the ideal output and work efficiency you're aiming for.

What Is Work Visualization?

Work visualization is simply the practice in which all aspects of work and workflow information is presented in visual form, hence the name. It involves presenting this information to all team members, managers, and stakeholders so that they can consume and process information quickly, and use it to be reminded of what needs to be done, who needs to do it, and where the team is in terms of progress.

Work visualization practice is a relatively modern practice. Traditionally, information about project status and direction cannot be easily accessed. People had their reports, project plans, and PowerPoint slides in their own desks and file cabinets. You had to request data from individual members manually, which takes time. In addition, some of the information is bound to be outdated. With work visualization, a more transparent manner of working is made possible.

Work visualization helps everyone in the company to see, know, and learn together. It is a simple and creative way of solving problems that can be used at every level of the organization. They enable everyone to see the differences between what was planned and what happened. Everyone can then help in finding root causes and developing countermeasures. It encourages people to work together on the problems and develop accountability towards achieving objectives without being overburdened.

Kanban is a work visualization technique that is aligned with Lean Thinking and Agile principles. Lean thinking, after all, is all about elimination of wastes, and Kanban is one tool that will highlight all the processes that produce waste. Agile methodologies, which Kanban falls under, focuses on maintaining quality and standards and controlling the total costs involved in the production of a particular product while

---

meeting the demands of the customers. It goes with the idea that the demands coming from the customers should be met effectively at a rapid pace. And in this book, you'll learn about how to use these tools for your business.

Kanban in Action

Kanban is a scheduling system being used in just-in-time manufacturing and lean manufacturing in Japan. It works by enabling you to spot areas having problems through performance indicators such as cycle time and lead time. This approach is so effective that several companies from all over the world such as Spotify, Auto Trader (UK), Pixar, Zara, and DJ Orthopedics have been known to us it.

Mattias Jansson, working as an operations engineer at Spotify shared that the main problem in their operations was scalability. The operations team just cannot keep up with the needs and demands of the company. By implementing Kanban as the workflow management tool, lead times became shorter, many internal tasks are completed, and the departments the teams work with became happier with the performance.

Auto Trader, a company based in Manchester, UK decided to use Kanban to their advantage when they realized that many of the issues they've been facing are brought by various teams (e.g. Sysadmins, Release Team, Service Desk) working against each other. Prior to using Kanban, the email system the company was using has been contributing to the lack of teamwork, and to make up for the inefficiencies and difficulties in prioritizing, employees had to work a grueling 70 hours a week.

Ed Catmull, the president of Pixar, has recognized the need for Kanban in film production. A finished movie is basically an organized sequence of events. To complete the projects, each team transfers the idea to the next team, until the idea is pushed deeper into the chain. Through using Kanban boards, everyone working on a project has an idea of what the others are working on and everyone has an idea as to how their work can affect the works of the other members.

Kanban systems are applied to the store level at Zara. The store managers are given the responsibility to determine what, when, and how much of a product will be produced. Data on what the loyal customers demand are the basis of the orders they send to the headquarters twice a week.

Hospitals can also benefit the use of Kanban. Seattle Children's Hospital, for example, has been experiencing shortages in various items such as surgical dressings, clamps, catheters, and specialized tubing. This led to the nurses having to stockpile the goods at random locations in the hospital to make sure that they have the necessary items whenever the situation calls for it. Unfortunately, this non-standardized way of inventory storing led to work delays, which reduced the time that can be allotted to treat patients. When Kanban was implemented, a designated storage area was established, and information is collected and this database is maintained so that supplies are available when needed and the amount of expired goods is minimized. When they do expire, they are disposed of quickly. As a result, medical practitioners are given more time to deal and treat their patients.

Sustainability is one of the hallmarks of Kanban and Lean thinking, and one of the companies who have been integrating this principle into their manufacturing process is Nike.

Kimberley-Clark Corporation, makers of Kleenex, worked with Unipart on enhanced staff development and engagement, which lead to a reduction of staff absenteeism and better staff morale.

John Deere, 2003 world's biggest agricultural machinery manufacturer, spent $100 million in transforming its Iowa, U.S. operation to lean manufacturing which led to employees being able to identify and eliminate non-value-added activities wherever possible.

Companies working following the agile approach have a large network of suppliers and related companies that aid them in delivering products of high quality, which also gives them the advantages of being able to increase production as the consumer demand increases while also being able to redesign the products with issues from consumers.

By implementing Agile, 3M gained the ability to create self-organized teams which are also reactive to customer requirements and also were able to push forward priorities that they seem fit.

ANZ, a banking company based in Australia, now has the capability of releasing new functions on their banking application as needed, and has enjoyed massive recognition as a result.

Google, by applying customer feedback to their improvements basing on Agile, allows users to participate in Beta testings, which help identify bugs, major issues, and reports needed to apply to further update their products.

Spotify applied an agile environment by organizing its employees into squads. As the agile scrum method emphasizes on dividing work into chunks, Spotify used that principle by assigning each squad different tasks at hand. Results from that make Spotify one of the leading music streaming services globally.

Applying these techniques to your business will help you achieve success. There's nothing to lose and everything to gain when you gain an understanding of these techniques.

Many companies that have started implementing these techniques in their companies and reaped success afterward. You can get in on the action by reading this book.

Thanks for purchasing this book, I hope you enjoy it!

Chapter 1. Kanban As A Way to Visualize Work and Maximize Efficiency and Output

"One who conquers the sea today is ready to conquer the ocean tomorrow." -

Matshona Dhliwayo

All successful companies out there started small, but they triumphed over adversities to become what they are today. Many of these companies out there which are experiencing tremendous success have at one point also suffered from disorganization, lack of efficiency from working processes, work delays, lack of teamwork, and a whole host of other problems. At one point, their managers or founders thought twice as to whether they will be successful one day.

The only difference is that they never quit. Instead, they started to look for ways to make things better. They looked up ways to fine tune processes. They used techniques to pinpoint bottlenecks easily.

All processes and various tasks in a company can be visualized at a micro and macro level. Being able to oversee every corner of the tasks helps not only the company be more successful and gain more profit, but it can also improve and maximize the potentials and capabilities of every employee in the company. By having the capability to identify issues that hinder progress from work, it saves the company a lot of time, energy, and resources.

Kanban originally served as a scheduling system from the Toyota Production System, developed by Taiichi Ohno who at the time was an industrial engineer tasked to improve manufacturing efficiency. However, by the start of the 21st century, Kanban was introduced to other sectors and is now utilized in the software industry, through commercial sectors such as IT, software development, and marketing.

Kanban Cards

The word is a literal translation of the term "visual card." This is the defining feature of this tool; it makes use of Kanban cards, which are a visual representation of a particular task or work item. For example, a Kanban card can say something like "Fix reported bug on attachments." Some cards can be so detailed as to include a detailed list of tasks that need to be performed related to the work item as well as performance metrics. These cards are laid out on a Kanban board.

The Kanban approach works as a pull system, wherein production depends on the demands by the consumers, instead of a push system wherein services and products are offered towards the markets.

To maximize process efficiency and achieve the output goal, you should always make sure the process goes smoothly. To do that, you should be able to monitor the progress of the workflow from start to finish. Kanban works perfectly for that. One of the main reasons Kanban is being used by several companies is that it helps them easily visualize and track the workflow.

Kanban Columns

The simplest Kanban board includes three columns - requests, ongoing, finished. Once kanban cards are made, placed, and monitored, employees then will able to visualize the workflow and progress at a macro level, giving them the idea which work should be prioritized and which work should be done at a later date. With the Kanban board at the place, employees are also able to identify causes for work delays and prevent loopholes and issues that may arise.

To-Do		In Progress		Done	
Task	Write quarterly report	Task	Develop Project X21201	Task	Review Developer Performance Metrics
Priority	Urgent	Priority	Critical	Priority	Medium
Deadline	12/23/2020	Deadline	11/20/2019	Deadline	11/30/2019
Completion	0%	Completion	90%	Completic	100%
Task	Review Project B20123	Task	Review Project A21203	Task	Review Project A21202
Priority:	Medium	Priority	Medium	Priority	Urgent
Deadline	1/18/2020	Deadline	2/6/2020	Deadline	12/13/2020
Completion	0%	Completion	35%	Completic	100%
		Task	Answer Support Emails **Must be performed daily		
		Priority:	Urgent		
		Deadline			
		Completion	10%		

Example of a Kanban board

Before the use of Kanban, many companies were not able to complete projects on time due to issues on prioritization. Back then, companies resorted to multitasking without placing a limit on how many works in progress should be addressed. However, contrary to popular belief, multitasking can do more harm than good.

So much time is lost when a team member loses focus due to context switching. In computing, context switching refers to the system of storing the state of a computer process so that it can be easily retrieved when needed and executed at the same point at which it was ended. It allows Central Processing Units to multitask. In humans, context switching refers to the process of switching from one task to the other, requiring mental effort to get to the state you were before you were interrupted. And it comes with a hidden cost. This is because it usually takes a while before you can gather your bearings and focus on the task at hand after your attention was diverted from it either by another task or a simple distraction such as your phone ringing or a colleague gossiping.

Sure, a team can focus on several tasks by optimizing what each one should be doing and when, and a team member certainly can work on multiple tasks; however, there should be a limit on how many tasks should be completed within a designated period. Employees are human too and having too many tasks to handle at once reduces the amount of attention they can give to each task, which causes them to work inefficiently and ultimately lead to project delays.

Kanban helps you visualize the projects you handle in an organized manner through the use of a Kanban board and Kanban cards. With the use of the Kanban board, you can help your employees organize the tasks they need to do for the day. It also helps them track the progress of the projects assigned to them, and determine which project to prioritize. Additionally, it helps them work efficiently since the overall workflow is monitored, making sure that causes for delays and other issues are pointed out and dealt with as soon as it is identified.

WIP (Work In Progress) Limits

With Kanban, the amount of work in progress is limited in all parts of the workflow. By setting the maximum amount of items per given stage, it is guaranteed that another task will only be dealt with once there's an available slot, making sure that the employees can focus on and work efficiently at the tasks they are handling at the moment. And because there are limits, you would need to evaluate which tasks are a priority. You will also be able to highlight problems in the workflow so you can resolve them.

To ensure production flows smoothly, you should always monitor the overall work progress. The use of visualization tools such as Kanban methodology makes monitoring the overall progress of the tasks a lot easier.

To make sure that the process works smoothly, overproduction should be avoided at all times. Kanban prevents overproduction by controlling the production rate using the demand rate. With one of its goals being prevention of excess inventory, a limit is placed at the start of the process based on the number of items waiting to be delivered at supply points.

Additionally, the inability to forecast demands from consumers causes vital problems in the production. It can lead to either producing over or less than what is being demanded by consumers. Kanban is utilized in this situation as a way to trigger demand signal that is immediately forwarded to the supply chain, so the supply chain responds to the demands required by the consumers. With that, there is the assurance that the inventory held in the supply chain is managed better and that they can deliver the demands of the consumers at the right pace.

The use of the Kanban gives your employees the ability to visualize the overall workflow and the ability to point out hindrances in the progression of the workflow.

Chapter 2: Lean Thinking

Lean thinking is a practice that promotes the idea that we should always on the lookout for things that can provide more benefit and value to society and individuals while reducing if not outright removing wastes.

Kanban is a fundamental practice in lean thinking because it allows you to identify where waste occurs in the workflow to prevent further unnecessary costs and use of resources. It enables employees to be aware of which projects need to be done right away while avoiding overproduction. Implementing Kanban is a great way to practice lean thinking, empowering employees to meet changes in market behavior.

The term was coined by Daniel T. Jones and James P. Womack as a representation for the insights they gained in-depth analysis of the Toyota Production System.

Toyota's way of training their managers throughout the years focused on developing its employees' abilities of reasoning instead of pushing them to follow systems developed by specialists. The company also has a group of elders and coordinators who are dedicated to aiding and teaching their managers on how to think differently and how to do better at their job by focusing on core aspects:

The Workplace

Focusing on the workplace entails making regular visits to the place where specific tasks take place. Being in the place and experiencing firsthand what happens there gives the managers and other employees the idea of what happens there. This also enables management to get a bird's eye view of the project. As a result, they acquire the capability to assess the works in progress and determine if there is rooms for improvement.

Additionally, being present also gives the employees an avenue to express their concerns regarding the work in progress and other things to the management. These concerns being addressed gives the impression to the employees that they have support and respect from the management.

Visiting the workplace and engaging your people leaves them the impression that you genuinely care, value and trust them. This also boosts morale, as it gives employees more confidence. Having confident and dedicated employees is good for your business.

Value

The Lean approach begins with a detailed understanding of what value the customer assigns to product and services. This is what determines what the customer will pay. Establishing value allows organizations to create a top-down target price. The cost to produce the products and services is then determined. The organization focuses on <u>eliminating</u> <u>waste</u> so that they can deliver the value the customer expects at the highest level of profitability.

Value refers to what a customer is willing to pay to acquire certain products or services. For a business to be profitable, it must create something of value at the least amount of cost. This requires a two-pronged approach. First, you must get an understanding of your customers. That way, you can create something that they would deem useful. You need to implement a system that would help prevent production and delivery of defective work. This is a way to prevent the likelihood of customers spending money on your products and being dissatisfied with them. Lean management practitioners refer to this practice as building value through built-in quality is tied to this.

Next, you should remove as much waste as possible. Make sure that you are conserving the company's effort, time, energy, and resources. This means putting a stop to something in the process once you see there is something wrong or doubtful in the process of the item being produced.

Value streams

A value stream refers to the entirety of the product's life cycle, which spans the collection of raw materials, the period in which the finished product is in use, and ultimately, the disposal of the product. This means that you'll need a good understanding of your "takt" time. Note that in management systems such as Lean, Takt time refers to the rate at which a production team should complete a product in order to meet demand. The takt time rhythm results in the creation of stable value streams in which the stable teams are tasked to work on stable sets of products with given stable equipment instead of optimizing the usage of specified machines or processes.

Lean thinking must be practiced to study this stream in detail. All processes must be examined to verify if it adds value to the product. Anything that does not contribute, be it steps, materials, or product features, must be reviewed. Note that any part of the value stream can be either of this three:

- Will clearly create value

- Will not create value but the waste is unavoidable due to the current technology

- Will not create value and is easily and immediately avoidable

Flow

Another aspect essential to the elimination of waste in the process is the complete understanding of the flow of processes. If the stream seems to have stalled at a certain point, that means waste will be or has been produced. Sometimes, that is unavoidable. It can, however be reduced, as highlighted in the previous section on waste by developing a value chain where each process is full in step with all the others.

Unfortunately, almost all traditional businesses are addicted to batch processes, wherein processes are aimed to produce as many items are possible with the goal of reducing the unit costs to a minimum value. Lean thinking approaches the matter in another way, wherein the focus is on the optimization of the workflow that the general cost of the business is reduced at a dramatic rate through the elimination of the need for transportation, subcontractor usage, systems, and warehouses.

Pull

Lean thinking has the goal of ensuring that every step in the process is executed because it is needed at a precise point in time. No step will be performed well ahead of time, preventing buildup of WIP inventory and bottlenecks. Synchronized flow will be maintained as a result. Rather than using the traditional American manufacturing approach of pushing work through based on a forecast and schedule, the pull approach dictates that nothing is made until there is demand for it.

This means that decision makers need to envision the differences between ideal and actual scenarios at any time in the workplace. This is where the use of visualization tools such as Kanban cards boards will be handy. With such a board, you can pull work from upstream depending on what you takt time dictates.

Additionally, it also requires efficient ways of voicing what is required in each step in the value chain. Sure, there is tension created because having a pull system requires flexibility and short design-to-delivery cycle periods. Nonetheless, pulling will enable the team to edge closer to single-piece-work. The team can identify issues as they show up, which can lead to the prevention of bigger problems. This can also contribute to complex situations being solved over time.

Excellence

Lastly, lean thinking is about instilling the kaizen spirit in every employee in your company. Kaizen refers to the notion of changing for the better albeit in small and sustainable ways. The kaizen spirit means looking for the 1% change for a hundred times from every team member instead of an instantaneous 100% change. Through the practice of kaizen, self and the collective confidence to face larger challenges is developed.

The ultimate goal of lean thinking is not to the application of the tools to all processes, but by seeking perfection by changing for the better. Smart systems or go-it-alone people are not the main contributors to perfection and are not sought after. It is the dedication from everyone in the company to improve things hand-with-hand little by little that matters.

By applying lean thinking in the overall workflow, the monitoring and reduction of wastes will be ensured.

Chapter 3. Agile And Scrum

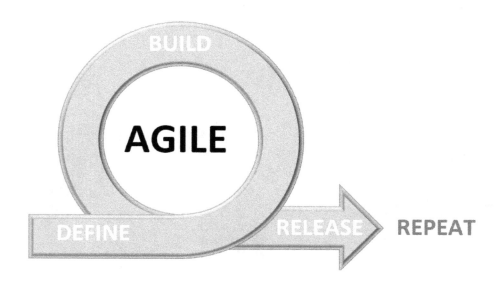

Agile is a compilation of methodologies focusing on the concept of iterative development, in which the requirements and solutions evolve or change by collaborating with teams capable of self-organization and are cross-functional. This management technique is often used in software development.

The advantages of Agile development are numerous. These include:

- giving the teams the capability to provide value
- having greater predictability,
- greater quality,
- greater skills to react to changes in demands from consumers, and
- faster delivery.

The most used agile methodologies are Kanban and Scrumban (Which is a hybrid of Kanban and Scrum). That's why this book will also cover Scrum and Agile.

The Benefits Of Going Agile

An advantage of an agile environment is that it promotes and develops teams to be self-organizing and accountable. Self-organization promotes initiative from employees and teaches employees to multitask while maintaining things in order. Being accountable means employees and teams recognize their responsibilities with the tasks appointed to them, that they can deliver what is asked of them, and if they are not able to do so, they can justify their actions and mishaps.

In an agile environment, engineering practices that are aimed to deliver high-quality items at a rapid pace is present. With these practices being employed throughout the processes, there's an assurance that consumer demands and expectations are met as fast as possible. This results to a great customer experience, and the positive impression increasing the likelihood that customers or clients will keep coming back.

The agile way of approaching business aligns the development of the products made corresponding with the demands from consumers and the goals of the company.

The 12 Principles

The modern Agile process is derived from the Agile Manifesto, which was developed by seventeen experts in software development. The manifesto presented the twelve principles that business should abide by if they want to improve their processes.

1. The highest priority should be satisfaction of the consumers, which can be achieved by punctual and continuous delivery of valuable software.

2. Be open to change. Accept changing requirements, even when they appear at the later parts of development. Agile processes should be able to help customers gain a competitive advantage.

3. Frequently deliver working software, and the preferred timescale should be as short as possible.

4. Developers and business people should work together daily for the whole duration of the project.

5. Continuously give the individuals in the team motivation, support, and trust that they can finish their tasks at the given timescale.

6. Keep in mind that face-to-face conversation has consistently proven to be the most effective and efficient means of discussing information to and with the team.

7. The primary measure of progress of the work-in-progress is working software. If you can develop prototypes, that's well and good, but you need to present something that actually works, rough edges and all, to be able to say that there's progress.

8. Sustainability is importance. Everyone involved including developers and users should be able to maintain a constant pace. The beauty of agile development is that the short bursts of activity keeps morale high. Burnout may happen but if you keep workloads at manageable levels, team members should be able to cope. However, if you bite off way more than you can chew, your team's motivation would be impaired.

9. To be able to enhance the agility of the processes, attention to good design and technical excellence should be maintained.

10. It is essential to have simplicity in the works, to maximize the amount of work not done.

11. It is from the teams that can self-organize that the best designs, architectures, and requirements spring from. This means that managers should be wary of micromanaging. The best course of action is to develop a team that can be trusted, and to foster that trust.

12. Twelfth, teams should reflect on how to be more effective, then adjust all behaviors corresponding from the reflections, all of that at regular intervals.

Incorporating all the twelve principles of the agile manifesto in your agile environment will not only aid ease the work processes, but also it will mold and develop the work ethic and dedication of the employees in the company. Having an effective and efficient work process plus dedicated employees will surely give the company the advantage.

The incorporation of the twelve principles of the agile manifesto in your agile environment makes the work a lot easier. It also allows everyone in the business holistically to develop themselves. Embodying the principles daily will improve the efficiency of the work and maximizes the quality of the product being made.

Customer demands change through time and employees find it difficult to deal with these. In an agile environment, however, accepting changes in requirements given by the consumers at an earlier or later notice is encouraged. Through the second principle of the Agile Manifesto, everyone is trained and developed to be able to adapt to the ever-changing customer demands.

Missing the deadline before getting the work done is a common problem in business for a long time ago. However, everyone can be trained to work quickly and efficiently through an agile environment. With the agile manifesto's third principle, employees are trained to deliver the required projects in the shortest amount of time possible.

There are occasions that the people working on a project are not able to agree with each other on the specifics in the project. This causes work delays and low product quality. To prevent issues, the fourth principle of the agile manifesto requires everyone involved in the project to work on it together daily for the whole duration of the product development.

It is unfortunate that sometimes, employees are not able to deliver their full potential to the projects given to them. Sometimes, tasks given to the employees are too simple, perhaps due to them being new to the company, leading to a waste of potential. These things can be fixed with the sixth principle of the agile manifesto, wherein every member of the team is given motivation and support.

Miscommunication can be a hindrance in workflow. The sixth principle suggests that a face-to-face conversation is the most efficient and effective way of discussing information with the whole team, wherein by having it regularly assures that no information is left not discussed.

In a project, an assurance that there is positive progress is the presence of a product that meets the quality demanded by its consumers. Without a product to show to investors or stakeholders, the support provided by these people might just be withdrawn from your company. Through the agile manifesto's seventh principle, everyone working in the project is required to deliver a product that satisfies the quality demands of the consumers.

The quality of the product is vital to the customers who will use it. Customers will choose your product when you can meet their expectations. The continuous giving of attention to technical excellence and good design, which what the ninth principle of the agile manifesto promotes, guarantee that the products you produce are at the optimum quality.

Extra attention to detail even though it is not required is an example of muda in lean thinking, referred to as over-processing. By applying simplicity to your work, which is through only doing work which is necessary to the overall workflow, maximizes the capability and time that can be allotted to projects that are yet to be done.

In an agile environment, teams are trained to be able to self-organize. They can decide on things and do their tasks without the frequent guidance and supervision of the management. With that, an environment build in trust exists. As what the eleventh principle of the agile manifesto pronounce, the best requirements, designs, and architectures come from teams who are cable of self-organization.

Like the concept of kaizen in lean thinking, the twelfth principle in agile manifesto promotes regular reflection on improving the employees' effectiveness and adjusting their behaviors in accordance to their reflections. By doing so, the employees are allowed to further enhance their skills and capabilities in their respective jobs. Everyone's improvement guarantees a greater overall workflow efficiency and maximization of the product quality.

Scrum

Scrum is a lightweight process framework and one of the many used in agile development. It is also the most preferred by many companies.

Process frameworks are sets of practices that should be followed to ensure consistency. Being lightweight means that the running costs of the processes are kept at the minimum as much as possible to maximize the amount of productive time that is available for getting valuable work done.

Scrum is often used in managing complex software and product development. It makes use of incremental and iterative practices, giving organizations the ability to adjust to rapid-changing requirements while producing products that meet the developing goals of the business.

A basic Scrum team consists of three members, the Product Owner, the Development Team, and the ScrumMaster. Each of these members has their specific roles in a project. In an agile environment that uses the Scrum framework, a scrum team is expected to be cross-functional and self-organizing.

Unfortunately, in some companies, teams are reliant on the management for the work that needs to be done. They only follow the orders of their higher-ups on the tasks that need to be taken care of. With the capability to self-organize, teams are allowed to choose which approach works best for them to get the task done at the projected deadline.

There are also cases that the teams ask outside help just to get things done. This comes with risks because there is no assurance that outside help provides a positive effect on the task that needs to be completed. Being cross-functional, teams are expected to have the capability to accomplish the task at hand without relying on outside help. With that, teams are trained to optimize their creativity, flexibility, and productivity.

Scrum teams carry out projects through iteration and increments, making sure that all factors coming from the feedback of the consumers are addressed. Through increment deliveries of the finished product, it guarantees that a tangible product is always available for use.

The implementation of the Scrum framework in an agile environment gives you the advantage of increasing the quality of the items to be delivered. In an agile environment, it is necessary to deliver the working product frequently and at intervals with short timescales. As a result, there will be an assurance that the product you will end up completing will be of high quality. This is because in an agile environment, products are regularly checked and changed based on the consumers' feedback.

The scrum framework also helps teams adjust and keep up with changes due to the access to certain information such as consumer feedback and demands regarding the products. Not only that, the framework is built in such a way that change is expected, which is a hallmark of agile development. In a software development setting, accepting the changes and working to address changing demands gives your clients a huge competitive advantage. The products you develop for customers will leave a good impression about the company and the teams behind it, and this could lead to more sales and profits.

Another advantage when using the Scrum framework is the ability make more accurate predictions, especially as regards consumer demands, meanwhile also spending less creating the products with the corresponding consumer demands. Having better estimates enables your organization to save a lot of time, effort, energy, and resources. As a result, you may redirect these resources toward other projects or endeavors that can generate value.

The defining characteristic of scrum is the ability to control the schedule and state of the projects. It gives you the idea as to which project needs prioritization and which projects can wait for a little longer. It also enables you to point out issues and bottlenecks in the workflow.

Maintaining an agile environment gives an assurance that the quality is met because regular inspections and developments are done, at a short time scale. For projects and tasks which include fast-paced changes through time, iterative development works better. An agile environment applying the Scrum framework makes it a lot easier to deal with feedback and demand from consumers which come at a rapid pace.

Kanban and other work visualization tools allow you to pinpoint problems earlier on so that efficiency is maintained. The following chapter is about how neglecting the issues in your company, be it in your employees, the management, the process flow, or equipment can bring you a lot more problems later on.

Knowing how important it is to address the problems in your company will give you insights on how you can improve performance from the individual to the organizational level.

Chapter 4. Why An Organization Needs Kanban: Overlooked Issues That May Cause Massive Problems

Kanban, as one of the Agile methodologies, has been developed with the ultimate goal of improving performance by giving an entire team a bird's eye view of what needs to be done, when it needs to be done, and who needs to do it. The beauty of Kanban is that it allows managers to see their team's capabilities and empowers every person in the team by setting limits, thereby encouraging sustainability.

Without tools such as Kanban, two things can happen: tasks will not be completed on time, leading to delays, or the team could fall victim to overwork, leading to burnout.

As Colin Powell said, "Never neglect details. When everyone's mind is dulled or distracted, the leader must be doubly vigilant."

Every aspect of the business should be checked regularly. Additionally, there are moments that the team is fixated on the tasks at their hand that they are not able to assess the bigger picture, wherein you can see it, so you must do something about it.

An essential part of a growing business is handling issues, whether they come from the consumers of the product or services being offered by the business, or from the team, the workflow, or the management. Being made aware of these issues allows you to make improvements on the products and services you offer. Neglecting these issues and being complacent will bring bigger problems, the worst of them being bankruptcy.

Poor management

One of the many problems being faced by businesses is the lack of Key Performance Indicators and the lack of monitoring of these indicators. These indicators provide criteria that give insights as to whether within the business, or a certain aspects of operation, is going well or taking a bad turn.

Neglecting these indicators will bring a lot of problems which include overproduction, lack of efficiency in the workflow, and work delays.

Overproduction is a common problem in businesses which occurs when companies are producing items more than what is demanded by the consumers. Failure to address this problem costs a lot, including money, energy, resources, and time. Companies that apply the push system are usually the ones who encounter this problem.

Another problem faced by companies is neglecting the reject ratio. This ratio measures the waste that was produced during the production of an item. Early on, a threshold should be set and alarm bells should ring if the amount of scrap that is being rejected is well below or above the ratio. After all, the goal of lean management techniques such as Kanban is to minimize waste in order to be more profitable. The reject ratio should be within acceptable limits.

However, a reject ratio that is too low might be an indicator of a lax quality assurance process, which could lead to customer satisfaction problems. Therefore, managers should constantly monitor these aspects.

Balancing production and the quality of work done by the employees is a headache if not managed properly. Growing companies tend to neglect one of the two while focusing on the other, which leads to several other problems later on. These problems include inefficiency, backlogs, low quality work offered, and the inability to keep up with the ever-changing customer demands in the market.

A study conducted on communication by the Society for HR Management includes four hundred companies with a hundred thousand employees each shows that lack of proper communication causes a loss of $62.4 million in average due to misaligned work, overhead, incorrect deliverables, and a lot more. The continuous lack of proper means of communication between all people in the company, not only a great amount of money will be lost, but also may lead to other worse problems, and eventually, bankruptcy.

Contributing factors to lack of proper communication include vague requirements, lack of enough experience, the fear of disappointment from the management's end, which may eventually lead to fear of losing one's job, poor processes and ego. Not establishing proper channels of communication may be detrimental to the growth and success of the company. It may also cause internal disputes between the employees and the management.

Retaining customers is also one of the many struggles in business. Businesses may lose customers if there is a decrease in product quality, a price increase of the product, and inability to meet the consumers' expected deadlines. Without customers, it will not be possible for companies to earn profit especially if there is intense competition.

Problems with employees

Motivating employees is a tough challenge, be it for startups or large corporations. On average, demotivated employees in startup businesses contribute about twenty percent of the total manpower. Not dealing with these employees may eventually lead to the bankruptcy of startup businesses.

For the case of large corporations, neglecting to motivate employees may lead to them providing only the bare minimum of effort, energy, and dedication at their tasks, having in mind that they work only to stay employed. These may lead to several problems, which include little to no quality provided at the work done, delays in the progress of the tasks at hand, missed deadlines, and absenteeism.

The presence of these problems will be costly for corporations as it may result to not being able to open up branches, extensions, or another business. The worst scenario is bankruptcy.

It is also a struggle for companies to train employees of the older generation with the new technologies present in society. Training is an expensive investment since it may take weeks, months or a year to make sure that the employees are properly oriented on how new technologies work. With that, companies may suffer overhead in operations, and eventually in the overall workflow.

Lack of proper utilization of employees is also a common struggle for different businesses worldwide. A mismatch between the employee's skills and the tasks assigned to that employee leads to work delays and low-quality work provided by the employee. Another example is not maximizing the potential of each employee in the company, which also leads to low quality work is given and work delays.

Iceberg of Ignorance

Sidney Yshido conducted a study dated 1989. The research showed that in many organizations, there is a disconnect among senior-level management. Many senior level managers seem to be unable to comprehend the processes and systems which can affect both the employees and the customers.

The iceberg of ignorance is in reference to this phenomenon in which senior level managers are aware of only 4% of the existing problems. Middle managers are aware of approximately 9%, with supervisors being aware of 74%, and the front-liners being aware of 100%. These are just rough numeral representations. The exact number may actually vary.

The most troubling thing from this study is that the people who are responsible and can solve the problems are the ones who don't even have the slightest idea of the problems that exist for the front-line employees, who are the ones responsible for serving the customers.

The executive-level leadership in the company must be aware of the problems that exist in the company, be it faulty equipment, an outdated computer software, or a broken process. These people should be aware of them to be able to help provide positive change for the employees and ultimately the consumers.

With a Kanban board maintained at various levels including the organizational level and front-line operations, individuals and management at every level can have a better look at how the business is doing.

Poor Customer Service

Customer service is another problem commonly encountered in all businesses. Multiple occasions of bad customer service will leave the consumers a bad image towards the company, which is detrimental to the growth and success of the company. The worst-case scenario will be shutting down the business.

No matter how good your products are, if you are not able to meet the consumers' expectations of your services, consumers will still not be satisfied with what is offered to them. If your customer service is not satisfactory for these customers, you will not have them as returning customers.

If you don't take the concerns, complaints, and feedback of consumers on your or your employees' performance, you will not be able to monitor progress. You will not be able to take action to rectify problems in a timely manner. This will only result to a negative impact on the reputation of the business.

With the presence of social media platforms such as Facebook, Twitter, Google Plus, Instagram, and a lot more, unsatisfied consumers will not hesitate to use these platforms to voice out their concerns and complaints that you have neglected. Negative comments posted on these platforms spread out at a rapid pace worldwide, resulting to massive damage on your brand's reputation.

Despite how established the business is, a bad reputation due to terrible customer services will leave a negative impact that will surely affect the business. Repeat customers, sales, and feedback from customers affect the growth and survival of your company. Poor customer service will result to a decrease in customer loyalty, brand value, and ultimately profits.

Muda

Waste reduction is one of the vital goals in lean thinking that is practiced to increase profitability. Muda, mura, and muri are the three types of deviation from the optimal allocation of resources which must be eliminated in order to increase profits.

Mura refers to inconsistence. With Kanban entailing a pull process, variation will be apparent. The sizes and types of requirements may vary on each iteration. Sometimes, variation cannot be avoided and is even encourages, such as in the case of design options being used to innovate. There is, however, variation that can be quickly avoided such as the use of various tools instead of a standard one, or adhering to different standards instead of establishing a universal set of standards.

Muri refers to overburden and this is in fact what must be dealt with first. This harks back to the principle of sustainability that Agile development promotes. Burnout must be prevented. If individuals and entire teams are overwhelmed, waste is likely to occur in the long run. Crazy work hours should be the exception, not the norm. This is why Kanban makes use of WIP limits, which sets a realistic workload for a specific iteration. With these limits, backlog is prevented, customers are satisfied, and the team would feel empowered that they are able to deliver.

In lean management, muda is typically used interchangeably with "waste." So it's the term that is often used whenever lean thinking principles are discussed. Its literal translation is wistfulness or futility. It is any hindrance that causes waste to be present in the production.

Taiichi Ohno, known as the father of the Toyota Production System, has seven hindrances or Muda identified, wherein when these hindrances are neglected, lessens the profits that can be earned by the company. These hindrances are transport, motion, waiting, inventory, over-processing, overproduction, and defects. An eighth Muda, termed as unused skill or talent, is later identified since dealing with this waste is a key factor in dealing with the original seven.

1. Transport, the first hindrance, is the movement of products even though it is not necessary to be done in the course of the overall process. By moving the products, it is exposed to risks of being damaged, delayed, or lost. Transporting products unnecessarily does not add anything to the value of the product and consumers are not willing to pay for that.

2. Motion, the second hindrance, is the unnecessary movement of the people or equipment during the creation of the product. It also covers the costs and damage inflicted on what creates the product. It includes repetitive strain injuries of the workers, wear and tear of the equipment, and unnecessary downtime.

3. If a product is not being processed or transported to a location, it is waiting. A large amount of time wasted is allotted to the waiting of the product to be worked on. Neglecting the increase in waiting time may lead to missing deadlines.

4. Inventory refers to all components, work in progress, and finished items that are yet to be processed. All of these represent a capital outlay which has yet to be converted to income. The longer the remain in the waiting stage, the more it will be damaging to the overall process and also to the company's profits.

5. Over-processing refers to doing more than what is required by the consumers. It also includes using components which are more complex, more precise, higher in quality and more expensive than what is only required. By doing so, it results in the delay in the production of the item and the spiking at high levels of production costs.

6. Production in large batches often results in creating more of a product than what has demanded leads to several wastes. It should be noted that the needs of the consumers change regularly and it changes quicker than the time that is consumed in creating large batches of products. Overproduction is considered as the worst kind of waste that can occur in a business.

7. Defective works or components are either discarded or reworked to achieve the demanded quality by the consumers. Inspecting and fixing defects not only cost effort, but also energy, time, and resources that should be allocated to other tasks. Defects result in additional delays and costs, which decreases the company's profits.

8. Unfortunately, there are circumstances wherein companies do not efficiently utilize their workers' skills, talents, and capabilities,

which is also a waste. There are even situations that for knowledge to be not shared, workers are permitted to work in silos. Without taking into account the proper matching and utilization of the workers' skills miss companies the opportunities that lie with it.

You should take note of the issues your company is facing, whether you are an employee or you are an owner. Problems should be addressed as soon as you see them. The following chapter will talk about how dealing with the issues will provide growth and success to the company.

Chapter 5. Taking Control: How To Use Kanban to Deal With Issues

Neglecting your problems will only give you a lot more problems to deal with later on. In this chapter, we will be talking about the benefits of dealing with the issues in the company.

Problems, in a way, help businesses grow. You can continuously bring satisfaction to the consumers despite issues. Dealing with the issues bring growth to each and everyone in the company, resulting in better performances, higher profits, and ultimately, success.

Using Key Performance Indicators

Key Performance indicators give you insight as to how the performances in the business go.

Note that the KPIs that would be most beneficial for your monitoring efforts may vary depending on the kind of project you're working on. For example, for social media marketing projects, engagements e.g. likes, comments, and retweets would be a good KPI. If you're in website development, Average Lead Time is a good KPI.

Here's a list of KPIs that are likely to be useful for businesses engaged in digital technology and marketing:

- **Average Lead time**
  This refers to the time it takes you to transform an idea into an actual product. In some industries, this spans the time during which a prototype has been developed and is ready to be moved to production. In others, it refers to the span of time during which an idea is formed and a product that is ready for use is developed. However, it usually does not take into account the time an idea is left in the "waiting period." You can even classify the items to

organize your data. You can set ALT per priority, or per project size, or per customer.

- **Queues**
  This refers to the list of items that are waiting to be processed, so they're supposed to be "waiting in between stages."

  Let's say your Kanban board has a column for "For completion", another for "For Review" and another for "For delivery". Once a project has been completed, it will be moved to the For Review section. If too many projects get completed because there are many members taking care of that task, a queue might start to form in the "For Review section if the project reviewers cannot keep up. Now, project delivery typically requires minimal effort and can be quickly performed, so it's not likely that a queue will form in that section even if it's manned by just one person. Nonetheless, queues are an indicator of where the bottlenecks are.

- **Work in Progress (WIP)**
  These refers to tasks that have been started but have yet to be finished. When you are able to track these tasks, you can help improve flow. Keep in mind that technically, all WIP do not add value to the customer. After all, customers won't be able to use unfinished work. You can only really consider the value when a project is completed and ready for the customer's use.

- **Reject Ratio**
  As mentioned, this measures the scrap that was produced during the production of an item, which spans the entire cycle. A threshold should be set earlier on and ideally, action should be taken if the reject ratio is too high.

- **Blockers**
  In Kanban, blocking refers to the art of marking an item as "frozen." These are the things that have completely stalled. This is

457

different from items that are just waiting to be processed (i.e. those in a queue). These are the items that are in limbo, awaiting an external dependency. For example, a client placed an order but part of the instructions is vague and requires clarification. Work is stalled until the client can provide clarifications.

- **Average Cycle Time**
  This refers to the amount of time it takes to complete a particular stage. So if a project requires multiple steps, the cycle time refers to the time it takes to complete one step. The time it takes for all the steps to be processed is the lead time. In Kanban, the goal is to optimize cycle time which means that you also have to consider the amount of work and resources that each step of the process requires. Be careful when optimizing cycle times because messing with one can result to dire consequences for another.

One of the indicators companies use is the reject ratio, wherein it measures the scrap that was produced during the production of an item. Through the Kanban method, monitoring of this indicator and other indicators will be easy since the by using a kanban board and kanban cards, you will be able to monitor the overall processes and the specifics of each part of the process.

By setting these indicators in your business, you will immediately know as to which part of the business needs changes or improvement. Every business, to be successful, places a handful of these indicators for them to know whether they made any progress at all and act accordingly depending on what these indicators show. Monitoring the overall workflow includes monitoring KPIs since these indicators will save you from problems that include overproduction, work delays, and lack of efficiency in the workflow.

Avoiding Overproduction

It's tempting to produce as many items you can during times wherein there is an idle equipment time or workers. However, by doing so, it does not do you any good and leads to a lot more problems later on which includes higher storage costs, work delays, product defects, higher capital expenditure, and excessive lead time. By eliminating overproduction, you can save a lot of money, time, resources, and energy that can be allocated to doing other tasks or projects.

Knowing as to how much product you should produce is essential and producing more than what is demanded will not do you good. By producing only what is required, you will be able to save a lot of time and resources which can be allocated to other tasks or products in the future. Avoiding overproduction is a must and you should never allow any instances of this in your business.

There are instances that scrap products are present in the production and there are a lot of factors that can attribute to that. Companies set reject ratios into the production of their products to regulate the production of scrap products. By following the established reject rations, companies can save resources, energy, and time which can later be used for other purposes.

Company growth and the quality of work done by the employees should go hand-in-hand. If you buy new equipment to improve your services, you should also train your staff to handle the new equipment efficiently. By doing so, you can be assured that the quality of services being offered to the customers is what you have perceived when you bought that new equipment for your business.

If it's the case wherein you bought new machinery for your factories or facilities having in mind that it will improve the rate of production of the items you sell, you should train your employees as to how to properly handle these types of equipment and you also need to make changes in the overall workflow. By doing so, you will be able to guarantee that the quality of the item being produced with the new equipment will be what the consumers are demanding.

Maintaining A Culture of Communication

Proper communication is necessary to assure that everything works fine in the business. Setting up proper channels of communication, be it through meetings or regular check-ups of the facilities gives the avenue for both the workers and owners to express their concerns and ideas, which will be for the betterment of the business. It is also through these communications that owners and workers will have engagements with each other wherein owners can show their support and gratitude to workers which will surely give workers the morale boost they need to work hard.

Retention of loyal customers in business is hard nowadays due to the presence of competitors. Making sure that retain loyal customers is a must since these customers give you a stable profit. They also give you an avenue to attract potential customers due to good impressions which are brought by the positive feedback of these loyal customers.

Keeping Employees Motivated

Boosting your employees will not cost you anything. After all, these employees work their selves to their limits to meet not only your expectations but also the expectations of the customers. Boosting their morale can be through engaging with them regularly, or providing incentives after a job well done. Motivating your employees will ensure that they give their full dedication in achieving their tasks, which in turn will surely boost the company's sales.

If you are in a startup business, it is necessary to make sure that your colleagues are fully motivated at all times. Demotivated employees may take up around twenty percent of the manpower of the whole team, which surely when left demotivated will cause a big disaster in the overall progress of the work being done. Motivating your colleagues every once in a while will make sure that they are working at their full potential, making things easier for the whole team.

For cases of large corporations, demotivated employees only work at their bare minimum having in mind that they do things for them to be still employed in the company. If you're having colleagues that are not motivated, it will affect the progress of the work you're both in. By keeping them motivated, it will assure you that the tasks appointed to your team will be done on time.

If you're a team leader, a supervisor, or in any managerial position in the company and you have colleagues under you which are demotivated, it will give problems not only to the work assigned in your team but also to the company when these employees will be ignored. By boosting the morale of these employees in any way you can, you will be sure that the whole team will work efficiently and that deadlines will surely be met at an earlier time. With that, company operations will go smoothly and the company goals will surely be achieved.

Newer technologies lead to newer techniques and approaches on how to make a job done in the shortest time possible. Training your employees, especially of the older generation, on how to properly handle these new technologies can be a struggle at times, and may cost you a lot of time. Adjusting the work processes and introducing a new comprehensible workflow will ensure that there will be no delays in the work being done since every employee will be able to understand it.

Employers should also know the capabilities, talents, and skills of their employees and that these skills should be utilized in the right way. A good match between the employees' skills and the tasks provided will surely shorten the time it takes to get the job done. With that, resources and energy will be saved while there is no need for the quality of the work to suffer.

Ensuring Quality

Consumers demand high-quality products and by producing defective items, not only you don't meet their expectations, but they also cause you delays on work. By making sure that the quality of the products you produce are at the quality demanded by the consumers, you can save a lot of time and money.

Providing Excellent Customer Service

Consumers want excellent customer service from businesses. A bad experience will leave the consumers a bad impression of the company. Maintaining excellent customer service, on the other hand, leaves a good impression on the consumers. Chances are they will surely return to your company as loyal customers. Loyal customers provide companies a stable income.

Concerns, complaints, and feedback from consumers of your products or services should be handled. Kanban, being an Agile methodology, enables you to take this further by enabling your company to meet changing customer demands.

Happy customers will spread the word of their experience to other people. With the presence of social media platforms such as Facebook, Twitter, and Google Plus, these happy consumers will not think twice of talking about their experience. Positive comments posted on these platforms spread out at a rapid pace worldwide, not only leaving your company a good reputation but also attracting potential customers.

Keeping a good reputation through excellent customer service can contribute to greater profits. Not only that, but it can be an avenue also for potential investors and business partners to open offers to your business.

Waste Elimination

By minimizing transport, or the unnecessary movement of products and people in the duration of the process, it prevents products from being exposed to damage and defects. It also prevents unnecessary workload, wears, and tears of equipment, and exhaustion of employees. Transport does not affect the value of the product and its elimination will prevent unnecessary expenses for the company.

Elimination of motion, or the movement of the people or equipment during production when it is unnecessary to do so, will save you a lot of time that can be allotted to do other tasks. By making sure that you have a well-organized workspace, the equipment that you will use is placed near the location of the production, and that the materials you need are placed in an ergonomic position, you will not only save excess time that you might use for a motion, you will also save energy.

Eliminating waiting time can make the work needed to be done at a shorter time scale. With having the work done at a quicker pace, another work that needs to be done can be worked out sooner. It also prevents excess inventory since raw materials will be used before it degrades and it also prevents overproduction since there will be no excess inventory.

Buying raw materials only when it is required and only in the required quantities will eliminate excess inventory. By its elimination, additional expenses, inefficient use of energy and resources, and work delays can be prevented. The materials that are conserved with its elimination can be used in other work that needs to be done.

Eliminating over-processing, or the excessive addition of any component in a workload or production despite not necessary prevents unnecessary expenses. It also conserves time and energy.

The next chapter will be talking about situations wherein you can improve your managing skills with the help of Kanban, Lean Thinking, Agile, and Scrum. Being in you're A-Game will surely lead your whole team into success in the future.

Chapter 6. Using Visualization Tools To Lead Your People To Success

Managing your people is not an easy task and issues in the business make things a lot worse. You'll need the right tools to deal with various issues. Implementing Kanban, Lean Thinking, Agile, and Scrum to your business will aid you in those endeavors.

Using the Kanban method

Kanban is a method used for workflow management which is designed to help you to visualize the work you have and maximize the efficiency of the work you are doing all the while being agile in doing the work. A Kanban board can have as many columns depending on the process of work you are planning to do. The simplest form contains three columns - Requested, In Progress, Done.

Key Performance Indicators aid you by providing criteria that determine whether the performances in the business are going well or not. Unfortunately, some companies do not apply these indicators in the business and some are not able to monitor these indicators. Either way, it causes these companies a lot of money, resources, and time.

By placing your projects in a Kanban board and setting up a limit in the "In Progress" column, you will be able to multitask projects. As long as you set up a limit in the "In Progress" column, which is based on the amount of work your team can handle at the moment, it is likely that the work will be done at the projected deadline you set. Additionally, Kanban's flexibility allows you to still point out problems that need to be addressed despite you are handling several projects at one time.

Identifying problems in your business can be easier through setting up your projects in a Kanban board. In a manufacturing setup, you will be able to see the bigger picture and identify the issues, be it knowing what causes the delay in the production of the item you sell or learn whether the overall process of producing your product is efficient. In an office setup, you will know as to what causes your team to not meet their deadlines, or you will be able to create a better-standardized process of dealing with projects since you have learned the previous one does not work efficiently.

Seeing the bigger picture lets you see what goes well and what needs improvement or change. Using the Kanban method in your business helps your team work out efficiently and maximize the output of your work. With that, you will be assured that everything goes well for your business.

Implementing Lean Thinking

Taiichi Ohno's original seven wastes can be eliminated if everyone in your company is adept in lean thinking.

Transportation can be prevented both in a manufacturing setup and in an office-based setup through different means. Workers who are working together in a project in an office-based environment should be close together. In a manufacturing setup, materials that are needed for the production of an item should be placed near the location of the production. In a manufacturing setup, transportation wastes can also be eliminated by setting up a U-shape production line, which creates a flow between the processes and also prevents overproducing work-in-progress products.

Excess inventory can be prevented whether you are working in an office or a manufacturing plant. You should only purchase raw materials when it is needed in the production, especially if the quantity of the raw materials is not enough for the production to proceed. By doing so, you can prevent work delays between production steps due to the excess amount of materials that need to be utilized.

Aside from purchasing materials only when necessary, you should also create a queue system. Having a queue system prevents the chances of overproduction to take place in your business.

Motion wastes include any movements of people, equipment, or machinery that are unnecessary. To prevent this, you should make sure that the workspace, be it in an office or a factory is well organized.

Additionally, materials and equipment should be placed at ergonomic positions to reduce stretching and straining. In a manufacturing plant, equipment should always be placed near the location of the production.

Waiting wastes can be eliminated by designing a process, wherein the process guarantees the flow of the production to be continuous. Another way is through leveling the workload in the business by utilizing a set of standardized work instructions. It can also be through the development of workers that are flexible and possess multiple skills, that are also capable to adjust quickly to the demands of the work provided to them.

One way of eliminating overproduction is by time takt thinking. By calculating the ratio of the time of open production to the average consumer demand, you will know the needed capacity to have the flow of production to be steady. Through takt time thinking, you will be able to make sure that the manufacturing rate throughout the stations is even. Another way of eliminating overproduction is to reduce the time needed to set up everything and by doing so enables a continuous flow of the process. Additionally, by having a pull system, like Kanban, can prevent overproduction by controlling the number of Work-In-Progress projects being handled at the moment.

Over-processing can be eliminated just by simply understanding the work requirements based on the customer's perspective. Before starting your work, you should always bear a customer in mind, producing the item or doing the job at the level of expectation and quality the customer desires. Also, only produce items at the specified amount by the customers.

Defects can be eliminated is to look for the most common defect and give it more focus. You should identify what causes it to happen frequently. Then, provide solutions that prevent the defect to happen again during production.

Another thing that you can do to eliminate defects is by making sure that no defective items pass through the production process. You can do that by designing a process that determines abnormalities that can be found in the production. With that, you will be able to prevent more defects that can come out later in the production process.

Redesigning your process is another way of eliminating defects. By designing a process that takes into consideration the defects that may arise, you will be able to save money, time, and resources that may be wasted due to the defects that may occur. Using standardized work guarantees a consistent manufacturing process. Having standardized work guarantees that the overall process is defect free.

By eliminating wastes, you can be guaranteed that you are working efficiently. By training everyone in your business in applying lean thinking in daily business, you can be assured that the work that needs to be done not only will be done at the projected deadline, but it also does not cost you unnecessary resources, energy, and money.

Maintaining an Agile environment

An agile environment helps everyone in your company design and build the right product that is demanded by the consumers. By its iterative approach, you are allowed to analyze and improve the product you are working on throughout its development. Having an agile environment enables your business to produce a high-value product that will let you stay competitive in today's market.

Retaining loyal customers is hard nowadays, especially since in every type of business you will not only deal with the ever-changing demands by the consumers but also you will have to deal with emerging competitors. Through disciplined project management, items are regularly inspected and adapted corresponding to the feedback from the consumers. With that, the assurance of products made with quality is ensured. Quality products not only retain loyal customers, but they can also attract potential customers.

Demands by customers change throughout time and it can be a hard thing to deal with. Having an agile environment, however, makes it easier to deal with. Accepting changes in requirements no matter be it early or late in the project it was asked is one of the principles in Agile. Despite how hard it is, training and working in an agile environment develop the whole team to adapt to changes asked by customers.

One of the problems faced in companies is the lack of leadership which greatly affects the performance of the team. Through the application of and training of leaders with Agile, leadership philosophies that promote teamwork will be embodied by the leaders which will surely boost up team performance. Teams working together and lead by efficient leaders make tasks easier to accomplish.

Applying the Scrum Framework

Remember that a Scrum team consists of three roles, the Product Owner, the Development Team, and the Scrum Master. The supervisor or the manager is usually given the role of either the Product Owner or the Scrum Master. Both roles have different tasks in a Scrum environment, however, both roles are fundamental to the success of the Scrum.

The Product Owner has the responsibility of the work of the development team and the maximization of the value of the product the Scrum team is working on. He or she is also responsible for managing the product backlog. Their job includes expressing clearly the items in the Product backlog, achieving the goals and missions through ordering items in the Product backlog, optimizing the value of work the Development Team is working on, and making sure that the Product Backlog is transparent, visible, and clear to everyone.

The Scrum Master, on the other hand, is responsible for making sure that everyone in the team understands and puts into action the Scrum theory, practices and rules. He or she works as the servant-leader for the team through guiding them as to how they incorporate the Scrum daily. He also guides the people who are not part of the Scrum team as to which of their interactions with the team helps and which do not.

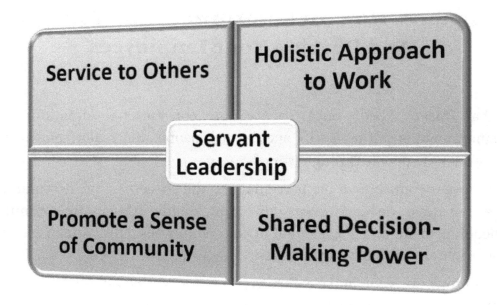

Balancing the growth of the company and the quality of work done by the employees is a headache if not managed properly. Growing companies tend to neglect one of the two while focusing on the other, which leads to several other problems later on. These problems include inefficiency, backlogs, low quality work offered, and the inability to keep up with the ever-changing customer demands in the market.

Through the Product Owner and the Scrum Master, the quality of the work being produced by the team will not suffer as the executive level management focuses on the growth of the company. The Product Owner provides the work requirements to the development team, making sure that the development team works on the product having in mind the requirements demanded by the customers. The Scrum Master guarantees that the Development Team and the Product Owner do their corresponding tasks at their maximum potential through encouragement and guidance of the whole Scrum framework.

Chapter 7. How To Kanbanize Your Workplace And Develop Your Employees

Agha Hasan Abedi once said, "The conventional definition of management is getting work done through people, but real management is developing people through work."

Employees contribute a big percentage to the success or the downfall of the business, depending on how you handle them. By training, encouragement, and engagement to your employees daily, you guarantee the brighter future of your business.

By training everyone in the company, everyone will eventually make their contribution in the identification and elimination of waste. It will not happen overnight, but there will be improvement day by day, little by little.

Training For Managers

Senior management and middle management should be trained regarding the importance of how things operate from the frontlines. They should have a firsthand experience of what is happening in the workplace. They are tasked to find out the facts themselves, and not only rely on reports submitted during boardroom meetings.

Engaging with the front-line employees and their work should be regularly done by the supervisors and managers to get a full grasp of the situation. By doing so, they can think and offer solutions to these problems as quickly as possible. It is also by them spending time at the workplace and with the employees that they can point out factors that may contribute to problems that may arise later on.

If you are a manager or supervisor, being able to point out bottlenecks in the process will save time, energy, and resources that might be allocated for the process had these bottlenecks were not pointed out earlier. The energy, time, and resources that were saved can then be used for other processes.

Fixing Skill Mismatch

Given the ability to visualize the overall and each specific part of the workflow, you can identify bottlenecks that can affect the work progress. There are occasions that these bottlenecks come from employees. It may be caused by them not being properly oriented of their tasks or how the equipment works, a mismatch between their skills and the tasks handed to them, absenteeism, and many more.

One of the bottlenecks that may arise in the process is the lack of knowledge of some employees of the older generation with new technologies present in society. Assigning them to other tasks that they are capable of at the moment is the best way to go. At the same time, you should train them to handle these new technologies introduced to the business.

Teaching them new things improve their performance and capabilities. Older generation employees work their selves out with full dedication to your company. Helping them improve their work by maximizing their capabilities will boost their confidence, shows them that you trust them, and surely will increase your sales later on.

Quality circles

This refers to a team of people who work on similar tasks. These groups are formed in order to discuss problems with the workflow particularly quality issues and to develop solutions for improvement. They're usually small and are led by a mentor. Ideally, they are given training in problem solving methods like brainstorming and cause-and-effect diagrams. They will present their findings and recommendations to management and when solutions are approved, these teams will be handling the implementation.

Kaizen spirit

Kaizen operates on the principle that improvement is a normal part of a job, and it is not something you only do when there is only available time after you've done everything else. Quality circles and individual suggestions can help improve the work within the normal working day. Encourage employees to be on the lookout for ways in which the system can be improved. Be open to suggestions. One of the ways in which this can be implemented is by making use of Andon.

Andon, a Japanese word used in the lean production approach, is a system of notifying the management, other workers, and maintenance of problems concerning quality or process. It can be through manual activation of a worker through a button or pull cord and can be also automatically activated by the production equipment itself. The work will be stopped until the problem is solved.

Most businesses utilize software or machines to do work. Despite having these things, automated work still needs specified human judgment to have things done the right way. With that, a lot of machines cannot be left alone to do the work provided since there's a possibility that things could go wrong if no one monitors them.

The practice of continuous imparting of human judgment to the system so that the system can monitor by itself without the unnecessary calling out of a human whenever it feels there is something wrong is known as automation. It is important since it separates the people from the machines, and prevents humans from doing the work tasked to the machines. It teaches lean thinking everyone in the company to look for ways to design smarter and lighter machines that cost less on capital expenditure.

Implementing lean thinking in the workplace means promoting the idea that everyone thinking together and that no one should be left with a problem to face alone. The practice of Andon enables knowledgeable employees to stop the production of a product once a defect is identified and call for assistance to resolve the issue. Andon teaches lean thinking to employees by pointing out on-the-spot obstacles to the lean aim of having zero defects at all stages of the process throughout the entire process, at all times.

Use the PDCA technique

This is an acronym for Plan-Do-Check-Act, the four steps in the iterative management approach developed by William Edwards Deming, an American statistician who spent time in Japan to train leaders of notable businesses. It can be used a problem solving technique.

Let's say that you're facing a major issue with how fast your customer support team can handle complaints. Many customers are unhappy with how much time it takes for them to receive any response. Here's how you can use PDCA to try to solve the problem

1. Plan. In this stage, you do just that – develop a plan for what needs to be done. If it's a large project, chances are, planning alone will take a lot of time and effort. You can make this undertaking manageable by taking smaller steps or dividing it into manageable chunks. In this stage, you will need to identify the core issues that need to be resolved, the resources you already have, and the resources you will need to acquire. In the event that it's not possible to acquire certain resources you also need to create a plan about what you can do with what's available.

    You also need to set the "win condition." This refers to a concrete goal that would allow you to know outright if your plan is working. For example, your win condition could be that "Only 3% of customer complains mention slow response rate as a problem" or "10 work hours have been spent on customer support".

    Go through the plan with your entire team a couple of times before you start the next stage.

2. Do. In this stage, you apply everything that has been discussed in the previous stage. It's best to implement your plan on a small scale because unpredicted problems may still arise.

    For example, if the problem is the rate at which customer concerns are handled and during the planning stage, you have determined that it's because there is no workforce that is dedicated for this task, consider training a few of your employees to allocate more time to customer support instead of building an entire customer support department. Keep in mind that this will have repercussions on your entire system because the time allocated for customer support will be removed from existing tasks.

3. Check. This is a crucial phase of the PDCA process. Audit how the plan was executed and check if it actually worked. Check if the win condition has occurred. Did the amount of customers complaining about slow response decrease? If it did, you still need to check if the number of customer complaints is actually the same in comparison to previous numbers. Did the employees really spend more time on customer support? Perhaps, there was a reduction in complaints because business was slow in the first place. Perhaps, the employees really did increase the amount of time they spend on customer support but it wasn't enough.

   You need to know if the problem has been resolved and if it wasn't, you need to analyze it and pinpoint the root cause.

   Act. If everything seems to have worked out, it's time to apply your initial plan on a larger scale.

The next time you face an issue about customer support, you can go through all these steps again and make small changes.

The PDCA cycle is a powerful tool for fixing problems at any level in your organization. And because it's iterative, your team can keep on finding and testing solutions over time and make small improvements. Just keep in mind that it takes time so it's not ideal to use this method to deal with an urgent problem.

SMED

SMED, which was originally known as Single Minute Exchange of Die or the changing of tools under ten minutes, is a fundamental practice in lean thinking which directly focuses on flexibility.

Flexibility is the ability to quickly switch from one project to another. SMED teaches lean thinking by seeking to improve flexibility all the time until a continuous flow at the right order which can respond to immediate demands by customers.

Standardized Work

Standardized work refers to the graphical illustration of the smooth flow with zero or one work-in-progress and having a clear location for everything including steps. This can help when implementing lean thinking management methods. After all, lean thinking is all about going for the smoothest workflow in every project through identifying and resolving problems one by one, leading to the development of both the workflow and the autonomy of the employees.

When there is standardized work, you are providing your employees guidelines on how work is executed. However, over time, these guidelines would have to be updated due to the nature of Agile development. Changes occur and improvements are made, and you need to make sure that the entire team is on board. When a team member is lagging and a bottleneck is form in the parts of the board that he is working on, the entire team will be affected.

Here are some steps in making sure that standardized work is practiced in an Agile environment.

1. Prioritize the routines that directly add value to your process – the things that affect quality and production speed. Of course, there are things that do not add value but must still be complied with, such as safety standards.

2. Develop best practices for executing tasks. This can be done through workshops with the staff. The routine should be as clear as possible and the recommended processing time for each step should be indicated. Include checkpoints that employees could use to be aware of deviations. Test to make sure that the guidelines or instructions are reasonable.

3. Present the task and flow in visual form. This is where Kanban boards can come in handy. Employees and managers should be able to tell outright what needs to be done and whether it's getting done properly. This can also make it easier to check what can be improved.

4. Training every team member to the standard. Make sure that everyone knows they're expected to follow the guidelines. Make it clear that you want everyone to raise a signal immediately if a problem arises.

5. Team leaders should be aware that they're expected to initiate improvement work. It's best to standardize certain aspects of the manager's tasks as well. A manager should always consider whether there's anything that will hinder the work flow for a specific day.

6. Utilize an improvement process. The board could use indicators that a task has been performed to standard. For example, green cards can be used to indicate that something went smoothly, and red could indicate that there was deviation. This way, you could spot problems that recur. Conduct meetings regularly to talk about problems and improvements.

Standardized work allows employees to identify tricky quality points such that they can visualize which matters to the customer, able to distinguish what goes right or wrong at every stage, and can confidently proceed from one stage to another. It teaches employees lean thinking through the visualization of every hindrance to the smoothness of the work and pointing out topics for Kaizen.

Consider training your employees with lean thinking so they can improve their skills and capabilities, which then can be used to identify and resolve issues in the business. When used with the application of the Agile Manifesto, overall performance will be improved. When the Scrum Framework is integrated into your system, it allows work to be easier through the members of the scrum teams having their specific roles and contribution to the success of the project.

Conclusion

I'd like to thank you and congratulate you for transiting my lines from start to finish. I hope this book was able to help you to visualize the overall workflow and maximize the efficiency and output of the overall work process through the application of Kanban, Lean Thinking, Agile, and Scrum to your business.

Kanban is a method that gives you the ability to visualize the overall workflow and spot problems that hinder the progress of the workflow. This is done through various techniques such as standardized work and the use of indicators such as lead time and cycle time.

To maximize the efficiency of the process and achieve the output goal you have in mind, you should make sure that the overall workflow goes smoothly. With the use of the Kanban board and cards, you will be able to get a good picture of the workflow, which gives you then the idea of which processes work well and which processes have problems.

Kanban also maximizes efficiency by enabling your team to multitask to an extent. Multitasking can do harm when done poorly so kanban places a limit on the work-in-progress, which depends on the capability of the workers and the capacity of the equipment. With the limit present, you will also be allowed to work in a sustainable manner. This also boosts employee morale.

As a lean thinking tool, Kanban promotes the identification and elimination of waste, resulting to more profits. The fact that lean thinking encourages managers to focus on the frontlines and develop the employees also help maintain morale and create an environment that promotes accountability and productivity. The regular workplace visits enable them to stay attuned to what's going on and what can be done to make sure that the workflow goes smoothly.

As an agile development technique, it also helps you keep customers satisfied, thanks to the flexibility that it allows and the pace with which it can keep up with customer's demands.

The next step for you to do is to apply what you have learned here in your business. By doing so, it will be a guarantee that you will be able to visualize every aspect of the workflow, assuring the smooth flow of the process. By having a smooth flow, you will then maximize the efficiency of the work being done, and finally, maximize the output quality to the levels demanded by the consumers.

If there is one thing that I want to happen, that is the success of your business through the tips provided in this book. Start making assessments in your business and apply the things you learned in this book and secure the success of your business in the coming days. I wish you the best of luck!

Book #8

Kaizen

How to Apply Lean Kaizen to Your Startup Business and Management to Improve Productivity, Communication, and Performance

Introduction

Thanks for purchasing this book, *Kaizen: How to Apply Lean Kaizen to Your Startup Business and Management to Improve Productivity, Communication, and Performance.* This book expounds the Japanese concept and contains a comprehensive guide on how to apply it in managing your startup.

More than half of startups fail within 10 years after their launch. This fact remains true regardless of how good or bad the economy is. Poor management is one of the top reasons behind the said phenomenon.

Starting Is Easier than Before

These days, it only takes guts for some people to start a venture. Besides, generating business ideas isn't that much of a problem when you can simply search and copy online. Or, you can visit the nearest commercial district and discover what essential product or service is missing.

When it comes to getting funds, you can find another work and save your income from that. You can also sell your own things online and on a garage sale. Borrowing money from family and friends is another option. Don't forget taking loans from banks or lenders. You can try crowdfunding as well.

What about land and equipment? Well, you don't have to buy everything at once. You also don't need brand-new equipment. If location matters in your business, you can rent for the meantime. In case your offer can be provided online, you can work anywhere as long as your computer is connected to the Internet.

Downloadable and web-based programs make it easy to perform functions like planning and accounting. There are also available templates that you can use to create proposals and contracts. If you don't know how to operate the programs or what to include in the documents, you can just search for guides online. When you start your business, you can practically do all tasks on your own.

Getting Your First Customer

Creating a social media page for your business doesn't cost a thing. You won't even waste precious time for it. You can do it while waiting in line, riding the subway or relaxing in your couch. Yet, doing so allows you to promote your business for free.

Several tasks involved in operating a startup are easier and cheaper than ever. Consequently, the competition is fiercer as aspiring entrepreneurs take the plunge every now and then. As a result, getting the attention of prospects is more challenging than before. How are you going to draw your first customer then?

Novelty and curiosity could lure your first set of customers. However, you can't depend on those two factors as time goes by. What will you do next?

Managing Your Business

Whether your launch succeeds or fails, you're bound to think about your next move. It's the first step in improving. Planning and implementing improvements form part of good management. Furthermore, good management strikes a balance between learning from the past, implementing changes in the present, and preparing for the future.

Improvement is both a way and an end-goal in managing a business. How does that make sense?

Introducing Kaizen

Kaizen is originally a Sino-Japanese word denoting improvement. As it got adapted into western use, the meaning evolved into continuous improvement. The qualifier isn't just a fancy addition though.

Continuous improvement and respect for people summed up the guidelines known as The Toyota Way. Published in 2001, the guidelines were sought and studied by western entrepreneurs, managers and even political leaders. All of them hoped to learn how one Asian company became one of the frontrunners in a market dominated by North American companies.

As a startup owner myself, I was eager to learn from successful companies like Toyota. I wasn't alone in feeling that way. I know you're also curious, and so are other aspiring entrepreneurs who want to be prepared before they begin operating their businesses.

This isn't the first book discussing management lessons from Toyota. However, this stands out for making the said lessons appropriate for running a startup. It doesn't shy away from discussing the challenges that make kaizen difficult to apply.

You see, The Toyota Way stresses good relationship between managers and subordinates. However, that doesn't seem valuable when you're outsourcing instead of hiring your own employees.

Outsourcing is beneficial in many ways, especially for startups. It's cheaper than hiring full-time employees because you don't have to pay for monthly salaries and benefits. You don't need to spend time on recruitment. Without employees, you won't deal with labor disputes and office politics as well.

As your startup grows, however, you can't rely on outsourcing alone. You have to stop doing everything on your own so you can devote your time and skills on important functions. Sooner or later, you'll require talented people to help you improve your venture.

Administrative and marketing assistants usually comprise the first hires of a startup. Next, you'll get employees in-charge of operating and maintaining your equipment. If you're providing services, you'll need specialists to further get ahead. Even if your startup is about selling digital products and services, you're going to make a technical team as you expand.

As you open another branch, you'll need a new set of employees. Who makes an ideal manager for the new branch? Between a qualified applicant and a long-time employee, the latter tends to be more preferable.

Why? Hiring in-house boosts employee morale. After all, the promotion can serve as recognition of hard work and loyalty.

It also saves time. Your long-time employee doesn't need a lengthy orientation before handling his or her new job. If you hire someone else, you'll have to introduce him or her to your company values, vision, and culture first.

Going back to managing a startup, better funding and equipment can get you ahead of the pack. However, topnotch human resource is one of the biggest factors that gets you far. You can read a lot of books and attend many classes. Yet, it's still more time-efficient to hire people and hone their skills as you improve yours.

Continuous improvement begins with the leader and subordinates. Get to know how it happens with the help of this book on kaizen.

Chapter 1: Demystifying Kaizen

"Open the window over there and take a look. It's a big world out there." (Sakichi Toyoda)

By this time, you've probably heard or read about the humble beginnings of well-known companies like Google, Apple, Starbucks, McDonald's, and Kentucky Fried Chicken. Their stories of starting with nothing and changing the world in some ways, as Boitnott (2014) described it, are a great source of inspiration for aspiring and struggling entrepreneurs. However, it's worth noting that all of the said companies started and thrived in the US.

Donilon (2016) asserted that the US had territorial advantage. The same can't be said about other countries that went or are still going through territorial disputes with their neighbors. The said edge was even more evident when the two world wars happened. With vast oceans and countries on its sides, Uncle Sam was practically untouchable.

The US dealt with crises along the way. Yet, it remained politically and economically better than many countries. The stability and positive view on the country helped American entrepreneurs more than they're willing to admit. Can you imagine the challenges that a foreign company faces when it competes on the world market?

The Unconventional Asian Company

For more than 70 years, General Motors was dubbed as the number one automaker in terms of sales. Ford came next and held the position for five decades. However, things changed when Toyota entered the picture in 2008 (Bunkley, 2008).

Founded by Sakichi Toyoda, the Japanese automaker began as a part of a loom-manufacturing company in the 1930s. Aside from automatic looms, Toyoda also introduced and implemented the concept of jidoka (Rosenthal, 2011). Originally meaning automation with a human touch, the said concept would later serve as one of the two pillars of the Toyota

Production System. The other pillar was just-in-time and it was developed by Taiichi Ohno, one of Toyota Motor Corporation's industrial engineers.

It was unusual for a company to make concepts for its production system and management approach. However, Toyota made it acceptable. It only reflected the company's creativity and willingness to handle challenges.

From Toyoda's Challenge to an Unprecedented Success

Toyota's success in the automotive industry wasn't earned overnight. In 1937, the Toyota Motor Company was established as an independent entity from Toyoda Automatic Loom Works. Years before that, Sakichi Toyoda initiated a challenge to invent a durable and efficient battery that's dependent on hydropower, not petroleum (Hasegawa, 2008).

Sakichi Toyoda's son, Kiichiro, spearheaded the establishment of the Toyota Motor Company. By the time the younger Toyoda did that, US and Russian-based researchers were already working on innovations for their automobiles.

Toyoda's challenge was given more importance when World War II began. Petroleum supply to Japan became scarce. That time was also difficult for Japanese researchers and their foreign counterparts to exchange ideas.

Without much choice, Toyota solely depended on professors from Japan's top universities. Despite having dozens of experts in one roof, the automaker still failed in creating the battery that Sakichi Toyoda wanted. Nevertheless, the discipline and dedication fostered in the research became instrumental in the development of the company's management approach.

The postwar period almost drove Toyota to bankruptcy in 1949. It survived, thanks to a loan from a consortium of banks. However, the company had to lay off 2,000 employees. Kiichiro Toyoda didn't want to fire employees, but he didn't have much choice as it was stipulated in their loan agreement. He stepped down as president when the mass layoff happened (Assembly, 2007).

Toyota's researchers gradually went back to work on Sakichi Toyoda's challenge. Japan's oil crisis and introduction of emission regulations in the 1970s further served as motivation for the company to innovate.

By 2008, Toyota still failed to accomplish Sakichi Toyoda's challenge. However, the innovations they developed paved the way for hybrid cars. Despite the unprecedented feat, then-company president Katsuaki Watanabe downplayed it and asserted that they're concerned with their automobiles' performance (Hazegawa, 2008)

Innovation, Not Competition

Who doesn't want to be the frontrunner in an industry? Imagine the number of investors lining up to offer you funding. You can finally help more people than before. Above all, the recognition is bound to make you feel good.

However, one of the important lessons you should learn from Toyota is that ranking first shouldn't serve as your main motivation in managing your business. It's true that the Japanese automaker beat Detroit's Big Three (GM, Ford, and Chrysler) in total sales in 2008 (Vlasic, 2011). The success was relatively short-lived, though. In just a couple of years, the American companies reclaimed the throne as their Japanese competitor had to deal with recalls. The rise, fall and return of the Big Three just prove that records are made to be broken.

A few years later, however, Toyota's sales went up and defeated the American automakers again. In fact, it's the number one automaker as of 2017, according to the Organisation Internationale des Constructeurs d'Automobiles. GM and Ford ranked fourth and fifth respectively.

Toyota's secret to success is out in the open. In his book, David Magee (2007) emphasized kaizen (continuous improvement) as one of the factors that helped the Japanese automaker become number one.

The Influence of Oriental Culture on Kaizen

Have you ever visited a nearby Chinatown, K-town or J-town? These Asian communities in foreign lands like the US reflect how tight their ties are. Likewise, they also signify the oriental culture's emphasis on social harmony. When western culture stresses individualism, its eastern counterpart gives more importance to group dynamics. Jeffrey K. Liker and Michael Hoseus (2008) further elaborated the differences of western and eastern cultures in many aspects of managing a business.

Culture played a role in the development of Toyota's management style. Instead of encouraging individuals to do differently, eastern culture dictates to try fitting into a group. Instead of recognizing an individual's accomplishment, it gives credit to teamwork.

Such attitude is beneficial in handling errors in business operations. For Toyota, a problem means deviating from standard while western culture views it as a result of someone's mistake. To manage the problem, the Japanese automaker encourages employees to ask for help. In contrast, western culture lets the individual who made a mistake to take the blame and resolve the issue on his or her own.

Ensuring harmony in the workplace enables kaizen to happen. Employees resolve problems more efficiently when they do it together and when they refuse to pin blame on anyone. By continuously resolving issues, they can improve processes. That's easier said than done though.

The Challenges of Implementing Kaizen

To be clear, you don't have to fully embrace oriental culture to apply kaizen. However, you should be prepared to do adjustments if you want to overcome the biggest challenges in applying the approach.

Resistance is among the hurdles against kaizen (Rodrigues, 2018). While you may warm up to the idea, do you think your employees will? Time will help weed out employees who don't share the same vision as you. However, time won't be enough to overturn how others view kaizen. One way to resolve this is by training your employees about continuous improvement.

Lack of communication tends to trigger and worsen resistance as well. As an employer and a manager, make sure your employees can easily talk to you about problems, suggestions and opinions. Being able to communicate with you helps them become more accepting of your ideas and decisions. Additionally, better communication speeds up crisis management.

Misconceptions are another challenge against the implementation of kaizen in startups. Continuous improvement isn't synonymous to continuous successes. The positive results won't be quick as well.

Be prepared to experience losses as you focus on improving your offer. That's just part of taking risks. Moreover, applying kaizen discourages you from minding the trends. Trends come and go, don't they? Sometimes, they favor other startups and cause yours to lag behind. But at the end of the day, the well-developed product and service take the lead for a longer time.

Failure to define important process is also an obstruction to kaizen's efficiency. In the latter chapters of this book, you'll learn about the types of waste in business operations. Some of the said waste are related to processes.

Three Principles Behind Effective Kaizen

Kaizen's efficiency has a lot to do with its three principles, namely process and results, systematic thinking, and not blaming (Magee, 2007). Under the first principle, both the process and results are considered equally significant. It's important for Toyota to sell well, to make quality cars and to improve their production processes. Think about this: What's the point of being number in sales but also having high operational costs and facing the possibility of recalls?

Process and results affect each other. If there are no problems in your process, you're likely to create polished products or offer refined services. Ideally, that leads to positive results as evident in increased sales and improved brand awareness. Such kind of results can motivate both the management and workforce to keep on doing well. It can also prompt investors to consider funding one of your business proposals.

The second principle, systematic thinking, is all about seeing the big picture. This means you don't just see the problem as it is. Dig deeply and look widely. In the next chapter, you'll find out the root cause analysis that serves as basis for crisis management.

You should also apply this to every action you do for your business. Always consider the short-term and long-term repercussions of every action.

Such principle prevents you from acting recklessly. Thoughtless actions put your startup's reputation at risk. Instead of having one problem, you end up with a lot. You can even cause disruptions in your operations, which can mean losses.

The third principle is something that many managers fail to do: not blaming. Blaming is useless. A lot of people know it but they still do it. Why? It's simply because it's easy to do. It also serves as a blanket excuse for the mistake and bad results.

Blaming wastes time and effort. Instead of using that time and effort to work on the mistakes, you'll end up managing ill feelings and unpleasant atmosphere at work. If that unpleasantness resulted in defects and operational disruptions, you'll deal with additional problems and waste more of your resources.

No matter how grave the error is, don't blame. Communicate with the person who committed the mistake and work things out. Depending on the gravity of the mistake, you may impose sanctions but make sure they're still legal, ethical and proportional to the error.

How to Start Continuous Improvement

Continuous improvement starts somewhere. Ideally, it should begin right when you plan your venture.

What are your short-term and long-term goals? If your startup is to succeed, you should first define what success means to you. You should determine key performance indicators (KPIs), but make sure they're realistic. However, you shouldn't get hung up over KPIs. Dwell on a challenge instead.

Just like Sakichi Toyoda, state a challenge that you wish your startup will accomplish. Make sure the dare is bound to benefit a lot of people without directly causing damages and injuries.

Accomplish the challenge using courage and creativity. Don't be afraid of mistakes. They're going to happen no matter how careful you are. Even if you're using equipment, there can still be errors.

What if you don't have the equipment needed to meet the challenge? Let creativity take over. Make the most out of your workforce, but be sure to keep them well-compensated. Take advantage of free resources. Learn from your competitors' mistakes.

Lenders and angel investors are also there to provide financial backing to your startup. Have the guts to apply for loan or ask for funding from someone you know.

It may take years before you can accomplish the challenge. This means some of your attempts will end up in failures. However, those failures aren't fruitless at all. They can serve as training for both you and your team. They can also teach about what processes and changes don't bring out good results.

Once you succeed, create another challenge. You might not realize it but you're already applying kaizen at that point.

Notes:

- Focus on innovation, not on competition.
- Resistance, misconceptions and failure to determine important processes are obstruction against kaizen implementation.
- The three principles behind effective kaizen are processes and results, systemic thinking, and non-blaming.
- To start continuous improvement, determine and meet challenges.
- Courage and creativity help you meet challenges.

Chapter 2: Relating Kaizen to Managing a Startup

"Great discoveries and improvements invariably involve the cooperation of many minds." (Alexander Graham Bell)

Kaizen is applicable to many aspects of business. After all, each aspect of business management requires continuous improvement.

Key Phrase: Important Business Process

So, your office's bathroom sink drains slowly every time someone uses it. Imagine the time and effort that some users devote in attempting to resolve the problem. Then, your employees spend more time complaining and suggesting instant remedies. When things get worse or when you see the problem yourself, perhaps you'll give it attention and hire a plumber yourself. How do you stop the problem from recurring? Are you also going to apply kaizen on it?

Obviously, you don't have to obsess over continuous improvement on your bathroom's functionality. There's no need as long as the bathroom is safe and sanitary, the fixtures are in good condition, and there are enough stalls and features for your employees.

Focus kaizen on important business processes. These processes differ from one industry to another. For manufacturers, the manufacturing procedure is clearly the most important one. If you're into retailing, providing choices, allowing customers to select, and processing orders forms part of the significant business process. Offering topnotch customer experience sum up the important process in the service industry.

A business process is basically the structured set of activities involved in delivering the product or service to customers. It involves creation, selection, payment and delivery. Under creation, you'll have to deal with supply management and quality control. Marketing forms part of providing choices for your customers. Payment involves accounting while delivery covers customer service.

By understanding your key business process, you can allocate your resources more effectively. You can also choose which business functions you should continuously improve. These are more manageable when you're operating a startup as the process tends to be simpler.

As your business grows, the business gets complicated. Aside from your main business process, there'll be management and supporting processes (Scheer, von Rosing & von Scheel, 2014).

Familiarizing yourself with your important business is pretty simple yet beneficial. Unfortunately, not a lot of aspiring and struggling entrepreneurs know this. Some of them add steps like gathering feedback and informing their customers about other products and services. If customers are rushing, the last thing they'll need is listening to an agent's marketing spiel.

Three Steps to Remember in Developing Kaizen Culture in the Workplace

Upon determining your key business process, you can initiate continuous improvement by performing three steps (Magee, 2007). The steps are as follows:

1. Identify problem.
2. Find out the root cause.
3. Formulate a solution.

The aforementioned steps don't look groundbreaking at all, do they? There are similarities with how doctors diagnose conditions and how students solve Math problems.

The difference of kaizen, however, is how it underscores the second step. This isn't to say that doctors don't exert effort in pinpointing the root cause of their patients' conditions. For kaizen's root cause analysis, you have to remember two concepts: the five whys and genchi genbutsu.

The Five Whys

The concept of five whys is basically about asking why for five times in order to reach the root cause of a problem (Ohno, 2006). This practice is applicable on business operations and even on your personal life.

Here's an example on applying five whys in your personal life:

1. Why did you oversleep? Because I was tired.

2. Why were you tired? Because I had to walk home.

3. Why did you have to walk home? Because I couldn't book a ride.

4. Why couldn't you book a ride? Because my phone broke.

5. Why did your phone break? Because the phone slipped and got dropped from my pocket.

Based on the above scenario, the root cause of oversleeping was dropping the phone. That appears illogical. But when you think about the root cause, you can assume that it has a lot to do with clumsiness and dependence on one's phone. Then, you develop a solution. It could be fixing the broken phone, buying a new one, or bringing a power bank.

Below is an example of applying the five whys in your business operations:

1. Why did customers refuse buying your products? Because your products weren't sealed.

2. Why were your products not sealed? Because the machine for sealing broke.

3. Why did the machine for sealing break? Because the seal got stuck in between the gears.

4. Why did seal get stuck in between the gears? Because the seal was too thick.

5. Why was the seal too thick? Because the wrong seal was used.

In the said scenario, the solution should cover removing the obstruction and replacing the wrong seal with the correct one. Once tested and fixed, make sure your products are sealed accordingly.

Don't try to dig deeper than the five whys. In the above scenario, asking another why is likely to give human error as the root cause. (This doesn't have to apply when you're trying out the five whys on a personal issue.) The analysis should never end up with such kind of root cause because you or your employees will blame one person.

Be mindful of your reasonings as well. Never jump into conclusions when asking each of the five whys. The answer to one of them should be a direct cause. For example, if you wonder why the machine broke, you shouldn't say it was because it's old. Wear and tear increase the risk of machine breakdowns. However, it's the damage they bring that could serve as direct cause to malfunctions.

The root cause shouldn't be another symptom of the problem as well. Going back to the aforementioned scenario about the machine, when you're answering why the seal got stuck, don't say it's because the machine also stopped the day before.

As much as possible, use a pen and paper (or marker and whiteboard) when asking and answering the five whys. Don't do it on your computer or phone. Otherwise, the autocorrect and autofill functions of your devices may end up doing the analysis for you. Writing, in contrast, gives you a bit more time dwelling on the possible causes. You can also do mind maps better when you do it on paper or whiteboard.

To realize if your root cause analysis is logical, one trick is to recite the answers minus the word because. Start from the answer for the fifth why. Afterwards, say "therefore" followed by the fourth answer. Repeat that until you reach the first answer. For the above scenario, your answers should be like the following: The wrong seal was used. Therefore, it was too thick for the machine's gears. Therefore, it got stuck in between the gears. Therefore, the machine for sealing broke. Therefore, the products weren't sealed.

Below are additional examples of applying root cause analysis specifically for managing a startup:

Scenario 1: Your ecommerce site has high traffic. However, your website's lead conversion rates are low.

1. Why were your lead conversion rates low? Because the majority of your leads didn't click the Buy button.

2. Why didn't the majority of your buyers click the Buy button? Because they didn't see it right away.

3. Why didn't they see it right away? Because the button didn't stand out.

4. Why didn't the button stand out? Because it was located far below the page.

5. Why was it located far below the page? Because it was placed below the lengthy product details and description.

Scenario 2: You're handing out flyers for your upcoming launch. However, you notice that the receivers throw them away in the nearest trash bin.

1. Why did the receivers throw away your flyers? Because you only forced them to receive flyers.

2. Why did you force them to receive the flyers? Because you didn't have enough time to distribute properly.

3. Why didn't you have enough time to distribute properly? Because you were rushing to distribute a box of flyers.

4. Why were you rushing to distribute a box of flyers? Because you printed a lot.

5. Why did you print a lot? Because you had plenty of unused paper and ink.

Scenario 3: You have a coffee shop in a busy street. You provide a selection of flavorful and affordable drinks, along with special and expensive ones. Queues are starting to become a normal sight in your establishment. While this looks like a sign of popularity, it can also be viewed as a problem that warrants a root cause analysis.

1. Why were there queues in your coffee shop? Because customers in front spent a lot of time ordering.

2. Why did the customers in front spend a lot of time ordering? Because they had to ask the available flavors, quantities and prices.

3. Why did they have to ask the available flavors, quantities and prices? Because they couldn't read your menu overhead.

4. Why couldn't they read your menu overhead? Because it was poorly lit.

5. Why was it poorly lit? Because there were too few light bulbs.

Scenario 4: You develop a food delivery app. After an upgrade, the number of users suddenly drop.

1. Why did the number of users suddenly drop after the upgrade? Because many of them chose other food delivery apps.

2. Why did many of them choose other food delivery apps? Because your app became confusing to use.

3. Why did your app become confusing to use? Because you changed the layout of your app's interface.

4. Why did you change the layout of your app's interface? Because you found it too plain.

5. Why did you find it too plain? Because it had no other functionalities aside from processing order and accepting payment.

Scenario 5: You already sent a customer's order. Afterwards, the customer complains about receiving the wrong product. You check your record and discovered the ordered and delivered products are the same. Instead of asking assurances from your customer that he didn't commit the mistake, consider doing the root cause analysis first.

1. Why did the wrong product get sent? Because the customer placed the wrong order.

2. Why did the customer place the wrong order? Because the packaging of the products looked the same.

3. Why did the packaging of the products look the same? Because you lacked designs.

4. Why did you lack designs? Because you didn't have much time designing packaging for other products.

5. Why didn't you have much time designing packaging for other products? Because their development and production were only given a month.

Genchi Genbutsu

Literally meaning "real location, real thing", genchi genbutsu serves as another guiding principle on how Toyota handles problem. The concept is fittingly known as go and see. After all, it encourages you to go to the problem's source and see it for yourself (Magee, 2007).

This is something that many startup owners should perform. Unlike big companies, you don't have many executives, supervisors and managers who have both the power and function to resolve issues in their respective areas. As a startup owner, you won't have many eyes and hands helping you spot problems.

Here's a simple example of applying genchi genbutsu: You notice a commotion in the restaurant you own and manage. It involves an angry customer talking down on a server. Instead of allowing the poor employee handle the brunt of the customer's emotion, step in and find out what it's all about. Make sure you ask both sides.

That sounds like a normal reaction for restaurant managers. However, there are managers who don't feel the need to do such an obvious task. Some even blame and shame their servers publicly.

If you're an app developer, you can apply genchi genbutsu when your users report bugs. You should download, install and use your app yourself. Do what the users did before they encountered the bugs. Experience how the bugs affect user experience. From there, you can ask the five whys and develop a solution afterwards.

Applying genchi genbutsu gets a little complex as your business expands. As you provide managerial powers to one or two employees, should you still go and see the problem yourself?

The answer is yes, especially if your employees are new to having managerial power. When you see the problem yourself, however, you shouldn't just observe and formulate your solutions right after.

Genchi genbutsu requires you to ask the employees who are working in the area where the problem originated. You can inquire about what happened right before the problem or the symptoms showed up. It's an integral step in collecting data at the actual site of the problem.

When everything in your business goes smoothly, you shouldn't settle down. Find a problem and treat it as a challenge. Moreover, think of it as a chance to improve. In the next chapter, you'll get a better understanding of the benefits of continuous improvement.

Notes:

- Before you aim for continuous improvement, determine your business's important process.

- The three steps in developing kaizen culture in the workplace are: identifying problem, finding out the root cause, and formulating a solution.

- To find out the root cause, ask five whys and apply genchi genbutsu.

- When asking five whys, make sure you're stating the direct cause for each why.

- Genchi genbutsu means go to the problem's source and see for yourself.

- Treat problem as a challenge and a chance for improvement.

Chapter 3: Highlighting the Benefits of Kaizen

"Isn't it funny how day by day nothing changes but when you look back, everything is different?" (C. S. Lewis)

Kaizen is instrumental in shaping Toyota's legacy. The same could happen to your startup if you and your employees fully embrace the concept. But before you start thinking of becoming the frontrunner in your industry, below are the benefits you should expect from doing continuous improvement.

Effective Management-Employee Communication

This is both a requirement and a benefit of applying kaizen. You need effective communication to instill your goals and strategies to your employees. You also need that in collecting information about problems and in getting feedback for the changes you introduce.

Teaching your goals and strategies right from the start helps ensure that you and your employees stay on the same page as you expand your business. This also gives your employees insights on the possible career growth they can have with your startup. Having such insights let them consider if they're going to stay with you for a long time.

Eliminating the blame game and encouraging them to inform you about problems speed up crisis management. These actions, along with allowing them to give feedback, boost their confidence and make them feel less stressed at work.

According to the Canadian Centre for Occupational Health and Safety, work-related stress causes short-term effects like headaches, chest pains and muscle tensions. It can badly affect sleep as well. This further causes employees to make poor judgment and neglect their duties at work. Such effects mean losses on your part. Imagine paying for their time, but not getting the work you required them to do.

In contrast, having a great workplace environment makes employees want to work better and stay longer. This can also be beneficial in your branding efforts later on.

Furthermore, effective communication is needed in reviewing your kaizen efforts. This turns into advantage as you or your employees can alert about the possibility of getting sidetracked. The sooner you realize it, the sooner you can work your way back to accomplishing your goals.

Elimination of the Seven Types of Waste

A complex manufacturing procedure and product surplus make it look like your business is doing well. Does your revenue increase though? Are you able to achieve your long-term goals as well?

What seem like signs of business doing well are actually forms of waste. As they're kinds of waste, it's only right to eliminate them. To eliminate them, you should be able to identify them first. According to Ohno (1988), there are seven types of waste in the business process. You can remember them as TIM WOOD.

1. Transport

From the delivery of raw materials to the shipment of finished products, several movements are involved. In the case of manufacturing food products, the steps include cleaning produce, processing, packing, labeling and warehousing. The plant should be organized with the first station being the cleaning area. Next to it should be the processing area, followed by the packing and labeling stations. The next should be near the entrance to the warehouse.

Organizing that way is a no-brainer. However, one of the common mistakes of inexperienced manufacturers is that they organize with maximizing space in mind. They try to fill as much space as possible. Others focus on keeping manual labor in one part, while the steps involving machines are on another area.

A problematic workplace setup creates the transport waste. This type of waste refers to the unnecessary movement of products. Aside from wasting time, the unnecessary movement puts your products at risk of mishandling. They may get misplaced as well. The complex setup may also cause collisions between workers.

2. Inventory

Raw materials, work in progress and finished products signify costs until they're delivered to the consumers. After all, you're paying for the supply of raw materials, the electricity for powering up machines, the delivery of your products to consumers and the labor needed to carry out the steps in your business process.

If you store excessive raw materials, unfinished products, and finished ones, you're bound to deal with the second type of waste: inventory. The surplus is deemed as a waste because warehousing alone costs money but doesn't give you anything in return. Perhaps, you can say it gives you assurance that you can use the extras in case there's a disruption in your production. But there's also the possibility that, when a finished product is discovered to be defective, that means you're less likely to sell your surplus unless you lower the costs.

Moreover, if there are no disruptions in your production processes and the demand for your products remains the same, the surplus will stay in your warehouse for a long time. Some manufacturers end up offering the extras as bundles just to clear their warehouses. The "buy 1, take 1" marketing strategy seems like a good one until you realize how you have to reduce the price to get rid of surplus.

3. Motion

The third type of waste happens when the equipment and workers are inefficient in what they're supposed to do. It's somewhat related to the transport waste. Their main difference though is that transport waste is about damages from moving products, while motion waste is about the damages from the workers and equipment that directly make the products.

Wear-and-tear damage in equipment is a classic example of motion waste. Equipment breakdowns are another example. You can also consider overworked and injured workers.

4. Waiting

Also known as delays and idle time, the fourth type is all about wasted time in the production process. Waiting can happen when you're understaffed or when work is poorly distributed.

Excessive delays in the production are bound to adversely affect your delivery of goods. Consequently, they can result to complaints and cancellation of orders.

5. Overproduction

Dubbed as the worst type of waste (Perrin, 2015), overproduction can trigger and worsen the other six. As its name suggests, this refers to the excessive production of goods when there is low or even no demand at all.

Overproduction is the number one cause of inventory problem. If you don't address the overproduction problem, you're going to worsen your inventory waste. Disposing the surplus means additional work later on.

Instead of delivering newly finished products to retailers or to the consumers, you may also end up storing them for the meantime and shipping the surplus from the previous production. This becomes a form of transport waste.

As a remedy to the surplus, you may lower production in the next few days or weeks. This means some of your employees will free up some of the work time you're paying them for.

Overproduction can trigger quality control problems as well. This is especially true if you're in the food manufacturing industry. When you're storing the excess, you need to be more mindful of expiry dates. Otherwise, they may end up rotting in your warehouse.

6. Over Processing

Front and back cameras are one of the advantageous features of smartphones. One in front and another one at the back are enough. Why add more? Shouldn't phone manufacturers just improve the quality and features of dual cams instead?

Such is just an example of over processing. Adding the extra camera means costs and another step in the production process. Perhaps, the only advantage of having such is that when one camera breaks, you can still have a couple left. You won't feel the need to fix the broken cam. But, as it is a feature you paid for, will you just leave it like that?

Over processing refers to the addition of unnecessary steps in your production. This waste also covers the use of raw materials that are more expensive and of higher quality than what you required for your production. If you're ordering the materials from overseas despite having local suppliers, you'll also deal with over processing, transport, and waiting waste.

7. Defect

Out of all the types of waste, defects are the easiest to understand. Defective products mean you can't recoup your expenses for their production. You wasted time, raw materials, electricity, and your workers' efforts. Depending on the severity of the defects, the goods could be considered literal waste as well.

It's only right to issue recall for defective goods. If you refuse to do so, you risk good reputation. Moreover, you lose loyal customers in the process. But just like Toyota's journey, it's still possible to bounce back and become better than before.

Getting rid of the seven types of waste helps you maximize your resources. Consider the reduced operational costs. You can use the capital you saved for paying loans or for investing on necessary equipment. When it comes to labor, you can use the waiting time for training in a more advanced work.

Eliminating waste is one of the objectives of lean manufacturing. Lean is basically a methodology. It involves streamlining your processes.

By knowing the seven types of waste, identifying areas you need to improve on becomes more manageable. The term lean kaizen denotes an approach of ensuring continuous improvement and eliminating waste.

The production is the most crucial step in a business process. In the case of providing software, the development phase is the most important part. If you're offering services, training and customer service are the most essential. In these steps, you can actually find the abovementioned types of waste. For service providers though, the defect refers to unsatisfactory work while overproduction may be equated to extensive service hours without extra charge.

Some types of waste can also be found in other business functions. You can relate them even in the administrative work that doesn't have direct involvement with products and customers. Delays and inefficient employees (motion waste) are the two common types of waste in non-production steps in your business process. Below are some examples:

- Keeping several boxes of printing paper for administrative work is an example of inventory waste.

- Erroneous data in reports is a form of defect.

- Buying, using and maintaining the most expensive computers when there are affordable and equally efficient options form part of over processing waste.

- Printing more flyers than necessary is an example of overproduction.

Safer Work Environment

With effective communication, your employees can inform you about health risks in the workplace. You can address them right away to avoid accidents. While it's true that your insurance may cover hospitalization costs of an injured employee, nothing can protect your startup from the backlash from the other employees. If news of the accident becomes public, you'll earn bad reputation as well. The results are worse when there's death involved.

Instead of the repercussions of workplace accidents though, you should ensure safer workplace because it's only ethical. Your workforce is a valuable resource. As a resource, you should give them an environment that helps them maximize their performance, and protects them. Value them and make them feel valued.

Better Customer Experience

As an entrepreneur, you shouldn't think you're only offering products or services. You should keep in mind that you're providing customer experience.

Many products these days are more of luxuries, not necessities. Smart TV is one of the notable examples. It's mainly for entertainment. You can use it for video conferences, too. However, a smartphone or high-tech laptop can be enough for such task.

Yet, people still buy smart TVs because it allows them to watch live broadcasts of games. The bigger screen and better video quality make them feel like they're part of the audience.

Some smart TV ads show a family watching together or one adult relaxing on the couch. They're basically selling the experience you can have when you use the product.

Luxury bags are worth noting as well. Some ladies just want them because the brands make them feel like they're members of the elite. The bags can also give them the notion of elegance.

How about your offer? What kind of experience do you wish your customer will have when using your product or getting your service?

Lean kaizen helps you improve the customer experience you can provide. The continuously improving product is the biggest reason. Having confident and efficient employees, especially those who directly deal with customers, is another factor.

Notes:

- Kaizen needs and enhances effective communication between management and employees.

- Kaizen helps eliminate the seven types of waste in the business process. These types of waste are transport, inventory, motion, waiting, overproduction, over processing, and defect.

- Kaizen can help ensure a safe and efficient work environment.

- Thanks to continuously improving product and service, you can give better customer experience.

Chapter 4: Applying Kaizen in Managing a Startup

"The man who moves a mountain begins by carrying away small stones." (Confucius)

Fostering kaizen culture in your workplace won't happen just because you want to. It requires effort, consistency, patience and cooperation. To overcome resistance, you also have to start small. People are more receptive to minor changes after all.

You also have to follow the 5S program to make your workplace environment conducive to kaizen and to help ensure that the changes last for a long time. While this was developed for Toyota's manufacturing procedure, this has been adapted for other steps in the business process. The 5S were originally Japanese words but they had English counterparts as they became one of the bases of lean manufacturing.

The 5S to Remember

1. Sort (Seiri)

This step is about differentiating what's valuable and what's not. To carry this out, you have to go to the location and find out what doesn't belong.

Under the first S, you have to identify obstructions. You need to ensure safety and maximize resources, particularly time, space and manpower.

You can accomplish the said goals by removing obstructions unless these have a lot do with the structure of your workplace. You can ask an interior designer to help you redo your workplace's floor plan in such a way that doesn't involve demolitions. But if the obstructions are furniture or equipment, you can rearrange them.

Collect items that don't belong in certain areas, too. Compile them in all on a table or in a corner. Put them in their respective areas later on.

Try to put yourself in the shoes of your employees as well. They should be able to move comfortably in the workplace. They shouldn't have to squeeze their way through. Maximizing space doesn't have to mean filling every square inch. The freed space can serve as wider walkway. A more spacious walkway helps prevent collisions and speed up transfer of goods.

2. Set in order/Straighten (Seiton)

This refers to putting things in their respective places. If the first S focuses on what to be eliminated, the second one underscores keeping the needed equipment and employees where they're supposed to be. Its goal is to make sure the workflow goes as smoothly as possible.

To implement this, make sure you have the needed work stations to perform key steps in your business process. They should be positioned in such a way that limits delays and transport waste. Next, fill the work stations with the right equipment and people. Even the storage for the equipment and supplies should be within those work stations.

3. Shine (Seiso)

Basically, this concept is about maintaining cleanliness and ensuring that your equipment is in optimal condition. Maintenance is needed because it also helps ensure the safety of your employees.

Inspection of equipment and procedure is an integral step in the third S. Random visits in your employees' respective work stations are also recommended.

4. Standardize (Seiketsu)

This step is all about creating rules and summing up your procedures. Defining such makes your employees understand what they need to do. This also involves modifying steps.

5. Sustain (Shitsuke)

It's pointless to improve a step then revert back to your old ways. The final step aims to prevent that from happening. Sustaining is about maintaining and aiming for improvement over and over.

Application of 5S in Production

What do your customers say about your product? As a startup, you can give your initial set of products to a control group. Take note of the negative feedback. Compile them and identify the most complained about issue. Ask the five whys and go to the area in the production where the problem first occurred.

From there, sort out the things that aren't meant in the area and bring the tools you needed for the job. Repair whatever needs to be repaired. Modify the wrongful step that trigger the flaw in your product's design or functionality. Maintain the new procedure. If that doesn't fix the problem with your product, go back to the modifications you introduced.

Going back to the sample problem of unsealed products, the first thing you should do is remove the box of wrong seal. Next, bring the box of correct seal in the packing area. The third step is to inspect and repair the machine. The employee concerned should be alerted about the problem as well. To avoid repeating the mistake, the employees in-charge of supplies should double-check if they're of the correct size. Sustain it by adding the said task for every transaction.

Introducing Kaizen Board

Search for productivity tips in Pinterest and Google Images. There's a great chance that you'll see boards with three columns known as To-Do, Doing and Done (Kniberg & Skarin, 2010). Over the years, people put their own spin on the said productivity tool. There are even apps based on it. Such tool is actually called the kanban board.

Ohno (1988) also developed the scheduling system known as kanban. The main difference between kanban and kaizen is that the former focuses more on logistics while kaizen puts a lot of emphasis on people and improvements. Yet, both can be used together. The kaizen board is a fusion of the two.

The Rationale Behind a Kaizen Board

You and your employees shouldn't wait for problems and their symptoms to occur before you carry out root cause analysis and solutions. However, encouraging your employees to find trouble isn't as easy as it seems.

Sometimes, you have to set up a reminder for you and for them to spot possible problems. That's what a kaizen board does. Aside from identifying progress, this tool lets you see the progress for the changes you introduce.

Tips on Designing and Using a Kaizen Board

The basic kaizen board has four columns. The first one is entitled the Idea column. It's followed by To-Do, Doing and Done.

Your kaizen board doesn't have to be fancy. You can use a pinboard or a whiteboard. To put entries under each column, you can use sticky notes, memo pads, or simply pens.

Make sure employees (even the lowest in the ranks and temporary ones) have a say on what you need to improve on in your startup, main offer, and management style. To make this possible, the kaizen board should be visible in the workplace.

The board should be at least 2 square feet. The ideal place is also near the entryway or the lounge.

Keep the pens, sticky notes, memo pads and pins right beside or under the board. Add a note encouraging your employees to use the said materials to enter their suggestions in the Ideas column.

Afterwards, organize a weekly meeting to process the Ideas. It can be as short as 30 minutes, but make sure it's part of the work period, not on breaks. If you do it on breaks, your employees may not treat your kaizen board seriously.

During those meetings, you can also update the kaizen board. Those in-charge of planning and working on certain ideas should provide entries in the To-Do and Doing sections respectively. If the work is finished, there should be updates on the Done column. The entries in the Done column should be kept for at least a week.

If you have more than 20 employees, you should provide a separate kaizen board for each team. Consider the number of members for each team when deciding the size of the kaizen board. You can collectively discuss the ideas from the different kaizen boards. But if your business starts to branch out and have more teams, separate discussions are better.

If your business is into software development, you can further modify the kaizen board by adding Testing column in between the To-Do and Doing columns. The Testing column is beneficial when you have two or more ways of accomplishing the To-Do entries.

Notes:

- Remember the 5S: sort, set in order, shine, standardize and sustain.
- Make a kaizen board to generate ideas.

Conclusion

I'd like to thank you and congratulate you for transiting my lines from start to finish.

I hope this book was able to help you in carrying out kaizen in your startup business. The management approach is based on both scientific evidences and common sense. It's not that surprising that you can apply it regardless of the industry you're in, the location of your business and the nationality of your employees.

Additionally, kaizen is applicable no matter how small your business is. It's even more ideal for startups than large corporations. The former has limited capital for funding operations, after all. Streamlining the business process helps a startup save and utilize the savings for further improvements.

Hopefully, this was able to help you appreciate the importance of teamwork as well. It's been reiterated many times how valuable that factor is. However, some people who attain success tend to think they're able to do so without anyone's help. As a result, the people who helped turned their backs against them.

Part of being a good entrepreneur is managing human resource well. Give them the support they need. You can start with moral support. Encourage and reassure them as a group. Ensure them a safe environment. Afterwards, train them in handling new tasks and taking leadership roles.

Don't forget to pay them well. This may mean increasing your operation costs and reducing your profit. However, the long-term benefits may include employee satisfaction and loyalty. Satisfied employees can promote your brand without asking for additional payment from you. Your customers will consider them more reliable as they've been with you for quite long.

Moreover, you can further attract skilled people if you know how to recognize hard work. However, you shouldn't distinguish individual efforts.

By introducing you to kaizen, I hope you're also able to identify your key business process. Remove the steps that don't add value to the way you serve your customers. Refining your business process is bound to improve your customers' experience with your brand. To help you decide whether a change or an existing step forms part of your key business process, ask yourself, "How does it benefit my customer?"

Continuous improvement doesn't have a definite ending, which is a good thing because you'll keep on striving for it. While it doesn't have an ending, it always begins with a challenge.

Long-term goals can be broken down into manageable challenges. Aside from that, you can use a kaizen board to generate ideas for challenges and set reminders for changes.

You can also try to spot the seven types of waste in all aspects of your business operation. To get rid of the seven types of waste, you should perform the following:

- Get rid of unnecessary steps in your business process.

- Avoid buying and storing extra materials.

- Strive to simplify complex steps.

- Invest on equipment and talents.

- Don't make more than what your customers need.

- Don't do more than your customers want.

- Avoid mistakes in the production.

Market analysis is required to carry out some of the above steps. Get to know the potential demand and the features that your target customers are hoping for. You can conduct an online survey, A/B testing, and interviews. You can study the leading ventures in your industry. Assess what features their products or services that don't add value to customers, and make sure they won't form part of your own offers.

Feedback forms and customer review sections in your site are also gold mines for possible challenges. During your meetings, you can also collect information about potential issues from your employees.

Part of teaching your employees about kaizen is training them to consider challenge as an opportunity for improvement. After determining a challenge, ask the five whys. Go to the source of the problem and consult the employees concerned as well.

After determining the root cause, develop a solution and implement them using the 5S: Sort; Set in order; Shine; Standardize; and Sustain. Get rid of the waste in the area where the problem started. Keep the needed equipment and people in the said area. Inspect and do necessary repairs. Train the workers there as well. Afterwards, modify the procedures to prevent the possible recurrence of the problem. Finally, sustain the newly introduced changes.

To test the 5S, try organizing your computer's desktop. Remove files, folders and programs in your desktop that you don't use for work.

For the second S, put the folders and programs you use for work on the desktop or taskbar. Compile important files in properly labelled folders as well. Buy the necessary program licenses, too.

Next, scan your work folders and programs for possible malware. Delete useless files and folders as well.

Every time you use your computer, you may create and save new clutter in your desktop. Make sure you sort, set in order, and shine before you shut down your computer. This way, you're standardizing and sustaining the organized desktop.

From organizing your desktop, try out the 5S in decluttering your work desk. From there, apply them in your office or shop.

Just like Toyota, don't settle. Keep on improving your main offer, workforce, work environment, customer service and marketing strategies. Continue refining your processes. You may still incur losses along the way, but they won't last long if you aim for improvements.

It can take time. Your competitors may take the lead as you keep on improving. You may fall behind the trends. However, you should remember that leads and trends aren't permanent. If you aim for kaizen, you might become the next Toyota that introduced the hybrid age in your own industry. It's better to set the trends than follow, right?

The next step is to commit yourself on improving. Do it, not just for your venture, but also for your life. Encourage your employees to do the same.

Don't worry about failures. There are more things you can learn from failures than from successes. Make sure you keep records of what failed so you won't have to repeat them again.

I wish you the best of luck! Don't forget to celebrate your successes but don't let them get into your head.

Thank You

Before you go, I just wanted to say thank you for purchasing my book.

You could have picked from dozens of other books on the same topic but you took a chance and chose this one.

So, a HUGE thanks to you for getting this book and for reading all the way to the end.

Now I wanted to ask you for a small favor. ***Could you please consider posting a review on the platform? Reviews are one of the easiest ways to support the work of independent authors.***

This feedback will help me continue to write the type of books that will help you get the results you want. So if you enjoyed it, please let me know!

Resources

Lean Six Sigma Simplified

Books

M. Adams (2004). Lean Six Sigma: A Tools Guide. Air Academy Associates

T. Stern (2018). Lean Six Sigma: International Standards and Global Guidelines. Productivity Press

N. Decarlo (2007). The Complete Idiot's Guide to Lean Six Sigma. Alpha Books

D. Pomfret (2009). Lean Project Management: A Study of Application. Project Management Institute

T. MacAdam (2009). Lean Project Management: Slashing Waste to Reduce Project Costs and Timelines. Project Management Institute

M. Thomsett (2005). Getting Started in Six Sigma. Wiley

L. Tang (2003). Six Sigma: Advanced Tools for Black Belts and Master Black Belts. Wiley

J. Arthur (2007). Lean Six Sigma Demystified. Mcgraw-Hill

R. Pirasteh-R. Fox (2011). Profitability with no Boundaries: Optimizing TOC, Lean, Six Sigma Results: Focus, Reduce Waste, Contain Variability. ASQ Quality Press

M. George (2002). Lean Six Sigma: Combining Six Sigma Quality with Lean Speed. McGraw-Hill Europe,

Videos

TECOEnergyinc. (2016. June 10). Lean: 8 Wastes. Retrieved From: https://www.youtube.com/watch?v=VWN8NrJ7LE8

fkiQuality. (2018. April 1). 5 Steps DMAIC Overview: Green Belt 2.0 Lean Six Sigma. Retrieved from: https://www.youtube.com/watch?v=go7KMaKV-W8

Gemba Academy. (2009. March 10). Learn What 5S is and How it Applies to Any Industry. Retrieved from: https://www.youtube.com/watch?v=c0Q-xaYior0

Lean Lab. (2017. April 24). What is Continuous Improvement? 4 Points to Create the CI Culture. Retrieved from:

https://www.youtube.com/watch?v=sWj9MowzDV0

Websites

Six Sigma Daily. (2014. June 12). Six Sigma Belt Levels and Related Training. Retrieved from: https://www.sixsigmadaily.com/six-sigma-training-belt-levels/

Kainexus Blog (2018. September 27). 13 Indispensable Lean Six Sigma Tools and Techniques. Retrieved From: https://blog.kainexus.com/improvement-disciplines/six-sigma/six-sigma-tools/13-indispensable-six-sigma-tools-and-techniques

Lifehack.Org (2019. May 28). How to Declutter Your Life and Reduce Stress (The Ultimate Guide). Retrieved from: https://www.lifehack.org/articles/lifestyle/how-to-declutter-your-life-and-reduce-stress.html

Lean Analytics

Alistair Croll, B. Y. (n.d.). *Use data to build a better startup faster*. Retrieved from Lean Anaylitcs Book: http://leananalyticsbook.com

Brekel, B. (2017, April 11). *Why Lean Startup Doesn't Always Work in Corporates as it Does in Startups*. Retrieved from Revel X:

https://www.revelx.co/blog/why-lean-startup-doesnt-always-work-in-corporates/

Burgstone, J. (n.d.). *What's Wrong With the Lean Start-up*. Retrieved from Inc.: https://www.inc.com/jon-burgstone/flaws-in-the-lean-start-up.html

DeMeré, N. E. (2016, July 8). *Lean Analytics: Why the "One Metric" is more complicated than it sounds ft. Notion Data* . Retrieved from Use Notion: https://blog.usenotion.com/lean-analytics-why-the-one-metric-is-more-complicated-than-it-sounds-7ba02d2aa718

DigitalPrinciples. (n.d.). *Be Data Driven*. Retrieved from Principles for Digital Development: https://digitalprinciples.org/principle/be-data-driven/

Innov8rs. (2018, February 12). *Let's Get Real: Why Lean Startup Is NOT Right For Everyone*. Retrieved from Innov8rs: https://innov8rs.co/news/lets-get-real-lean-startup-not-right-everyone/

Jongen, R. (2018, November 6). *What Is Lean Analytics, and How Do You Apply It*. Retrieved from Revel X: https://www.revelx.co/blog/what-is-lean-analytics/

Lownie, K. (2013, October 7). *Minimum Viable Service: Why Less is Best When it Comes to SaaS Customer Service*. Retrieved from Open View Partners: https://openviewpartners.com/blog/minimum-viable-service-less-best/

Patel, N. (n.d.). *Neil Patel*. Retrieved from Using Lean Analytics Principles to Build a Strong Company: https://neilpatel.com/blog/lean-analytics/

Reies, E. (2011, June 14). *Open Innovation in DC*. Retrieved from Startup Lessons Learned: http://www.startuplessonslearned.com/2011/06/open-innovation-in-dc.html

Reis, E. (n.d.). *Principles*. Retrieved from The Lean Startup Methodology: http://theleanstartup.com/principles

RevelX. (2017, March 10). *Medium*. Retrieved from Why Lean Startup Doesn't Always Work in Corporates as it Does in Startups: https://medium.com/@RevelX/why-lean-startup-doesnt-always-work-in-corporates-as-it-does-in-startups-35a6a3c7f606

Sanon, M. (2017, April 28). *4 Reasons Why Data Analytics is Important.* Retrieved from Digital Vidya: https://www.digitalvidya.com/blog/reasons-data-analytics-important/

Lean Enterprise

5S Today. (n.d.). What is 5S? Retrieved November 9, 2019, from https://www.5stoday.com/what-is-5s/

American Society for Quality. (n.d.). What is lean? Retrieved November 5, 2019, from https://asq.org/quality-resources/lean

APB Consultant. (2017, September 7). Lean enterprise. Retrieved November 9, 2019, from http://isoconsultantpune.com/lean-enterprise/

Aslinger, G. (2014, November 17). Lean six sigma for beginners. Retrieved November 9, 2019, from https://www.processexcellencenetwork.com/lean-six-sigma-business-performance/articles/continuous-improvement-with-lean-six-sigma-for-beg

Do, D. (2017, August 5). The five principles of lean. Retrieved November 7, 2019, from https://theleanway.net/The-Five-Principles-of-Lean

EnPower Group. (n.d.). Lean enterprise management. Retrieved November 4, 2019, from http://enpowergroup.com/lean-enterprise/

GoLeanSixSigma. (n.d.). DMAIC: The 5 phases of lean six sigma. Retrieved November 9, 2019, from https://goleansixsigma.com/dmaic-five-basic-phases-of-lean-six-sigma/

Ingram, D. (2017, November 21). Key Issues for the Implementation of a Lean Manufacturing System. Retrieved November 9, 2019, from https://smallbusiness.chron.com/key-issues-implementation-lean-manufacturing-system-75390.html

Investopedia. (2019, October 6). Lean startup. Retrieved November 5, 2019, from https://www.investopedia.com/terms/l/lean-startup.asp

Jansson, K. (2017, May 2). "Lean thinking" and the 5 principles of lean manufacturing. Retrieved November 4, 2019, from https://blog.kainexus.com/improvement-disciplines/lean/lean-thinking-and-the-5-principles-of-lean-manufacturing

Johnson, J. (2019, July 30). Lean vs. six sigma: What's the difference & use cases. Retrieved November 9, 2019, from https://tallyfy.com/lean-vs-six-sigma/

Kanbanize. (n.d.). Kanban explained for beginners. Retrieved November 9, 2019, from https://kanbanize.com/kanban-resources/getting-started/what-is-kanban/

Lean Manufacturing Junction. (2019, October 14). Benefits of lean manufacturing: What can it do for your company? Retrieved November 9, 2019, from https://www.lean-manufacturing-junction.com/benefits-of-lean/

LeanKit. (2018, October 8). Lean, kanban, and how they work together. Retrieved November 9, 2019, from https://leankit.com/learn/lean/lean-kanban/

Martin, J. R. (n.d.). Lean company vs. lean enterprise. Retrieved November 5, 2019, from https://maaw.info/ArticleSummaries/ArtSumWomackAndJones94.htm

McArdle, C. (2017, December 27). 10 benefits of applying a lean methodology. Retrieved November 9, 2019, from https://www.kaizenkulture.com/blog/10-benefits-of-applying-a-lean-methodology

Proqis. (n.d.). An introduction to the Toyota production system and principles. Retrieved November 6, 2019, from http://insights.btoes.com/lean-resources/toyota-production-system-principles-introduction-to-tps

Rastogi, A. (n.d.). A brief introduction to lean, six sigma, and lean six sigma. Retrieved November 9, 2019, from https://www.greycampus.com/blog/quality-management/a-brief-introduction-to-lean-and-six-sigma-and-lean-six-sigma

Rever Team. (2019, May 16). Lean thinking: Principles to scale effectively. Retrieved November 5, 2019, from https://reverscore.com/lean-thinking/

Rodriguez, T. S. (2018, November 3). LEAN production: The method that made Toyota the most valuable car brand in the world. Retrieved November 6, 2019, from https://medium.com/drill/lean-production-the-method-that-made-toyota-the-most-valuable-car-brand-in-the-world-13279db0b224

Terry, J. (2019, September 10). Lean thinking: The foundation of lean practice. Retrieved November 5, 2019, from https://www.planview.com/resources/articles/lean-thinking-lean-practice/

Terry, J. (2019, November 6). What is kanban? Retrieved November 9, 2019, from https://www.planview.com/resources/articles/what-is-kanban/

The Lean Startup. (n.d.). The lean startup principles. Retrieved November 5, 2019, from http://theleanstartup.com/principles

Universal Class. (n.d.). Lean thinking concepts. Retrieved November 5, 2019, from https://www.universalclass.com/articles/business/lean-thinking-concepts.htm

Wastradowski, M. (n.d.). What is 5S? Retrieved November 9, 2019, from https://www.graphicproducts.com/articles/what-is-5s/

Womack, J. P., & Jones, D. T. (2014, August 1). From lean production to the lean enterprise. Retrieved November 4, 2019, from https://hbr.org/1994/03/from-lean-production-to-the-lean-enterprise

Lean Startup

Farbrot, A. (2014). Entrepreneurs Are More Single-Minded. Retrieved from https://partner.sciencenorway.no/bi-business-entrepreneurs/entrepreneurs-are-more-single-minded/1407583

Vojinovic, I. (2019). Thirty-Nine Entrepreneur Statistics You Need to Know in 2019. Retrieved from https://www.smallbizgenius.net/by-the-numbers/entrepreneur-statistics/

Entreprenoria. (2016). Top 10 Successful Entrepreneurs without a College Degree. Retrieved from https://entreprenoria.com/personal-development/top-10-successful-entrepreneurs-without-a-college-degree/

Price, R.W. (2011). What Is Entrepreneurial Management? Retrieved from https://news.gcase.org/2011/10/24/what-is-entrepreneurial-management/

Ries, E. (2011). The Roots of the Lean Startup. *The Lean Startup: How Today's Entrepreneurs Use Continuous Innovation to Create Radically Successful Businesses*, 28.

Pope, E. K. (2019). Startup vs. Small Business: What's the Difference? Retrieved from https://www.fundera.com/blog/startup-vs-small-business

McGowan, E. (2017). What Is Lean Startup Methodology – And How Can It Help You? Retrieved from https://www.startups.com/library/expert-advice/lean-startup-methodology-can-help

Expert Program Management. (2019). Book Summary: The Lean Startup by Eric Ries. Retrieved from https://expertprogrammanagement.com/2019/04/book-summary-lean-startup/

Peerbits. (2019) The Definitive Lean Startup Guide: Everything You Need to Know. Retrieved from https://www.peerbits.com/blog/everything-you-need-know-about-lean-startup-methodology.html

The Lean Startup. (n.d.). The Lean Startup Methodology. Retrieved from http://theleanstartup.com/principles

Ries, E. (2011). Batch. *The Lean Startup: How Today's Entrepreneurs Use Continuous Innovation to Create Radically Successful Businesses*, 182.

Sheth, S (2019). Four Ways to Efficiently Manage Employees in a Lean Startup. Retrieved from http://customerthink.com/4-ways-to-efficiently-manage-employees-in-a-lean-startup/

Ganti, A. (2019). Employee Stock Ownership Plan (ESOP). Retrieved from https://www.investopedia.com/terms/e/esop.asp

Agile Project Management

Books

R.Wysocki-Wiley (2009). Effective Project Management: Traditional, Agile, Extreme.

K. White (2009). Agile Project Management: A Mandate for the 21st Century. Center for Business Practices.

R. Russell-Bernard, B. Taylor (2017). Operations and Supply Chain Management. John Wiley & Sons.

J. Malik (2013). Agile Project Management. Schroff Publishers and Distribution.

M. Layton, D. Morrow (2018). Scrum for Dummies. John Wiley & Sons.

K. Rubin, A. Wesley (2013). Essential Scrum: A Practical Guide to the Most Popular Agile Process.

K. Laudon, J. Laudon (2013). Essentials of Management Information Systems. Pearson.

J. Sutherland (2015). Scrum: The Art of Doing Twice the Work in Half the Time. Rh Business Books.

D. Astels, G. Miller, M. Novak (2002). A Practical Guide to Extreme Programming. Prentice Hall PTR.

J. Pinto (2007). Project Management: Achieving Competitive Advantage. Pearson/Prentice Hall.

S. Pautsch, C. Hanser (2014). Lean Project Management. Verlag GMBH.

D. Pomfret (2009). Lean Project Management: A Study of Application. Project Management Institute.

S. Cimorelli (2017). Kanban for the Supply Chain: Fundamental Practices for Manufacturing Management: Second Edition. CRC Press.

M. Hammarberg, J. Sunden (2014). Kanban in Action. Manning.

D. Summers (2009). Quality Management: Creating and Sustaining Organizational Effectiveness. Pearson/Prentice Hall.

Videos

Infoworld. (2018, March 19). How the Agile Methodology Really Works. Retrieved from: https://www.youtube.com/watch?v=1iccpf2eN1Q

Mark Shead. (2016, May 31). What is Agile? Retrieved from: https://www.youtube.com/watch?v=Z9QbYZh1YXY

Jim Sterling. (2016, April 18). The Jimquisition: Crunch. Retrieved from: https://www.youtube.com/watch?v=Z8RCV0UWJgE

Kim Justice. (2017, May 8). The Agony and Ecstasy: The Story of Duke Nukem Forever. Retrieved from: https://www.youtube.com/watch?v=dfV4rI_gR1g

Henrik Kniberg. (2012, October 25). Agile Product Ownership in a Nutshell. Retrieved from: https://www.youtube.com/watch?v=502ILHjX9EE

Development that Pays. (2017, January 18). Scrum vs. Kanban: What's the Difference? Retrieved from: https://www.youtube.com/watch?v=rIaz-l1Kf8w

CA Technologies. (2016, June 7). The Difference Between Lean and Agile. Retrieved from: https://www.youtube.com/watch?v=aUd3xTdtXqI

Scrum Mastery

Association for Project Management. (n.d.). Agile Methods. Retrieved November 11, 2019, from https://www.apm.org.uk/resources/find-a-resource/agile-project-management/agile-methods/

Green, P. (2012). Adobe Premiere Scrum Adoption. Retrieved November 12, 2019, from http://blogs.adobe.com/agile/files/2012/08/Adobe-Premiere-Pro-Scrum-Adoption-How-an-agile-approach-enabled-success-in-a-hyper-competitive-landscape-.pdf

O'Connor, G. (2016). Agile must-haves: three requirements for a great agile team. PM Network, 30(1), 26–27.

Schwaber, K., & Sutherland, J. (2017, November). The Scrum Guide: Retrieved November 9, 2019, from https://www.scrumguides.org/docs/scrumguide/v2017/2017-Scrum-Guide-US.pdf#zoom=100

Sims, C., & Johnson, H. L. (2012). The Elements of Scrum [Epub]. United States: Dymaxicon.

Sims, C., & Johnson, H. L. (2014). Scrum: A Breathtakingly Brief and Agile Introduction [Epub]. United States: Dymaxicon.

Sliger, M. (2011). Agile Project Management with Scrum. Paper presented at PMI Global Congress 2011—North America, Dallas, TX. Newtown Square, PA: Project Management Institute.

Sutherland, J., & Sutherland, J. J. (2014). *Scrum: The Art of Doing Twice the Work in Half the Time* [Epub]. New York: Currency.

International Scrum Institute. (2019). The Scrum Framework. Retrieved from https://www.scrum-institute.org/contents/The_Scrum_Framework_by_International_Scrum_Institute.pdf

Sutherland, J. (2014, January 23). Scrum Done Right: How Spotify Takes On Industry Giants | OpenView Labs [Blog post]. Retrieved November 17, 2019, from https://openviewpartners.com/blog/spotify-great-agile-example-scrum-done-right/#.XdUvE1cza00

Takeuchi, H., & Nonaka, I. (1986). The New Development Game. Harvard Business Review, 3–10. Retrieved from https://ullizee.files.wordpress.com/2013/01/takeuchi-and-onaka-the-new-new-product-development-game.pdf

Kanban

Agile Vs Scrum: Know the Difference. (2019, September 21). Retrieved November 4, 2019, from https://www.guru99.com/agile-vs-scrum.html

Amjal, S. (2018, May 4). How Agile Scrum Training Transformed These 5 Companies. Retrieved November 4, 2019, from https://www.quickstart.com/blog/how-agile-scrum-training-transformed-these-5-companies/

Goldman, L.,Nagel, R.L., & Preiss, K. (1995). Agile Competitors and Virtual Organizations - Strategies for Enriching the Customer, *Van Nostrand Reinhold.*

Gonçalves, L. (2019a, September 16). What is Scrum Methodology, Everything You Need To Know About. Retrieved November 4, 2019, from https://luis-goncalves.com/what-is-scrum-methodology/

Gonçalves, L. (2019b, October 5). What Is Agile Methodology. Retrieved November 4, 2019, from https://luis-goncalves.com/what-is-agile-methodology/

Highsmith, J. (2001a). History: The Agile Manifesto. Retrieved November 4, 2019, from https://agilemanifesto.org/history.html

Highsmith, J. (2001b). Principles behind the Agile Manifesto. Retrieved November 4, 2019, from https://agilemanifesto.org/principles.html

Jansson, K. (2017, May 2). "Lean Thinking" and the 5 Principles of Lean Manufacturing. Retrieved November 4, 2019, from https://blog.kainexus.com/improvement-disciplines/lean/lean-thinking-and-the-5-principles-of-lean-manufacturing

Kanban Explained in 10 Minutes | Kanbanize. (n.d.). Retrieved November 4, 2019, from https://kanbanize.com/kanban-resources/getting-started/what-is-kanban/

Landeghem, L. (2015, January 4). Why is Overproduction the Worst Muda? |. Retrieved November 4, 2019, from http://www.consulting-xp.com/blog/?p=546

Leading Edge Group. (2018, October 12). Key Performance Indicators for Production Monitoring - Leading Edge. Retrieved November 4, 2019, from https://www.leadingedgegroup.com/key-performance-indicators-for-production-monitoring/

Lotich, P. (2014, October 7). Internal Problems Can Impact Your Customers - Are You Aware? – The Thriving Small Business. Retrieved November 4, 2019, from https://thethrivingsmallbusiness.com/small-business-problems/

Mathew, A. (2015, April 20). The Impact of a Poor Customer Service. Retrieved November 4, 2019, from https://www.liveadmins.com/blog/the-impact-of-a-poor-customer-service/

Naydenov, P. (2019a, October 10). Top Reasons Why Companies Use Kanban [Infographic]|Kanbanize Blog. Retrieved November 4, 2019, from https://kanbanize.com/blog/why-use-kanban-infographic/

Naydenov, P. (2019b, October 11). Kanban in IT Operations: 5 Real-Life Examples. Retrieved November 4, 2019, from https://kanbanize.com/blog/kanban-it-operations/

Ohno, T. (June 1988). Toyota Production System - beyond large-scale production. Productivity Press. p. 29. ISBN 0-915299-14-3.

Peshev, M. (2019, February 23). The 31 Biggest Business Challenges Growing Companies Face - Mario Peshev. Retrieved November 4, 2019, from https://mariopeshev.com/business/the-biggest-business-challenges-growing-companies/

Schonberger, R.J. (2001). Let's Fix It! Overcoming the Crisis in Manufacturing. New York: Free Press. pp. 70–71.

Shingō, S. (1989). A Study of the Toyota Production System from an Industrial Engineering Viewpoint. Productivity Press. p. 228. ISBN 0-915299-17-8.

Skhmot, N. (2017, August 5). The 8 Wastes of Lean. Retrieved November 4, 2019, from https://theleanway.net/The-8-Wastes-of-Lean

Smartsheet. (n.d.). Understanding Kanban Inventory Management and Its Uses Across Multiple Industries. Retrieved November 21, 2019, from https://www.smartsheet.com/understanding-kanban-inventory-management-and-its-uses-across-multiple-industries

The Leadership Network. (2015, November 10). How Kanban systems are used in different industries. Retrieved November 21, 2019, from https://theleadershipnetwork.com/article/kanban

Top 10: Lean manufacturing companies in the world. (2017, April 26). Retrieved November 4, 2019, from https://www.manufacturingglobal.com/top-10/top-10-lean-manufacturing-companies-world

What is Agile/Scrum. (2019, October 22). Retrieved November 4, 2019, from https://www.cprime.com/resources/what-is-agile-what-is-scrum/

Womack, J. P. & Jones, D.T. (1996) Lean Thinking.

Womack, J. P., Jones, D.T. & Roos, D. (1990) The Machine That Changed The World.

Kaizen

Assembly. (2011, December 28). The Creators of Toyota's DNA. Retrieved November 3, 2019, from https://www.assemblymag.com/articles/84596-the-creators-of-toyota-s-dna

Boitnott, J. (2014, October 22). 6 Startups With the Most Humble Beginnings and the Greatest Successes. Retrieved November 3,

2019, from https://www.inc.com/john-boitnott/6-startups-with-the-most-humble-beginnings-and-the-greatest-successes.html

Bunkley, N. (2008, April 24). G.M. Says Toyota Has Lead in Global Sales Race. *The New York Times*. Retrieved from https://www.nytimes.com/2008/04/24/business/worldbusiness/24auto.html?_r=3&ref=business&oref=slogin&oref=slogin&oref=slogin

Canadian Centre for Occupational Health and Safety. (n.d.). Workplace Stress - General. Retrieved November 3, 2019, from https://www.ccohs.ca/oshanswers/psychosocial/stress.html

Donilon, T. (2019, August 14). Advantage, America. Retrieved November 3, 2019, from https://www.foreignaffairs.com/articles/united-states/2016-06-28/advantage-america

Hasegawa, Y., & Kimm, T. (2008). *Clean Car Wars: How Honda and Toyota are Winning the Battle of the Eco-Friendly Autos*. Chichester, United Kingdom: Wiley.

K. Liker, J. K., Hoseus, M., & Center for Quality People and Organizations. (2008). *Toyota Culture: The Heart and Soul of the Toyota Way* (Rev. ed.). United States of America: McGraw-Hill Education.

Kniberg, H., & Skarin, M. (2010). *Kanban and Scrum: Making the Most of Both*. United States of America: C4Media Inc.

Magee, D. (2008). *How Toyota Became #1: Leadership Lessons from the World's Greatest Car Company* (Rev. ed.). New York, United States of America: Portfolio.

Ohno, T. (1988). *Toyota Production System: Beyond Large-Scale Production* (Rev. ed.). United States of America: Taylor & Francis.

Ohno, T. (2006, March). "Ask 'why' five times about every matter." Retrieved November 3, 2019, from https://www.toyota-myanmar.com/about-toyota/toyota-traditions/quality/ask-why-five-times-about-every-matter

Organisation Internationale des Constructeurs d'Automobiles. (2017). *WORLD MOTOR VEHICLE PRODUCTION: OICA correspondents survey*. Retrieved from http://www.oica.net/wp-content/uploads/World-Ranking-of-Manufacturers-1.pdf

Perrin, X. (2015, January 4). Why is Overproduction the Worst Muda? Retrieved November 3, 2019, from http://www.consulting-xp.com/blog/?p=546

Rodrigues, E. (2018, November 7). How to overcome the Biggest Obstacles to Kaizen Implementation [Blog post]. Retrieved November 3, 2019, from https://prodsmart.com/blog/2018/11/07/how-to-overcome-the-biggest-obstacles-to-kaizen-implementation/

Rosenthal, M. (2011). The Essence of Jidoka. Retrieved November 3, 2019, from https://web.archive.org/web/20110714222919/http://www.sme.org/cgi-bin/get-newsletter.pl?LEAN&20021209&1&

Toyota. (n.d.). Toyota Way 2001. Retrieved November 3, 2019, from https://www.toyota-global.com/company/history_of_toyota/75years/data/conditions/philosophy/toyotaway2001.html

Vlasic, B. (2011). *Once Upon a Car: The Fall and Resurrection of America's Big Three Automakers--GM, Ford, and Chrysler*. United States of America: HarperCollins.

Von Rosing, M., Von Scheel, H., & Scheer, A. W. (2014). *The Complete Business Process Handbook: Body of Knowledge from Process Modeling to BPM*. United States of America: Elsevier Science.

CPSIA information can be obtained
at www.ICGtesting.com
Printed in the USA
LVHW011224270121
677612LV00008B/399